Foundations of Wellness

Foundations of Wellness

Bill Reger-Nash

Meredith Smith

Gregory Juckett

Human Kinetics

Library of Congress Cataloging-in-Publication Data

Reger-Nash, Bill, 1942-
Foundations of wellness / Bill Reger-Nash, Meredith Smith, Gregory Juckett.
    pages cm
 Includes bibliographical references and index.
1. Health--Textbooks. 2. College students--Health and hygiene. 3. Young adults--Health and hygiene. I. Smith, Meredith, 1981- II. Juckett, Gregory, 1955- III. Title.

RA776.R36 2014
613--dc23

2014025427

ISBN: 978-1-4504-0200-2 (print)

The web addresses cited in this text were current as of July 2014, unless otherwise noted.

Acquisitions Editor: Ray Vallese
Developmental Editor: Ragen Sanner
Managing Editor: Anne E. Mrozek
Copyeditor: Bob Replinger
Indexer: Dan Connolly
Permissions Manager: Dalene Reeder
Graphic Designer: Joe Buck
Cover Designer: Keith Blomberg
Photograph (cover): © IsaacLKoval/iStock
Photographs (interior): © Human Kinetics, unless otherwise noted
Photo Production Manager: Jason Allen
Art Manager: Kelly Hendren
Associate Art Manager: Alan L. Wilborn
Illustrations: © Human Kinetics

Printer: McNaughton & Gunn

Printed in the United States of America

10 9 8 7 6 5 4 3 2 1

The paper in this book is certified under a sustainable forestry program.

Human Kinetics
Website: www.HumanKinetics.com

United States: Human Kinetics
P.O. Box 5076
Champaign, IL 61825-5076
800-747-4457
e-mail: humank@hkusa.com

Canada: Human Kinetics
475 Devonshire Road Unit 100
Windsor, ON N8Y 2L5
800-465-7301 (in Canada only)
e-mail: info@hkcanada.com

Europe: Human Kinetics
107 Bradford Road
Stanningley
Leeds LS28 6AT, United Kingdom
+44 (0) 113 255 5665
e-mail: hk@hkeurope.com

Australia: Human Kinetics
57A Price Avenue
Lower Mitcham, South Australia 5062
08 8372 0999
e-mail: info@hkaustralia.com

New Zealand: Human Kinetics
P.O. Box 80
Torrens Park, South Australia 5062
0800 222 062
e-mail: info@hknewzealand.com

E5301

Writing *Foundations of Wellness* represents a 20-year effort. This period coincides with the time that my wife, Jan, and I have been together. I dedicate this work to Jan, our daughter Emily, and to my deceased mentor Kennard McPherson, all of whom have facilitated my personal and professional wellness journey.

–Bill Reger-Nash

To my family and friends who supported me on my life journey to follow my dreams. I also want to give thanks to Bill Reger-Nash for being an invaluable mentor and my husband, Sean, for being my solid ground when I need it. Finally, I dedicate this book to the wonder of the human spirit, may we all continue to grow and know ourselves better.

– Meredith Smith

To my wife, Elizabeth, my wisest counselor, who has loved me unconditionally from the very beginning.

–Greg Juckett

CONTENTS

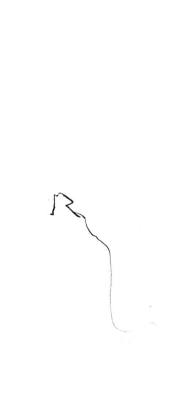

In a century transformed by the digital revolution, too often we live on automatic pilot. We rush from one activity to another, eat on the run, drive in a hurried manner to class or work, finish meals having overeaten but still hungry, communicate far more with screens than directly with others, and accumulate experiences that tend to be a kilometer wide and a centimeter deep. Is something wrong with this picture? Being unaware enables dysfunction to permeate life. There is a better way to live. Challenges represent opportunities for growth and development (Donaldson, Csikszentmihalyi, and Nakamura 2011). We need to find a way to move forward and mindfully embark on a balanced wellness journey.

This book provides a roadmap about how to develop the motivation and capture the time to experience deeper life satisfaction. A major objective is to grow more in touch with the texture and pleasures of your personal, interpersonal, school, and occupational lives—all at once and all together. *Foundations of Wellness* focuses on 18- to 30-year-old adults, roughly the age of millennials, but the content is applicable to people of all ages. Young adults are vibrant, open to change, and living fully. During this period of change, one develops lifelong thoughts, attitudes, beliefs, and behaviors. Young people transition from the structure of home, parents, and high school to college, independence, career, family, and beyond. The patterns established during these transitional periods are likely

patterns of a lifetime. Every day is an opportunity for a new beginning.

WELLNESS

Wellness is a journey into personal transformation. New information is of little value unless it is applied to living. "Wellness is the integration of body, mind, and spirit—the appreciation that everything you do, think, feel, and believe has an impact on your state of health and the health of the world" (Travis and Ryan 2004, p. xvi). Travis and Ryan use the image of an iceberg (figure 1) to show that the most visible aspects of health are above the water. What lies below the surface has a substantial influence on your wellness. Lifestyle behaviors, psychological beliefs, and motivations all affect your health. At the bottom of the iceberg are spiritual truths. These invisible dimensions have a profound effect on everything about us.

The key issue for your wellness journey becomes how you capitalize on what exists around you and below the surface. The authors have constructed a pathway that incorporates mindfulness (Kabat-Zinn 1994, 2003, 2005, 2012, 2013) and positive psychology (Donaldson, Csikszentmihalyi, and Nakamura 2011), which are powerful resources for your journey.

Wellness is often confused with specific aspects of health. Frequently, college campuses call their fitness centers "wellness centers." Others identify wellness

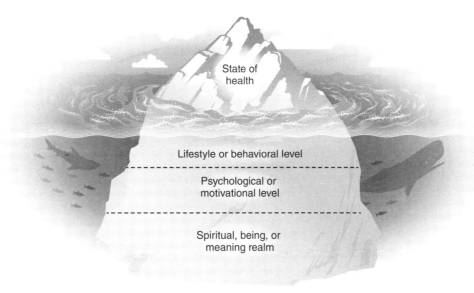

FIGURE 1 Iceberg model of health and disease.

with good nutrition. Still others believe that wellness means good mental health. These aspects are important, but wellness includes and supersedes all of them. Wellness can also be confused with prevention, although overlap exists with all these components.

MINDFULNESS

Mindfulness is a form of Buddhist meditation, but you do not need to be Buddhist to benefit. Dr. Jon Kabat-Zinn (2013) and his colleagues at the University of Massachusetts Medical Center helped translate mindfulness into a secular psychological application. According to Kabat-Zinn (2003), mindfulness is defined as "the awareness that emerges through paying attention on purpose, in the present moment, and nonjudgmentally to the unfolding of experience moment by moment" (p. 145). The practice is a recommended foundation for living with greater awareness and more equanimity.

Not surprisingly, the constructs of mindfulness and meditation overlap. According to the American Cancer Society website, "Meditation is a mind–body process that uses concentration . . . to calm the mind, . . . the intentional self-regulation of attention, a mental focus on a particular aspect of one's inner or outer experience" (Meditation 2014). For the purpose of this volume, you will focus on the practice of mindfulness as translated by Jon Kabat-Zinn (2013).

Attitudinal Foundations

Kabat-Zinn (2013) prescribes the following seven **attitudinal foundations** to undergird formal and informal mindful practices:

- **Nonjudging** is the mindful ability to see and to experience impartially, without labels or indictments.
- **Patience** permits everything to evolve in its own time.
- A **beginner's mind** enables you to see objects afresh, as if for the first time.
- **Trust** represents confidence in yourself.
- **Nonstriving** is being present with whatever is happening, without the need for goals, objectives, or outcomes to justify the process.
- "**Acceptance** means realizing how things are and finding ways to be in wise relationships with them. And then to act, as appropriate, out of that clarity of vision" (Kabat-Zinn 2012, p. 130).
- **Letting go** is the ability to let be, to relinquish attachment, to be nonattached to outcomes, and not to cling to what you hate or detest (Kabat-Zinn 2012).

These attitudinal foundations permeate each chapter and serve as beacons to guide your life journey. You build all mindfulness practices on these attitudes, to further enrich your day-to-day activities. The seven attitudinal foundations are as relevant to stress, physical activity, nutrition, sleep, interpersonal relationships, addictions, and preventive health care practices as they are to mindful sitting and yoga.

POSITIVE PSYCHOLOGY

Positive psychology promotes happiness and fulfillment (Seligman and Csikszentmihalyi 2000). Whereas much of modern medicine addresses illness, this discipline focuses on strengths and asset building. Positive psychology is defined as a new discipline "that studies mental health rather than illness, seeking to learn how normal life can be more fulfilling, and to identify the practices that individuals and communities can use to foster greater happiness" (Siegel 2013, p.41). Components include flow, gratitude, compassion, kindness, love, selflessness, generosity, and mindfulness (Siegel, 2013). The aim is to promote optimal human and community functioning. As these realms harmoniously come together, positive change is more likely to occur (Donaldson, Csikszentmilhalyi, and Nakamura 2011).

BOOK ORGANIZATION

This volume is divided into three sections. Each chapter builds on and extends the previous one, but each can stand alone. The chapters begin with wellness objectives and a vignette illustrating a wellness challenge. Wellness concepts are based on our observations of students or their reports. The authors have taken liberty with the reporting to preserve student anonymity and emphasize teaching points. The stories are intended to be illustrative rather than historically accurate.

Part I, encompassing chapters 1 through 5, establishes the basic problems that confront us in the modern world and introduces the tools you can use to rediscover your wellness and inner peace. The prevailing systems are predicated on a throwaway culture that encourages conspicuous consumption (Assadourian and Prugh 2013). Yet you all have a role to play in determining your future. You have options to conserve resources and to pursue a more healthy lifestyle. The more you are constructively engaged in the various components of life, the healthier you are (Donaldson, Csikszentmilhalyi, and Nakamura 2011).

Chapter 1, "Wellness Beyond Health," points out that the American "illness care system" dominates most health-related conversations and consumes an inordinate amount of resources. Your goal is to move beyond the absence of disease and achieve higher levels of living. Although one size does not fit all, a number of positive psychology practices can make personal growth and relating to others easier and richer (Boehm, Vie, and Kubzansky 2012).

Chapter 2, "Living the Attitudinal Foundations," applies the seven attitudinal foundations of mindfulness to daily living. Awareness becomes meaningful only if it is incorporated into day-to-day values, behaviors, and activities.

Chapter 3, "Using Mindfulness to Enhance the Experience of Life," discusses how to practice mindfulness in your wellness journey. Formal and informal mindfulness practices establish a solid foundation for living here now.

Chapter 4, "Changing Your Perspective With Your Thoughts," considers the importance of your thoughts, the working of your mind, and the relevance of the mind–body connection. Your mental diet is as important as your food diet.

Chapter 5, "Social Capital, Connections, and Support," explores the benefits accessible through social networking and social support from family, friends, and community. "Joys shared are doubled, and sorrows shared are halved," according to a time-tested saying passed down through generations.

Part II, chapters 6 through 9, addresses the physical dimensions of wellness. We examine the role of physical activity, nutrition, sleep, and body maintenance needs. It is estimated that as many people die from lack of physical activity and poor nutrition as from tobacco (Mokdad, Marks, Stroup, and Gerberding 2004).

Chapter 6, "Getting Started With Regular Physical Activity," addresses the benefits of regular physical activity and ways to integrate it painlessly into your life. The more physical activity you incorporate into everyday living, the less often you need to go to the gymnasium to work out.

Chapter 7, "Nutrition," examines why optimal nourishment is associated with eating more plants, namely, vegetables, fruits, legumes, and whole grains, along with reducing intake of salt, sugar, and saturated fat. The abundance of foods high in fat, sugar, sodium, and calories, combined with a sedentary lifestyle, is making many Americans overweight or obese, contributing to depression, premature disease, and diminishing overall quality of life (Moss 2013).

Chapter 8, "Sleep Balance," examines the role of sleep in a wellness lifestyle. We look at the data and suggest approaches to achieve better sleep.

Chapter 9, "Health Care Advice to Live Well," focuses on the medical resources available in the United States. These assets are unparalleled, yet U.S. health outcomes lag behind those of other developed nations (Brill 2013; Anderson, Davis, Hanna, and

Vincent 2013). Access to care has historically been limited for those without health insurance coverage. With health care insurance, patients often receive too many treatments and drugs (Abramson 2004), which contributes to iatrogenic illnesses (those caused by the health care system). This chapter also addresses complementary and alternative health practices.

Part III, chapters 10 through 12, discusses strategies for achieving a higher level of living. Lawrence Kohlberg (1973), building off Jean Piaget's (1965) developmental psychology, described six stages of moral development. The highest, final stage fosters life in its fullest sense for all. This principled living should be your ultimate goal.

Chapter 10, "Understanding Addictions," addresses compulsions and addictions in a positive manner. Stress can throw people out of balance, and some may develop maladaptive coping strategies, such as excessive alcohol consumption. Addictions, however, can also lead to an inner journey and high-level wellness.

Chapter 11, "Sustaining Environmental Heath," examines your ecological footprint on the physical world. We have severely damaged planet earth and are now reaping the consequences. But you can mitigate this damage in several ways. Mahatma Gandhi (1869–1948), admonished us, "Live simply so that others may simply live."

Chapter 12, "Spiritual Foundation," serves as a culminating experience for the entire book. We look beyond the constraints of your bodies, your emotions, and your psyche.

The concepts of wellness are simple, but the implementation is difficult. One of the authors (B.R-N.) coached high school basketball in Trumbull, Connecticut, with Vito Montelli (Ferhman 2014), masterful coach and teacher. Vito had written on the wall of his office, "Tell 'em once and have 'em do it a million times." It was always understood with Coach Montelli that you needed to do it *correctly* a million times. Similarly, you master the various levels of wellness skills and concepts by practice, practice, practice.

Instructors who use this book will have access to an online test package. There they will find sample multiple-choice, true–false, and essay test questions. The authors developed these questions to allow instructors to assess students' learning for the wellness management topics and tools found throughout this text.

GOALS AND THE EXPERIENCE

One of the goals of this book is to broaden the current, popular perception of health and wellness. Why just settle for freedom from identifiable diseases when an equally achievable goal is balance, harmony, and peace of mind? This book does not focus on the absence of illness; neither does it assault the reader by depicting one horrible disease after another. Instead, much of the book focuses on enhancing self-actualization, self-responsibility, peace of mind, attitudinal change, and balance at several experiential levels. Exploration in each of these separate realms—physical, mental, emotional, social, environmental, and spiritual—is life enhancing. Collectively integrated into a daily pattern of living, these realms are synergistic.

This book's orientation is toward wellness and ways that people can make themselves more well. The positive psychology messages of the book are as much process as content. Up-to-date health information is the starting point. Within all is wisdom, which can serve as your personal guide. Mindfulness is a tool for heightened consciousness. The more cognizant you are of your inner wisdom, the easier you can see possibilities and free yourself from feeling victimized.

The reader is advised that this book's orientation is toward what people can do to make themselves more well. The authors certainly recognize that those with acute and chronic illness will benefit from working with licensed medical doctors and other health professionals, which is emphasized in chapter 9. Those who

are dealing with serious physical, mental, emotional, or psychological health issues should consult with a certified health professional. Not uncommonly, health problems have a physiologic basis that a medical professional can help improve.

Learning activities are interspersed throughout the book. We ask that you set up a journal, with sections for each of the 12 chapters. Include your general reflections as well as the specific written exercises throughout the volume. This tool will enable you to build a portfolio of wellness experiences that you can access later.

We are all teachers and learners. We expect that readers will become fellow travelers toward improved health and wellness. The authors represent a variety of ages and life experiences, but in no way do we see ourselves as having *the* answers. We, the authors, collectively know a lot, but our recommendation is to walk together to fine-tune insights, attitudes, and skills; to try new behaviors; and to form habits through the steps of mindfully living well (Horton and Freire 1990).

The motto for this book is this: Be curious, trust yourself, have fun.

Part I

Challenges and Opportunities in Living Well

© Mandav

Chapter 1

Wellness Beyond Health

Objectives

After reading this chapter, you will be able to

- identify two barriers to wellness,
- differentiate between health and wellness,
- explain how mindfulness can undergird overall wellness,
- list the six dimensions of wellness,
- list and describe three positive psychology practices that promote wellness,
- describe the importance of balance in all areas of daily life, and
- describe the primary prevention role of mindfulness for telomere length.

Rachel was confused. As a 23-year-old undergraduate exercise physiology major, she was committed to good health and wellness. She knew the health promotional literature. Nonuse of tobacco products, regular exercise, and a good diet are the keys to good health. She never smoked. Her fitness was as good as it had ever been. She trained every day, including two track workouts weekly. She was running 5K races in 19 minutes, lifting weights two days a week, and stretching after each of her daily training sessions. Her diet included vegetables, fruits, whole grains, and lean protein. Her body fat was 16 percent, and her body mass index was 21. She felt at the top of her game.

But when her mother became ill near exam time, Rachel became distressed and depressed. She could not believe how terrible she felt. What else could she have possibly done to avoid feeling this way?

Do you live in a bountiful world? Your domain is diverse, stimulating, and accessible, if you have the right resources and motivation. Travel, knowledge, immigration, and intercultural communication afford exposure to amazing adventures. The planet continues to shrink to bring you exotic new foods, values, and social events. You can have friendships not only in your neighborhood but anywhere in the world. The sophistication of medical technology increases on a daily basis.

With all these resources, you may be wondering why you are not taking better care of yourself. The United States spends at least 40 percent more per capita than the next most generously spending nation (Brill 2013), yet Americans' life expectancy is low compared with that of other countries (*United Nations World Population Prospects Report* 2011). One in every three adults in the United States is currently obese, and this crisis has not been successfully addressed. People seem to be mindlessly reacting to what the environment enables and reinforces, and the U.S. environment is conducive to **obesity**. Making an unhealthy lifestyle choice is far easier for young adults than making a healthy one. All too often, time outside school and work is spent eating fast food, sitting on a couch, drinking alcohol or sugar-sweetened beverages, watching television, attending to a computer screen, and identifying **health** with regular medical check-ups.

Much of what systemically weighs on you today contributes to your feelings of personal overload. Much of your world is cluttered with misinformation that overwhelms your ability to discern. As an individual, you are no match for a mass media that perpetually plays on your appetites and feeds your fears.

Often, the response is to acquiesce to the status quo and suppress what you cannot address. The left side of figure 1.1 illustrates a reactive cascade of stimuli leading to maladaptive coping. External stressors alert you to danger. But you are no longer running from saber-tooth tigers in 21st-century America. Rather, you often bury the things that bother you inside yourself, while not addressing your stress in productive ways. Your physiologically based **fight-or-flight** reaction is no longer appropriate when impatiently sitting in traffic.

Your body may not be able to tell the difference between acute emotional stress and the immediate threat of a robber holding a gun to your head. In both cases you are hyperaroused. Your body's endocrine system releases a flood of chemicals that physically, emotionally, and mentally empowers action. Common reactions include verbally attacking the perceived perpetrators or even innocent people who happen to be present. Other people suppress their fear only to

have it haunt them later. Habitual repetition of these responses leads to being out of balance. You may end up chronically stressed and suffer from high blood pressure. You may be unable to sleep soundly. You may even become depressed over time. In reacting in these ways, you deny yourself pleasure, satisfaction, opportunity, and power.

"**Wellness** is the integration of body, mind, and spirit—the appreciation that everything you do, think, feel, and believe has an impact on your state of health and the health of the world" (Travis and Ryan 2004, p. xvi). Wellness includes and supersedes physical considerations. Physical inactivity, a poor diet, and tobacco use account for most deaths in the United States (Mokdad et al. 2004). But assuming that optimal health is achieved only by avoiding these three pitfalls is incorrect. In fact, toxic mental, emotional, spiritual, social, environmental, and community norms precipitate illnesses (Ornish 2007).

Mindful awareness is the cornerstone of our optimal wellness program, informing positive psychological, behavioral, and communitywide well-being. **Mindfulness** is defined as "the awareness that emerges through paying attention on purpose, in the present moment, and nonjudgmentally to the unfolding of experience moment by moment" (Kabat-Zinn 2013, p. 145). Mindfulness leads to inner peace and increased alertness. Through this calm awareness, you can better appreciate what is happening and act more deliberately.

The top right side of figure 1.1 illustrates the responding pathway. Given a regular practice of mindfulness, you can grow in nonjudgmental awareness and develop an appreciation for what is happening in your life. Thus, you have more latitude to make conscious decisions. With the regular practice of mindfulness come patience, self-trust, acceptance, and an ability to let go of things that you cannot control. Throughout *Foundations of Wellness*, we present evidence of how this responding pathway can break the cycle of ill health, addictions, and self-defeating behaviors while setting the stage for high level wellness.

Every chapter of this volume has experiential exercises that you will be asked to write about. You may wish to set up a journal to record those written exercises on your own, or your instructor might assign those more formally as part of your coursework.

PREVENTION

All too often, health is defined as the absence of disease. Societal resources focus on preventing disease. **Prevention** refers to those planned measures that are taken to forestall diseases or other health problems.

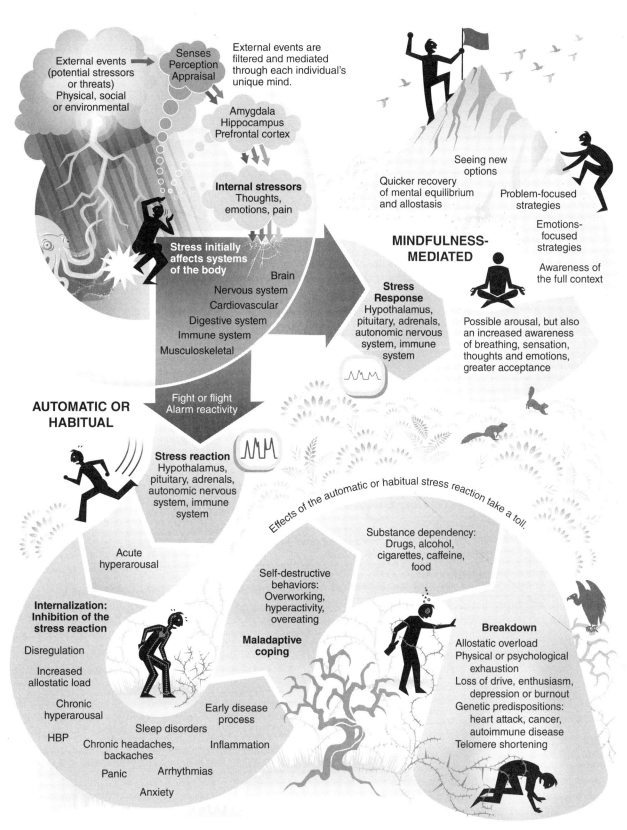

FIGURE 1.1 Stress-reaction cycle. Humans instinctively react to stress. When stress persists, such automatic reactions can lead to a cascade of ill effects and more stress. Alternatively, you can become mindfully aware. Note the two pathways, namely the "AUTOMATIC OR HABITUAL" compared to "MINDFULNESS-MEDIATED." Practicing mindfulness provides mental, emotional, and intellectual "space" to generate options. Mindfulness does not eliminate life challenges but makes them more manageable.

Based on Kabat-Zinn 2013.

Three levels of disease prevention exist:

- **Primary prevention** activities are those taken to forestall any disease process from occurring. It is well known that 60-90 minutes of daily **physical activity** helps people control their body weight. This primary prevention strategy addresses overweight and obesity.

- **Secondary prevention** refers to those measures taken to detect an illness condition early and to treat any diagnosed condition promptly. For example, blood-pressure screenings can detect increased risk for heart disease and stroke. A person might be counseled to consume more vegetables and fruits, to eat fewer animal products and dairy products, and to reduce sodium to 1,500 milligrams daily. These actions represent secondary prevention.

- **Tertiary prevention** represents those measures taken to retrain, reeducate, and rehabilitate a person with an illness, injury, or other impairment. After suffering a heart attack, a person might be referred to cardiac rehabilitation for regular supervised exercise, dietary counseling, and stress management. These educational and rehabilitation efforts would be intended to help the person regain function. The majority of prevention dollars are spent on tertiary prevention.

HEALTH CARE: MANAGING CRISES

Hospitals in the United States are good, medical technology is excellent, and medical professionals are usually dedicated and compassionate (Blank 2006). But something is still missing. Is our health care system focused on disease prevention through a long-term plan that includes wellness, or is it primarily concerned about treating illness after people become sick? As you look around, the answer is obvious: the medical system thrives by primarily addressing illness, disease and disability (Brill 2013). How much does this approach cost, not only in terms of money but also in terms of unnecessary suffering and lives?

This complex and costly "illness care" system consumes an inordinate amount of resources. American health care focuses on critical and specialized care, such as saving gunshot victims, replacing joints, conducting heart bypass surgeries, and excising cancerous tumors. These procedures serve an important need, but the evidence suggests that too many medical procedures are conducted in the United States and that too little emphasis is given to primary care and wellness (*Prostate-Specific Antigen Test* 2013; Haythorn and Ablin 2011).

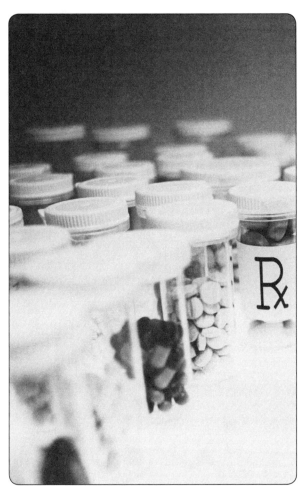

Health care should include a balance of primary care and wellness as well as appropriate medicines and use of medical technology.

© Super Stock

America spends more money per capita on health care and as a percentage of gross domestic product than any other nation in the world (*Kaiser Health News* 2012), yet it lags behind other high-income countries in terms of good health indices (Moses et al. 2013). Although the United States is the wealthiest industrialized nation, the 2010 U.S. infant mortality rate and life expectancy were 34th and 36th in the world, respectively (*United Nations World Population Prospects Report* 2011). Nearly 18 cents out of every dollar in the U.S. economy is spent in the health care sector, which employs 15.7 percent of the total U.S. workforce (*Occupational Employment Statistics* 2013).

Fee-for-service medicine, overuse of hospitals, sophisticated technology, and new designer pharmaceuticals drive up health care expenditures (Moses et al. 2013). Ill-directed health care reimbursement incentives to providers promote an overmedicated and overdosed society, rather than a system that consistently delivers judicious and effective treatments (Abramson 2004; Ornish 2011). For example, physician compensation for visits managing the complications of diabetes is far more generous than for visits aimed at preventing the disease through the promotion of wellness lifestyles.

Over the years, the language related to wellness and primary prevention has been coopted by the medical community (Starr 1982). The health system is **medicalized**. Illnesses amenable to lifestyle change, such as heart disease, some cancers, stroke, obesity, diabetes, hyperlipidemia, and **mental health**, are all medicalized; that is, they are treated with drugs and medical procedures (Coffey 2001; Pischke et al. 2010). Lifestyle advice, although fundamental to addressing the root causes of many illnesses, is given as a cursory recommendation at best. Wellness lifestyles are rarely taught in medical school (Mian et al. 2013) and are not reimbursed by insurance for **young adults**. Consequently, health promotion and wellness are given little attention or time in doctors' offices and other medical facilities.

People confuse health care and health. People might say, "I see my doctor regularly," "I am healthy because I have not missed a day of work in years!" or "My doctor examined me, and I am fine. My blood pressure, cholesterol, and heart checked out okay."

SOCIAL CONTEXT

Relatively few wellness programs are implemented in the United States. Little public money is available to promote wellness education, environment, and policy changes. Public health and wellness accounted for less than 3.5 percent of the $2.7 trillion health care expenditures for 2011 (*National Health Expenditure Data* 2014), despite the well-known aphorism that "an ounce of prevention is worth a pound of cure." Fifteen billion dollars over 10 years were earmarked for prevention and wellness in the 2010 Affordable Care Act health care reform legislation, but funding has not materialized (Preston and Alexander 2010).

The consequences of the lack of investment in wellness and primary care are disastrous. For example, overweight and obesity are nearly 100 percent preventable, but the U.S. epidemic continues. For the first time in U.S. history, young adults are projected to have a shorter life expectancy than their parents (Daniels 2006). The overweight and obesity crises could be controlled and even reversed if significant resources were allocated toward primary care, wellness education, investments in walking and bike trails, and retooling the food industry. For example, the U.S. Department of Transportation (2013) has a monumental budget for transportation infrastructure, but only a tiny percentage is spent on bicycle and pedestrian pathways. Such investment could encourage physical activity, promote body-weight maintenance, decrease traffic congestion, and save fossil fuels (Mulley et al. 2013).

Wouldn't it be incredible if everyone could safely walk or bike to the local market to buy a few items or if schools were built in neighborhoods with trails so that students could walk or bike safely to them? What would it be like if the choice to be well became easier, or the irresistible option across physical, mental, and emotional health domains? This has not happened, and no evidence indicates that it is about to happen.

DEFINING HEALTH VERSUS WELLNESS

What precisely is health? Are wellness and health the same? Historically, medical professionals described health as the absence of disease (Starr 1982). This definition is congruent with an illness care system. In contrast, we propose a broader definition consistent with the World Health Organization (1947): Health is "the state of complete mental, physical, and social well-being; not merely the absence of disease or infirmity" (p.1). This definition is closer to, yet distinct from, our concept of wellness. Both wellness and health exist on a spectrum. The illness–wellness continuum, figure 1.2, elucidates this. The more you do to be aware and to promote your growth results in moving toward high-level wellness.

Few people embody high-level wellness in all domains. Wellness is not equal to physical health, and vice versa. A person can be well and have mental illness. Heart attack, stroke, and cancer victims can be well. This concept is important. A person may have cancer and have robust mental health, extensive **social support**, and strong **spirituality**. In sum, such a person may be further along the wellness continuum than a stressed and anxious marathon runner.

Illness can even serve as a wake-up call to improve health. In a study of 652 women with breast cancer, positive changes in mental health, social support, and spirituality were observed within eight months after diagnosis and at the two-year follow-up (Danhauer et al. 2013). Consider the meaning within the title of the book *Now That I Have Cancer I Am Whole* (McFarland 2007). Wellness supersedes the body. A commitment to wellness is health enhancing, but no single aspect of ill health precludes a person from being well.

Implementing a wellness program in your life can result in what Don Ardell (1986) calls "rip-roaring good health," that is, living with high levels of energy,

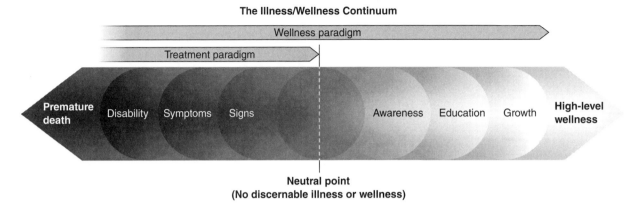

FIGURE 1.2 The illness–wellness continuum.

Used with permission, from *Wellness Workbook,* 3rd edition, John W. Travis, MD, and Regina Sara Ryan, Celestial Arts, Berkeley, CA. © 2004 by John W. Travis, page xviii.

pleasure, satisfaction, insight, and joy. This concept includes the six dimensions of wellness—physical, spiritual, emotional, social, mental/intellectual, and environmental—as popularized by the National Wellness Institute (see figure 1.3). Balancing each domain within the whole is paramount.

Wholeness and Balance

Wellness is balance. The more you engage in wellness practices, the better off you are. For example, even 10 minutes of daily physical activity is better than none, and the totally sedentary are at greatest risk. *Physical Activity Guidelines for Americans* (2008) recommends 30 to 90 minutes of daily moderate-intensity physical activity. The optimal macronutrient intake (Omni) and the dietary approach to stop hypertension (DASH) diets recommend 8 to 11 servings of vegetables and fruits per day (Swain et al. 2008; Greenland 2001).

The more vegetables you eat, the more you exercise, and the more you practice mindfulness, the higher your wellness will be, but only up to a point. As will be explained in the discussion of addictions in chapter 10, problems are associated with both abstinence and excess. Rip-roaring good health involves more than just being disease free. Wellness is associated with peace of mind, an abundance of physical and emotional energy, a positive outlook, and a deep-seated feeling of self-worth, safety, and security. Your positive thoughts about the present, hope for the future, and **optimism** can promote your health (Boehm, Vie, and Kubzansky 2012). Balance in being is important, and the balance you achieve is an "inside job" (Pransky 2003).

COMMITMENT

Although the content of wellness is modest, making the commitment to live a wellness lifestyle is monumental. This commitment requires attitudinal and

perceptual shifts—a reframing that permits seeing through the clutter in your life and acting with sensitivity to your day-to-day choices. Choosing balance within the holistic domains of wellness means that you will enjoy better health than you ever expected possible. There are no absolute prescriptions about what you must do or what results you will realize. Health challenges do not preclude you from attaining high-level wellness.

We do not want to overstate the following outcomes, but when you are well, you are more likely to

- feel good,
- have good friends,
- be close to your ideal body weight,
- feel harmony,
- have energy to do whatever you want to do,
- think clearly,
- sleep well, and
- enjoy life.

Being well doesn't happen by default, but the dividends are greater than the investment. You are worth the effort.

Some professionals make onerous wellness prescriptions, such as "Eat only organic vegetables and fruits," or "You must exercise for 60 to 90 minutes a day." This is not the best approach. A better approach is to provide information, principles to follow, skills to practice, and goals to seek. You have the free will to determine what will work for you now, or even 10 years from now.

You can unconsciously make a wellness program an end in itself. In doing so, you can become divorced from living. Good health practices are not a substitute for living a wellness lifestyle. If the process is not fun, if you are reluctantly engaged in health promotion, if

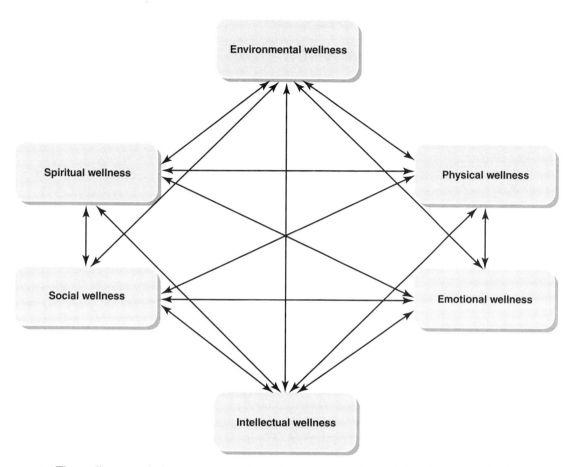

FIGURE 1.3 The wellness web. The six dimensions of wellness are interrelated. You should strive to balance these dimensions in your life so that they can work together to keep you well.

Adapted, by permission, from N. Tummers, 2013, *Stress management: A wellness approach* (Champaign, IL: Human Kinetics), 5.

you are not enjoying yourself along the way, then the wellness value of the behavior is compromised.

Eating, touching, moving, sex, poetry, and music are pleasurable activities that provide their own intrinsic rewards (Diamond 1997). Without the immediate and pleasant feedback that they can provide, you would likely lose interest in all activities. When Jon Kabat-Zinn (2013) defines life as "embodying the full catastrophe," a phrase drawn from the film *Zorba the Greek*, he sees it positively, including all the challenges, beauty, capacities, pride, frustrations, and thrills that make up who you are.

Here are a few examples:

- Walking the dog for a half hour can be a lot more fun than walking eight laps around an athletic field.
- Eating a sumptuously flavored Chinese stir-fry is delicious and nutritious. Eating can be made more varied and adventurous through the exploration of ethnic cuisine. The foods of the world have an array of savory spices, flavors, and scents. Try recipes with new ingredients.

- Focus on the joy of the moment. This moment is really all there is. It is all you ever really have. You can find satisfaction in your current situation if you are present to experience it. In this way, satisfaction in life is accessible to all.
- Look out the window and savor a previously undiscovered glimpse of nature.
- Lose yourself in a bike ride along a waterway.
- Dance as if no one were looking.

LIFE'S BOUNDLESS CLASSROOM

When you make your life experience a journey, rather than a destination, your life becomes a boundless classroom in which you continuously learn lessons. In this classroom, you can mindfully learn through trial and error. In this classroom, you make no mistakes; you only learn lessons. Living in such a classroom means (1) you cannot fail, and (2) you cannot make final judgments on the actions of others or even your

© BOLD STOCK / age fotostock

You must discover for yourself the activities and lifestyle choices that work best for you in your quest to remain committed to balanced living.

own actions (Diekmann, Tenbrunsel, and Galinsky 2003). You may make errors, but that is merely the method of learning. If you become irritated with your romantic partner, accept the shortcoming and own the experience. Apologize and move forward. Experiences that you once deemed failures are as much a part of the wonderful texture of wellness as the ones that seem to succeed.

Live right here, right now. Planning is fine, but after you make a life decision, relax and engage fully in the process. Yogi Berra (2001) wrote a book titled *When You Come to a Fork in the Road, Take It!* There is value along every path you consciously walk. What happens in life is not all that matters. What you do with what happens is more important. Physical illness, great sunsets, relationship challenges, a sumptuous meal, business failures, a sudden windfall, and job changes are events. Are you present for the experience?

MINDFUL AWARENESS

Mindfulness is the art of paying attention. It serves as a foundation for happiness and living well. What could be better than being attentive to where you are and what you are doing! Mindfulness is a practice enjoyed by people throughout the world no matter what their religion. Many think that mindfulness is limited to monks, nuns, clerics, and mystics who

are cloistered away from the world. Nothing could be further from the truth. Mindfulness is zoning in, which then increases your capacity for life, living, love, and pleasure.

The 10-minute activity Mindful Observation provides an introductory mindfulness experience as a means of demystifying the practice for those who are uninitiated.

Establishing Priorities

Because many of your life decisions are reactive, having a framework for prioritizing can be helpful. Stephen R. Covey (1995) depicts choices as residing in one of four quadrants which include urgent and important categories. We depict an alternate form of these priorities in figure 1.4. Level 1 represents the critical (urgent) and valuable (important). For example, you may critically need to see a health professional after cutting your arm with a kitchen knife. If you do not take action quickly, the consequences can be dire. Level 2 includes the valuable but not critical. For example, regular physical activity is valuable for **quality of life**, but nothing catastrophic will happen if you skip it today. We recommend spending as much time as possible in level 2, because it is here that your life is in balance. Level 3 refers to those critical but not essential behaviors that consume a disproportionate

Activity

Mindful Observation

Find a window facing outside that you can sit in front of for five minutes without being disturbed. This exercise involves mindful observation, paying attention without making judgments. The viewscape might include plants and other living creatures, but the content is less important than the process (Kabat-Zinn 2013). This exercise may feel awkward. You do not need to call attention to yourself. Act normally, relax, and engage.

1. With your eyes open, take two long, slow, deep breaths and relax. Then breathe normally and notice your chest wall rising and falling with each in-and-out breath.

2. Now, make a mental note of one object within your viewscape. Keep your attention present. Be aware. Breathe mindfully as you continue your observation experience. If your mind wanders away from the body sensations or the viewscape, note where your thought has gone and return your attention to your breath.

3. When you are ready, and without hurrying, move on to the next visible object. Refrain from making judgments about what you see, or noting what you see as good or bad. Stay present, focused, and relaxed. Breathe normally.

4. Patiently, mindfully, and deliberately move your eyes from one object to the next. View each as if for the first time. In fact, this is the first time you are seeing this object at this time in this setting. Stay with the observation for a while. Pause, and then move on to the next object in view.

5. You might be feeling insecure about this exercise; let go of those concerns and trust in yourself. You have nothing to do other than to be mindful of your experiences. You are bringing increased attention and nonjudgmental awareness to an aspect of your life.

6. Move slowly and patiently from one object to another, repeating the process of experiencing, noticing, and letting go.

7. You will undoubtedly become distracted. Your mind will move to thoughts other than this mindful observation exercise. This wandering of the mind represents an excellent opportunity for acceptance. Distractions are part of who you are and part of the mindfulness practice. If your mind wanders a hundred times, bring it back a hundred times. These distractions are an intrinsic part of being mindful. When you become aware of a thought, make a mental note of it and return to the observations.

8. After several minutes of this process, pause with two more long, slow, deep in-and-out breaths. Take a moment for self-acceptance and lose yourself in the experience. Your life is richer for performing this exercise in increased attention and mindfulness.

For all the mindful practices, resist the temptation to jump up and do something new. Instead, sit with the experience for a full minute after completing the mindful activity.

---

amount of your time, resources, and energy. Meetings, phone messages, e-mails, and popular activities fall into this category. Something may be critical for others, such as co-workers and friends, but not necessarily for you. Level 4 includes activities that are not valuable and not critical. You may choose to watch a television show, engage in social media, or call someone, but such activities are frequently neither valuable nor critical. When we prioritize, everything can become an optimal wellness experience and helpful to living in a more aware, focused, and peaceful manner.

Much of Western medicine is considered critical and valuable. The preceding example about the laceration needing immediate attention illustrates this point. However, when you live in balance at the individual or population level, there are fewer critical and valuable issues. For example, scientists are convinced that global warming would not be so dire had we better managed our natural resources (Assadourian and Prugh 2013). Understanding these levels can help you be more deliberate about the use of your resources as you mindfully make decisions.

I. Critical and valuable Behaviors: Medical emergencies Disasters Project deadlines	**II. Not critical, but valuable** Behaviors: Eating fruits and vegetables Regular physical activity Reduce, reuse, and recycle material Mindfulness practices Expressing gratitude and love
III. Critical, but not valuable Behaviors: Interruptions Some email, mail, phone calls, deadlines Internet searching	**IV. Not critical and not valuable** Behaviors: Most emails, phone calls, social media, browsing the web, television

FIGURE 1.4 Covey's framework provides help in establishing priorities when making decisions. The grid shows examples of common behaviors and the degree to which the behaviors are critical and valuable.

Based on Covey 1995.

LIFE CHALLENGES

Your thoughts, emotions, and motivations are crucial. If you do not keep yourself in balance, disappointments can increase to the point where you substitute symbols for happiness. The loss of 30 pounds (14 kg), for example, may draw enough compliments to distract you from negative thinking. Given powerful distractions, you may momentarily think all is well. Similarly, drinking a lot of alcohol, altering your mood with drugs, and flitting from one relationship to another can be associated with immediate pleasure. Gratification is commonly achieved by smoking, driving too fast, idle texting during class and work, shopping for things you do not need, spending money you do not have, and taking unwise risks. Such imbalances may involve excitement, but they also contribute to stress, can exacerbate sexual dysfunction, and increase the likelihood of unhappiness (Travis and Ryan 2004). At many levels, you keep yourself out of balance with your reactions. But you cannot hide from your own mind.

Part of being aware is realizing that dominant societal norms keep you focused outside yourself. The practices of wellness enable you to be present with yourself so that you can appreciate your being. When you are in balance, you have focus, quiet, and calm. In contrast, when you lose balance, you are extending an invitation to illness and disease. The choice is yours.

CHOOSING BALANCE

To live your life in mindful balance is to make a conscious choice to be your own best friend. You need to take even better care of yourself than your mother would! Such choices are valuable but never easy. Many of the decisions made along this path are common sense. Being nice to others feels good and is the right thing to do. Do you sweep the leaves off your porch with a broom or buy an electric-powered blower to do the job? Physical movement in this case is healthful, reduces pollution on planet Earth, and feels good. Humans often do better when they are physically inefficient as excess calories are burned and **fitness** improves.

When you are mindful, you have far less inclination to abuse your body, mind, and emotions. Many unhealthy lifestyle habits are ineffective coping mechanisms. You may be overeating out of unhappiness or because your diet is loaded with fat, sugar, and salt (Moss 2013). These latter foods stimulate the appetite and sabotage your body's appestat, the food intake regulatory mechanism (Sclafani and Ackroff 2012). You may smoke cigarettes as a distraction from life stressors (Mackey, McKinney, and Tavakoli 2008). Knowledge alone may not be enough to solve a lifestyle problem. Being tranquil, knowing how to prioritize, learning to identify barriers, staying away from risky environments, and developing self-enhancing strategies can help you take charge.

Life challenges occur minute by minute. The *Foundations of Wellness* model helps you reclaim your natural state of joy, happiness, meaning, and fulfillment (your life homeostasis). Those things that promote good health also promote pleasure and positive emotions (Ornstein and Sobel 1989). **Positive**

Rachel's mother's illness was a major challenge to her social and emotional stability. Vigorous exercise and a disciplined diet were not enough to sustain her. Rachel became stressed, depressed, and pessimistic. She desperately needed additional coping tools. Rachel went to see a university student health counselor, who provided her with instruction in mindful awareness and expressing gratitude. After beginning to implement those recommendations, Rachel immediately experienced the hope that there was an answer.

emotions comprise trust, compassion, gratitude, awe, forgiveness, joy, hope, and love (Vaillant 2013). With positive emotions come increases in vitality, improved immunity, and perceptions that are more nurturing (Seligman 2011). Like a child who cannot walk well until he or she first develops the proper muscles by crawling, you cannot move to the next higher level of consciousness without having mastered previous ones. These changes evolve naturally from awareness.

Similarly, when you accept who you are and where you are in life, you are more likely to feel good about yourself and not be threatened by change. When you are serene and have the physical, mental, emotional, environmental, and spiritual supports that you need, change will occur naturally (Seligman and Csikszentmihalyi 2000). This positive approach represents a sea of change for psychology.

POSITIVE PSYCHOLOGY

Positive psychology is the recently developed branch of psychology that focuses on identifying and promoting people's genius and talents. The field studies optimal human functioning to promote societal changes that make people and communities thrive (Sheldon et al. 2014). Emphasis is on strengths and finding meaning, inner peace, and fulfillment, not sickness and disability.

Seligman (2011), a founding member of positive psychology, maintains that positive emotions, engagement, meaning, self-esteem, optimism, resiliency, vitality, self-determination, and positive relationships enable people to flourish. Research is demonstrating the efficacy of this approach in promoting asset-building skills and higher well-being (Siegel 2013; Reichard et al. 2013). Fordyce (1977) was one of the first to demonstrate a dose response for happiness intervention tactics in quality of life. The more that people committed to the tactics, the greater the benefit they gained (Fordyce 1983). Seligman, Rashid, and Parks (2006) demonstrated that engagement, positive emotion, and meaning are means of improving mood, preventing stress, and alleviating depression. These positive psychology practices are not only associated

with an improved emotional state and higher levels of wellness but also lead to healthier behaviors and a lower death rate from heart disease, kidney disease, and HIV–AIDS (Chida and Steptoe 2008).

Inner Strengths

"Strengths are built-in capacities for certain thoughts, feelings, and behaviors" (Siegel 2013, p. 13). Everyone has talents in all areas to some degree. Curiously, most people have little appreciation for their character strengths. Yet your strengths can easily dominate your time and priorities. You rarely count the time when you are doing something that you are passionate about. You might be passionate for teamwork and center your life on organizing, coaching, and officiating soccer. Others might express a passion for teamwork by promoting a community orchestra. Such activities undoubtedly link to a personal strength.

Not surprisingly, inner strengths are associated with greater personal happiness. The Values in Action Program (www.viacharacter.org) has a 20-minute, 120-question Inventory of Signature Strengths Questionnaire to help people rank their five most dominant strengths. Just knowing your strengths does little good. You need to use them to have a positive effect on happiness.

In one study, young people were assigned to one of two groups (Seligman et al. 2005). Group 1 was directed to write about early memories. Group 2 was assigned to implement something daily with one of their top strengths for a week. At the end of two weeks, the implementers were happier and less depressed. These changes remained in place for the next six months, compared with the control group.

Flow

Flow, another construct of positive psychology, represents being immersed in a challenging and rewarding endeavor without distraction, sense of time, or self-consciousness, and feeling one with and having control over the outcome (Donaldson, Csikszentmihalyi, and Nakamura 2011). Awareness, action, and mastery merge.

Activity

Identify Your Inner Strengths to Work Towards Happiness

This activity will enable you to identify your inner strengths and provides an opportunity to implement them over the course of a week. This assignment has a two-week time frame.

1. During week 1, go to the Values in Action link, www.viacharacter.org, and complete the 120-item questionnaire. The computer program will analyze your responses and provide a list of your five key signature strengths.
2. In 200 to 300 words, summarize what you learned about yourself from this exercise.
3. During week 2, implement a different strength in your life each day for five days.
4. In 200 to 300 words, summarize how you felt about implementing your key strengths.

Keep your Values in Action results because you will be using these materials in subsequent chapters. Place the two summary statements and your Values in Action results in chapter 1 of your journal.

Csikszentmihalyi began studying flow after observing painters and other crafts people intensely absorbed in their activities, often losing track of time, interest in eating, and taking breaks. Film director George Lucas reported starting work at 9 a.m. and not finishing until 10 p.m., totally losing track of time (Siegel 2013). Some attribute the basketball accomplishment of LeBron James with his ability to flow. His intensity, skill level, and control in the game are legendary. Martial artist Bruce Lee recommended being like water to achieve flow with the environment (Lee 1975). To flow is to pursue a goal yet to become immersed without conscious awareness of the goal, objective, or the need to apply skills. The activity is intrinsically rewarding.

Happiness

Happiness refers to life satisfaction (Schwarz and Strack 1999). Alternatively, it is a "subjective sense of well-being . . . as well as the sense that your life is worthwhile" (Siegel 2013, p.7). Indeed, happiness is one of the overarching goals for wellness, that is, to be happy and to do those activities that promote and maintain happiness. According to Dr. Martin Seligman (2011), happy people are resilient, flexible, and optimistic and have positive emotions.

Happiness is promoted by attentiveness. Killingsworth and Gilbert (2010) determined that mind wandering occurs about half the time for all people regardless of the activity (except for making love), but that people are happier when their mind is on task. Happiness is also associated with being meaningfully engaged and helping others. Volunteers report higher levels of happiness and well-being (Borgonovi 2008). Optimistic people are happier, healthier, and tend to be more productive (Seligman 2006).

People can learn to be optimistic by challenging their negative views, that is, by changing their pessimistic self-assertions and challenging negative ideas. After doing poorly in a test, a pessimist might conclude that he or she cannot master the content and will likely repeat the poor test performance. An optimist will choose to see the causes of failure as something that he or she can manage, such as additional test preparation or locating a tutor. Optimists almost universally perform better than pessimists (Seligman 2011).

Learned optimism is the cultivation of skills that permit a person to be able to see and experience joy, happiness, and well-being (Seligman 2006). These skills can reduce heart disease by 30 percent (Tindle et al. 2009). Happy people are more likely to participate in physical activity compared with less happy people (Baruth et al. 2011). Blanchflower, Oswald, and Stewart-Brown (2013) demonstrated a strong relationship between positive emotion and vegetable and fruit consumption.

Gratitude

Gratitude is a key personal strength and represents how we feel when we receive an undeserved benefit from another (Emmons and Stern 2013). Gratitude is somewhat of a transcendental experience in that you recognize goodness outside yourself (Siegel 2013). This signature strength has been shown by positive psychology research to be among the most positive attributes that a person can have (Seligman 2011). Writing letters of gratitude to people living and deceased can improve happiness (Seligman, Steen, Park, and Peterson 2005). Similar results are realized by regularly counting blessings (Emmons and McCullough 2003). Behaviors

© iStockphoto

Helping others can be fulfilling and lead to your own happiness.

related to kindness included performing numerous acts of kindness in a single day, engaging in a high variety of kind acts, and keeping track of acts of kindness (Otake et al. 2006). Kabat-Zinn (2013) encourages his clients to recognize that there is more right than wrong with them.

Even if you are not predisposed, gratitude is a skill that can be nurtured. Acts of gratitude positively influence blood pressure, immune function, happiness, and well-being (Emmons and Stern 2013). A study by Emmons and McCullough (2003) demonstrated improvements in optimism, happiness, and physical health after participants daily wrote for one week about positive experiences in their lives, compared with a control group.

Engagement

Active participation in life is healthful. Engagement leads to higher levels of meaning and personal satisfaction (Seligman 2011), which are major components of well-being. One study encouraged young adults to use their cameras to capture 9 to 12 images that made their lives feel meaningful. After just one week, these young adult participants manifested higher levels of meaning and satisfaction in their personal lives (Steger et al. 2013).

Activity

Gratitude in Everyday Life

This exercise requires 10 days.

1. For 10 consecutive days, identify and describe something different for which you are grateful. Entries do not need not be particularly extensive (50 to 100 words per day will suffice).

2. Daily share your gratitude orally with a friend, classmate, or a loved one.

3. After 10 days of recording your gratitude, summarize your reaction to the experience in 200 to 300 words. Was keeping track difficult? Did you enjoy doing so? How do you feel about sharing your gratitude with another person?

4. Insert your daily log and your summary statement into your journal.

Rachel encountered a trial that served as a springboard to a higher level of well-ness. Similar to many of her classmates, she thought that she was doing fine with her health behaviors. She was coping with most of the eventualities of life. Her regular exercise and vegetable-based diet served her well. Nevertheless, her mom's illness at exam time challenged her beyond her capabilities. She could have spiraled down to a lower level of living and experienced the onset of chronic disease. But instead, she used the challenges as an opportunity to incorporate mindfulness and gratitude into her life. She set aside 10 minutes daily for mindful awareness and maintained a daily gratitude log. The log provided a means for her to identify positive experiences in her daily life that she could easily have overlooked.

Through active engagement and reflection with the content of the book and the challenges presented in your everyday life, you may gain better understanding of your identity and power. This process will enable you to recognize your inner strengths and resources, and to appreciate the relevance of personal goals, jobs, and daily functioning to life. The more consciously you actively participate in the processes of life, the more fulfilled you will be (Donaldson, Csikszentmilhalyi, and Nakamura 2011).

EVIDENCE TO SUPPORT WELLNESS PRACTICES

Of course, there is always a question of whether or not wellness practices make a difference in people's lives. Throughout the volume, we will refer to the research to substantiate the effects.

The following discussion is technical but important as it substantiates benefits associated with the recommended wellness activities. As will be presented throughout the chapters, stress can be reduced and well-being promoted by mindfulness and positive psychology practices.

Investigations have examined **telomeres**, which are the specialized ends of chromosome structures that provide constancy to DNA molecules. Telomeres enable the DNA molecules to replicate safely. Stress damages and shortens the telomeres (Boesten et al. 2013). If telomeres are shortened below a critical threshold, the telomeric protection is lost and chromosomes can be damaged (Donate and Blasco 2011). Such damaged chromosomes are associated with a depressed immune function, premature aging, decreased life expectancy, and increased chronic disease (Georgin-Lavialle et al. 2014).

Stress reduction and mindfulness interventions are demonstrating modest but promising results regarding the reversal of telomere shortening (Daubenmier et al. 2012; Epel. 2012). In a small study of cancer and aging, Biegler et al. (2012) observed statistically significant increases in telomere length after the stress reduction intervention, as compared to baseline telomere length.

The goal of the Foundations of Wellness approach is the promotion of high-level wellness and health. By performing the recommended mindfulness and positive psychology practices, we would be preventing stress-related telomere shortening. Preventing the onset of disease is more cost effective than attempting to reverse physiologic damage (Ornish 2007).

SUMMARY

Major **social** impediments exist to the incorporation of a wellness lifestyle. The medical profession often sees health as the absence of disease. The focus on illness care and health crises consumes inordinate resources in the United States, leaving little available for health promotion and wellness. Wellness lifestyle problems are medicalized, that is, defined within a medical framework. Health care reimbursement to physicians favors procedures and drugs.

Wellness is choosing to maximize internal and external resources toward a balanced integration of body, mind, and spirit within a health-promoting environment. *Foundations of Wellness* begins with the application of mindful awareness. The desired outcomes may not happen in a week, a month, or even a year. But committing yourself to the process of optimal wellness living can occur in a millisecond and last a lifetime. The commitment is but a monumental first step.

Positive psychology provides tools for living well and removes you from the prevalent 21st century ill-ness orientation. These tools make you aware, resilient, and capable of flourishing in a toxic world. Wellness involves being an active participant in life. Perfect execution is not required. The more you nurture the body, mind, and spirit, the more inner strength you have to live fully and maintain peace of mind. The better you take care of yourself, the more likely it is that you will be resilient, happy, and fulfilled.

Growth is not foreign to you. Your life is constantly changing. Sometimes you feel in charge of the direction of the movement; sometimes it feels as though the changes are directing you; at other times, it seems too difficult to try to figure out what is happening. Clearly, however, the more you are present with and engaged in life, the more you can learn, appreciate, enjoy, and be well.

Fundamentally, you are all right just as you are. Appreciating your assets sets the stage for a high quality of life. Your body may be damaged or broken, but the composite of your mind, body, and spirit is whole. Positive psychological well-being capitalizes on your assets to promote a high level of functioning.

Chapter 2

Living the Attitudinal Foundations

Objectives

After reading this chapter, you will be able to

- identify two barriers to moment-to-moment awareness,
- identify the importance of living with mindfulness,
- define each of the seven attitudinal foundations of mindfulness,
- describe how each of the attitudinal foundations can be applied to daily living,
- apply the attitudinal foundations in everyday living on at least three occasions per day, and
- list four instances when mindful awareness resulted in an improved quality of life during the past week.

Aryne is a 24-year-old graduate public health major. She woke up this morning to see the sun shining. The yard is filled with wonderful signs of life. The birds are out, and the plants are abloom as never before. She feels truly blessed.

Aryne frequently suffers from cluster headaches that last anywhere from 4 hours to 12 weeks. Today she woke up without a headache. What a wonderful nonheadache day! She has often taken things for granted, but she will not take them for granted today.

Aryne gained her new perspective after enrolling in a psychology course as part of her undergraduate education. During the course, her professor emphasized how the attitudinal foundations of mindfulness and positive psychology could improve people's lives. Aryne began doing brief daily mindful awareness practices, focusing particularly on incorporating the attitudinal foundations into her everyday life. Now, even her cluster headaches remind her to be nonstriving, that is, to engage 100 percent with her activities and not to second-guess herself. As she practices, she is more meaningfully engaged and her life has more flow. Aryne realizes that the pain will pass.

She attempts to do the best she can, be at peace with herself, and not make the situation worse. Mindfulness has helped her accept herself. She is no longer as uptight as she once was. She understands that her pain does not define who she is. Even at the worst times, she knows that she is all right and has much for which to be grateful.

A wellness goal to strive for is to become more aware of every moment. The seven attitudinal foundations of mindfulness (nonjudging, patience, beginner's mind, trust, nonstriving, acceptance, and letting go), as defined by Jon Kabat-Zinn (2013), establish a solid base for such awareness. Day-to-day living involves thousands of demands and tasks. Almost everything going on keeps people focused outside themselves. Further, people spend about half their time thinking unrelated thoughts of past or future events, which is to say that mind wandering is pervasive in modern life (Killingworth and Gilbert 2010). During mind wandering, people are less happy and have reduced energy (Seligman 2011).

Every instant can become a meaningful wellness experience. Understanding the role of the seven attitudinal foundations is an important first step. These are the guiding principles for the practice of mindfulness, whether that is mindful sitting, body scanning, walking, eating, or everyday living. Practicing the attitudinal foundations presents opportunities to reclaim control of attention and happiness. This chapter will help you live with more awareness and satisfaction.

Seventeenth century French author Blaise Pascal (1623-1662) wrote, *"Le cœur a ses raisons que la raison ne connaît point."* This is translated to mean, "The heart has reasons that the mind can never know." Knowing concepts intellectually is not enough. The French have two words for knowing, namely *savoir* and *connaître*. *Savoir* refers to a cognitive understanding, whereas *connaître* is used to refer to something with which there is intimate experience. It is said the distance between the head (knowledge) and the heart (experiences incorporated into beliefs, values, attitudes, norms, and behaviors) is indeed the longest distance in the world. The goal is to traverse that chasm in a way that makes the attitudinal foundations a force for improved mindfulness. Living draws the body and mind in different directions. The attitudinal foundations are effective means to cut through the clutter and to focus on living well.

FOUNDATION FOR MINDFULNESS

Attitudes are established beliefs that guide thinking, behaviors, and responses. Attitudes set the stage for moments that determine what a person is, sees, and

© Tomasz Nieweglowski - Fotolia

Upsetting things happen to everyone. Don't let that stop you from trying to have a positive attitude. Just trying to see the brighter side will help to make the situation seem less grim, whereas focusing on how awful it is will make it seem even worse.

feels. Many experiences are taken for granted, even though ongoing "miracles" are occurring. For example, the billions of ongoing interrelated biological processes within you are worthy of appreciation, even though they might not technically qualify as miracles. In the presence of a variety of health conditions, diagnoses, and physical limitations, far more is right than wrong with any person. Rarely is this appreciated.

Think about the intricacies of physical and mental functions, actions, reactions, and interactions; the appeal of an apple; or chewing, swallowing, digesting, absorbing, and gaining energy associated with eating that apple. Think about the relationships in life that bring food, shelter, and friendships; the enjoyment of art, music, and quiet; the sensuousness of a sunset, the rustling of autumn leaves, the awesomeness of life forms everywhere. Each is cause for celebration and generally underappreciated.

Much can be done to maximize quality of life. Attitudes unlock the texture of experiences. There is almost always something to do. Options might include reading a good novel, writing a poem, working in the garden, walking the dog, swimming in the river, bicycling through the woods, cuddling with a sweetheart, volunteering at the animal shelter, or generally being engaged in life. The choices involve the activities and accompanying attitudes.

You may feel tense, fragmented, inadequate, guilty, or frustrated when ruminating about the past or projecting into the future. Emmons and McCullough (2003) remind you to focus on those life processes that are working well. Do you want to emphasize limitations or resonate with assets? What you experience is essentially a choice.

Attitudes affect your overall quality of life and health. For example, optimism and a positive attitude can make the sun appear brighter and everyday events more pleasant (Forgeard and Seligman 2012). By contrast, dark and pessimistic moods color the perception of all experiences. Almost anything can become awful, even when it is not that bad (Borysenko 2007). A negative attitude affects the biochemistry of your emotional response, which further reinforces the low mood, initiating a vicious cycle (Pert 1997). Stressed and depressed people are more susceptible to the common cold and liable to experience other, even more serious, health problems (Cohen et al. 2012). Changing your attitude can change your health.

Personal change need not be forced. Considering what is important is worthwhile. Attentiveness and trust are central to personal serenity. Rather than letting highly charged negative emotions lead you to pursue elusive materialistic goals, adopting different

© Corbis

Don't take any experience for granted. Stay present in the moment and appreciate the wonder around you.

attitudes can transform life (Dalen et al. 2010).

How joyful can life become? Perceptions create reality (Wubbolding 2002). Being open and viewing things as they are, rather than catastrophizing, can change your world (Borysenko 2007). Even the nature of fear changes when brought into consciousness (Kemeny et al. 2012). Perception change means healthier, happier lives. Thus, your attitudes constitute important elements for health and wellness.

Each day has 24 hours. How you use that time is your choice. Becoming short and impatient with your friends and family, for example, does not serve anyone. In discussing highly effective people, author Stephen R. Covey (1989) recommends taking time to "sharpen the saw," as he called it. If personal and interpersonal skills do not permit you to live effectively, you need to take time "to sharpen the saw," that is, to learn those skills that provide better coping mechanisms.

SEVEN ATTITUDINAL FOUNDATIONS

Jon Kabat-Zinn (2013) defines the seven attitudinal foundations of mindfulness. These represent a skill set that enables you to embrace your life in a whole new way. The utility of these skills becomes clearer and more effective through practice. These attitudinal foundations are often applied together. They have been shown to work with sick people in a medical setting (Kabat-Zinn 2013) as well as with healthy people (Williams et al. 2001). But they work only if you use them.

Nonjudging

A major goal for life satisfaction is to be aware and to not judge. **Nonjudging** is the mindful ability to see and to experience impartially, without labels or indictments. Your mind judges continuously. These judgments can serve good purposes, such as assessing what is in the refrigerator to determine what to eat for dinner. Most people continually evaluate their experiences, and doing so can be helpful. For example, you need to judge where you can safely pass another automobile on a curvy two-lane road.

A judgment can also be an indictment and associated with guilt. Perhaps you conclude your friend cannot be counted on to help. Such an indictment may evoke a negative emotion as you are placing yourself above others (Bordenhauser, Shephard, and Kramer 1994). The default mode for thinking appears to be negative ruminations with indictments of self and others (Killingsworth and Gilbert 2010). Not uncommonly, you experience negative thoughts unrelated to the task at hand. Your negative opinions appear factual.

As I write this text, it is fall and a spectacular kaleidoscope of color pervades the landscape. The experience changes dramatically after you label the various kinds of trees, grasses, and flora. Labeling everything is not necessarily wrong or bad. It is simply removed from absorbing the fullness of the fall landscape. Nonjudging does not detract from experiences. Rather, such behavior is intended to help you be part of what is going on by enabling involvement without the uneven shading caused by your labels and judgments.

By standing back, placing matters on hold and taking time to observe, you free yourself to experience a broader spectrum, to see differently and thus potentially live more fully and clearly. By being open, you have the opportunity to appreciate what you may have otherwise labeled, indicted, or overlooked.

Activity

Nonjudgmental Observation

Set aside 10 minutes. Find a place where you can comfortably observe without being disturbed. Sitting or standing is all right. You will need 3 minutes to read these directions and organize, and then 7 minutes for the observation activity. A timer will help you keep track of time.

Take a few minutes to observe your thoughts in action. Begin by being quiet for two minutes with your eyes closed, following your breath all the way in and all the way out. Be present where you are.

1. As you continue to breathe with awareness, pay attention to your thoughts. Do not judge them.

2. Next, open your eyes, look around the room, and observe each item within view, one by one. Remain nonjudgmental.

3. Often, you will evaluate each thing along the lines of "I like this," "I do not like that," "This one is pretty," and so on. These judgments become emotionally charged by the memories associated with them. Note that the judgments within your perceptions create your reactions, as opposed to the actual object that you were examining.

4. Be present without labels and without indictments with whatever you perceive.

5. Now, think about your customary observation approach for events in your life. Think about what occurred this morning, afternoon, or evening.

How you perceive events creates your reactions to these events. Nonjudgmentally perceiving events will save you pain and suffering, providing you a more brilliant world with far more interesting texture and dimensions than you might otherwise allow.

Judgments create limitations for self and others. What you do to others, you do to yourself. If you can learn to be nonjudgmental with others, then you are more likely to do so with yourself. You will also be more likely to appreciate your own attributes.

Patience

Patience is the ability to see that "sometimes things must unfold in their own time" (Kabat-Zinn 2013, p. 23). You cannot rush time. You may become agitated when life's events do not go as you planned or when you are simply bored. Becoming impatient, you create impediments to personal serenity and balance.

After you become motivated to make changes, you might like to be progressing with your interpersonal relationships and mindfulness skills more rapidly than you currently are. You might believe that you should be able to be calmer, more attentive, or more comfortable. Paradoxically, these objectives are sources of further distraction. Patience, patience, patience—the important thing is to do the practice.

Many experiences require time to develop. If a bird is to hatch from its egg, you do nothing positive by attempting to accelerate the process by cracking open the shell prematurely. If you commit to 25 minutes of daily vigorous physical activity, 25 minutes is required. Similarly, do you savor the walk through the park on a sunny day, or do you attempt to save time by rushing?

Patiently participating in any activity can be transformational. An orange provides nourishment but also provides a sweet taste, a pulpy texture, and sensual pleasure. By being measured and patient with the eating process, every meal becomes a feast. Gulping down your food may require less time but will not give you any more nourishment. You may not benefit as much nutritionally or mentally when you rush eating, and the same principle applies to rushing your life.

A patient person is more able to make a rational decision based on a dispassionate view of what is. Once incorporated into your life, patience becomes an asset that allows you to appreciate both others and yourself. It allows you to see situations for what they are. Patience helps eliminate frustrations and increase well-being.

Not infrequently, you are most impatient with yourself, viewing your own thoughts, attitudes, and behaviors as unacceptable and even intolerable. Impatient reactions can be destructive, resulting in hasty decisions, foul moods, and saying unkind words to others, which further color the original experience.

All experiences can be openings to move forward. Instead of frustration and exasperation, a patient response sets the stage to handle the situation with greater consciousness. Using mindfulness techniques, you can take a moment to be mindful, following your breath all the way in and all the way out when feeling

Activity

Fostering Patience

Set aside 10 minutes—3 minutes to read these directions and organize, and then 7 minutes for the exercise addressing patience.

In your mind's eye, visualize yourself in a frustrating situation from your past, such as standing in a checkout line at the supermarket while the shopper at the front seems to be taking forever to write a check, or being in a highway toll booth lane that is stopped while all the other lanes are moving. Things like this come up every day.

1. Visualize the setting, the feelings, the actions, the words, and your bodily reaction.
2. What were you telling yourself about the situation? Were you telling yourself that you were wasting your precious time being stuck in line? Were you wishing that the other person would hurry up because you have important places to be? Were you thinking about what actions you could take or how things could be different?
3. Were you feeling anxious, frustrated, or upset?
4. Now that you look back on the situation, was it as much of a challenge as you thought? Did you learn any lessons or recognize positive aspects to the situation? If you acted impulsively to change the situation, what happened? Were the results what you expected?

You become more patient by mindfully observing your impatience.

agitated or anxious. You do not need to muscle every event into a shape that meets your expectations. A patient response provides an opportunity to have a full relationship with what is happening.

Often when you look back on situations, you realize that they were not as bad as you thought they were. If you can foster patience in situations as they occur, you may be able to avoid saying or doing hurtful things to others. Every day is successful if you avoid making things worse.

You have only 24 hours in each day. How you use that time is up to you. Becoming impatient with your friends and family does not serve anyone. If your personal and interpersonal skills do not permit you to live effectively, your quality of life will be augmented by learning new skills that provide better coping mechanisms.

Beginner's Mind

Beginner's mind is the ability to experience things as if for the first time (Kabat-Zinn 2013). How many fail to appreciate the true nature of reality by taking life for granted! Bring beginner's mind to the morning oatmeal and transform breakfast. Listen to a poem with fresh ears and have it come alive unencumbered by expectations. Listen to the poem as if for the first time. Listening to the poet's voice resonating can provide a fuller understanding of the text. The whole is greater than the sum of the parts. Experience the whole by truly paying attention. A beginner's mind helps call attention to the fabric of life, whether taking out the garbage or mindfully taking in a view.

Ordinary everyday experiences can become miraculously transformed through the adoption of a beginner's mind. It is all too easy to approach situations and people with preconceptions that shade your perceptions and rob you of the fullness of life. Preconceptions happen without consciousness awareness. You lose sight of what is happening. Events become routine. Think about how you take your relationships for granted, even important ones. You may see your friend and say, "Oh, yes, it's Jane." But from that perspective, your interactions are usually dictated by your experiences with Jane, taking little account of what is presently happening between you and Jane. You also may not recognize the wonder of the moment as it is occurring right now because you are stuck in thoughts from your past.

For instance, what was ordinary about your friend or partner when you first met him or her? What was ordinary when you selected your first puppy? What was ordinary about your newborn daughter, son, sister, brother, niece, or nephew? What was ordinary about the drive home in that new car? What was ordinary about that rolling, tumbling thunder in last night's rainstorm? Such marvelous occurrences are powerful, but it is easy to lose the rich texture of life by seeing them as mundane.

Proceeding on automatic pilot is easy. One of the authors (M.S.) recounted driving home along the same route she has driven dozens and dozens of times. But on this one particular day, she noticed the setting sun casting a warm, beautiful glow across the rolling hillsides. She was in touch with the myriad subtleties of color and light intensity. The landscape was suddenly transformed from yesterday's mundane view into something new and extraordinary. By being open to your surroundings, you can increase your joy.

When was the last time you saw beauty in the natural or built environment? Even a rundown factory can have beautiful qualities. By expanding attentiveness to your surroundings, finding a new

Activity

Looking With Beginner's Mind

Set aside 10 minutes—3 minutes to read these directions and organize, and then 7 minutes for the exercise.

1. Pause for 60 to 90 seconds to become more aware of what is going on right now.
2. What do you particularly notice about the setting that you are in?
3. Can you transform something you see by looking with beginner's mind? Reflecting on this may help you develop a fresh perspective.

If you do this exercise with concentration, it may be the most powerful activity of your day. Think about the many things going on in your life that you literally do not see or remember. You would not want to prepare for a test with the level of mind wandering that often characterizes your commonplace activities.

Activity

Using Beginner's Mind to Let Go of Preconceptions

Set aside eight minutes—three minutes to read these directions and organize, and five minutes for the exercise. Recall a previous activity that was unpleasant. Identify what you were telling yourself about the situation.

1. Did your expectations cloud the experience with what you thought it should be?
2. Did the experience fit with your plans?
3. Might the situation have been better or worse if you had gone into it with no preconceived notions or expectations?
4. Would a beginner's mind have altered your experience?

The situation may have been challenging. But if your stress, anxiety, and frustration had been lower, then you would have had access to more internal resources.

---

lens to look at routines, and watching for differences along an oft-trodden path, you may be provided with entertaining, sensitizing, and profound insights that can greatly deepen your satisfaction. The grain of life increases when you take the time to experience life's events. Using a beginner's mind is but one tool to aid this process.

Trust

Trust means believing in yourself and your qualities. It is the ability to have self-confidence about who you are. The technically oriented 21st century can cause you to be defined by outside stimuli, lose touch with who you are, and trust everything and everybody but yourself. Nothing you learn has meaning unless you remain front and center to the process. Self-appreciation is critical. Your instincts can be your most important attribute.

Of course, distractions are myriad—tasks to be done and expectations to meet. By staying mindful in your day-to-day life, you can identify connections and wisdom. This process may involve believing that you alone can best define what contributes to your reality (Goldberg 2008). Self-trust involves recognizing that inner wisdom will guide you along your unique path.

Nonstriving

Nonstriving is the ability to be engaged with whatever is happening (Kabat-Zinn 2013). Yes, you may want more energy. Yes, you may want to be less obsessed by your thoughts. Yes, you may want to be closer to the "ideal" body weight. But most important is the ability to be present in the moment.

If, for example, you are undertaking a regular physical activity program to lower blood pressure, additional benefits accrue from doing so in a nonstriving manner (Ornish 2007). When preoccupied with

© Brand X Pictures

Engage yourself in the present. Don't strive to get some place or go faster than before; enjoy your surroundings and take in the fresh air.

Learning More About Self-Trust

Trust begins with the faith that you can achieve a fundamental unfailing belief in your core self. After you have talked yourself into trying the concept of "faking it till you make it," you can try a few approaches to flowing further down your river of believing in yourself.

Think of three people who exemplify the core concepts of self-trust:

- Belief in self (self-confidence)
- Belief in their unique abilities
- Peace in the situation in which they find themselves (good or bad)
- Listen to others but see the final decisions in their life as their own
- Appreciation for the self that they are
- Have instincts and trust them
- Mindful in day-to-day living
- Make strides to gain and maintain vitality, reality, and overall well-being
- See their journey as unique yet tied to others

Don't panic! No person has all these down pat. Many wise persons have a dedication to the journey. They take life one day at a time. They have used their experiences to learn lessons, not to define who they are. On a notepad, write the first names of the three people you identified.

Arrange an interview with one of the people on your list, perhaps the one who has time for a 30-minute heart to heart. Explain to your subject that you are working on self-trust and see him or her as someone who might offer some insight into your journey. Be sure to keep the interview to 30 minutes. Be respectful of the person's time.

You are welcome to use your own questions or to modify the ones that follow. Your interview should result in no more than a two-page paper (500 words) on what you learned. Be careful not to tell the subject's story. This exercise is about writing what *you* learned, particularly about self-trust, from the subject's story. Try to include the person's words to live by, or affirmations, that have helped him or her stay focused. Do not use family names. Who you interviewed is less important than the person's journey and what you learned. Think of the person as a sage. You have traveled to a mountaintop to gain his or her perspectives. Think before and after the interview. Then get typing!

Sample Questions

- How do you stay aware of and trust yourself?
- How do you witness things that happen to you and not become immersed in the chaos, sadness, or drama?
- How do you live in the moment and learn from it?
- You obviously have made many important decisions. When did you start trusting your instincts? How do you learn to "let it be"?
- If I want to give myself time and space to develop my best self and start trusting myself more than I do at present, how can I find both the time and the space to do it?
- Do you have any suggestions about how I can use the concept of trust in my life? I may think I know myself pretty well and am not always happy with what I see; how can I begin to see myself with acceptance?
- Have you had people in your life (friends, teachers, supervisors, family) who meant well but were unable to guide you? How did you determine which ones held meaning for your life?
- What do you do to rejuvenate yourself? Do you ever take time to be quiet? How do you make your life less of a to-do list and more of an adventure?
- How do you find inner conviction, not just for the hard stuff but also for the day-to-day journey?
- How do you handle the mistakes that happen in your life?
- How do you stay nonjudgmental when the world seems to judge everything?

Summarize your interview experience while focusing on how you can incorporate more trust into your life.

Activity

Nondoing, Nonstriving, Just Being

For this exercise on nonstriving, you need to set aside 20 minutes. You need comfortable shoes and outdoor clothing. This activity may be the most challenging one in the entire book because you are going to be involved in nondoing, nonstriving, and just being. This will be an exercise of intention and attention, of you simply being. You may want to set a timer so that you will know when the 20 minutes ends.

1. Go to a public open space, such as a park, forest, farm, or large field.
2. Begin by taking two long, slow, deep breaths in and then out.
3. For the purpose of orientation, identify a destination.
4. Proceed walking toward the destination. Reaching the destination is not important. Rather, stay present to your surroundings as you meander along. Covering a set distance is not important. Pace is not a factor. Think of yourself as a curious mature being, interested in everything but obsessed with nothing.
5. Keep your attention on where you are and what you are doing. Be attentive to the sights, smells, and sounds, as well as the texture of the terrain.
6. Your mind will undoubtedly wander off to unrelated thoughts. That is not a problem. The distractions are part of the awareness. Simply make a mental note of where your focus has gone (for example, your work schedule for this evening) and return to your journey.

The activity may seem trivial, but your life depends on it. This exercise demonstrates peace and joy associated with a normal, even mundane, activity. The approach is a way of returning your wandering mind to consciousness. Remember that people are far less happy when distracted than they are when their minds are on task.

---

exercising to normalize your blood pressure, you might actually increase your stress, which is counterproductive. Distractions are part of the mindful present. They can help you recommit to being aware. Awareness of the so-called distractions help you come back to the present to let the mindfulness process flow.

Nonstriving serves all dimensions of wellness. For example, think about the nonstriving value of taking a lunchtime walk outdoors, experiencing the scenery, being in touch with your moving body, and savoring your breathing in the open air. The restorative value of such an attitude is monumental because it transforms a walk from a simple physical act to a rejuvenating practice.

Nonstriving has many similarities with flow, as defined in chapter 1. When in flow, you are fully engaged. You can feel in control without obsessing about control. You have goals, but attention to them is not foremost in your consciousness.

For your everyday life, the more you see yourself as complete, whole, adequate, and capable, the more likely you can live with expanded awareness in the present moment (Kornfield 2011). By contrast, when you become a bottom-line person, preoccupied with making things happen the way you want them to, you

can rob yourself of the present joy. You should not obsess about improving. Rather, your aim might be to accept where you are and passionately engage with the flow. You cannot control some aspects of your life. Striving to control such matters can generate tension and stress, especially when you have expectations.

Predetermined expectations can be formed about your relationship with your romantic partners, children, parents, artistic pursuits, or work projects. You can waste a lot of energy attempting to mold a person or situation to your unrealistic ideas. Both short- and long-term negative consequences can arise from your inability to *just be* with what *is*.

Kornfield (2000) nicely illustrates nonstriving in his volume *After the Ecstasy, the Laundry: How the Heart Grows Wise on the Spiritual Path*. Each step of your life can be as valuable as the next, no matter the label. From the outside, the changes associated with inner peace are not necessarily observable. A Zen saying is relevant here: "Before Enlightenment, chop wood carry water. After Enlightenment, chop wood carry water." Nothing is different on the outside, even though the inside has been transformed. You continue along the road of your life.

As an alternative to struggling, you can cultivate

mindful nonstriving, a nature that is attentive to the present moment as a means of substantial satisfaction. In doing so, you can find that there is nothing that you need to become or that you need to force on others. Each moment needs the opportunity to unfold in its own time. Yes, you can design the garden, plant the roses, and take plenty of time to smell them along the way, even if they don't all bloom as you may have hoped. Truly, you have no place to go and all day to get there. You are already there.

You do not want to overidealize the notion of nonstriving awareness. Life is often messy. Your mind will wander, more for some than for others (Forster and Lavie 2014). That doesn't matter. In fact, these circumstances are opportunities to bring yourself back, to flex your mental muscles of control, which become more developed under these repeated acts of returned awareness (Dumontheil, Gilbert, Frith, and Burgess 2010).

Some people confuse nonstriving with not caring or not working to achieve goals, which is not what this concept is stating. Rather, nonstriving is being okay with what is present right now, and it is closely tied to acceptance. You can have goals and dreams that help you stay motivated, but you need not be consumed by them.

Acceptance

"**Acceptance** . . . means realizing how things are and finding ways to be in wise relationship with them. And then to act, as appropriate, out of that clarity of vision" (Kabat-Zinn 2012, p. 130). Often, you needlessly try to control situations, many of which are out of your control and some of which are none of your business. Of course, acceptance may be one of your most difficult challenges. You are not asked to do nothing. But if your life is in chaos, mindlessly reacting to the chaos will not help. You need to accept things as they are in the present moment and not contaminate them with a desire that they be different. You waste time resisting what is, and by so doing, you lock yourself in a hopeless conundrum.

Acceptance can aid everyday functioning by enabling you to see clearly. Acceptance is to use your energies to focus on what is, rather than to address imaginary problems created by your preconceptions. Take, for example, a fifth consecutive cloudy day in Seattle or a deep blanket of snow on the Illinois landscape. Obsessing over your desire for this day to be warm and sunny spoils an otherwise lovely day.

You can generate a mother lode of negative emotional energy lamenting any given situation. You

Activity

Accepting Disappointment

Everyone has had disappointments in their lives, relationships, schooling, or social activities. This activity on accepting disappointment requires 15 minutes. You need a laptop or paper and a pen or pencil.

1. Begin by taking two long, slow, deep breaths in and then out. Then breathe normally and rest mindfully for another two minutes, being aware of the air passing in and out of the tip of your nose. Note how much cooler the air is with the in breath than with the out breath. Just be aware.

2. Identify one recent disappointment and label it at the beginning of a journal entry. This event might be a horrible trauma or a garden-variety disappointment. Choose something meaningful but something that you are ready and able to deal with by yourself.

3. With your eyes closed, take two minutes to relive that disappointment.

4. Then take five minutes to write down the relevant memories.

5. Now, hold the thought of this disappointment in awareness where you are now. As painful as this may be, in this moment, you are here and you are all right. By so doing, you have enlarged the scope. Enlarging your perspective can help you consider that the disappointing event is in the past. Right here right now, things are not so bad.

6. Experience the relaxation in this moment. Doing so will color the next moment and the next. Being mindful can bring acceptance.

7. Insert your comments into Chapter 2 of your journal.

Again, do not jump into your next activity or assignment. Take a minute or so to transition mindfully.

ryne did not control her cluster headaches. She patiently accepted her life as it was, becoming less anxious. These changes seemed to be related to her daily mindful observation sessions. As she observed with a beginner's mind, she became aware of tension around her neck and shoulders. During her mindfulness sessions, she felt at peace. These positive feelings persisted even after her sessions. The headaches gradually diminished. Ultimately, she achieved a higher quality of life.

miss out on what you have right now. This is not to say that everything is wonderful. But you can benefit from recognizing that the good, bad, and indifferent happen. Most of these concerns are not monumentally important, even when upsetting and disappointing. Skilled special education teachers commonly exemplify acceptance. They have learned to accept challenging students where they are and to help them learn, no matter what their abilities.

Your attitudes change dramatically just by accepting where you are (Ellis 2006). Acceptance allows you to be less attached to absolutes. This conception does not mean that you do not have standards. Rather, acceptance enables you to see what is and to move away from an romanticized notion of what should be. Your energies can be freed up so that you can spend your time addressing life's requirements. Acceptance can translate into being able to work effectively and maintain personal equanimity—tolerance, integrity, inspiration, self-respect—all of which are prerequisites to wellness.

Letting Go

Letting go is the ability to let be, to relinquish attachment, to be nonattached to outcomes, and to avoid clinging to what you hate or detest. Much in life is beyond your control. The context of life is huge. Life

Activity

Loving Kindness—Letting Go

Set aside 15 minutes—5 minutes to read these directions and organize, and then 10 minutes for the loving kindness meditation. In this exercise, begin by invoking feelings of loving kindness toward yourself.

1. Close your eyes as you sit in a comfortable position and become aware of your breathing.
2. Invite a feeling of love and kindness toward yourself. You may want to remember a time when another particularly appreciated you or something you did. Let that feeling wash over you. Feel the love that radiated from the other person and the love you experienced.
3. Say quietly to yourself: "May I be free from inner and outer harm; may I be happy; may I be healthy; may I live with ease" (Kabat-Zinn 2013, p. 214).
4. Identify a person you particularly care about. While visualizing that person in your mind's eye, similarly invoke that he or she be free from anger, filled with compassion, and able to feel the kindness that is extended to him or her.
5. Identify a work colleague. While visualizing that person in your mind's eye, similarly invoke that he or she be free from anger, filled with compassion, and able to feel the kindness extended to him or her.
6. Next, think of someone with whom you have a particularly challenging time, maybe even someone you dislike. Direct loving kindness to that person, wishing him or her freedom from anger, freedom from hatred, and fulfillment with compassion and kindness.

Many people find it particularly difficult, even onerous, to send loving kindness to people for whom they hold strong negative feelings. However, to do so is to give yourself a chance to let go.

Aryne's life was changed by her practice of mindfulness. She is not locked in to her morning and early evening mindful observation practices, but she does them regularly. Moreover, when a cluster headache comes on, she reaches for her MP3 player and moves in a nonstriving manner through the guided mindful observation.

When Aryne incorporated mindful observation practice sessions into her daily schedule, she had the opportunity for more awareness. The attitudinal foundations guided her practice. As she observed herself with a beginner's mind, she noticed tension around her shoulders and neck that was previously unrecognized. Aryne's life did not undergo an immediate metamorphosis, but incrementally it improved. Although she would prefer not to have any cluster headaches, she accepted that they occur. She was able to move in closer to them and not fight them. Aryne is far more patient with herself. During her cluster headache episodes, she is less tense. Her headaches are becoming less frequent and less severe.

includes brilliance that manifests through the application of letting go. Many issues are best resolved by not fretting about them. You can do well by not holding on to your inflexible ideas about how things should evolve. What we resist customarily persists. When you let go of your expectations for how the world should be, you can begin to align yourself "with that domain of being that is awareness itself, pure awareness. . . . The more we let go in this way, the deeper our well-being" (Kabat-Zinn 2012, p. 133). This attitude is not only sensible it is liberating.

You often hold on to things that are comfortable, things that you have worked hard for, the remnants of good times. Old, long-lasting relationships fall into this category, as do grade school, high school, and college friends; family members; or long- or short-time friends with whom you shared precious moments. Then you may have attachments to possessions and habitual actions: a childhood diary or high school scrapbook, an old pair of comfortable shoes, an adorable shirt or blouse that is long out-of-fashion, a job or long-performed task that you have outgrown, or a lover from the distant past. Lastly, there are things for which you have an aversion or hatred. Aversion is simply a form of negative attachment. In all cases, it becomes true that whatever you obsess about holding onto, you get stuck with. When you let go of fixations, you can develop preferences that can be enjoyed.

Many people struggle with the dilemmas of attachments. How often are you unable to fall asleep or routinely wake up in the middle of the night because of worry? Much of this problem can be attributed to your inability to let go of what happened during your day.

The antidote to this is to recognize that you grow and change, that you grow in different ways, and that your needs change with time. Thus, if you devote too much effort and encounter too much stress to hold onto or maintain someone or something, then it may be time to just let go and let things be as they are. By accepting things for what they are, you replace considerable nervous tension with calm and open-mindedness.

SUMMARY

Many people pursue goals and neglect living. The optimal wellness approach involves rejuvenating life by incorporating the attitudinal foundations into everyday activities. These attitudes represent a new lens by which to recalibrate your sense of self. The new attitudes enable you to be part of the whole, amidst personal blemishes. From such a perspective, the blemishes lose their power and do not detract. You can be broken but still whole.

The attitudinal foundations facilitate a shift in focus toward the inner state. The goal is to pay attention. The attitudinal foundations are as relevant to everyday life as they are to the mindfulness practices.

Nonjudging awareness enables living fully, without unrealistic expectations for self and others. Patience may be the most overlooked attitude. It permits life to evolve without tension and frustration. Beginner's mind is to see and experience as if for the first time. Time, energy, and pleasure are wasted on preconceived perceptions. Trust is the ability to be self-confident with perceptions, values, beliefs, and actions. Nonstriving is living with life as it is. It embodies the qualities of flow, as identified by Csikszentmihalyi (2000). Acceptance facilitates forgiving self and others. Knowing everything about people, places, and things is impossible. By recognizing what is and being open to what is happening, a person can move forward. Letting go is the ability not to sweat the small stuff and to remember that on the cosmic scale, it is all small stuff!

© Photodisc

Chapter 3

Using Mindfulness to Enhance the Experience of Life

Objectives

After reading this chapter, you will be able to

- describe how mindful observations can enrich daily life,
- list three guidelines for successful mindfulness practice,
- describe the role of distractions in mindfulness,
- describe your personal experiences of five different mindfulness practices, and
- implement a daily (at least 5 days per week) 20-minute mindful sitting practice.

Jim loved being at the university. Although not a particularly diligent student in high school, as a first-semester junior he was now motivated to do well. His parents never completed high school, but they continually admonished him to study, telling him, "Get an education. Don't end up as we did." His dad was a blue-collar worker, his mom managed the household, and the family was low income by most standards.

Jim's freshman year in college was difficult. He lacked drive. His reading and writing skills were marginal, and his grades were below a C average. As a sophomore Jim developed a good relationship with his sociology professor, who was passionate about his discipline, his students, and life. Jim recognized how accomplished and content the professor was.

Jim wanted to be well, but he felt out of control. He signed up for an eight-week beginner's mindfulness class at the university wellness center. He studied and sought help with his term papers at the library. Jim became determined to do better. He studied hard but continued to play hard, too. He was not one to miss a party.

Jim's negative thinking was particularly problematic. He was quite critical of himself. The only times Jim felt calm were when he jogged and during his mindfulness practices. His morning and evening 10-minute mindful sittings became the parts of his day that were crucial to inner peace and improved sleep.

Life as a young adult is unpredictable. You survive by doing the tasks that are most obvious, seizing opportunities, all the while putting up with the banal demands of everyday life. Your activities are often energized with new and fascinating endeavors.

In addition, you may engage in counterproductive behavioral patterns as well. Young adults may drink alcohol to excess, feel incomplete without a romantic relationship, regularly participate in casual sex, spend money on clothes they do not need, eat well past satiety, occasionally ingest illicit drugs, and drink so much coffee that they do not sleep well. Where do these behaviors come from? Are you in charge of them, or are they in charge of you?

Most university students are busy with life and school agendas. You spend little time being mindful. Are you a human being or a human doing? Your preoccupation with material items, activities, and accomplishments keeps you focused outside yourself. You may seem to be driven by forces that you cannot see.

Reaching deep levels of awareness can be difficult. You can miss so much. It takes a bright, nonparochial fish to know that it lives in water (Bem 1971). Often, you may be like the fish and have little consciousness of what makes up your world.

What tools do you have at your disposal to learn more about what, where, and who you are? Are you in or out of control of your life? Mindfulness is a means of slowing down, pausing, getting in touch, and reminding yourself who and what you are. One goal is to increase attention, thereby transforming your daily activities into mindful ones.

Proficiency in the various aspects of mindfulness is a journey toward increased calm, acceptance, love, inner peace, and quality of life. You benefit most when the mindful approach permeates every experience, every moment, every cell, and every fiber of your existence. Eating for nourishment, for example, can be transformed into mindful eating by bringing conscious awareness to a meal. Psychologists see mindfulness as a skillful response to thoughts, emotions, behaviors, and habits (Davis and Hayes 2011).

Jon Kabat-Zinn helped translate mindfulness into a useful tool for the 21st century Western world. The practice dates back to the time of the Buddha, approximately 2500 BCE. Today, mindfulness is used throughout the United States as a tool to enhance control, quality of life, and pain management (Kabat-Zinn 2013) and to serve as an antidote to dysfunction (Davis and Hayes 2011).

Mindfulness practices are mainstream in psychology and religion. A 2014 search for "mindfulness" on the SCOPUS online scientific database retrieved more than 3,500 documents. Searching Google yielded more than 5,000,000 sources. Mindfulness and meditation are aspects of every religion in the world (Oman 2011). A 2007 survey revealed that approximately 13 percent of the adult U.S. population performed daily deep-breathing exercises (Barnes, Bloom, and Nahin 2008).

Enhanced attention transforms values, attitudes, intentions, and behaviors into deliberate responses. Regular skillful mindfulness practice results in dramatically improved quality of life (Siegel 2013). The *Foundations of Wellness* approach is a positive one, that is, we are emphasizing improving quality of life and promoting positive psychological well-being. We are not solely focused on disease, disability, and death as is common with most health discussions. However, mindfulness can also lessen the ill effects of acute and chronic illness (Bos et al. 2014; Pbert et al. 2012). That is, mindfulness promotes wellness and can decrease illness (Siegel 2013).

In this chapter, we examine mindful eating, sitting, full body awareness (body scan), walking, and hatha yoga. Our discussion is infused with practice opportunities. Performing an exercise does not mean you have mastered it. Some of the exercises practiced here will be repeated in later chapters.

LEARNING TO USE MINDFULNESS

Mindfulness skills can help you reach personal attributes that are often drowned out by the clutter in your life. Even if you are dealing with a health issue, you are intrinsically well. Mindfulness helps to remind you of that innate wellness. You have the capacity within for a full, fulfilling, and productive life. Your journey is to access those qualities. Mindfulness enables self-discovery, cultivation of inner resources, and fine-tuning of decision-making capacity.

Your mindfulness practice sessions are facilitated by accessing a quiet and comfortable location where anchor for awareness in most of the mindful practices. Quantum physics indicates that life is fundamentally energy, not just particulate matter (Vedral 2011). The desk where you are working, the computer screen you are viewing, and the chair you are sitting on are more energy than they are solid matter (Knox 2010). Most of us are preoccupied with the material aspects of everyday living. Attending to your breath with beginner's mind can shift your focus from matter to the vibrant energy within. The breath brings life to every cell of your physical body and energizes your spirit.

Remember, your breath is always with you. It is the first thing you do when you are born and the last thing you do as you leave your body. Many of us rarely give it a thought in between.

Practice

You are nourished by the actual mindful practice, not by study alone. Studying has a role, but it is not mindfulness. An example related to food might clarify this concept. You are sustained by eating healthy foods, not by reading brochures about vegetables and fruits or eating a menu.

You are encouraged to engage in the mindfulness practice as if nothing else exists. Total engagement is one of the six dimensions of flow as defined by Csikszentmihalyi (1990). In fact, you have nothing else to accomplish at this time. A nonstriving engagement with the practice might appear in contradiction to maintaining high levels of motivation. The goal is to enter the mindfulness process, to become one with your practice, not unlike the athlete who flows with the game. Motivation and skill are prerequisites. Performance is enhanced by intense engagement, not concentrated thinking. Mindfulness involves being mentally, physically, emotionally, and spiritually present. As you let go into the present, your flow paradoxically increases your attention and control in your journey.

Mindfulness looks quite different after you have been doing it awhile. Practice provides a better understanding of the concepts. The beginner may find the mindfulness practice descriptions difficult to comprehend. Merely going through the motions of practice does little good. Rather, you benefit to the degree that you are skillfully engaged. Remember beginner's mind! You may not be very good at first, but that does not matter. It's called practice. Your intention will dictate your attention. Without commitment, you will wallow in your distractions, preoccupied with your discomfort.

You can write about your self-discoveries after practicing mindfulness.

you are not likely to be interrupted. Warm and comfortable clothing is helpful. You should turn off the television, telephone, and other electronic devices, and ask family and friends not to disturb you. The duration of a practice is less important than the quality of your awareness. That being said, there are recommended durations for the practice sessions in this chapter. A timing device, such as that on a cellular phone, eliminates the need to watch a clock.

Incorporating the seven attitudinal foundations, as described in chapter 2, into your practice is essential. Your attitudes set the stage for success. Mindfulness is a nondoing exercise in awareness and nonjudging. The practice is mental and intentional. Just by committing to practice these simple mindfulness exercises, you have started contributing to your own well-being and you deserve a mental pat on the back.

Breathing

Attending to the breath brings you in touch with your inner energy (Chin 1995). The breath serves as an

Activity

Mindful Breathing

Set aside eight minutes—three minutes to read the directions and organize, and then five minutes for the awareness-of-breath exercise. Read the entire description before starting the practice.

1. Lie on the floor, sit in a chair, or stand. Close your eyes if you feel comfortable doing so, or cast your eyes down toward the floor to avoid being distracted. Making eye contact with others or focusing on specifics in your surroundings can be distracting.

2. Become attentive to your breath. Follow it all the way in and all the way out. Most relaxing or productive breathing is diaphragmatic or belly breathing. The air flows into the lungs as the diaphragm contracts and the abdomen expands. If you wish, repeat the words "breathing in" and "breathing out" aloud or quietly to yourself. Let the in-and-out breath resonate in your body for the five-minute mindful period. Follow the stomach rising and falling with each in and out breath. When your mind wanders, mentally note where it has gone and bring it back to the breath.

3. When you finish the breathing and concentration practice, take another minute to be present. There is no need to label or otherwise characterize the process. However, if the experience was satisfying, remember that you have access to this resource no matter where you are. If not satisfying, remember that your mind is accustomed to being active, problem solving, thinking, ruminating, and multitasking. Your mind often seems to have a mind of its own. No matter what the experience, can you look upon it in a nonjudgmental way?

4. Distractions serve to keep you out of touch but only if you wallow in them. Otherwise, the distractions are part of mindfulness, as you repeatedly bring your attention back to the breath. You are not responsible if a bird lands on your head, but the bird that builds a nest in your hair is another issue. Become aware of distractions and let them go.

5. You may feel anxiety during the mindfulness practices. This feeling is perfectly natural, because you ordinarily are on the go and your mind is a cascade of endless thoughts. Were you previously aware of how much your mind wanders? Understanding how frequently your mind wanders represents growth in awareness. It is only when you have awareness that you can facilitate the desired change.

Congratulate yourself for taking this time to be mindful.

Mindful Eating

You want to bring increased mindful participation to all aspects of your life. Eating is something you do 21 times per week. Attention to eating is a wonderful exercise, because it demystifies mindfulness. You often eat with limited attentiveness. You may eat while reading the newspaper, listening to the radio, watching television, working on your computer, having a conversation, and even while driving. In such instances, you are hard pressed either to enjoy or to regulate your food intake. Mindful eating can increase enjoyment of meals and also lead to healthier food selection and weight loss (Dalen et al. 2010).

Mindful Distractions

During mindfulness, your mind and body are a source of distraction. You can be distracted by thoughts, bodily sensations, recalling incomplete tasks, external noises, or even the quiet. You often ruminate about the past or worry about the future. Even in a short application, thoughts about the mindfulness practice will arise. You may think, "This is a waste of time," "I can't do this," "What am I doing here?" Those are just thoughts. Say to yourself quietly, "Isn't that interesting," and bring your focus back. Treat those thoughts the same as you would any other thought or distraction.

You become further distracted by judging your distractions as good or bad, desirable or undesirable. When you judge, you are twice removed from being mindful, namely, the distraction and the judgment. You are not trying to repress thoughts. Rather, distractions are transformed into an integral part of the mindfulness practice when you observe them nonjudgmentally, identify them, and return to the breath.

Mindful Raisin Eating

Set aside eight minutes—three or so minutes to read these directions and organize, and then five minutes for the mindful raisin eating. As an alternative to the raisin, you can use a grape or any other similar small food morsel.

1. Begin this exercise by placing two raisins on a napkin in front of you. Take one into your fingers and give your full attention to it. Take two long, slow, deep breaths to relax. Note the pause between each breath. Look with beginner's mind, that is, as if you were from outer space and seeing the raisin for the first time. In fact, this is your first occasion with this particular raisin.

2. Continue to breathe in and out while making a nonjudgmental examination.

3. Slowly and deliberately move the raisin around in your hand. Let the light reflect off it. Roll it between your fingertips. How does it feel on the outside? Can you feel anything inside it? Bring it to your nose and notice the fragrance. As you move the raisin around your fingers, identify the sensations, the texture, the appearance, even the sounds. Simply be aware and be present.

4. Now slowly place the raisin between your lips and front teeth. Pause. Resist the temptation to bite into it. Instead, move the raisin around your mouth—tasting, feeling, and generally experiencing it. Of course, your mind will wander. Having a strong intention to be present for the eating process will help. Stop and identify where your thoughts have gone and then bring your attention back.

5. Without rushing and while maintaining your awareness, bite into the raisin with your front teeth. Move it around your mouth and notice the change in taste and texture.

6. After 30 seconds or so, move the raisin to the back of your mouth and begin deliberately chewing with your molars. Are more flavors now available? Chew for at least a minute but resist the temptation to swallow. Rather, continue to savor the experience of the taste and texture.

7. Then, consciously and mindfully swallow the raisin, following the sensations as it passes through your throat into your esophagus and into your stomach. Be conscious of the physiologic changes in your body. Be aware that you are now one raisin heavier!

8. Remain with those sensations for a minute or so. Then, repeat the process with the second raisin, maintaining your beginner's mind and nonjudgmental awareness. Truly, each raisin is different as we examine, feel, smell, taste, and savor it.

9. After completing the second raisin, pause quietly for a minute before initiating your next activity.

Your practice of nonjudging has a way of transforming distractions into mindful awareness, causing them to dissipate, and even strengthening the cognitive control region of the brain (Brefczynski-Lewis, Lutz, Schaefer, Levinson, and Davidson 2007). You should recognize that having such thoughts and letting them go are just a normal part of the mindfulness process.

When you are distracted, you can easily indict yourself for not being adequately motivated. When you recognize distracting thoughts, your practice is to accept what is happening and then let the thoughts go. You can benefit from having trust in your commitment to practice. Even if the same thought keeps appearing, you maintain a nonjudgmental awareness that it is recurring, let it go, and bring yourself back to your breath again. If you fall 100 times, you can get up 100 times.

Mindful Body Scan

Kabat-Zinn (2013) observed how you can be "preoccupied with the appearance of your body and at the same time completely out of touch with it as well" (p. 75). The mindful **body scan** is an opportunity to experience full-body awareness, segment by segment. Calling attention to each body part seems to purify it of tension and stress incrementally.

You can progress through mindful full-body awareness in a variety of ways. You can do the full-body awareness scan in any position, whether lying down on your back, sitting, or even standing. Your attention to your body is important. Let go of expectations and permit the breath to flow naturally.

This process will be easier and make more sense when you listen to an actual body scan. Mindful body scans of 20 and 30 minutes are available at http://publichealth.hsc.wvu.edu/BillRegerNash/. We suggest listening to an audio recording for the first several body scans, because doing so will enable you to keep your attention on the process without regard to whether you are doing it correctly.

When completing any mindfulness practice, having an attitudinal foundation of acceptance is important. By acceptance we mean seeing and being at peace with things as they are. You are not trying to change your body segments during a mindful body scan or to

Activity

Body Scan

Set aside 25 to 35 minutes. You will need 5 minutes to read these directions and organize, and then 20 to 30 minutes for the body scan.

1. Lie on your back on a mat, the floor, or a mattress. Let your feet fall away from each other. Wear warm clothing or cover yourself with a blanket, if appropriate.

2. Take two long, slow, deep breaths, following the breath all the way in, being attentive to the pause, and following the breath all the way out, being attentive to the pause. Repeat.

3. Begin by moving your attention from your breathing down to the toes of your left foot. Focus your attention on each of the toes of the left foot. Keep your attention there for 15 to 30 seconds, being aware of the sensations or the lack of sensations. Notice the spaces between the toes. When finished, let go of this experience of the toes.

4. Move your focus to the ball of the left foot. Pause, keeping your attention there for 15 to 30 seconds. Then systematically move your attention to the arch of the foot, the heel, and the instep, being mindful of each for 15 to 30 seconds in succession.

5. Progressively move up from the foot, addressing the ankle, the shin bone, the muscles surrounding the front of the knee, the back of the shin, the knee, the thigh bone, the inner thigh muscles, the hamstrings behind the thigh, the outer thigh muscles, and finally the hip and large gluteus muscles (the muscles of your buttocks).

6. After completing the scan of the left leg, move your attention to the toes of your right foot, the ball of the foot, the arch, and the heel. Sequentially move up through the right hip and gluteus muscles.

7. From the right hip, slowly, mindfully, and progressively move your attention to the region of your pelvis and genitals. Bring your attention into the lower and midback, areas of discomfort for those who sit in vehicles and at desks. Move your attention into the abdomen, chest, upper back, and shoulders.

8. After completing the shoulders, move to the fingers and thumb on the hands (do both left and right at the same time), being attentive to the fingers and the space between them before moving to the palm of the hand, the wrist, forearm, elbow, front of the upper arm (biceps muscles), and back of the upper arm (triceps muscles). Return to the shoulders, neck, chin, cheeks, mouth, nose, eyes, and finally the scalp.

9. Finish with a series of long, slow, deep breaths. Breathe in through the bottom of the feet up into your chest and then exhale through an imaginary blowhole (like a blowhole of a whale) at the top of the head. Breathe back in through the blowhole back down into the chest, and then breathe out through the bottom of the feet. Continue this breathing for three to five minutes.

Upon completion of the body scan, remain quiet and without judgments. However, you may notice a difference in the sensations throughout your body. Savor that awareness of your body.

Jim was a good guy, but he wasn't particularly productive during his first two years of college. He was going through life reasonably unaware of what was influencing his attitudes and his behaviors. He noticed that his motivation began to change when he enrolled in a mindfulness class. He increased his mindful sitting time to 20 minutes. He also initiated an every other day 30-minute body awareness scan which provided the opportunity to accept what was.

change food intake patterns through mindful eating. Rather, your focus is on being aware as you bring attention to your body and your mind, moment by moment.

Mindful Sitting

Mindful sitting may be the most established mindful practice (Kabat-Zinn 2013). It involves taking a seat, establishing yourself, and setting a foundation with nonjudgmental awareness. We recommend sitting in a dignified, erect, and upright position in a place where you are unlikely to be disturbed (see figure 3.1). The most important aspect is to find a posture that works to keep you alert. You can sit on the ground, on the floor, or in a chair. If you sit in a chair, sit forward on the seat so that you do not slouch. If you sit on the floor, you may want to use a 6-inch (15 cm) cushion. You can place your hands on your knees, in your lap, or however else is comfortable. Generally, you should wear comfortable, loose-fitting, warm clothing that does not constrict your body.

Depending on your flexibility, you may want to cross your legs or have one leg folded in front of the other so that both knees touch the floor, forming a triangle of support. Try to settle in and be physically still for the duration. Notice impulses to move and fidget. Mindful awareness is the key. If the posture is causing discomfort, it is all right to move, but do so with attentiveness. If an itch is overpowering, you can mindfully scratch the area. Alternatively, you can bring your attention to the source of irritation and make it part of the mindfulness exercise.

Your mental state is more important than your physical position! Nonstriving clearly fits into the sitting practice when you focus your attention on being present in the moment—right here, right now, just this. You do best when you let go of your expectations and permit yourself to engage (Kabat-Zinn 2013).

Initially, being still may present challenges, but the more you are mindful, the easier the sitting will become. Mindfulness works only if you work at it. There is nothing mindful about sitting for 20 to 30 minutes if your attention is elsewhere. Awareness of distractions is integral to the practice. Make a mental note of the distraction and bring your mind back to

© Vision Images

FIGURE 3.1 Maintain a straight back and open chest for mindful sitting. This posture will keep you alert and attentive while allowing space to breathe from your diaphragm.

your breath. You become more aware through practice. Although it is not unusual to feel anxious or unsettled with such new experiences, mindfulness can cultivate the quiet within. Within is the only place where true peace exists.

Beginner's mind is a crucial skill for mindful sitting. With practice you will find that you are developing your ability to resonate with your breath. Because you usually breathe without thinking about it, you tend to take your breath for granted. But holding your breath for a mere 60 to 90 seconds will make you more appreciative of the process! Your breathing will become far more interesting. The truth is that you can make almost any activity of daily living more interesting simply by increasing attention.

You may want to observe your breath from the tip of the nostrils, or perhaps by observing your abdomen rising and falling with each in-and-out breath. Initially, choose one area to follow your breath and stick with it for that practice session. This exercise is an opportunity to be. It is natural to become bored, to want to stop, or to want to engage in something else.

Your body also wants to move. Remember, mindfulness is your guide to inner peace, and achieving it requires commitment.

When you are beginning your sitting practice, we recommend using the audio recordings available at http://publichealth.hsc.wvu.edu/BillRegerNash/ (Quick links: sitting meditation and body scan). Another idea is to join an established community sitting group. Most college towns have such a group, and most groups are not heavy handed about the kind of meditation you practice. Do an Internet search or check with local mental health professionals, a local

Activity

Mindful Sitting Practice

Set aside 10 minutes—3 minutes to read these directions and organize, and then 7 minutes for the sitting.

1. Take your seat on the floor, on a cushion, or on a chair. Close your eyes, if that is comfortable. If not, keep your eyes cast down toward the floor.

2. Focus your attention on your breath. Take two long, slow, deep breaths to settle in, and then breathe normally. Follow each breath all the way in, notice the pause, and follow it all the way out. You may find it helpful to anchor awareness on the breath passing the tip of your nostrils. You may notice that the in breath is cooler than the air passing out of your nostrils. You want to anchor in the present. Of course, thoughts and other distractions will arise. Make a mental note of the scattered thoughts, bodily sensations, or noises, whatever they are, and return to the breath.

3. Commit to being with this process and being at peace. Let go of all other concerns and preoccupations. They will be just fine as you take this time to nurture yourself.

4. Rather than acting on impulses, observe nonjudgmentally. This is part of mindfulness, not a distraction from it. This is an opportunity for awareness. Observe as the member of an impartial jury.

5. You might say to yourself, "Isn't that interesting!" and then return to the breath. This strategy helps you to become aware of your experiences but not make them a further source of distraction. You may not be in touch with how much your brain attaches to thoughts or how much you customarily fidget.

6. Your brain tends to keep you in a perpetual state of distraction. You likely jump from one thought to another. Do not be attached to your thoughts and sensations; just be aware. Don't give any value to them as they arise or view any particular thought as being good, bad, happy, or sad.

7. Your body may initially feel discomfort with mindful sitting. This practice is also an occasion for awareness and nonattachment. Identify the source of discomfort, stay with it for a while, and if necessary adjust your posture. Most important, remain at peace.

8. You can welcome discomfort as a reminder of your commitment to be right here, right now. This approach will help to cultivate flexibility, that is, to recognize every moment-to-moment experience as a facet of the practice.

9. Being in touch with and relaxing into discomfort is a means to change your perspective on pain, boredom, and life. The mindful practices can help with trusting yourself. Know your physical limits.

10. Return to the breath.

Pause at the end of the sitting to appreciate your dedication to life, your life with more nonjudgmental awareness.

food cooperative, or even the people who coordinate the local farmers' market.

Patience is an inner attribute that permits everything to evolve in its own time. When you start a mindfulness practice, rushing serves no purpose. Skill develops over time with commitment and practice. As you become distracted, patience can enable you to persevere. Every moment and every distraction are essential components of the practice. The act of mentally noting distractions and then returning your attention to your focus serves to strengthen that portion of the brain.

During mindfulness, keep your attention on the uniqueness of each breath, whether it is the air passing through your nasal cavity and through your larynx into your lungs, your chest wall and then your abdomen rising with each in breath, or the exhalation associated with the falling of the chest wall and abdomen (Suzuki 1992). This is beginner's mind. Your intention will enable you to take a fresh view of the experience. You can notice the movement of your clothing across the surface of your skin as well as the pulsation in your arms, hands, legs, and feet with each in and out breath. Your entire body is breathing.

Initially, 5 minutes of daily sitting will suffice, although more is fine. Soon thereafter, you will benefit from increasing your sitting time to 10 and then 20 minutes. The longer-term recommendation is to sit for 20 minutes two times per day, after you awake in the morning but before you become engaged in the activities of the day, and again in the early evening after the completion of your major obligations but before dinner. Five minutes of mindful eating at lunch is also recommended. Do not postpone your mindfulness until you are ready for bed, because that schedule is an invitation to fall asleep. Falling asleep is all right, but it is not mindfulness.

Mindful sitting does not occur when you place your body on the chair or cushion. Your intention and commitment are crucial elements. Curiously, mindfulness requires an effort, but concomitantly, you do best when you remain nonstriving and engage with no goal other than to be present. Mindfulness will not reduce your blood pressure if you obsess about it during your practice! You may have embarked on the process of mindfulness to help relieve stress in your life, to sleep better, to become less anxious. These goals are all laudable, and evidence substantiates that these benefits occur (Grossman et al. 2004). But the process will not work unless you can trust yourself and become nonstriving. Meditating to reduce your anxiety by obsessing with what is happening with your anxiety during mindfulness is counterproductive! You need to forget about your outcome goal orientation and focus on the goal

of moment-to-moment awareness. You move forward in mindfulness by being present right now.

Mindful Walking

Mindful walking is an opportunity to transform an everyday experience into something extraordinary. You take walking for granted. More than 20 percent of Americans have a disability. Some of the disabilities are so severe that the person cannot walk or does so only with great pain and discomfort.

The general mindfulness guidelines also pertain to walking. Your goal is to bring attention to this commonplace activity. We suggest locating a place where you will not be disturbed. To grow in mindful walking skill, we suggest starting by walking slowly and deliberately. Walking is a grounding activity. If possible and depending on the weather, you may want to walk without shoes or socks, but wearing shoes is just fine.

You begin with your eyes modestly cast down and generally gazing 5 to 10 feet (1.5 to 3 m) in front, so as not to be distracted by the surroundings. Your walking speed can vary, but we suggest moving at somewhere

© Bernd_Leitner

Mindful walking can help give you awareness of your body and the way that it feels in motion.

Activity

Mindful Walking Practice

Set aside 15 minutes—5 or so minutes to read these directions, organize, and determine a suitable location, and then 10 minutes for the actual practice. Mindful walking ideally occurs in a place where you are unlikely to be disturbed. You can walk around in a circle outdoors, back and forth in a room in your home, or even in a garage. With mindful walking, you have no place to go and all day to get there. The mindful-walking process is the goal—simple but powerful.

1. Begin by standing with both feet together. Take two long, slow, deep breaths, deeply into your belly. No destination, no hurry. With your arms comfortably at your sides, take a slow step forward with your left foot and leg, being aware of leg swinging while your weight shifts to the other side of your body. Consciously and slowly, place the heel of the left foot on the ground in front of you. Move your body forward. Your weight is momentarily equally distributed on both legs and hips as the right foot and leg slowly move forward and your foot makes contact with the walking surface.

2. There is nothing magical about the pace of the walk, but to begin, we recommend taking one second for each step. Be aware of the sensations in your feet, legs, hips, abdominal region, shoulders, and head. Keep your eyes cast down or soften your gaze to avoid being distracted. If someone else is around, avoid making eye contact.

3. This exercise involves paying attention. Make a mental note where your eyes and thoughts have gone if you are distracted. Identify the distraction and then bring your attention back to your walking and your body. Remember that a distraction is really just a movement of your attention away from the mindful walking. Note where your mind has gone. Bring your attention back. Every aspect of this process is intrinsic to mindful walking. Be committed to consciousness, not an absolute way of doing the practice.

You have transformed this most common form of physical activity among humans into a component of your mindfulness practice. You will practice mindful walking again during the chapter on physical activity. Take a moment to appreciate what you are feeling. Give yourself a mental pat on the back for taking these steps.

between 10 and 25 percent of your normal speed. This recommendation is not a fixed guideline. Start mindful walking at a slow pace, not at the speed of doing errands. The goal is mindfulness.

The process involves paying attention to your body—your feet as you plant them on the ground, the shifting of your weight from one leg and foot to the other as you balance yourself, your arms as they hang at your sides, the weight of your head on your neck and shoulders. You can be present to the winds, be they gentle or otherwise, and to the sounds that surround you; you are a passive recipient of these experiences. You can see yourself as the open field that receives sunlight, rain, and falling leaves but remains unchanged.

After you have practiced mindful walking in a controlled environment on several occasions, you can transition to walking with awareness across the spectrum of opportunities. In this time you can be present to nature, whether in the woods, a field, or a parking lot. You can walk to get to work, to perform errands, and to take breaks. In any case, the process of walking mindfully can transform each step of the day.

Walking is an ongoing opportunity to be mindful. Nothing is mystical about the process. You are bringing awareness to this everyday act. Mindful walking may be easier than mindful sitting or a body scan because your body is moving. A sustained mindful walk is ideal for the person who finds sitting meditation difficult. The good news is that mindfulness comes in all shapes and sizes. The key is to engage.

HATHA YOGA

Yoga is series of practices aimed at bringing tranquility, peace, calm, and insight to the mind of the practitioner. Yoga was developed over 5,000 years ago as a means to enlightenment. In the West today, yoga has become different things to different people—anything from healing, physical exercise, and stretching to wellness and spirituality. **Hatha yoga** is one particular form of practice that

Sun Salutation

You need 15 to 20 minutes for these five poses, which make up this variation of the sun salutation. Wear loose, comfortable clothing. A mat or blanket is helpful but not necessary. We recommend engaging in yoga with bare feet.

   This form of the sun salutation is a series of yoga poses in sequence. Repeated several times in a row, sun salutations are challenging. Follow the five-step sequence that starts by standing in the mountain pose:

1. Mountain pose (see figure 3.2a): Stand tall. Keep your feet hip-distance apart and point your toes and knees straight ahead. Keep your knees slightly bent (soft or relaxed). Keep your legs, core muscles, and gluteus muscles (the muscles of your buttocks) strong. Keep your chest open and lifted. Now move into the next pose.

2. Quarter moon pose (see figure 3.2b): From mountain pose, extend your spine long and straight while keeping your core strong and your feet firmly planted on the ground. Reach your arms overhead with your hands clasped together and your index fingers pointed together to make a steeple. Exhale. Stretch to the left side and point the steeple toward the side wall. Check your breath to make sure that it is full and deep. Then find just the right amount of stretch. If your breath becomes tight at all, back off a bit. Inhale. Come back to reaching your arms overhead; keep your legs and feet firm. Exhale. Stretch to the right side and point the steeple in the other direction. Finish by moving back into mountain pose with your arms at your sides or your hands folded over your heart.

3. Forward fold pose (see figure 3.2c): From mountain pose, bring your arms up overhead and "touch the sky." Lift both arms toward the sky. Fold forward and dive forward, hinging at your hips and reaching your arms forward and then down. Let your arms and head hang down. Gently, even imperceptibly, shake your head side to side so that your neck is released. Keep your knees bent so that they are soft and relaxed. Hold on to each elbow, hold on to your legs or ankles, or let your arms just hang like a rag doll. Finish by gently bending your knees even more and gently rolling up your spine with your head coming up last into mountain pose.

4. Chair pose (see figure 3.2d): From mountain pose, place your feet hip-distance apart, keeping your feet and knees pointed straight ahead. Sit down as if sitting in an imaginary chair. Keep your knees bent, drop your gluteus muscles down, and keep your tailbone pointing straight down at the ground. Reach your arms overhead and look at your fingertips or straight ahead. Lift your chest and relax your shoulders. Finish by holding the chair pose for five full, deep, relaxing breaths.

FIGURE 3.2 Sun salutations with (a) mountain pose, (b) quarter moon pose, (c) forward fold pose, and (d) chair pose.

(continued)

Hatha Yoga Activity   *(continued)*

5. Start while you are still in the chair pose. Squat as far as possible in the chair, keeping your feet and knees straight ahead. Bring your hands in front of your chest in steeple position (hands clasped with index fingers pointed together). Count 1, 2, 3 and then straighten up with the hands held high above your head. Finish in mountain pose.

These five poses represent an important and sophisticated beginning in hatha yoga. We strongly encourage you to participate in yoga with a trained instructor, as this can decrease your risk of injury and advance the physical and mental benefits of the practice.

Adapted, by permission, from N.E. Tummers, 2011, *Teaching stress management: Activities for children and young adults* (Champaign, IL: Human Kinetics), 117-118.

emphasizes specific body postures (asanas) and awareness of breathing (pranayama). Although mastering the discipline could take a lifetime, a person does not need to achieve mastery for hatha yoga to be beneficial.

The art of hatha yoga can help you learn to flow with the energy of the body as you move through various postures. When infused with mindfulness, the postures are transformed from physical stretching to a powerful form of mind–body integration. Our students often find yoga a comfortable form of mindfulness because the mindful movements are engaging.

Hatha yoga engages the body, the breath, and the energy that follows the breath. It has a powerful role. When done mindfully, hatha yoga can expand your perspectives and consciousness. Whereas mindfulness generally serves to remind you of who you are, yoga helps to remind and to "rebody," that is, to grow your consciousness of the role of your body in your existence. It is not unusual to take your body for granted.

Our hatha yoga practice starts by bringing awareness to your body. You will be doing mindful stretching, strengthening, and **flexibility exercises** with a heightened sense of wakefulness with each movement.

Your ostensible work is with the body, but the practice has deeper implications than physical fitness. You are also reenergizing your mental, emotional, and spiritual selves.

Practice needs to be carried out carefully in a nonforced, nonstriving manner. The movements are gentle but powerful. The practice of yoga can be a classroom for reminding yourself of the need for trust. You trust the strength and wisdom within. You are in charge; you are the captain of your own life. Like the captain of any vessel, you will make mistakes, but you accept responsibility.

As with any form of physical exercise done improperly, yoga has the potential for injury to your body parts, especially the joints (Dacci et al. 2012). Trust is crucial for optimal functioning in all realms of your life. Yoga is a wonderful arena for learning to trust yourself by being mindful. Breathing into the poses can elucidate your limits, not as a constraint, but as an indication of who you are. A skillful teacher is invaluable in guiding a student safely through the poses.

We consider mindful sitting, eating, and walking, the body scan, and hatha yoga the formal components

Initially, Jim became interested in mindfulness because he was feeling desperate for positive change in his life. The mindfulness course at the student recreation center led him to begin attending a weekly sitting group that met at a local mosque. He was surprised to run into his favorite sociology professor there. The group did an hour of mindfulness that included 30 minutes of sitting, 10 minutes of mindful walking, a short reading, another 10 minutes of sitting, and a brief discussion.

At first, Jim found the hour with the group a challenge. Little by little, he became more comfortable. He was glad to have the opportunity to participate in the sessions because they made him more peaceful. The people were kind. He often had dinner with them after the mindfulness sessions. His personal practice increased. He has since graduated from the university. He earned a 3.3 grade point average for his last two years of school, a success that he attributes to mindfulness. This turnaround was impressive after his dismal academic performance during his first two years.

of mindfulness. These form the foundation of our recommended life transformational processes. Increased awareness can facilitate cutting through the clutter of your everyday lives, such that you regain possession of your mind, body, and spirit. All too frequently people are walking automatons, on automatic pilot as they move from one task to another. Mindful awareness can breathe life into your actions, relationships, thoughts, and into your entire being. Learning the fundamentals of mindfulness through the formal practice sets the stage for a richer, deeper, and more meaningful life.

SUMMARY

As you slow down, you can experience increased calm even with the occurrence of what may appear to be interruptions. As you slow down, you may recognize that your mind jumps from one disconnected thought to another. As you slow down, you can feel the demands of the insatiable material reality gnaw at you. As you slow down, you can gain a level of awareness not otherwise appreciated.

Often, you are not in touch with how distracted your mind is, even when you are not consciously thinking about something. Mindfulness can be like an anthropologist's notebook in that it can define your established values. Strong motivation can keep you centered and help bring you back to the here and now.

The sitting practice is a foundation for all forms of mindfulness. This practice helps to ground you where you are. Although your mind can be restless, awareness can transform the "distractions" into an integral part of mindfulness.

Physical practices provide you with various mindfulness experiences. The body scan helps increase appreciation of your body, which serves you well, no matter what challenges you experience. Hatha yoga practice is an opportunity to luxuriate in an ancient therapeutic movement practice.

This chapter has provided some guidance on how to live in peace, that state of mind where things can be whirling around you but you are not thrown off balance. Peace of mind occurs by experiencing your thoughts without attachment, by growing in awareness, and by better appreciating your bonds with others. We encourage you to pursue these practices in more detail, but you should recognize that everyone can experience quiet and inner peace.

Chapter 4

Changing Your Perspective With Your Thoughts

Objectives

After reading this chapter, you will be able to

- define the concepts of the consciousness continuum,
- explain how thoughts can affect feelings and actions,
- identify how thoughts affect wellness,
- apply Maslow's hierarchy of needs to behavior,
- understand how perceptions influence reality, and
- differentiate between thought, perceptions, and projection.

Malcolm, a 20-year-old psychology major, was having a difficult time balancing the stress of school and work with the enjoyment of life. His work manager's overbearing style put Malcolm in a foul mood. Malcolm's school work was increasingly difficult. He was having trouble keeping up with his assignments. With the stress associated with his academics and work, he was worried, anxious, and not sleeping well.

Every night Malcolm went to bed obsessing about what had gone wrong during the day. These worries made his school work all the more difficult because he was unable to concentrate, and his grades dropped. He felt overwhelmed. A friend recommended that he see a counselor at the student health center. He met with a counselor on a weekly basis for six weeks. Malcolm also attended a mindfulness workshop that promoted living in the present moment.

Whatever your level of wellness, Norman Cousins (1989) figuratively recommends that you start with the *Head First*, which is also the title of his book. Your entire life experience passes through the lens of your consciousness (Pransky 2007). Thoughts are pivotal to your well-being. Positive evaluations of everyday events, a hopeful attitude, and optimism promote a healthier life. These factors have been shown to be significant for cardiovascular health (Boehm, Vie, and Kubzansky 2012). If you seek the highest levels of rip-roaring good health, thinking positively is a must.

Your consciousness and thoughts profoundly affect everything about your life (Darling et al. 2007). Think about times when you received an academic grade that was higher or lower than you expected. How did this change your happiness? Didn't the higher grade provide a sense of euphoria and a better mood? Alternately, a nagging thought can plunge you into a negative mind-set. People identify specific aspects of life to make sense out of the world. To label something is to give it power. Thinking that you are going to fail or to succeed at something predisposes you to do just that.

Of course, thoughts do not exist in a vacuum. Rather, your consciousness is influenced by the state of your relative needs as well as by interpersonal, institutional, social, and environmental factors (Sallis, Owen, and Fisher 2008). Thinking about higher levels of artistic expression is impossible if your thoughts are obsessed with basic food and safety. Only after your basic needs are satisfied can you confront other obstacles. For instance, marketers often create "needs" that are not in line with your best self-interests. Commercial advertising often communicates that personal fulfillment is to be found in a luxury automobile, designer shoes, or the like. But trying to achieve sustained happiness through material possessions is like trying to hit a home run in a soccer game. It simply does not work, yet many people relentlessly pursue

material sources of happiness without realizing that there is a better way (Opree, Buijzen, and Valkenburg 2012).

This chapter explores the roles of mind, consciousness, and thought in your wellness journey. Previous chapters discussed practicing mindfulness, the seven attitudinal foundations, and incorporating positive psychology into daily living. This chapter adds one complementary component to the optimal wellness program: Your thoughts are powerful. What you perceive, what you believe, and what you tell yourself make up your world (Perrone-Bertolotti et al. 2014). None of these concepts stands alone. They work together to shape who you are.

The demands of everyday life include the clamor of print, radio, television, and web; interactions with colleagues; myriad responsibilities; and a cascade of random thoughts. These powerful external influences can distract you from fully understanding your own mind or from focusing on your deepest personal needs. Remember that your wellness goals include happiness and inner peace. An unfocused, wandering mind is an unhappy mind. A centered, focused mind responds purposefully instead of wandering repeatedly from one random thought to another.

LOWER- AND HIGHER-LEVEL CONSCIOUSNESS

The mind operates on a continuum of consciousness (see figure 4.1). At one end of the continuum is the primitive brain stem that has survival functions shared with other animal life forms. These functions are especially related to self-preservation and procreation. Functioning in this realm is instinctive and reflexive—fight or flight (Cannon 1932). This lower brain involves visceral reactions, providing information

Activity

Improving Focus

Before proceeding further, quiet your mind and body with a 10-minute mindful session.

1. Sit, stand, or lie down and grow attentive to your breath. Remember that mindfulness is an exercise in zoning in and increased awareness.
2. Mentally watch the breath all the way in and all the way out.
3. Becoming quiet enables you to gain better access to your inner wisdom and to achieve a higher level of consciousness as you move forward through this chapter.

Mindfulness establishes a foundation for greater awareness and joyous, fulfilled living.

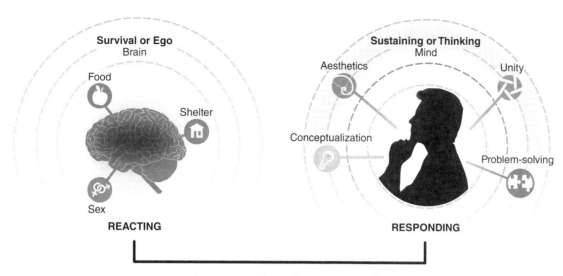

FIGURE 4.1 Consciousness continuum.

that stimulates behaviors essential to your physical survival. The survival-oriented lower-level brain comprises the competitive and reproductive instincts. This realm espouses that you are a separate physical being, that you have little in common with others, and that you must fight to survive and win. Many mass media advertisements incorporate these instincts as one means of selling their product (Astrup et al. 2006). Advertisers link basic drives to products being sold, thereby hijacking your thinking.

Many people become immersed in survival reactions. Different types of personalities manifest "survival reactions" in different ways. One set of personalities are classified as type A and type B. Type A personalities, for example, are often described as goal oriented, time conscious, compulsive, and hostile. By contrast, type B personalities are less competitive and less self-absorbed. Research indicates that type A personalities are predisposed to coronary heart disease (Williams 1989). Their association with heart disease is mediated through hostility and anger (Haukkala et al. 2010), which have the power to taint life experiences. Hostile people seem to be telling themselves that others are mean, selfish, undependable, and threatening, rather than intrinsically good (Kovácsová, Rošková, and Lajunen 2014). Such hostility imprisons people by their own thoughts. Obviously, being hostile can lead to social isolation. You undoubtedly know people whom you prefer not to be around. Research shows that social isolation predisposes people to illness and makes it more difficult for them to recover (Uchino 2006).

By contrast, higher levels of consciousness permit more sophisticated thoughts, feelings, emotions, and behaviors. These focus on the refined dimensions of human beings (Edelman 2001). The thinking, or reasoning, mind makes extensive use of the cerebral cortex, which is the most highly developed brain structure of all animal forms. It is the seat of abstract and intricate thinking.

The cerebral cortex allows humans to think with latitude and devise alternatives. Mental flexibility makes humans highly adaptable to their environment, which includes their relationships with other people. In this part of the brain, self-absorbed thoughts are tempered, and happiness is sought through connection with others. Here also is the center of appreciation of spiritual elements, including cooperative relationships, truth, beauty, art, music, and social justice. Functions of the responding mind can be superimposed over the reacting brain. Both are available for your use and exist in an infinitely delicate balance. This balance is an inside job, meaning that this kind of balance must come from within the deepest parts of your being (Pransky 2003).

HIERARCHY OF NEEDS

Abraham Maslow (1954), the renowned 20th-century psychologist, describes a continuum of consciousness called the **hierarchy of needs** (see figure 4.2). Your needs influence your thinking. According to Maslow, human motives can be arranged in a hierarchy that is stronger and "lower" at one end and weaker and "higher" at the other. The lower basic survival needs are the more potent driving forces. If your thoughts are preoccupied with fulfilling basic physical needs such as food, shelter, or safety, you may find it difficult, or even impossible, to think abstractly about higher aspirations.

Creating Your Own Hierarchy of Needs Triangle

Set aside 30 minutes—5 minutes to read these directions, organize, and set up your own hand-drawn Maslow hierarchy of needs triangle; 5 minutes to list 15 life concerns; 5 minutes to rate their importance and how well they are being fulfilled; 10 minutes to discuss your results; and 5 minutes to summarize the experience.

1. On a sheet of paper, draw a Maslow hierarchy of needs triangle with four horizontal lines dividing the triangle into five sections. Thus, you will have a triangle representing (1) physical needs at the bottom, (2) safety, (3) belongingness and love needs, (4) esteem needs, and (5) self-actualization needs at the top.

2. List 15 life concerns. This list is not definitive, but it can serve as a point of reflection and discussion.

   1. Label each life concern on the list A through O.

   2. Next to each item, rank the importance of each of these to you on a scale of 1 to 10 (with 10 being most important).

   3. Rank how well the need is being fulfilled on a scale of 1 to 10 (with 10 being totally fulfilled).

3. Looking at figure 4.2, place the letter corresponding to each item in the triangle where it fits into the Maslow hierarchy (physical needs, safety needs, belongingness and love needs, esteem needs, self-actualization needs).

4. Where are your concerns on the hierarchy of needs triangle [(1) physical needs, (2) safety needs, (3) belongingness and love needs, (4) esteem needs, (5) self-actualization needs]?

5. There are no right or wrong answers. No matter where you place your concerns, remain nonjudgmental with your new awareness.

6. Share your results with someone you trust—a friend, classmate, roommate, partner, or spouse.

7. Write a 100-word summary of the experience and enter it and your 15-concern hierarchy of needs triangle into Chapter 4 of your journal

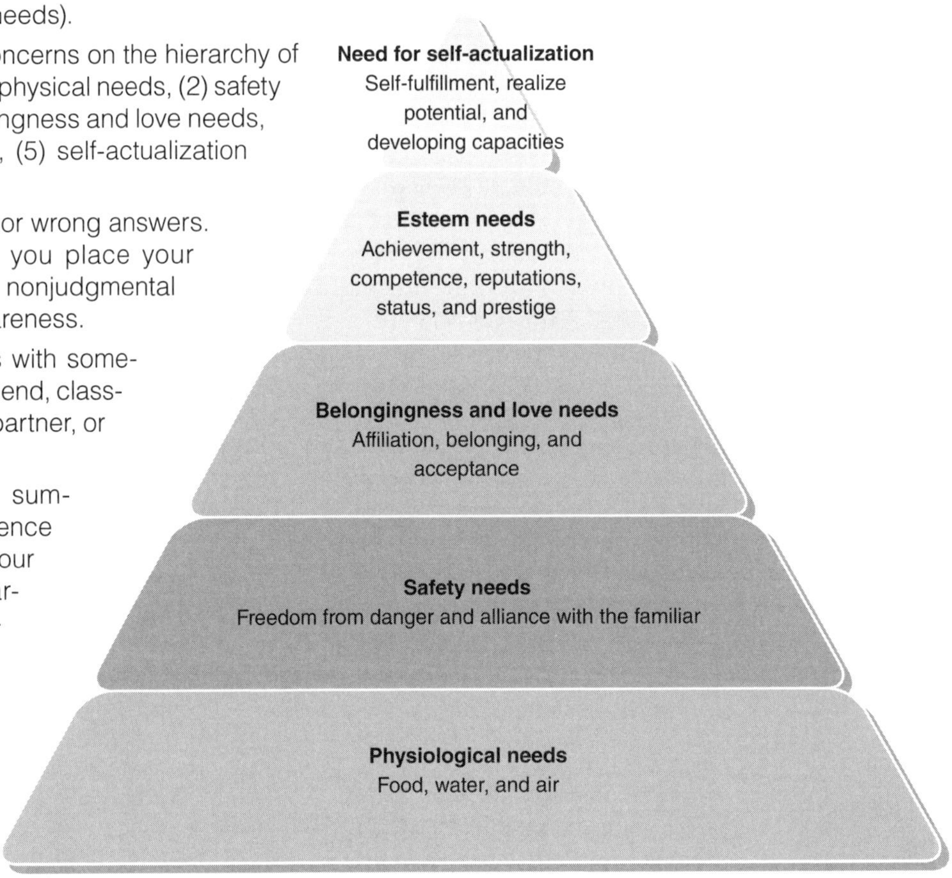

Need for self-actualization
Self-fulfillment, realize potential, and developing capacities

Esteem needs
Achievement, strength, competence, reputations, status, and prestige

Belongingness and love needs
Affiliation, belonging, and acceptance

Safety needs
Freedom from danger and alliance with the familiar

Physiological needs
Food, water, and air

FIGURE 4.2 Maslow's hierarchy of needs.

Based on Maslow 1954.

Activity

Lower- and Higher-Level Consciousness: Peaceful Decision Journal Entry

Set aside 15 minutes—3 minutes to read these directions and organize and 12 minutes to do the journal-writing exercise involving peacefulness and a decision.

Think back to a recent time in your life when you were particularly peaceful with yourself and when you made a decision that took into account your needs as well as the needs of someone around you.

1. What was this experience like for you? Was it enriching or depleting?
2. Describe the effect it had on your well-being. If it had a negative effect, reflect on why the experience was negative. Use knowledge you gained after the experience to help you understand the negative interaction.
3. Was the decision based on love or based on fear?

This activity can elucidate insights about how your mood dictates your thoughts. (Professors are encouraged to use this activity to explore the consequences of the interaction of moods and thoughts.)

Some people become stalled at the stage of fulfilling their basic needs, even though objectively their physical safety no longer represents a problem. Without higher awareness, lower-level drives can cause physical, mental, emotional, social, and spiritual problems. After all, there is only so much stuff to go around on planet earth. You can become obsessed with scarcity and allocate an inordinate amount of energy into stockpiling. Competition, fear, and feelings of isolation can distract you from who you really are and from your inner wisdom.

You need to differentiate between real demands and perceived needs. For some, this distinction may involve a leap of faith, because you typically see all your experiences as real. When you perceive that your survival needs are not being met, the spectrum of available choices may seem insufficient. The immediate demands of life may engulf you.

When you have attended to your physiologic and safety needs, you are freer to choose what you want to think. You can see choices, explore options, and access your innate wisdom. What you focus on is often up to you.

None of this is meant to suggest that life is binary. Rather, you live and move back and forth along the spectrum of consciousness. You make decisions based on what you think about where you are. In the realm of function, you always have a choice. But the better you are at taking care of your basic needs and taking time for mindfulness, the less likely you are to experience fear (Jampolsky 2011). With inner quiet, you are more

likely to be at peace, in touch with your higher self, and able to make responsible decisions.

Attribution

Your thoughts promote what is often called a self-fulfilling prophecy, meaning that what you choose to believe can happen. When you attribute characteristics to yourself, your feelings, expectations, and behaviors are likely to follow (Lewis and Daltroy 1990). Remember, you are not always what you think you are. But what you think, you are.

Attribution theory describes how people explain events to themselves and what consequences come about, in terms of behavior and emotions, because of those personal explanations (Lewis and Daltroy 1990). A consequence of explanatory thoughts is the belief in your ability or inability to carry out a plan. When you say that you are good at something, you are more likely to work hard and achieve success (Beckmann et al. 2012). The concept of self-fulfilling prophecy comes into effect here. If you see yourself as being a regular exerciser, research demonstrates that you are more likely to exercise (Beacham et al. 2011).

By contrast, if you tell yourself, "There is no way I can ever correctly assemble this computer work station," you are unlikely to succeed. Similarly, if you perceive that success in school is a question of luck or otherwise not within your control, you will generally not expend as much effort trying to make a difference in the outcome. Life experiences are created through your thoughts (Pransky 2003).

For decades, positive psychologist Martin Seligman (2011) studied the effect of thinking on health. His research led him to conclude that negative and pessimistic thoughts not only influence your fulfillment but also place you at risk for ill health. Those with a major illness, such as cancer, who are pessimistic tend to experience a poorer prognosis or die sooner than optimists do (Seligman 2006). Optimistic people tend to think about specific consequences of events in a positive manner. This optimism has a wellness-promoting effect.

Coherence

If you have a sense of **coherence**, the ability to find meaning in every aspect of life, you perceive a crisis as less problematic, which enables you to perceive the situation as potentially meaningful and comprehensible (Richardson and Ratner 2005). Those perceptions help you experience negative events as potentially beneficial, making you more resilient to stress. People who feel a sense of meaning and understanding within events may have the motivation to do whatever is necessary to be at peace with the situation. Their rich cognitive framework, that is, their resilient thinking, provides them with additional coping tools.

STRESS

Stress results from an overload of demands made on the capacity of a person. Stress itself is not negative. Stressful situations do not make you unhappy or ill. Rather, it is the power of the human mind, your perceptions, that influence your reality. The Yerkes–Dodson stress curve (1908) demonstrates that performance increases as stress increases, an obvious benefit. But after stress reaches a certain elevated state, performance levels off and then decreases precipitously (see figure 4.3). High levels of perceived stress often negatively affect health (Holmes and Rehe 1967).

Think about how your consciousness can complicate your life. Perceptions can create stress (Gerin et al. 2012). Perceived stress can increase the intensity of physical pain thereby making it more debilitating (Choi, Chung, and Lee 2012) and exacerbate other health conditions. After you are in such a cycle, the pain can escalate until you choose to do something, such as those things being suggested throughout this volume.

The relationship of these thoughts on wellness can go either way, either toward or away from optimal health. Psychoneuroimmunology, also known as mind–body health, has demonstrated the relationship between positive and negative thoughts and subse-

© Willie B. Thomas

Go into difficult tasks with the positive mind-set that you can succeed, and note how much more likely you are to finish the task!

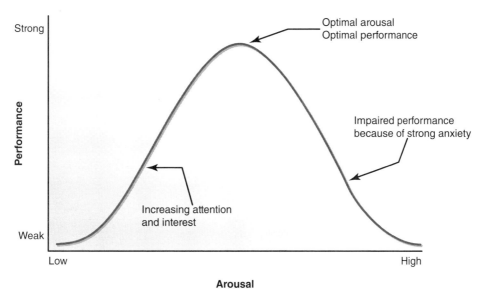

FIGURE 4.3 Yerkes–Dodson curve. As stress increases, so does performance, up to the point where stress becomes overwhelming and performance begins to deteriorate.

Reprinted from D.M. Diamond et al., 2007, "The temporal dynamics model of emotional memory processing: A synthesis on the neuro-biological basis of stress-induced amnesia, flashbulb and traumatic memories, and the Yerkes-Dodson Law," *Neural Plasticity* 2007: 1-33. Copyright © 2007 David M. Diamond et al. This is a an open access article distributed under the Creative Commons Attribution.

quent physical, emotional, and mental health (Pert 2006). Just as you are more likely to catch a cold when feeling stressed (Heikkinen and Järvinen **2003**), so also you have the ability to bolster your immune system by your thoughts (Knox 2010). You can modulate the effect of stress by the way you view it. Your brain, under the influence of conscious thought, is indeed a pharmacopoeia of potential coping resources.

Awareness of Thoughts

Happiness is only one thought away (Pransky 2003). This notion is challenging. It suggests that you can be your own persecutor, prosecutor, and helper, depending on your mindset. You literally create your own reality by focusing on select thoughts and perceptions.

Dealing with this knowledge can be disturbing. Creating your reality gives you enormous power and

alcolm's counselor helped him look at his thoughts differently. Malcolm's situation was exacerbated by the demands made by what he perceived as an overbearing boss at the same time that he was struggling to succeed in school. The young worker kept count of the number of (perceived) times his boss insulted him. Malcolm decided that he was going to get into an argument with his boss when the number reached 50.

Fortunately, the counselor was able to help Malcolm see that his life overload was causing him to think negatively. They examined the overall context of the issues plaguing him. The student-worker needed tools to be able to experience his life differently and not feel overwhelmed and reactive.

Malcolm experienced a metamorphosis through counseling and mindfulness. After he got in touch with the effect of his perceptions on his reality, Malcolm transformed his life. He felt more empathy for himself and his boss.

makes you responsible, which of itself can feel threatening. Nevertheless, it is through your own power and responsibility that you have a powerful solution to many of life's disappointments. You can focus on nurturing thoughts, not self-defeating ones. Each person chooses his or her thoughts and life direction.

Thoughts can precede emotions, even though you may be unaware of which thought sponsored your emotions (Talbot et al. 2009). For example, when you are studying for a test or working to meet a deadline, you may overeat with little awareness of your underlying anxiety. Awareness of your mental state gives you more control over the experience. If you find yourself feeling anxious, focus on being present right here, right now. Bring your attention to your breath. Bring your attention to what you are experiencing, your bodily sensations, the sounds, your thoughts. If you are in touch with the cause, let go of what sparked your anxiety. Such an approach might reduce your emotional response to the situation. This enhanced awareness may liberate you from the oppression of your own expectations, judgments, emotions, and social environment. This possibility has substantial implications for your health.

Members of Alcoholics Anonymous and other similar fellowships demonstrate how success can be found in changing the way that you think. Recovering alcoholics come to learn that they primarily have a thinking problem, not just a drinking problem (*Alcoholics Anonymous* 2001). Likewise, Al-Anon, the support group for the family and friends of alcoholics, emphasizes that each member is in charge of his or her own happiness and peace of mind (*Courage to Change* 1992).

To be clear, this is not to say that policies, social systems, and environments have no influence on your thoughts or your health. But the bottom line is that life experiences are mediated through your perceptions.

Projection

Projection is the outward picturing of an inward condition. Projection is also known as social projection or egocentric bias (Bazinger and Kühberger 2012). This "out-picturing" is associated with the way you view yourself, seeing what you want to see. It involves attributing your own attitudes, feelings, or suppositions to others and then allowing those thoughts to create what you see.

Swiss psychologist Carl Jung (1958) suggested that people are predisposed to project a "shadow side," a self perceived to be unlovable, undesirable, and unacceptable. When you focus on those aspects, you then also see people and situations unfavorably. Conversely, if you see yourself as doing the best you can, you are more likely to view others as doing their best.

Activity

Empathy and Acceptance

Set aside 10 minutes—3 minutes to read these directions and organize and 7 minutes to do the exercise involving empathy.

Close your eyes and visualize yourself in a crowded environment, such as a bus, train, doctor's office, or standing in line at a movie theater. You encounter a source of irritation, such as unruly children, a person speaking very loudly, or a cashier who is slow.

1. Get in touch with your sense of annoyance with the other person. Feel the tension that builds in your chest, neck, arms, or hands as you impatiently bear the irritation. You know your body, so you know best in which physical areas you store your tension.
2. Pause and mentally follow your breath all the way in and all the way out. Repeat this act of breathing awareness for approximately one minute.
3. Again mindfully visualize the situation. Make an effort to identify with the "offending" person or persons. Look nonjudgmentally.
4. Stay with the breath for several additional minutes. Has the tension in your body disappeared? Do you feel more empathy for the other(s)?
5. Practice this exercise in your everyday life at least once within the next week.

This exercise is not only about empathizing with the other person but also about accepting yourself with your reactions to others. This change in thought can free you to live your life with more joy and less tension.

In this way, projections create positive perceptions. What is within also becomes what is outside. If you are feeling upbeat, optimistic, and loved, you project that outside yourself (Seligman 2006). When two people fall in love, they are likely to see what they want to see, rather than an objective picture.

A gloomy mood can further lead to feeling pessimistic, and this state can affect your perceptions and subsequent actions (Banks 1998). The Monday morning blues may be a stereotypical example. After a high-energy weekend, you might wake up for classes or work feeling as if you are living inside a dark cloud or as if you had been thrown under a bus!

In such a mood, a teacher, indeed anyone, might be impatient with the normal behavior of students and all others. Making major decisions at this time is unwise. Remember that moods change. We suggest doing a mindfulness practice, such as focusing on the breath. The mood that created the negative thoughts may pass. If the mood does not pass, accept yourself for where you are. At least you are not aggravating the situation by cursing yourself or others because of it. An inappropriate reaction exacerbates existing problems.

You can be nonstriving with what is happening by having trust in yourself and in the processes of life. By contrast, impulsively reacting to persons, places, and things while in a low mood can begin a cascade of events that is other than what you may have intended. When your thoughts are projected on the outside world, they dominate your reality. With angry thoughts, you project a hostile mood and see

© Eduard Titov - Fotolia

You can lessen the effect and amount of stress that you feel from a potentially stressful situation by projecting a positive mood instead of feeding a more negative reaction.

Activity

Projection, Mirror

Set aside 15 minutes—3 or so minutes to read these directions and get organized, and then 12 minutes for the exercise:

1. Gather a pen and paper or your computer keyboard. Sit quietly for several minutes, concentrating on awareness of your breath.

2. Think of a person toward whom you are holding a grudge or whom you simply dislike.

3. Write down a characteristic (quality) about the person that you find most disagreeable.

4. Now quietly and with a sense of curiosity, reflect on how you may be displaying some of the same characteristics yourself. This activity will take some motivation. Smile at yourself. See what you can learn and begin the process of acceptance (for yourself and others).

5. During the exercise, when you become aware of a trait that you don't like, just say, "Isn't this interesting." Be nonjudgmental.

Write a 100-word summary of this experience in your journal. Include this and your reflections about the person you choose for this exercise.

negative qualities in others, become intolerant, or attribute ill intention (Lowe 2013). The mood comes from a thought, a perception.

Scores of illustrations come to mind here: a perceived insult by a coworker, a deli coffee served without the proper combination of milk and flavoring, getting cut off in traffic, being delayed for an important meeting because your partner was not yet ready to leave, being asked at the last minute to do just one more thing. Many of these circumstances do not fit with what you think should be going on at the time, and they deflate your energy. In such situations, you can easily choose a way that makes yourself and others unhappy. The next person you encounter can be the recipient of an unintended snub.

In contrast, a positive, bright mood can lead us to feeling loved, seeing only good qualities in others, and attributing goodness to everything around us. As Jon Kabat-Zinn (1994) reiterates throughout his book of the same title, "Wherever you go, there you are," you take your mind with you at all times.

The mirror exercise that follows may help you uncover hidden or repressed qualities. As you go through the process of increased self-awareness, you may be able to celebrate what you formerly saw as an unacceptable part of yourself. The more aspects of self you recognize, accept, and reclaim, the more you experience yourself and your world in balance. This exercise can serve to remind you who and what you really are.

Self-Victimization

Acting as a victim (self-victimization) involves getting caught up believing that life just happens without recognizing how you perceive, contribute, or fail to act on choices available. Further, seeing yourself as a victim can keep you stuck in pain, discouragement, and even illness from which you see no escape.

Seeing a way out is easier when you understand

Activity

Perceiving Relationships to Avoid Self-Victimization

Set aside 10 minutes—3 minutes to read these directions and then 7 minutes for the activity.

1. Imagine yourself as an "A" student in public health. You may think that you can never do enough. People recognize that you do well on tests; thus, they often ask you for assistance studying, not considering the implications of the extra work of helping out. You have a lovely relationship, but your significant other is never satisfied with the time you give. Your parents would like you to visit or call them more frequently. In addition, you are working 20 hours per week. You ask yourself, "When have I done enough? How can I get it all done?" You are experiencing chronic overwhelm.

2. Now imagine you are at a party with your romantic partner. You notice your love interest spending a lot of time chatting with someone else. Your partner seems quite happy and even flirtatious. You assume that your significant other may be thinking of leaving your relationship. This possibility is both hurtful and frightening. You become angry. Your instinct is to confront your partner immediately about the perceived behavior.

3. Can you see any aspect of your own life in the preceding situations? Take a few minutes to be mindfully quiet and feel these demands. Can you feel the frustration, anger, and indignation?

4. Now take a few additional minutes to be present with your breath. Be right here right now. Let your body relax.

5. Think about the perspective of your romantic partner. Getting in touch with a different view may alleviate some of the angst that you are feeling. Your partner may be less than thrilled about your preoccupation with the demands of your life. But wallowing in self-victimization is not doing either of you any good. Because you are stressed, you are more likely to think negatively.

6. Recognize that conflicting feelings may be a cue to chat with your significant other about your relationship. Approach these conversations from a place of peace and calm. Recognize his or her commitment to you. Speaking when you are angry is unlikely to promote good will. Instead, take time to be present with yourself. When you no longer feel frustration, speak about your concerns. Use "I" statements and avoid accusations. If you value the relationship, you may be unable to continue at the frenetic pace to which you have become accustomed.

Malcolm had limited his entire life with his thinking. Unlike many who become stuck in a negative pattern of behavior, he took the important step to see a mental health counselor and initiated mindfulness. With mindfulness, Malcolm experienced tranquility unlike never before. He recognized that his thinking was more problematic than the outside world.

Malcolm began to feel more empathy for others. He discovered that his boss was also struggling. The boss's wife had filed for divorce and moved out with their children. This situation didn't necessarily excuse inappropriate behavior on the part of his boss, but it did help Malcolm build an understanding of why his boss sometimes acted the way he did. By making an effort to know his boss better, Malcolm had found a powerful tool that he could use to gain better understanding of all the relationships in his life.

Ten-minute twice daily mindful sitting sessions enabled Malcolm to start and finish his work day in a positive manner. He began to appreciate the importance of inner peace. His sleep improved almost immediately. He was studying better, and he became more patient with his boss. Malcolm became more accepting of the challenges with himself, his boss, and his school work. He began to do better in all three arenas of his life—as a student, as an employee, and in his romantic relationship. He looked on his overall situation with a beginner's mind, and he was even able to feel some sense of commonality with his boss.

how your thoughts screen your reality (Tarlaci 2013). When you perceive yourself as a victim, you blame others for your unhappiness. In situations in which a person is blaming others, we usually find that the person is actually discontented with her- or himself.

Self-victimization is a pitfall to your wellness. All of us know people who self-victimize. If you look closely enough, you may see this in yourself. Powerful thoughts overlay self-victimization experiences. You may hear statements such as, "Oh, look what happened to me. Poor me!" The innocent victim posture can generate the secondary gain of empathy and sympathy. In normal conversation, many of us may seek a bit of sympathy now and again. Such self-pity is a different matter, however, when it dominates our lives or becomes a primary means of communication.

When you perceive yourself as a victim, you can easily blame others for your unhappiness. You can get caught up in persistently criticizing yourself. People are often harder on themselves than they are on others. As a result, fear, anger, and feelings of isolation can become dominant. In this situation, you become angry because of what is happening. Everything and everyone seem to work against you. You lose your power to generate positive thoughts. The power of your perceptions and choices are tremendous.

Every day, you encounter stressors. Your responses to these stressors determine their influence in your life.

A goal for mindfulness is to become more deliberate, to learn to *respond*, not react. To have a deliberate response means to exercise your choices. You may not have control over all the circumstances in your life, but how you respond is within your domain. You can choose to do things differently.

When you become aware of how you are responding through mindfulness, you tend to feel contented and have a better self-concept and better health (Prazak et al. 2012). Most important, you are less anxious than you would have been if you perceived life as beyond your resources. You have choices every moment of your life. The challenge is how to recognize and exercise them.

Be aware of your thoughts. They are yours. You do not have to believe all of them. You can focus on what brings inner peace and happiness.

SUMMARY

Your thoughts determine what you see and how your approach your life. But you need to be aware of societal influences that affect what you are thinking. Awareness of the power of your thoughts provides one more tool in the journey toward optimal wellness.

You do better when you live in the present moment, that is, when you refuse to let thoughts infringe on what you are experiencing right now. You do better when you take time to practice mindfulness in sitting, body scan, walking, and yoga practices.

The concepts in this chapter are central to understanding how your thoughts affect your wellness. When at peace, you can consciously frame your thoughts about both your everyday reality and your cosmic existence within the greater universe. You can build your life using mindfulness and positive psychology to be more predisposed to think clearly and positively.

Your lower and higher levels of consciousness are vastly different. At the lower levels, you are reactively focused on survival. When stressed, anxious, and overwhelmed with life demands, you are more likely to be negative in your thinking and ineffective with meeting your life goals. Pessimistic thoughts can make you sick. Optimistic thoughts can add to your feelings and experiences of well-being.

Your mental consciousness is linked into the Maslow hierarchy of needs. Unmet basic needs preclude thinking about anything other than food, shelter, procreation, and safety. But anyone can get stuck in lower-level thinking. If you believe that every situation is a survival situation, then you become trapped by your thoughts, which can create a self-perpetuating malicious cycle.

You project what is within yourself onto life. Taking time to respond mindfully enables you to move beyond merely reacting to what you think is happening (or making yourself a victim). You can become more involved with living your fullest, most fulfilled life.

© Corbis

Chapter 5

Social Capital, Connections, and Support

Objectives

After reading this chapter, you will be able to

- define social networks and social support,
- explain how social support can improve the quality of life,
- discuss the importance of solid relationships for emotional stability,
- identify strategies to improve the quality of relationships,
- identify the role of social capital in promoting good health,
- list three self-help groups that promote wellness, and
- describe mechanisms of social support.

Mia was stressed. She had many relationships in her life, but the two-year relationship with her boyfriend, Max, was in trouble. He was insensitive. She was impatient. Mia was unsupported and alone much of the time. Max was struggling with recreational substance abuse.

Mia was having difficulty concentrating in class. She was not sleeping well and was no longer taking time for her customary daily walks. She felt the need to save her boyfriend from himself. Max was controlling, just as his own parents had been. He "knew" that relationships did not last and was constantly bracing for the breakup.

Mia and Max each needed different things at this critical time in their young lives. The challenge for them was to determine together if they could support each other on separate journeys to a common goal. Mia agreed to start walking again and to see whether this activity would help her sleep. Max agreed to contact student health for an assessment or counseling to see whether his recreational drug use was really recreational or turning into something else. They both agreed that they would seek the advice of several long-term couples who appeared to be happy. They would ask them a series of agreed-upon questions regarding what a healthy relationship might look like.

Can you identify a recent experience that was improved by sharing it with others? For most, the answer is yes. You have close bonds with friends, family, schoolmates, and work associates. They are almost an extension of who you are. When you share positive experiences with them, your perceptions and emotions are magnified. When sadness and negative experiences are shared, the hurt diminishes.

You live, move, and define your being in a social world (Bandura 2011). What you learn and how you experience the world are influenced by the people, networks, organizations, institutions, communities, and environments that surround you (Sallis, Owen, and Fisher 2008). In return, the world is influenced by your connecting to it (Bandura 2011).

As social creatures, humans need companionship. Connecting can have positive implications for health and well-being. Some feel their strongest connection with a spouse, family member, or friend. Others feel their closest connections with a spiritual community (Widmer et al. 2013) or in **prayer** or meditation (Dyer 2007). Others connect with the natural world, such as when they walk in the woods. Pets can contribute to well-being, lower blood pressure, and increase longevity (Headey, Na, and Zheng 2008). Life expectancy can be extended by caring for plants (Shibata 2004). Online relationships are central for young adults (Subrahmanyam and Greenfield 2008). Connections are available when you reach out, and these experiences can immensely enhance your reality.

Whether you already have a strong social support or seek more, this chapter can further your journey. It provides guidance to enhance social connections and to build social capital, regardless of your past socialization, your habits, or current beliefs about yourself.

SOCIAL RELATIONSHIPS AND CATEGORIES

The wellness and health of individuals depend not just on their own biology, behaviors, and environments, but also on the biology and actions of others in their communities (Smith and Christakis 2008). We are all interdependent. Both illness and wellness are nonbiologically transmitted.

House (1981) describes categories of social support. These can buffer physical, mental, and emotional challenges and augment quality of life (Thoits 2011). They include:

- Emotional—perception of being cared for
- Instrumental—aid and services to another person
- Informational—advice to help solve problems
- Appraisal—evaluation and constructive feedback

Smith and Christakis (2008) describe **social network** categories, which include primary relationships with other people, are as follows:

- Individuals—family, friends, romantic partner, colleagues, associates, classmates, neighbors
- Organizations—classes, support groups, civic clubs, sororities, fraternities, service clubs, religions
- Interactions—weekly book clubs, meeting friends for lunch, reunions, online social networks, family dinners

Your interactions are as varied as the various forms of communication, including coffee with a grandparent, a romantic dinner with a sweetheart, a telephone call from an old friend, a text message from a schoolmate, a meeting of colleagues, a self-help meeting, or a community protest of global warming. All can contribute to the quality of your life. The bottom line is that having even one close relationship is associated with better health, happiness, and inner peace (Smith and Christakis 2008).

Having support is vital for change and living well. James Prochaska (1994) suggested that people can reverse undesirable life patterns at any age and helping relationships and social resources are central to this process. People sometimes want to fix themselves before reaching out to others. But fixing yourself and attaining fulfillment often require first reaching out to others. Social support and social networking come together to promote social capital.

COMMUNITY AND SOCIAL CAPITAL

Social capital refers to the connections between people, the resources that accrue from social networks and social support, all of which enhance health, productivity and quality of life in community (Putnam 2000). For individuals, social capital requires trust, commitment, a sense of being valued, confidence in what is being achieved, and a shared purpose in the community (Reger-Nash et al. 2006). According to Putnam (2000), civic virtue is enhanced with an established dense network of reciprocal social relationships.

Communities with high social capital have a common shared vision. A classic high-social-capital, high-trust society would be the Amish. If your barn burns down, an entire Amish community will pitch in to rebuild it in a day or two. Of course, you, in turn, would be obligated to do the same for your neighbor if his barn burned.

From the beginning of human existence, humans have lived in extended families, clans, tribes, and geographic communities. Gathering, hunting, self-

Getting involved in the community can increase quality of life.

protection, basic needs, and the synergy for problem solving were all enhanced through group effort. Quality of life is higher in communities where social capital is prevalent. Communities and groups can be defined and recognized by their levels of positive social capital.

During the 1950s in Roseto, Pennsylvania, heart disease rates were observed to be half the national average and below the levels of two neighboring communities. All three communities shared the same health care facilities, physicians, and drinking water supply (Egolf et al. 1992). The social cohesion of the many three-generation households with deep Italian cultural traditions and civic commitment seemed to serve as a buffer to heart disease and other forms of ill health for the residents of Roseto. Unfortunately, those protective effects dissipated with significant family structural changes that occurred in the 1980s and thereafter. Families no longer lived together in the same households. Close family ties dissolved as adult children moved elsewhere. With those changes, the state of good heart health also declined (Wolf 1992).

The Roseto effect was also observed in an industrial region of Japan (Hanibuchi et al. 2012). The region was originally designed to serve one particular large manufacturing industry. At about the same time people moved to the region to engage in industrial work. Thus, the families shared common bonds and better health in four of nine domains assessed, versus the comparison regions (Hanibuchi et al. 2012).

The landmark Ni-Hon-San study (Japan, Honolulu, and San Francisco) looked specifically at the strong bonds common to traditional Japanese culture and the way in which those connections affect the health of Japanese people living in Japan, compared with those living in Hawaii and San Francisco. Heart disease prevalence was lowest in Japan and highest in San Francisco (Marmot et al. 1975). The traditional close-knit Japanese family experienced high levels of social support and lower rates of heart disease. Even subgroups in Hawaii or San Francisco who maintained the cultural traditions experienced one-third the rate of heart disease compared with that of the United States in general (Marmot and Syme 1976). But for those Japanese in Honolulu and San Francisco who intermarried and did not maintain their cultural and family traditions, the rate of heart disease equaled that of their American counterparts. For these Japanese Americans, living without cultural and social support was as much of a risk factor for heart disease as high **cholesterol**, high blood pressure, or smoking.

In addition to towns and cities, a number of non-geographic communities exist, including trade or industrial unions, political parties, fraternal organizations, youth and religion-based groups, virtual self-help groups, veterans groups, and support groups. Each grows and thrives out of the shared interest of members. These communities serve the function of assisting members in defining their personal values, facilitating relationships with others, and finding personal meaning. High levels of social capital are common in these types of communities.

Greek fraternities and sororities on college campuses represent social networks that can promote reciprocity, social trust, and academic excellence. The companionship for students involved can be helpful because they support each other and work to address mutual needs in the academic and general community.

The social environment of some organizations, however, can foster group think. Organizations, Greek or otherwise, can become counterproductive when it comes to drinking to excess, partying, and manifesting insensitivity to others. Your choice of groups to belong to, now and as you age, will require discernment. Remember, your social environment can strongly influence your individual behavior, for better or worse. Often you become like the people you associate with the most.

Businesses, agencies, corporations, workplaces, and governments constitute communities well equipped for social support and networks. Their importance lies in the consistency of contact with the other people present. They present opportunities for interpersonal skill development and conflict management. Many of these groups have highly formalized goals, structures, and rules, and they often define themselves in relation to their members' shared interests and values. A number of large organizational structures (multinational corporations) and institutions (religious, educational, finance) have positive features for individual members and for society. These entities serve as major sources of employment, ensure that work is accomplished, and consequently provide social networks in which many people function well, contribute, and feel needed.

You should recognize the power that institutions hold on your life, for good and for ill. Both your perceptions and your values will aid in maintaining balance. To maintain optimal health through social support and social networks through established institutions, you need to

1. be aware of their influences,

2. discern whether those influences are desirable, and

3. brainstorm ways to strengthen or weaken their hold on your best interests.

Volunteering

Volunteering means to give personal time and talents to perform tasks to a community for which you receive no financial payment (*Volunteers* 1982). Americans have a rich history of volunteering and provide more community service than do citizens of other nations in the Western world (Putnam 2000). This propensity was described nearly 200 years ago by Alexis de Tocqueville ([1835] 2003).

Although the number of volunteer hours in the U.S. has waned compared with 50 years ago, the number of people providing volunteer service has not decreased (Putnam 2000). Note that such time investment not only helps the community but also contributes to the physical and psychological well-being of those engaged as volunteers (Thoits and Hewitt 2001). This kind of service is a component of positive psychology (Donaldson, Csikszentmilhalyi, and Nakamura 2011). Volunteering enables people with different levels of social status to interact with equivalent status, thereby facilitating cooperation and social capital within a community (Ferlander 2007).

The most substantial volunteer-related influence on personal well-being occurs when you help others in need. The positive effects include increased happiness, life satisfaction, self-esteem, sense of control, good health, and less depression (Thoits and Hewitt 2001). The mechanisms for the beneficial effects might be that the volunteers feel appreciated by those being served (Thoits and Hewitt 2001), have an enhanced sense of purpose (Thoits 1992), and find the engagement intrinsically rewarding (Donaldson, Csikszentmilhalyi, and Nakamura 2011). Volunteering represents a worthwhile investment because it is the right thing to do.

RELATIONSHIPS

The number and quality of your relationships is protective against illness and premature death (Berkman et al. 2000). Although relationships are not perfect measures of wellness, they reflect a person's well-being.

Dyads are the simplest form of networks and they demonstrate an interdependent impact on health. Married couples experience lower premature mortality than the unmarried (Hu and Goldman 1990). Consistent with this, there is an increase in mortality following the death of a spouse (Elwert and Christakis 2006). Hospitalization of one spouse increases the likelihood of a premature death in the partner (Christakis and Allison 2006). Curiously, providing good end-of-life care to a partner has been shown to decrease the risk of death in the surviving spouse (Smith and Christakis 2008).

The effects go beyond individuals. Weight loss and gain and tobacco and alcohol use are transmitted socially. Wing and Jeffery (1999) demonstrated the improved effectiveness of interventions targeting groups of people compared to individuals alone. An analysis of the Framingham Heart Health Study demonstrated that obesity spread through social networks with up to three degrees of separation, meaning that an obese person's friend's friend would be negatively impacted by the obesity. Although this relative negative impact is threatening, it works for the good of the cluster as well. For instance, the propensity for people to stop smoking, exercise regularly, and visit doctors, among others, likely spreads through social networks as well (Smith and Christakis 2008).

One aspect of social networks is close friends. Close friends are the ones you confide in and trust. These are the gems in your life, and they promote longevity (Guilley et al. 2005). Women seem to have more close friends than men do, which might reflect the tendency of women to confide. This practice may well be mediated by empathic understanding (Heaney and Israel 2008). You are more likely to confide in another and accept assistance if you perceive the support person as socially similar and as one who has experienced similar challenges (Thoits 1995).

Friendships and close relationships generally make a profound contribution to wellness (Kernes and Kinnier 2005). Many people center their lives on others, and this focus contributes to their well-being. For example, adolescents who have more friends are not only happier but also more likely to make healthy lifestyle decisions (Mahon, Yarcheski, and Yarcheski 2004).

Family

The debate continues about whether health is primarily a product of nurture or nature (Pléh 2012). How you define who you are and how you relate to others comes primarily from your relationship with parents (Fraser 2013). Families have a direct effect on how you navigate through the world. You often live out patterns of social interaction by selecting friends and partners who have characteristics similar to your parents and who treat you like your parents treated you (Boman et al. 2012).

You are the product of all your experiences, but the nurturing role of the family is paramount (Ji et al. 2010). Infants who had a loving bond with at least one parent were shown to have fewer emotional and behavioral problems later in life (Kim and Kochanska 2012). These children exhibited better emotional stability and were less troubled and aggressive, regardless of family income, education, and race. Children learn key dimensions of social adjustment, emotional intelligence, and coping skills from their parents (Papageorgiou et al. 2011).

When you perceive that you are cared for, you feel better about yourself. You are also more likely to cope successfully with stress, anxiety, and depression

© Monkey Business

A healthy relationship with family can have a profound influence on the socialization of children into the community and provide a sense of support throughout life.

(Custers et al. 2010). Families provide a blueprint on how to interact with others (good or bad) and help you identify acceptable behaviors.

In a long-term study, two classes of Harvard alumni were questioned about parental support. A follow-up 35 years later revealed that 91 percent of respondents who initially reported a lack of feelings of warmth or closeness toward their mother and father were diagnosed with physical illness in midlife, whereas only 45 percent of those rating their parents high in warmth and closeness had a diagnosed disease (Russek and Schwartz 1997). Feeling loved by your parents sets the stage for better self-care. Parents who trust and support their children deserve much credit as their children learn to trust and empathize with others (Wray-Lake and Flanagan 2012).

No formal training is offered for becoming a parent, yet parenting may be the most important job that any human being undertakes. Some parents are ill-informed about the care and feeding of a child. Some highly educated and nurturing parents raise troubled kids. Many events can interrupt the intended nurturing of children. If a parent is present, stays alert, communicates, listens, and exhibits unconditional love, his or her child will escape the battlefield of growth and development with fewer wounds.

Intimate Relationships

Your primary relationship can be romantic, although it need not be so. Improved health and happiness are associated with treating your intimate partner well (Proulx and Snyder-Rivas 2013). Married couples, for example, experience better health and immune function and reduced risk of dying from chronic diseases or all causes (Proulx and Snyder-Rivas 2013).

When romantic relationships are built on a solid foundation of love, they have the potential to represent what is best within us. For many people, nothing feels better than experiencing the unqualified love of another, especially when it is mixed with genuine mental, emotional, spiritual, and sexual bonds. The intimacy of the deeply interpersonal relationship enables people to feel as one as they move through the challenges of life. Ideally, these bonds enable the partners to live in unison as they share their vulnerabilities and aspirations.

Intimacy begins and ends with respect. For two people to journey together, they must value and accept what the partner represents. Obviously, every two individuals will have differences, but high levels of respect and acceptance set the stage for both to be themselves. Intimate partners can be open and honest with each other. Indeed, they must be open and honest. If they are to trust each other, they must not have

hidden agendas. Sharing differences are opportunities to know each other better and learn different perspectives and values.

At times one partner must take the lead, but that does not diminish the need for equality and sensitivity. Perceived slights may occur. When they happen, open communication will enable the partners to work toward resolution.

The seven attitudinal foundations of mindfulness can serve as a lighthouse to steer an intimate (or any) relationship safely toward fulfillment. Nonjudging is always in order. People are different. Being quietly aware of the other person in a nonjudgmental manner will enable each to grow into the person she or he wishes to be. Patience enables each to resist reacting to whatever the other is doing. Of course, taking your partner for granted may occur after you have been together for an extended period. Beginner's mind reminds you to see your significant other as if for the first time. Stay aware of your partner's charm and unique inner and outer beauty.

Before being able to trust others, you need to have faith in yourself, your intuition, and your values. Trust is a two-way street. Doubting either yourself or the other places a roadblock to being open with each other. To be fully engaged in the challenges and fulfillment of the relationship is to be nonstriving. Intimate relationships are opportunities to flow. Quietly accepting where you are serves as a base to grow, to address the challenges mindfully and skillfully. And lastly, you need to let go of many perceived aspects of the relationship that do not fit with your particular preconceptions. All this requires commitment, motivation, and the intention to live well together.

Even with this understanding it remains easy to take your partner for granted, particularly when you see her or him every day. Some couples spend considerable time planning their wedding and then do little subsequently to nurture their relationship. An axiom of health is that you lose whatever you don't use. If you do not nurture your special partnership, whether that be marriage or any other such union, your relationship can atrophy from inadequate attention. Therapist John Gottman (1998) suggested that four factors contribute to rancorous intimate relationships, namely criticism, stonewalling, defensiveness, and contempt. It is not your job to do your partner's inventory. Your job is to keep your own side of the street clean. Deal with your own issues. What can you do to make the situation better? While there is life, there is still hope. Avoiding all four of these pitfalls is advisable.

Patiently accept yourself and practice your mindfulness. If avoiding all four pitfalls isn't possible, understand that we are all human and make mistakes. Then be nonjudgmentally aware of what is going on. Taking action to combat negative behaviors will likely prevent the derailing of your relationship. People who seriously practice mindfulness experience higher-quality relationships, which may be mediated through improved personal well-being, empathy, enhanced sexual satisfaction, emotional stability, and better stress management (Kozlowski 2013).

Romantic and intimate relationships are not for everyone. It may not be the right time or circumstance for romance to be your primary source of social support. Many people have primary relationships that are not romantic. These primary relationships take on many shapes and forms. Life is intrinsically complicated. You need to make do with what you have at this time in your life. Thus, you may find that your primary relationships are your college roommate, best friend from home, brother, sister, parent, or grandparent.

At this juncture in your life, these people make up your primary relationships and can provide social and emotional support. Among these people—family, friends, and so on—a particular person may not be your only support. Be aware of the dangers of placing too many emotional demands or unrealistic expectations on any one person. Many well-rounded people have a bevy of people to turn to depending on the need. Some are good to exercise with; others have good advice, make you laugh, or are fun at a party. Remember, whatever you need is mostly found within yourself using the mindfulness training strongly advocated in this book. But do not overlook your social networks to help you further your progress as a human "being" (nondoing). Stepping out of your comfort zone to explore the possibilities of what others might hold for you is necessary and rewarding.

The person with whom you have a bond is much more than a reflection of your thoughts about her or him (Kabat-Zinn 2013). More often than not, you are drawn to someone who magnifies or brings out your best. These people may be your best teachers as you discover latent or previously unknown interests and skills. Or they may challenge you with their thoughts, values, and behaviors. Give every relationship a chance to evolve.

With life, change is constant. Few relationships

Activity

Beginner's Mind in Relationships

This 15-minute exercise is appropriate for exploring and evaluating any type of relationship. Take 3 minutes to read the directions for this activity and organize yourself. Then take 12 minutes to do the exercise.

Identify and visualize your partner, spouse, or another key person in your life. Experiencing one of these people with beginner's mind is an excellent avenue for increased appreciation.

1. Take two minutes to be quiet with your breath. You may do so sitting, standing, or even walking around. Focus on the breath. Be present.

2. In your mind's eye, visualize the person as if he or she were with you. Considering the overall personhood, hear his or her voice, see the person walking, and imagine feeling the touch of the person's hand on your shoulder.

3. Take another minute to savor those experiences.

4. Write down the unique and distinguishable traits that made this person who he or she is. Do not rush. Identify three aspects of this key person in your life, aspects for which you are grateful.

5. Now take another three minutes to sit quietly with your breath. As thoughts come to your attention, just be with them. Let go of any judgment; just be with your thoughts and your breath.

6. As you conclude this activity, keep your fresh beginner's mind perspective with you as you move about your activities. Take that perspective with you when you next experience the person.

7. You can choose to do this exercise with each key person in your life to gain greater understanding of your most important relationships.

8. Include your notes from item 4 above in your journal entries for chapter 5.

You do well to renew your appreciation of all aspects of your life with beginner's mind.

Mia had a family but somehow felt alone. This feeling carried over to her life and relationships, not just with Max but in all her interactions. Max realized he was not tuned in to Mia's insecurities, and his need for control was not helping either. He began to appreciate that being a man might mean listening and attempting to understand, rather than reacting as his father did.

last forever as they were initially. Most relationships mature or need to be rebuilt; some need to be discarded with respect. Each relationship should make you ready for the next one. Endeavor to learn the lesson to either move forward together with this person or to find the courage to move on without him or her.

Toxic Relationships

Some relationships can be hurtful or toxic. You sometimes find yourself involved with a person or group that is no longer positive to your life. Perhaps a once loving and accepting person or group has become a source of distress. Realization of the underlying issue is the first key. After mindful consideration of your

options, you may need to set this relationship aside. Relationships that are draining and not rewarding should be limited significantly, if not completely ended.

Depending on the type of separation needed, your options and strategies should be considered. If there is threat of harm or if you are in a domestic violence situation, see whether your community has an organization to help you extricate yourself from the situation. Some community resources provide a safe shelter where you can stay and will support you in your efforts to leave the dangerous situation.

For less toxic situations, you might talk with a mentor, close friend, or trusted family member for

Toxic relationships can create lasting damage beyond just physical danger. You have the right to protect yourself by getting out of the situation. If you or someone you know needs help in a domestic violence situation, you can contact the National Domestic Violence hotline at 800-799-7233 or visit www.thehotline.org. The Childhelp National Child Abuse hotline is 800-422-4453 or visit www.childhelp.org/pages/hotline-home.

advice. You may need help to sort out your feelings and further decide whether to end the relationship abruptly. Ask for strategies on how best to end the relationship, if you think that advice would be helpful. A conversation with the offending person or people may or may not be useful. You can definitely reorder your priorities. You can reorient your thinking to focus on the positive aspects of your life.

Marital relationships are a special case, especially if children are involved. Divorce should always be a last resort unless violence or abuse is involved. Love typically waxes and wanes, and married couples often struggle through difficult times. Don't give up too easily! Marriage counseling and 12-step programs have saved many relationships.

When a troubled relationship ends, a wide array of feelings can emerge. Some people second-guess the ending of a relationship, and others even regret it. Most, however, immediately experience a release of tension and relief from unwanted obligations. But coming to peace with your decision might take some time.

Do mindful sitting and walking sessions, because they can provide inner calm to accept where you are and move forward with quiet wisdom. Give yourself the emotional support you need by believing that you did the best you could in a difficult situation.

Mentoring Strengths

As you evolve in your life and career, you will find that having access to mentoring is a key dimension to your quality of life in several realms—academics, professional career, and personal life. Many inner-city neighborhoods have mentoring programs for people of all ages. Labor unions are adept at mentoring those who work as apprentices in a specific trade. In the field of addictions, many recovery programs are predicated on members having a sponsor (*Alcoholics Anonymous* 2001). In some situations, a group of people support each other in their work, academics, and family life. Herbert Benson (1987) suggests important benefits result from having a maximal mind guide, as a facilitator for optimal performance in life.

A mentor is regarded as an experienced and trusted advisor to a student or other person. We think of mentoring as a two-way communication relationship in which each serves to augment the resources of the other in some manner. Personal rewards accrue to volunteers who gain experience working with kids in middle school, for example. Evidence shows that as young people attend these programs, fewer drop out. At the worksite, partnerships can enhance relational wealth for both employees and the employer (Leana and Van Buren 1999). These relationships promote sustainable human capital (Banerjee 2013).

Mentoring has been somewhat formalized in many regions of the country. The Mentoring Partnership of Southwestern Pennsylvania (2014) is a nonprofit organization that provides a variety of free services to local mentoring projects. It is one of over 30 mentoring partnerships in the United States that is affiliated with MENTOR/National Mentoring Partnership. They report that mentored students are 52 percent less likely to skip school than their peers are. But one in three children in their service area reach the age of 19 without having a mentor. Most mentors are volunteers who commit to a specific period of service, typically a year or less. Although the experience is rewarding as an interpersonal relationship for both the student and the mentor, many more volunteers are needed. If you become involved as a mentor or mentee, you will receive far more benefit than you give.

Social Environment

The actions of others and whatever you pay attention to, including advertising, affect your feelings, attitudes, values, and behaviors, and can even trigger immune reactions. People change behavior based on their observations of others and the prevailing social norms (Bandura 1988). Role modeling works. Social relationships and your environment can significantly affect health behavior and health status (Heaney and Israel 2008).

The positive influence of others is explicitly addressed in the social cognitive theory of behavior change (Bandura 1991). This effect was demonstrated when a film of Mother Theresa working with the poor was shown to students. Before and after assessments established an increase in antibodies among viewing students, compared with students who did not see the film, as documented through a change in norepinephrine in saliva and by salivary immunoglobulin A (McClelland 1989). Exposure to this inspirational film provoked a measurable enhanced immune response.

Although you learn from the context in which you live, perception and projection are largely autobiographical, that is, you see through the lens of your values and beliefs. Remember that projection makes perception. In this case, the students observed behaviors that were consistent with their own experiences, character, and values, thereby reinforcing their own beliefs. Seeing love and kindness in the world had a positive effect on immune function. Believing is seeing, and it can do a body good!

A social support network that reinforces your commitment to contribute is fortunate and commendable. Finding people you like, who are supportive and friendly, while doing something that you believe in and champion, can be a health booster. When surrounded by supportive people, you function at a more optimal level when engaged in something bigger than yourself.

Self-Help Groups

Peer support self-help networks demonstrate efficacy in helping people with physical, emotional, and mental health challenges (Repper and Carter 2011). Such self-help groups are a powerful tool for health and wellness. Tom Ferguson (2007) spent the majority of his medical and wellness career as a physician furthering self-help groups in cities, states, and online in both the United States and other countries. Ferguson also helped establish networks of lay people and medical professionals to assist when needed.

In self-help groups, people learn to support each other on their journey toward a higher quality of life. Intimacy, empathic understanding, and unconditional acceptance are health enhancing, whereas feeling lonely detracts from health (Hutcherson, Seppala, and Gross 2008). Many of these groups—community based, self-directed, and with no leading therapist—originated with the 1935 founding of the Alcoholics Anonymous fellowship.

Alcoholics Anonymous (AA) is a fellowship that has made a substantive contribution to physical, mental, emotional, and social health of alcoholics (El-Guebaly 2012). The fellowship was based on the principle of alcoholics helping other alcoholics. Relationships are reciprocal, as is the case with social capital.

Newcomers, those still struggling with stopping drinking, rely on the wisdom and sobriety of older members for support and guidance. Those with years of sobriety serve as sponsors and are motivated to maintain their own sobriety by hearing the stories of pain, loss, and devastation shared by the newcomers as well as by telling their own stories.

Alcoholics Anonymous pioneered what is known as a 12-step recovery process. The recovery process steps are a logical and sequential approach to help members address life challenges. More important, the steps are a guide to a new way of living. Significant improvements and reductions in health care costs were observed after regular participation in 12-step recovery programs. For each meeting attended, adolescents realized a 4.7 percent reduction in health care costs during the seven-year follow-up (Mundta et al. 2012). These results are similar to the cost savings observed for adults in other 12-step programs by Humphreys and Moos (2001, 2007). These programs will be further discussed in chapter 10, "Understanding Addictions."

Twelve-step self-help groups also serve drug addicts, gamblers, family members coping with addicted relatives, heart attack and stroke victims, parents of children with attention deficit disorder, sexual assault victims, and those victimized by other forms of violence (Donovan et al. 2013). The empathy, informal counseling, sponsorship, and peer support made available by those who have experienced the same turmoil themselves enhances the lives and coping skills of participants (Hutcherson, Seppala, and Gross 2008). These self-help groups are separate and distinct from formal therapy groups. Formal therapy can also play a crucial role in health and recovery from disease.

Social Media

In this age of electronic connections, communities of people come together with common visions. People who have never met but share a passion, mission, and interest can gather in cyber space, which complements the traditional geographic place gatherings. Urban and rural people from every part of the globe can gather by telephone, e-mail, conference calls, online social networking, or any combinations of these. FaceTime and Skype provide face-to-face communication across any distance. Similarly, clubs and organizations constitute communities and may provide virtual chat rooms, where the communication may be brief, sporadic, or ongoing.

The Internet and cell phone use provide rich social networking opportunities. Nearly three out of four (72 percent) 18- to 29-year-olds regularly use social networking websites (Social Life of Health Information 2011). Social media represent an effective means to connect, engage, stay in touch, and advocate for change. This enhanced level of participation might be healthful in and of itself. The 1986 Alma Ata Charter of the World Health Organization stated, "People cannot achieve their fullest health potential unless they are able to take control of those things which determine their health." To be engaged is to take charge, and to take charge is to enjoy better health.

Connecting, participating, and volunteering opportunities are now at our fingertips. You have more opportunities to influence others and to be influenced. Separate and distinct benefits are associated with physically volunteering in projects (Thoits 1995), but cyber space participants also experience nurturing aspects of social capital. But it is not yet known whether online activism will realize the same health-related connection benefits or be as effective in influencing the rest of the world. Certainly the revolutionary wave of the Arab Spring would not have occurred without the change in networking power originating from social media (Tudoroiu 2014).

Research has demonstrated a dose response for the density of social media exposure and the level of social capital (Centola 2011). The greater the exposure is, the more likely it is that young people will be prompted to engage and act collaboratively, as would be expected.

This social media field is relatively new to science. Briscoe and Aboud (2012) demonstrated the potential

Today's social media means that you can stay connected with friends and family much easier than you could in the old days of snail mail and long-distance phone calls. Be smart about what you post, though; assume that nothing online is ever truly anonymous and, once posted, is never truly removed.

for social media to engage participants at the social and behavioral levels. Social media enables communication across a wide cross-section of the population without regard to race, education, or access to health care (Chou et al. 2009). Connected people can be mobilized for any number of purposes. Health outcomes research is beginning to demonstrate the influence of social media on overall quality of life (Hether, Murphy, and Valente 2014).

WELLNESS BENEFITS OF SOCIAL CONNECTIONS

The effect of social connections on disease is significant. Quite simply, humans are hard wired to be social. A study of heart attack patients showed that low levels of social support were detrimental to life expectancy and that high levels were protective of a longer life (Leifheit-Limson et al. 2010).

The relationship of a parent to his or her child is foundational. Additionally, the relationship of long-term couples has the potential to develop deep emotional and psychological bonds that directly and

profoundly affect the health of the physical body. Dr. Redford Williams and colleagues (1992) at Duke University identified marriage as having a protective effect. When the researchers evaluated men and women undergoing coronary angiography, unmarried persons without social support were three times more likely to die within five years, compared with married or otherwise supported individuals. Williams' team was unable to identify any other possible causes for the differences.

More recent and more robust studies have again demonstrated the protective effect of marriage (Rendall et al. 2011). Men at high risk of heart disease fare better if they see themselves as having the loving support of their wives (Nakhaie and Arnold 2010). The men experienced a nearly two times greater rate of angina if they reported that their wives did not love them compared with men who perceived themselves as being loved by their wives. Similarly, healthy men who reported an absence of spousal love were three times more likely to develop ulcers compared with those reporting loving support from their wives (Medalie, Stange, Zyzanski, and Goldbourt 1992).

A recent Finnish study reported that having a partner was equally protective for both women and men. Among unmarried men and women, coronary events were 58 to 66 percent and 60 to 65 percent higher respectively, compared with those who were married or had a regular partner (Lammintausta et al. 2013). An even more marked difference was observed in the one-month post coronary death rate. Compared with married men and women, deaths were 60 to 168 percent higher among unmarried men and 71 to 175 percent higher among unmarried women (Lammintausta et al. 2013).

Social relationships are strongly linked to cancer (Pinquart and Duberstein 2010) and life expectancy (Holt-Lunstad, Smith, and Layton 2010). David Spiegel and colleagues (1989) conducted a social support intervention with women with metastatic breast cancer. Their study illustrates this effect. Breast cancer participants were randomly assigned to either a social support group intervention that met weekly for 90 minutes for one year or to a control group. After 10 years, the women who had been in the support group were shown to have lived twice as long as those in the control group. Nothing else explained why the supported women did so well (Spiegel et al. 1989). Interpret these results carefully because the study has not been replicated.

Another similar intervention with malignant melanoma patients demonstrated results that are even more dramatic. Patients were randomly assigned to a six-week 90-minute support group intervention or a control group. Treatment group participants were found to have had better survival rates six years later (Fawzy et al. 1993). More recently, social and emotional support has been demonstrated as the most positive predictor for quality of life among HIV-positive gay men in the United States (Slater et al. 2012).

USING ACCEPTANCE TO MAKE CONNECTIONS

Some of you have the social support you need, whereas others do not. Some find it easy to make friends, and others find this a difficult task. Self-acceptance can enable you to develop and maintain relationships (Dagaz 2012). Accepting yourself opens the door to see others without judgment. Acceptance of a person right here and right now will help provide a solid foundation on which to build a relationship.

What makes high-functioning families unique is love and acceptance. Use the same acceptance model that you use with high-functioning families and exhibit it toward colleagues, associates, neighbors, and friends. When another person seems different and does something perceived as offensive, many people quickly and unnecessarily take offense. "How dare they do that!" is a common refrain. Note that this is a statement, not an inquiry. Take care to avoid condescension. When you forgive, do so from the heart.

People are much the same. Our similarities are far greater than our differences. The more you recognize this fact, the sooner you can feel and experience a genuine connection with others. Acceptance is a wonderful enhancement to forgiveness. When you accept another's uniqueness, you have nothing to forgive. When you accept that we are all part of the same oneness, the same cosmic consciousness, you are more predisposed to feel good about others and to accept their positive regard (Tolle 2005).

Mia and Max are not yet through all the challenges of their relationship, but they both recognize that the other is doing his or her best. Perhaps the most profound enlightenment occurred for Max. He no longer believes that all relationships end. He is not altogether sure that this relationship will survive, but he remains committed to trying. He cares very much for Mia and respects the person she is. And this revelation has proved life changing for him.

Mia is no longer fixated on saving Max from himself. She cares a great deal for him, but she too understands that not all relationships are forever, and that is all right. She has learned a lot since they both committed to personal growth. She walks almost every day, and her walks have taken on a more mindful quality.

Max and Mia jointly committed to being accepting of self and nonjudgmental toward each other. Their relationship became less important than their exploration of their own personal needs. As a result, their relationship has morphed into something more than it was, and for that, they are both grateful.

Activity

Loving Kindness Meditation

This 10-minute exercise is appropriate for exploring various relationship. Take 3 minutes to read the directions for this activity and organize yourself. Then take 7 minutes to do the exercise.

1. Take a long, slow, deep breath in as you close your eyes and become quiet. Exhale slowly. Repeat this three times and thereafter stay aware of your normal breathing for three minutes.

2. Think about a special person in your life, such as a romantic partner, friend, or family member. Keep an image of that person in your mind for two minutes and then say quietly to yourself, "May she be loved, blessed, peaceful, and happy."

3. Now think of an acquaintance. Keep an image of that person in your mind for two minutes and then say quietly to yourself, "May she be loved, blessed, peaceful, and happy."

4. Now focus on someone that you are not particularly fond of. Keep an image of that person in your mind for two minutes and then say quietly to yourself, "May she be loved, blessed, peaceful, and happy."

5. Return to the breath. Breathe in and out. Stay focused on the here and now.

After the exercise and as part of your quiet reflection, notice what feelings emerge when you think about someone you love or a valued acquaintance, as opposed to someone you are not fond of. Simply notice these feelings and thoughts. Do not dwell on them. Rather, continue to focus your attention on your breath and the image of the person. Note the difference in your feelings and breath when you consider sending love and light to the person you are not fond of. You might be surprised by what you find.

Excerpt(s) from FULL CATASTROPHE LIVING by Jon Kabat-Zinn, © 1990 by Jon Kabat-Zinn. Used by permission of Dell Publishing, an imprint of Random House, a division of Random House LLC. All rights reserved.

SUMMARY

Social support may be the most underappreciated influence on good health. As a society, we are prone to look for simple answers to complex problems, such as physician prescriptions. Many times the answer to real peace and happiness requires the support of another person, not a pill.

At least one strong source of social support is required for children to develop and for adults to function well. Networks are also valuable. Seeking appropriately supportive relationships begins with a thorough understanding of yourself. Without this knowledge, you will not be as successful in finding the social support and networks you need to nurture your growth. Connections are available through many portals.

Family, friends, peer groups, and work colleagues are good places to observe and make inroads towards your goal of obtaining more support. Advocacy through a group or a cause you believe in can be an excellent source of connection to others. The Internet is often an underused tool for connection. Take advantage of every resource to strengthen yourself through relationships.

Toxic relationships can challenge your coping skills. Although being nonjudgmental is important, a relationship may not be healthful. This realization does not necessarily represent failure. After spending time in quiet awareness and possibly consulting with your mentor or other advisor, decide whether to reorient your priorities and focus your energy on positive relationships and useful activities. The ending of one activity or relationship and the taking up of new ones take place in everyone's life fairly often.

Social capital involves maximizing the resources of a community. People feel appreciated and supported. A common interest brings people together in such communities. As a result, they support each other for better health and a high quality of life. People spend time with each other and work together to satisfy basic needs and personal fulfillment.

Quiet and mindfulness are the practical and readily available sources for accepting yourself and others. After you befriend yourself, you are more able to be open to others. You are in a stronger position to interact healthfully with others after you learn to appreciate your own inner peace. By having strong social support and social networks, you will find that your well-being may be improved by means of the social capital that develops.

Part II

Physical Dimensions of Wellness

© Monkey Business – Fotolia

Chapter 6

Getting Started With Regular Physical Activity

Objectives

After reading this chapter, you will be able to
- differentiate between exercise and physical activity,
- define light-, moderate-, and vigorous-intensity physical activity,
- list and describe the four FITT components for physical activity,
- list five resistance-training exercises, and
- describe the relationship between regular physical activity and wellness.

Haslyn was a first-semester senior. He strongly desired to go to medical school and spent most of his time studying, preparing for exams, and filling out applications. He was overweight and getting winded easily. His physician recommended walking for 30 minutes every day and weightlifting two times a week. He thought that doing these activities was impossible because he spent all his time attending classes, completing assignments, and studying. On those few occasions when he was able to relax, he simply wanted to watch TV or a movie and zone out. But his doctor stressed the importance of physical activity and told Haslyn that three 10-minute aerobic bouts had the same benefit as one 30-minute walk and that he could do the weightlifting at his apartment.

Haslyn now takes his dog for a walk in the morning for 10 minutes. During the midafternoon lull, he refreshes himself by going around the block two times while his friends are at the student union. He walks to classes and parks his car farther away when he shops. For resistance training, he bought four inexpensive sets of hand weights, which he uses twice a week. His weightlifting takes only 5 to 10 minutes each time.

Haslyn cannot believe how well he now feels. After six months, he is back to the same body weight he enjoyed as a senior in high school. When asked how much activity he does on a daily basis, he replied that he really didn't know because he wasn't doing anything special. "It just seemed to work. I'm invigorated by the short breaks for exercise throughout the day. It's not something I feel I have to do. Regular physical activity is now just a part of my life."

Regular physical activity is vital to wellness. The more you move your body, the better you feel. The closer you are to your ideal body weight, the more energy you have available. Even your mental health is better when you move more. No other form of health promotion seems to have as much effect on health as regular physical activity. It is a key to good health.

In spite of this, according to *Healthy People 2020* (2010), less than half the nation's population is doing enough physical activity to contribute to good health, about a third (36.3 percent) are totally sedentary, and only one-fifth (18.2 percent) meet minimal recommended standards for resistance and **aerobic** training. Although an exercise revolution took place in the United States 40 years ago when Ken Cooper popularized aerobic activity (Cooper 1970), we now have more labor saving devices and encounter more barriers to everyday physical activity than ever before.

This chapter provides background information and tools to improve the quality of your life by engaging in **physical activity** and **exercise**. The strategies are intended to help surmount these pervasive barriers to activity. There is no free lunch; you do need to make an effort. By following these recommendations, you can make regular physical activity, muscular and bone strength training, and flexibility a painless part of your life.

PHYSICAL ACTIVITY AND EXERCISE

The difference between physical activity and exercise may not always be clear. Most people use the two terms interchangeably. Physical activity is the larger category and includes any health-enhancing bodily movement, such as gardening, washing the car, swimming, jogging, walking to the bus stop, or walking to class. Exercise is activity that you do repetitively and purposively to promote your fitness, such as aerobics, dance, swimming, jogging, brisk walking, and lifting weights. Typically, you jog or go to a fitness center for exercise. For most of the discussion in this chapter, the more generic term *physical activity* is used.

Regular physical activity requires commitment, but you need no specialized equipment to benefit (Loprinzi and Cardinal 2013). Joining a gym or exercise center is unnecessary to maintain fitness, although such facilities serve many well (Tappe et al. 2013). Fitness, the ability to perform different types of physical work, is the product of targeted physical activity and exercise that promote aerobic capacity, muscle strength and endurance, bone strength, and flexibility. Lifestyle options abound. Walking behind your lawnmower for an hour every week in the summer may be something you want to do, much like your grandparents did. You may choose to walk to work and class to save money, decrease air pollution, and avoid traffic congestion. The benefits of the activity accrue no matter what.

BENEFITS OF PHYSICAL ACTIVITY

Regular physical activity can be a gateway behavior to other wellness practices. It might diminish craving for tobacco products (Peters et al. 2009), facilitate healthy dietary changes, and improve sleeping patterns (*Physical Activity and Health* 1996). Of course, being regularly active reduces your risk of obesity, heart disease, stroke, diabetes, osteoporosis, and cancer. Regular physical activity provides a sense of accomplishment and the knowledge that you are doing something positive for yourself (Haskell et al. 2007). Exercise increases self-efficacy and self-esteem (Deslandes et al. 2009). You look and feel better. Regular physical activity improves the quality and quantity of your life. It adds years to your life and life to your years.

Physical activity offers not only physical benefits but also important mental health benefits (Conn 2010). When you feel better, you are more likely to take better care of yourself and to need less medical care. Anxiety and depression are among the most costly of health conditions and represent barriers to living well (Goetzel et al. 2004). People who are regularly physically active have less stress, anxiety, and depression than those who do not exercise regularly (*Physical Activity and Health* 1996). Regular walking alone serves as an antidote for mild and moderate depression (Dresler et al. 2013).

Research on exercise in the area of mental health is extensive. According to Kim et al. (2012), men and women engaging in 2.5 to 7.5 hours of physical activity per week reported better mental health (odds ratio=1.39, p=0.006). The evidence is sufficiently strong to indicate that meeting the guidelines for regular physical activity, as well as achieving even lower levels, prevents and treats depression (Mammen and Faulkner 2013).

Physical activity is associated with cardiovascular benefits. Body fat is diminished with physical activity, and lean body tissue is increased (Levinger et al. 2009). These changes are often associated with increased levels of **high-density lipoprotein (HDL)**, or good cholesterol (McArdle, Katch, and Katch 2009). Physical activity and exercise have also been shown to decrease low-density lipoprotein (LDL), also known as bad cholesterol (Levine and Miller 2007). Exercise also significantly decreases triglyceride levels, the circulating fat in the blood stream (Dunstan et al. 2012). Vigorous activity reduces risk for some cancers (*Physical Activity Guidelines for Americans* 2008).

In general, the more physical activity you do, the more health benefits you will realize (see figure 6.1). However, going to extremes with anything, including physical activity, can cause problems. Overuse injuries, for example, can occur if your activity level becomes excessive. The greatest health gains from physical activity occur as a person moves from the inactive to active category and continues to increase with additional physical activity, but less dramatically.

Those who do little or nothing have the greatest risk of becoming ill. They are more likely to be overweight or obese, to have less energy, and to feel "blue" more frequently. Getting off the couch and going for a daily 15-minute walk can change everything (Wen et al. 2011). For the most sedentary people, the first steps are the most important. But you don't have to be a marathoner or even a jogger to receive immense health benefits. "Those who think they have not time for bodily exercise will sooner or later have to find time for illness" (Edward Stanley, Earl of Derby, 1826–93).

Improvement comes from regular physical activity, and many opportunities are available every day to engage in activities. Leaving your study cubicle to deliver a message to a friend who is studying a minute away may seem a waste of time, but the health benefits add up. Sitting makes you lethargic. Research has demonstrated that sitting is an independent risk factor for ill health, including cardiovascular disease, diabetes (Wilmot et al. 2012), and kidney disease (Bharakhada et al. 2012), and sitting can reduce life expectancy (Veerman et al. 2012). Standing burns twice as many calories as sitting does. Those who spend a lifetime average of 6 hours per day sitting to watch TV can expect to shorten their lifetimes by 4.8 years (Veerman et al. 2012). Is your TV time really worth 5 years of your life? The take-home message is to avoid being sedentary for prolonged periods. Some physical activity is better than none. To moderate the effect of too

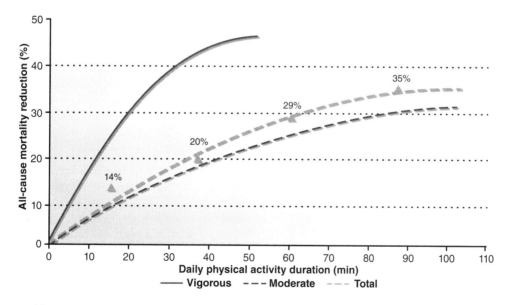

FIGURE 6.1 All-cause mortality risks are reduced substantively with the first 15 minutes of daily activity. Additional benefits are realized up to 100 minutes daily.

Reprinted from *The Lancet*, Vol. 378(9798), C.P. Wen et al., 2011, "Minimum amount of physical activity for reduced mortality and extended life expectancy: A prospective cohort study," pgs. 1244-1253, copyright 2011, with permission from Elsevier.

Activity

Start the Benefits of Physical Activity by Walking

Start the process of increasing your physical activity by taking 10-minute walking breaks.

Moderate-intensity walking is moving as if you are going somewhere. If you are walking a half mile (.8 km) to the drugstore or post office, you will self-select your pace at between 3 and 3.5 miles (4.8 and 5.6 km) per hour, which is a moderate intensity for most people. You will feel better with as little as a 10-minute walk!

1. In comfortable clothes and shoes, stop what you are doing and take 5 minutes to walk to a destination.
2. Then turn around and return to your reading area (10-minute round trip).
3. Many people experience feeling better with 10 minutes of uninterrupted physical activity. How do you feel now?

---

much sitting, it's best to limit TV watching to no more than two hours per day,

- break up bouts of sitting by standing for a few minutes at least every half hour,
- place your computer monitor and keyboard on a portable table so that you have a choice of working while standing or sitting, and
- stand during class (tell the professor in advance why you want to stand; she or he will be more accepting of this seemingly aberrant behavior if you communicate your intentions).

FITT PRINCIPLE

The four components of the FITT principle—frequency, intensity, time, and type—provide guidance for a safe, effective, and efficient personal physical activity program. The effectiveness of using these components is supported by a plethora of exercise science research, which is summarized in *Physical Activity and Health: A Report of the Surgeon General* (1996) and *Physical Activity Guidelines for Americans* (2008). The overarching recommendations are summarized here and are further explained in sections on each of the four FITT components.

Physical Activity Guidelines for Americans (2008) recommendations are as follows:

- Aerobic activity: 150 to 300 minutes of moderate-intensity or 75 to 150 minutes of **vigorous-intensity activity** per week
- **Muscle- and bone-strengthening activities:** Working the legs, hips, back, abdomen, chest, shoulders, and arms two or more days per week
- Flexibility activity: Working to elongate the muscle groups and improve range of motion in

the joints addressed in the aerobic and strengthening activities, two or more days per week

Frequency

Frequency refers to the number of sessions, or bouts, of physical activity performed in a week. To achieve the training recommendations, the goal is to perform at least three aerobic, two strengthening, and two flexibility sessions each week (*Physical Activity Guidelines for Americans* 2008). For the aerobic activity, minutes can be accumulated over the course of a day in 10-minute blocks. The goal is to increase the workload on your cardiorespiratory system, muscles, and bones sufficiently to stimulate an increase in fitness, all the while providing enough time for recovery. For weight training, you should take 36 to 48 hours for recovery, because muscle fibers need to grow during this period. But you can do aerobic training and stretching on consecutive days. Even then, however, it is desirable to rest at least one day a week to allow the body a chance to regain energy and recover.

Intensity

Intensity refers to the level of exertion. Monitoring your physical activity intensity is helpful in order to (1) be mindful of your physiological reaction to the increase in exertion; (2) exert yourself sufficiently to achieve your health, fitness, and quality-of-life objectives; (3) avoid injury; (4) maximize your benefits without undue stress; and (5) enjoy the process. Modern lifestyles and work patterns are more sedentary than is healthy. Most American adults watch three to six hours of television daily (Nielson 2012), and many sit at desks, in class, or at computers for several additional hours (Chau et al. 2012). The lack of physical activity is the greatest risk.

FITT Physical Activity Log

Determining your current physical activity is an important step in moving forward. For this activity, you need to develop a log like the one in table 6.A, except that it should be large enough for you to record your activity. Track your moderate- and vigorous-intensity aerobic, strength, and flexibility training for the week, whether at a fitness center or elsewhere. Specify the activity and the quantity in minutes or number of repetitions. For the aerobic activity, track only those activities of 10 minutes in duration or longer. Walking 10 continuous minutes between classes counts. Sum the minutes and sets across each row.

After you get into your routine, you can use this form as a daily physical activity log. A daily physical activity log is a form of journaling. People have been shown to be more successful initiating and maintaining healthful practices when they record what they are doing (Akers et al. 2012). You should log your physical activity using whatever device you have to track appointments and other daily activities. In addition, record whether you were able to flow, to become nonstriving in the bout of physical activity. The activity can become an end in itself if you become thoroughly absorbed by it.

Baseline Physical Activity Log

Date:_____	Sunday	Monday	Tuesday	Wednesday	Thursday	Friday	Saturday
AEROBIC ACTIVITIES							
What?							
Duration?							
MUSCLE- AND BONE-STRENGTHENING ACTIVITIES							
What?							
How much?							
FLEXIBILITY ACTIVITIES							
What?							
How much?							

Aerobic Activity Intensity Levels

Technically, light-intensity physical activity is exertion that exceeds sitting at rest and walking at less than 3 miles (4.8 km) per hour. This level of activity is substantively superior to being sedentary (Dunstan et al. 2012). Light-intensity energy expenditure is achieved by such activities as strolling around the mall, washing dishes, doing routine housework, and working in most occupational settings (Donahoo, Levine, and Melanson 2004).

Although little research has been conducted on the health promotion benefits of light-intensity physical activity, Healy et al. (2008) demonstrated a negative relationship with light activity and two-hour fasting glucose. Light activity is associated with a lower level of blood glucose than what is observed for sedentary people. Thus, any bodily movement represents caloric expenditure and therefore contributes to improved health and weight management.

A landmark wellness change occurred with the work of Pate et al. (1995) and the Surgeon General's publication of *Physical Activity and Health* (1996). These two documents were the first official professional recommendations for **moderate-intensity physical activity**. Before this time, the recommendation was for vigorous physical activity only, as advised by *ACSM's for Exercise Testing and Prescription* (American College of Sports Medicine 1986). Although the health benefits of vigorous activity are unquestioned, the scientific evidence demonstrated equivalent efficacy for moderate-intensity physical activity (*Physical Activity and Health* 1996).

Intensity can be self-rated on a relative scale of 0 to 10. Zero (0) represents your effort sitting, and 10 represents the most vigorous physical activity you have ever done. Moderate-intensity activity is rated at 5 to 6, and vigorous-intensity exercise is 7 to 8 (*Physical Activity Guidelines for Americans* 2008). A 9 or 10 on the relative exertion scale is **anaerobic activity** (triggers formation of lactic acid). Competitive athletes train at this maximal level, but doing so increases the likelihood of injury for the normal healthy person.

Moderate-intensity physical activity makes you breathe harder, increases your heart rate, and causes you to sweat. It can be sustained for a prolonged period. People walking to a destination generally self-select a moderate-intensity pace, which is between 3 and 3.5 miles (4.8 and 5.6 km) per hour. Other examples of moderate-intensity activity include tennis doubles, ballroom dancing, water aerobics, and bicycling on level terrain at less than 10 miles (16.1 km) per hour.

Vigorous activity entails breathing hard enough that carrying on a normal conversation is challenging. The Centers for Disease Control and Prevention (*How Much Physical Activity Do Adults Need?* 2014) lists the following activities as vigorous: "Race walking, jogging or running, swimming laps, singles tennis, aerobic dancing, bicycling 10 miles per hour or faster, jumping rope, heavy gardening (continuous digging or hoeing), and hiking uphill or with a heavy backpack." No additional health benefit is associated with exceeding the vigorous activity threshold.

Another means of determining whether you have exceeded vigorous physical activity is the talk test. If you are gasping for breath and cannot carry on a normal conversation, you are exercising with too much intensity. You are above the vigorous range. Exercising at that level may not be problematic for competitive athletes or young adults generally, but such intensity is not necessary and may even be counterproductive because it increases the risk of injury. To achieve proper benefit, reduce your pace if you find yourself moving uncomfortably fast. You have more to lose by being too vigorous than by not achieving moderate intensity.

Most healthy young adults can safely initiate a moderate- or vigorous-intensity physical activity program. (Important note: If you have any concern regarding

---

Haslyn quickly began experiencing the benefits of his regular walk to school. He lived slightly less than a mile (1.6 km) from the university, which took him about 15 minutes walking each way. First, he realized that little extra time was required for his walking commute (he did not have to search for a parking space), and he arrived feeling invigorated, mentally sharp, and ready to get things done. But sitting had become the bane of Haslyn's life. He was sitting in class, sitting in the library, and sitting at his hotel desk job for long stretches. So he made it a point never to sit for more than 30 minutes at a time, preferably even less than 15 minutes. He moved his telephone at home and work to a place where he had to stand to answer it. Haslyn is as productive as ever, if not more so. He certainly feels better.

Activity

Determining Your Aerobic Physical Activity Intensity

The following 20-minute learning activity will use walking as a physical activity to clarify moderate and vigorous intensity. Dress comfortably and wear shoes that will not be problematic during 20 minutes of walking. Find a flat area where you can walk for five minutes, about a quarter of a mile (440 yards, or 400 m), without stopping. The distance is less important than the time for this activity.

1. Moderate-intensity walking bout. Moderate-intensity walking is a pace you would self-select if you were going somewhere. This intensity should be associated with increased respiration and heart rate but should permit conversation.

    1. Select your destination and walk to that destination at a moderately intense pace, that is, your customary walking pace if you were going somewhere, such as walking from one building to another between classes.

    2. On a relative scale of 0 to 10 (10 being the most vigorous), how would you rate that intensity? Ideally, it should be a 5 or 6.

    3. Return to your starting point at the same pace. Again, rate your intensity on the 0 to 10 relative scale. Was it any more or less vigorous than the first time? You may have been able to go faster with the same exertion because of a modest increase in your body temperature which makes your body more efficient.

2. Perform a vigorous-intensity walking bout. Vigorous intensity involves walking at a faster pace than you would self-select. This pace will make it harder to carry on a conversation, your arms will be moving more energetically, and you will need to exert real effort to maintain this speed.

    1. Select the same destination and walk to that destination at a vigorous pace, that is, faster than your customary walking pace. Your breathing is more labored, and your heart is pounding harder. This intensity should be associated with an increase in respiration and heart rate.

    2. On a scale of 0 to 10, how would you rate that intensity? Ideally, it should be a 7 or 8.

    3. You might notice that it took less time to reach the destination. This is important, because on days when your time is limited, you can achieve the same health benefits in half the time at a vigorous intensity, compared with a moderate intensity.

    4. Return to your starting point at the same pace. Again, rate your intensity on the 0 to 10 relative scale. Was it any more or less vigorous than the first time?

Healthy people generally find it easier to incorporate moderate-intensity physical activity into their daily lives (Pate et al. 1995).

---

your health before, during, or after starting a physical activity program, check with a qualified health professional.) All exercise programs should be started gradually. Doing too much, too fast is counterproductive and may result in muscle soreness and exhaustion, although some discomfort from tender muscles should be expected when you first start to be active. Keep the intensity at a level you can enjoy. No pain, all gain! Be alert to unusual signs or symptoms that can result from overdoing your physical activity. Always trust yourself. Trust what your body is telling you. Do not try to push your body over its limits.

Muscle and Bone Strength-Training Intensity Levels

A public health bone density crisis exists in the United States, although little attention has been given to these concerns in government publications (Kelley, Kelley, and Kohrt 2012). Bone integrity is crucially important to preventing future osteoporosis, and the young adult years are a critical period for bone development. People typically lose 3 percent of their muscle mass each decade after age 30 (*Physical Activity and Health* 1996). Thus, resistance training is vital to preserving bone density.

The same resistance-training activities that increase muscle strength also augment bone strength. Although the health community previously advised regular walking as the antidote to osteoporosis, information that is more recent suggests that walking alone may not be adequate (Kelley, Kelley, and Kohrt 2012). Bone strength is enhanced by adequate consumption of vegetables, fruits, calcium and vitamin D, aerobic exercise, and resistance training (Hughes-Dawson 2010). Unfortunately, swimming and cycling seem to have little beneficial effect on bone structure. Bone mass increases up to about the age of 30, after which a gradual decline occurs. Weight-bearing activity is vital to bone growth. The space program has been concerned about bone density loss in zero gravity situations because astronauts lack opportunities for weight-bearing activity.

Only about 30 percent of the U.S. population report meeting the national strength-training guidelines (CDC 2011). Muscle strength permits the safe performance of routine daily living functions, such as lifting a bag of groceries into the car. Muscle strength also improves joint integrity. Increasing muscle strength around the knees enhances their stability.

Muscle- and bone-strengthening activities encompass resistance training and weightlifting, which force muscles and bones to work against an applied force or weight (*Physical Activity Guidelines for Americans* 2008). Activities for each of seven body parts (legs, hips, back, abdomen, chest, shoulders, and arms) need to be performed with sufficient intensity in order to benefit each part and with sufficient mindfulness to avoid injury. A set includes 8 to 12 repetitions of each activity. Each repetition is a complete activity movement (full contraction and return), such as a biceps curl. Perform each set with enough intensity (weight, resistance) that you cannot do another repetition without assistance after completing 8 to 12 reps (*How Much Physical Activity Do Adults Need?* 2014). For optimal benefit, do two or three sets at least twice per week.

A risk of injury exists with strength training. For this reason, you can benefit from guidance when starting out. Proper form is an indication of intensity: If you cannot do the repetition without distorting your form, you are doing too much weight or working with too much resistance.

Flexibility-Training Intensity Levels

Stretching increases flexibility and diminishes muscle soreness (Herbert and Noronha 2008). At no time should you do ballistic stretching (rapid movement). All stretches should be done gently and sustained for 10 to 30 seconds. You can finish your stretching in 2 to 5 minutes or flow with the practice in a nonstriving manner for more than an hour. Peacefully relax and breath into the stretch. At no time should you feel pain. Move to the level of mild discomfort and stop. Trust yourself and use common sense.

High-Intensity Interval Training

High-intensity interval training (HIIT) is performing repeated bouts of vigorous or maximal physical activity for short periods followed by a longer recovery period of light- or moderate-intensity activity. Most people are pressed for time. With high-intensity interval training, you save time in exchange for some short-term discomfort. Walking, jogging, cycling, or swimming for 30 seconds at vigorous intensity should be followed by a 2-minute recovery at light to moderate intensity. Several variations can be used with this approach (Siahkouhian, Khodadadi, and Shahmoradi 2013). You can do 1 minute of vigorous activity followed by 1 minute of moderate-intensity recovery, or 30 seconds at maximal capacity followed by 4 minutes and 30 seconds of low-intensity recovery (Gibala and McGee 2008). This approach has been demonstrated to evoke short-term appetite suppression in young women (Reger, Allison, and Kurucz 1984) and represents a welcome change of pace to sustained moderate and vigorous physical activity. A variety of approaches can make your physical activity sessions more interesting.

Time

Time refers to the duration of physical activity. For optimal health, *Physical Activity Guidelines for Americans* (2008) recommends 300 or more minutes per week of moderate-intensity activity or 150 or more minutes of vigorous-intensity activity for adults. Weight loss requires 60 to 90 minutes of moderate-intensity activity daily, on at least five days per week (300 to 450 minutes per week) (*Physical Activity Guidelines for Americans* 2008). However, all physical activity helps with energy balance and therefore weight management. If you are motivated to perform these higher levels of activity, you are to be commended. If you do not have the time or motivation, you are encouraged to follow the minimum guidelines of 75 minutes of vigorous-intensity activity or 150 minutes of moderate-intensity physical activity per week. This duration represents at least 30 minutes of moderate physical activity five days per week or 25 minutes of vigorous physical activity three days per week.

Remember that any bouts of 10 minutes in duration count toward your overall time goal (*Physical Activity Guidelines for Americans* 2008). Health benefits are associated with incidental physical activity, such as taking the stairs. Stand, stretch, and move anytime

Accumulating Physical Activity With Walking

If you can't find a 30-minute block of time for physical activities, an alternative is to put together 10-minute bouts of activity. These add up. Health benefits occur when you accumulate 30 minutes over the course of a day. Make the segment only 10 minutes long and choose activities such as the following:

- Walk around the block when you pick up the morning paper.
- After breakfast, take your dog, the "walking machine with hair," out for a few minutes.
- When you take a midmorning break, make it a stroll, either solo or with a colleague.
- Park several blocks from your destination and make your walk to school, work, the dry cleaner, or the grocery store a bit longer.
- Walk while meeting with colleagues instead of sitting around a stuffy office.
- Take a midday break and walk a couple of blocks.
- Walk with friends to talk about what is on your minds.
- Mix and match them all and more.

Doing 10 minutes of activity instead of having a doughnut or cookie will make a huge difference in your health over time. Although each person's unique makeup will affect specific gains, benefits include weight loss and enhanced productivity. Three 10-minute bouts make up 30 painless minutes every day. You will feel better—guaranteed!

---

you can, even if only for a few seconds. The human body was designed to move—it is the only machine that breaks down from disuse.

On any day when 30 minutes seems too daunting, you can do 20, 15, or even 10 minutes. The closer you can get to the daily recommendations, the better you will feel. Because the most commonly reported barrier to regular physical activity is time (Sherwood and Jeffrey 2000), you can increase the intensity when less time is available. Remember that 1 minute of vigorous-intensity activity counts for 2 minutes of moderate-intensity physical activity. Walking faster saves time. Vigorous activity does not mean running hard or even race walking. You can simply pick up the intensity of whatever activity you are doing.

Sedentary people, those doing less than 30 minutes of moderate-intensity physical activity per week, are most at risk for heart disease, stroke, high blood pressure, breast or colon cancer, obesity, and osteoporosis (*Physical Activity Guidelines for Americans* 2008). Irregular activity, more than 30 minutes but less than 150 minutes of moderate-intensity activity per week, results in a reduction of these conditions.

Many people report that they begin to feel better even with daily walks of 10 minutes. For this reason, you should incorporate physical activity into any setting while monitoring how you feel. A daily log can

nicely complement the physical activity while helping to reinforce it (Chambliss et al. 2011).

A nonstriving approach to physical activity is best. Physical activity is enjoyable in and of itself. Going for a walk in any setting, no matter what the weather, can be wonderful. There is no such thing as bad weather (within reason), only bad clothing. Dress appropriately for the conditions. Trust in yourself and in the process. Your health and outlook will improve. Walking in the woods in summer or even with the snow of winter can be pleasurable, sensuous, and restorative. This activity can be a form of walking meditation.

Type

Type refers to specificity of training, or the aspect of fitness (aerobic capacity, muscular strength or endurance, bone strengthening, and flexibility) that the activity or exercise focuses on as well as the body parts targeted, such as biceps or quads. Any physical activity can provide health benefits, although activities that use the large muscles of the lower body will burn more calories and provide enhanced cardiovascular benefit. Types include bicycling, walking, jogging, cycle ergometer (stationary bike), dancing, hiking, housework, cutting the grass, swimming, weightlifting, gardening, body resistance exercises, and yoga. The list could go on.

Activities consistent with your normal lifestyle and values, for example, active commuting, are more likely to be maintained (Ryan et al. 2008).

Obviously, many activities and exercises involve multiple aspects of fitness and numerous body parts. But you should recognize that doing just bench presses without doing bent-over rows could cause a muscle imbalance. Another example would be working the quadriceps but ignoring the hamstrings, thereby increasing the risk of hamstring strain.

You can engage in different forms of physical activity to prevent injury and burnout, such as going for a walk, cutting the grass, cycling, swimming, or raking leaves. You can also intersperse recreational weightlifting at home as an occasional break from your studies. Enjoyable activities are easier to continue.

Walking for Aerobic Fitness

Walking is an easy, convenient form of regular physical activity and the exercise of choice for most people ("Vital Signs: Walking Among Adults" 2012). Regular walking produces as many health benefits as any other form of physical activity. Wearing a comfortable pair of shoes is important, but unless you have orthopedic problems, you don't need to spend a fortune on them. Most stores offer specials. Try on several different shoes. After you narrow your choice to two pairs, place a shoe from each pair on your left and right foot. After walking around for a short time, you will immediately know which is more comfortable. Then, don your comfortable pair of shoes and start walking daily from your front door.

Walking offers many advantages, perhaps too many to address in one short chapter. Walking is inexpensive and fun. No special gear is needed, apart from good shoes. Walking areas, such as paths, sidewalks, shopping malls, and other off-street areas, are available in many communities. A wooded area where hiking is possible may be nearby. You may want to commit yourself to walking to the store or around an athletic field.

You can share walking with friends. The social support that comes from walking with others helps you stay committed to it (Coleman, Berg, and Thompson 2014). Kids are known to be more active if they have active friends (Jago et al. 2011). Perhaps the rest of us could take a lesson from them.

Your walking is influenced by your environment. People may decide to live in a specific area for many reasons. Cost is a major consideration when choosing where to live, and other factors include perceived safety and the relative distance to places of work, schools, shopping centers, and parks. A survey conducted by the National Association of Realtors found that 57 percent of Americans thought that shopping centers, businesses, schools, and homes should be located nearby to reduce automobile use (Cortright 2008). If people perceive the neighborhood as being aesthetically pleasing and more walkable, they walk more (Gebel et al. 2011). Women who lived in socioeconomically disadvantaged neighborhoods were more likely to walk if they believed that the area was safe (Van Dyck et al. 2013).

The evidence suggests that people will pay more to live in a house of the same quality that is closer to shopping centers, businesses, and schools, thereby making travel on foot a possibility (Cortright 2008). In 13 of the 15 housing markets studied, a positive correlation was found between the walkability of a community and housing prices. People prefer to live in a walkable community, and some realtors have started using this preference to their advantage.

Walking has many advantages:

- Walking is a weight-bearing activity, so it reduces the likelihood of osteoporosis (Byberg et al. 2009).

- Walking uses the muscles of the lower body. It's useful for burning calories because the large muscles of the lower body use a lot of energy. Regular walking provides an excellent cardiovascular workout.

- Walking (indeed, all exercise) has been shown to help prevent adult-onset diabetes (Francois et al. 2014). This effect occurs because better transport of glucose into the muscle tissues occurs with exercise.

- Walking has been found to prevent back injuries, and it is not as likely as some physical activities to cause injury (Houmard et al. 2004).

- Walking has been shown to help control high blood pressure (Murphy et al. 2007).

- Walking reduces the risk of hospitalization for cardiovascular disease and death (Hu et al. 2004).

- Walking can be protective even when people begin it later in life (Stessman et al. 2009).

- Walking produces fewer injuries and disabilities than other forms of exercise (Colbert, Hootman, and Macera 2000).

Muscle and Bone Strengthening

Muscle and bone strengthening can be effectively accomplished through weightlifting and other resistance training. An added benefit is that people maintain weight loss better when they add resistance training to their aerobic exercise (Peterson, Sen, and Gordon 2011). The current recommendation is to use strength training focused on the legs, hips, back,

Activity

Mindful Walking for Fitness

Bringing increased attention and consciousness to everyday activities is a form of mindfulness. You can easily lose the richness of day-to-day experiences when you are on automatic pilot. You go through the motions of living but miss life in the process. If you walk from the car to the office and fail to notice, much less savor, the spring flowers, you are out of balance.

Being mindful while walking is a unique opportunity to enhance everyday life activity and take yourself off the automatic pilot mode of living. Mindful walking requires no specific environment. You can do it while going from any activity to another. All you need is your commitment to be present with the process of walking.

1. Be mindful of the movement of your body as you walk. We suggest staying focused on your feet and legs.

2. Take at least 10 minutes so that you have time to become nonstriving.

3. Walking outdoors is great, but you can begin in an 8-foot-by-10-foot (2.4 m /x/ 3 m) room. The goal is be present, not to get anywhere.

4. Walking is a rather complex activity that has become so routine that we often have little awareness of what is involved. Slow yourself down so that you can experience a wonderful dimension of life that you take for granted. Open yourself to experience walking as if for the first time, using beginner's mind in your steps. Imagine that these are the first steps you have walked after a period of disability.

5. If you choose to do walking meditation in an area where you have to turn around frequently, do so with consciousness. Pause with awareness before beginning to turn. Pivot with attention. Then proceed along your path while being aware. Be mindful of your breathing, mindful of the activity, mindful of your body, mindful of your thoughts. As ideas percolate into your consciousness, observe them, note mentally what they are, and then return your attention to the process of walking. Your only goal is to be right here, right now. You have no place to go and all day to get there.

6. Do not judge how you are doing, which would be an active thinking process. Simply observe the ideas that come to mind and then return your attention to your feet, legs, and body in general. If you stumble, notice whether your mind stumbled before you lost your balance.

7. The walking activity should be one seamless motion. The walking, pausing, and turning should bring to life an activity that, like your breath, is always with you. You will end with a heightened awareness and be more at peace.

8. Be conscious of yourself and your surroundings. With the process, feel free to be as you normally are. You want to slow your mind down. Maintain your mindfulness. Focus on the process of walking.

Your awareness, not your thinking, brings you in touch.

Based on Kabat-Zinn 2013.

abdomen, chest, shoulders, and arms (*Physical Activity Guidelines* 2008).

Although specific aerobic activities such as brisk walking, jogging, and running build up the hips and legs, these muscle and bone strengthening activities can be tailored to your needs. For example, you do not need to do extra hip and leg workouts if your aerobic training already involves jumping rope, stair climbing, or downhill walking. Consider following the low-to-high axiom, that is, using "lower" (lighter) weights or resistance and a higher number of repetitions to start.

Free weights are excellent because they develop balance as well as strength. Modest danger is associated with weightlifting and using resistance bands. The safest weight training is done with weight-training machines (see figure 6.2) regularly available at health and fitness centers. Resistance bands anchored to an object like a tree, door, or even your feet, are also safe, although there is some danger if they are incorrectly anchored. But both weight machines and resistance bands eliminate the danger of dropping weights on your body, which could cause serious injury. A

FIGURE 6.2   Universal weight machines can be safe equipment for weightlifting.

knowledgeable trainer can help you learn the proper techniques.

The qualifications of the trainer are important. Express your concerns if the trainer seems inattentive during your sessions or if you seem at risk for injury. You are the employer in this situation; that is, the trainer is working for you. Be assertive yet polite about your needs. If you feel pain when doing a repetition, stop immediately. Trust what your body is telling you. Mild soreness the day after exercising, which fades away after a day or so of rest, is to be expected, but sharp or intense pain while exercising is abnormal and means that your body is telling you to stop. You are either lifting too much weight or your form (the manner in which you are lifting the weight) is incorrect. Many novice weight lifters inadvertently strain muscles and injure themselves by attempting to start with too much resistance or weight. With proper guidance you can avoid the patterns that lead to injuries.

If you become injured, discontinue what you are doing and consult with a health professional knowledgeable about strength and bone training. Take a break and wait until you have fully healed before returning. This need for down time to recover is an important reason to be measured as you increase weights or resistance. Another recovery option is to exercise other muscle groups. For example, if you injure an arm muscle, it is generally considered safe to focus on the legs for a while (in this scenario, as long as you are not using your injured arm in any way to

engage in leg exercise).

Experienced weight lifters may safely work out with free weights and dumbbell. If you use a barbell for the bench press (lying on your back and lifting the bar up), a spotter should be present, someone who is strong enough to help with the barbell if necessary. You do not want to risk a serious injury. Having an attentive spotter is critical. Never perform bench presses or similar potentially dangerous weightlifting activities alone.

Many alternatives to working out with barbells or dumbbells are available, and even a fitness center is optional. You can use your own body weight for resistance, such as by doing push-ups, pull-ups, or modified sit-ups. Note that for a full push-up you use your hands and toes as the contact points, for a modified push-up you use your hands and knees, and for an even easier push-up you can lean toward and push away from a wall.

You should perform these activities with weight or resistance proportionate to your strength. Repeat the activity in sets. Do not hold your breath during strength training. Holding your breath during exertion (the Valsalva maneuver) tends to raise your blood pressure. Instead you should exhale during exertion. Returning to the starting position in a slow, controlled manner is important for muscle and bone development.

For all strength-training activities, start with one set of 6 to 10 reps and build up to three sets of 8 to 12 reps over time. You need to be careful with these exercises and emphasize technique over the amount of weight. Make sure that you are aligning your body so that you can directly apply the bones and muscles to moving the weight or resistance. If you find that you are compromising your form, such as distorting your body position or swinging your body into the weight, you are likely attempting the repetitions with too much weight or resistance.

Start with exercises involving your legs before moving up to the arms. Always begin doing slightly less than you know you can do, because you do not want an injury. A mindful strength-training and bone-training program might take 30 minutes or as little as 10 to 15 minutes two days per week, depending on how much you decide to do. You can do more if you feel like it, according to physical activity recommendations and what you think is best for your body. But you need to make sure that the excellent does not get in the way of the good. If you are overwhelmed by the thought of doing moderate intensity aerobic activity for 30 minutes five days per week, strength training with a core workout two days per week, and flexibility training after every workout, you may just drop out. Doing something is always better than doing nothing.

Remember, sickness will capture your attention if you fail to integrate wellness into your life!

Much can be done to incorporate everyday activities and resources into your resistance-training program. Shoveling dirt in the garden is an excellent full-body workout. Jumping rope, as well as walking up and down hills and stairs, can stress bones enough to increase bone density. Forces are produced as your body strikes the ground. You can incorporate resistance bands into your training. Inexpensive and portable, bands are a great way to exercise in any environment. Also, you can repeatedly "stomp down" on your bicycle pedals (by standing and pushing down hard) as you make your way up hills.

You can also use gallon (3.8 L) milk or juice containers with screw-on lids. A gallon of water weighs about 8 pounds (3.6 kg). Filling these containers with varying amounts of water creates dumbbells of 2, 4, 6, and 8 pounds (.9, 1.8, 2.7, and 3.6 kg). The outpatient cardiac rehabilitation program at Wheeling Hospital in West Virginia used water-filled containers for bone and muscle strengthening. Such containers are an inexpensive means of adding to your workout.

Bench Press

Bench press works the pectoral (midchest), triceps, and anterior deltoid muscles as well as the bones in the hands, wrists, arms, shoulders, and chest. To perform the bench press with a barbell, you should have a spotter, a qualified person who stands near the barbell in case you are unable to support the weight. Remember to begin with less weight than you know for sure you can lift. The bench press bar itself often weighs 45 pounds (20.4 kg). When using free weights, we recommend that you begin with the bar only (with no extra weight added) until you learn the correct form and build up enough upper-body strength to maintain proper form at all times. Add light weights slowly and incrementally, according to what your body can handle. Going slow with less weight (beginning with the bar only) gives you the opportunity to be mindfully aware of your body and what it can and cannot do. You need time to acclimatize to the process.

Directions

1. Lie flat on the bench. The barbell is on the rack attached to the bench. (On a bench press machine, simply lie on the bench of the machine.)
2. Inhale and place hands slightly wider than shoulder-width apart on the bar or grab the handles of the machine. Carefully push the barbell up away from the chest while exhaling. Do not lock out the elbows.
3. Inhale as you return the weight slowly to just above the chest.

Recommendations

1. To begin, repeat with the bar only or with light weights (with less weight than what you know for certain you can handle, while maintaining proper form) 6 to 10 times. Do only one set for the first several weeks.
2. After getting acclimated (perhaps the third or fourth week), work until exhaustion with each set of 8 to 12 repetitions. Perform three sets.
3. Remember to exhale on exertion.

Biceps Curls

Biceps curls, using a light barbell or light dumbbell, work the biceps (i.e., muscles in front of the upper arms). This activity stresses and strengthens the bones in the hands, wrists, arms, shoulders, and chest. With a weight machine or the proper fitness center equipment, the biceps arm curl is safer. The goal is to stress the biceps.

Directions

If you have access to a biceps curl machine at your fitness center, follow the directions given. If you are using dumbbells or a barbell, follow these directions:

1. Start by standing erect but with your knees slightly bent (do not lock your knees in place).
2. Pick up the weights. Bend your knees while keeping your back straight, pick up the dumbbells or barbell, and return to the standing position.
3. Keep your back straight and erect (tighten the abdominal, gluteal, and spine muscles) and keep your elbows tucked into your sides.
4. Curl the two arms up together while exhaling.
5. Exhale as you slowly bend your arms back to beginning position. The return is just as important as the curl up. Alternately, you can curl one arm, while leaving the other arm in the extended position. Return the first arm to the extended position as you curl the other arm. Continue to do these alternating arm curls while breathing in and out with each cycle.
6. Perform each repetition cycle 8 to 12 times. You should exhaust your biceps muscles by the last repetition.
7. Do two to three sets.

Triceps Extension

Triceps extension works the triceps, which are the muscles in the back of the upper arms. This activity stresses the bones of the hand, arm, shoulder, and spine.

Directions

If you have access to a triceps extension machine at your fitness center, follow the directions given. If you are using dumbbells or a barbell, follow these directions:

1. Sit in a chair (or on a ball, which is more challenging) with a light dumbbell (one that you can comfortably lift) held by both hands behind your neck.

2. While contracting the abdominal muscles to prevent the back from arching, inhale and then extend the forearms up toward the ceiling. Do not lock out the elbow joint. Exhale on exertion.

3. Return the weight and forearms to the position behind the head, all the while maintaining the upper arms straight up toward the ceiling.

4. Inhale while returning the weight to behind the neck.

5. Repeat this process 8 to 12 times to exhaustion. Perform two to three sets.

Bent-Over Rowing

Bent-over rowing helps to strengthen back muscles and assists with posture. This activity strengthens the bones of the arms, shoulder, back, and vertebrae and balances the stress of bench press activities.

Directions

If you have access to a bent-over rowing machine at your fitness center, follow the directions given. If you are using a dumbbell or a barbell, follow these directions:

1. Place the right knee and lower leg on a bench and a manageable dumbbell in the left hand.
2. Lift the weight up toward the chest while bending the elbow to move it up toward the ceiling, while also moving the upper arm and elbow straight up toward the ceiling. Exhale on exertion. Slowly return the arm to the extended position (at rest).
3. Repeat 8 to 12 times or until exhaustion.
4. Then place the left knee and lower leg on the bench. With the dumbbell in the right hand, repeat the process.

Latissimus Dorsi Pull

Latissimus dorsi pull, also known as a lat pull, works the deltoid muscles (i.e., shoulder and upper back) and the latissimus dorsi muscles on both sides of the upper back. This exercise also works the teres major, biceps, and rhomboid muscles.

Directions

If you have access to a machine for latissimus dorsi pull at your fitness center, follow the directions given. If you are using dumbbells or a barbell, follow these directions:

1. Place your hands on the ends of a bar that is substantially wider than your shoulders.
2. Pull the bar down in front of your body (not behind your head) to the middle of the chest. Remember to exhale on exertion. Slowly return the bar to the starting position.
3. Repeat 8 to 12 times. Perform three sets.

Modified Sit-Up

Modified sit-ups (sometimes called curl-ups) are for the abdominal muscles (rectus abdominis and oblique muscles). A less strenuous option is to cross your arms across your chest or hold them flat along your sides.

Directions

1. Hold your arms beside your head with your hands touching your ears, or cross your arms on your chest.
2. Contract the abdominal muscles and come to about 30 degrees, keeping the lumbar vertebrae (or lower back) on the floor.
3. Exhale on exertion. Inhale as you return your head and shoulders to the floor.
4. Perform three sets of 10.

Squats

Squats are a good exercise to strengthen the legs and the entire muscular system, but you need to take care not to bend your knees more than 90 degrees. Note that squats can be done with or without weights.

Directions

1. With a barbell (begin with the bar only or with less weight than you know for certain that your body can handle without injury) resting on a squat rack that is 3 inches (7.5 cm) lower than the shoulders, move under the barbell and place it on your shoulders. Grip the bar slightly wider than the shoulders.
2. Inhaling deeply, remove the barbell from the stand while looking straight ahead.
3. Keeping the back straight, take a step back and then bend the knees and hips so that the barbell moves toward the ground.
4. Do not permit your knees to bend more than 90 degrees. Exhale and straighten the knees and hips to return to the initial position.
5. Start with one set of 6 to 10 reps and build to three sets of 8 to 12 reps.
6. After performing the repetitions, step forward and lower your body so that the bar is back on the rack.

Lunges

Lunges can be done instead of squats. They also work to strengthen the legs and the entire muscular system. As with squats, be careful not to bend your knees more than 90 degrees. Note that these can be done with or without weights.

Directions

1. Choose dumbbells you know you can comfortably handle. Keeping your back straight, exhale as you pick up the dumbbells and stand erect with your legs and feet shoulder-width apart.
2. Inhale deeply. As you exhale, take a large step forward (lunge) until your knee is at 90 degrees, but no more.
3. Exhale and return to the starting position. Start with one set of 6 to 10 reps and build to three sets of 8 to 12 reps.
4. Repeat with the opposite leg. Start with one set of 6 to 10 reps and build to three sets of 8 to 12 reps.

Core-Strengthening Workout

The popular term *core* refers to the muscles of the chest, abdomen, back, pelvis, buttocks, and hips (Phillips 2011). The core serves to stabilize the central body and spine (Akuthota and Nadler, 2004). Core development is important to proper functioning, reduction of lower-back pain (Bliss and Teeple 2005), and athletic performance (Paul 2007). Many people work diligently on aesthetics of chest and arm development, but equally important is performing exercises that provide for well-balanced core muscle groups.

The following are some useful exercises recommended for core muscle groups that will promote both muscle and bone strength. Regular performance of these exercises becomes surprisingly fun and rewarding. Good muscle tone feels great and simultaneously improves fitness and appearance. Performing these exercises can also help prevent injuries. Up to 85 percent of Americans experience a significant back injury during their lifetime, and many of these injuries could have been avoided (Freburger et al. 2009). Back injuries result in unnecessary pain, suffering, loss of work, and loss of ability to enjoy leisure pursuits. Regular aerobic activity is helpful, but proper strengthening exercises for the arms, legs, back, and abdominal muscles will further cut down on these debilitating problems. Stronger muscles and bones always pay dividends in terms of enhanced function and appearance.

One short workout for core strengthening includes the bridge, a front plank, opposite arm and leg raise, side squat with knee lift, and a full-body stretch (Phillips 2011).

Bridge

The bridge strengthens the entirety of the abdominal region, the gluteal muscles, and the lower back. This can provide balance as well. The goal is to provide stability to the lumbar spine which serves as a platform for the movement in other sections of the body.

Directions

1. Begin by lying on your back with your arms at your sides, knees apart and bent, and feet flat on the floor.
2. While exhaling, squeeze your buttocks and lift your hips up as high off the floor as you comfortably can.
3. Hold for a few seconds and return to the resting position on the floor. Repeat 10 times. Rest for 30-60 seconds between repetitions. Perform one to three sets.

Front Plank

The front plank involves some isotonic (movement) but mostly isometric (static) exercises that strengthen the abdominal and oblique muscles. This can also be called an abdominal bridge. Here your body weight is held by the forearms, elbows, shoulders, core muscles, legs, and feet. When performed correctly, the front lank promotes an upright and dignified posture by supporting the correct alignment of the spine.

<u>Directions</u>

1. Start face down with your weight on your knees and forearms. Place your forearms and hands out and in line with your body and keep your elbows under your shoulders.
2. Exhale while tightening the abdominal muscles. Shift your weight to your forearms and feet, and have your legs extended. Balance your body like this, straight and still as if it is a plank of wood.
3. Hold for 20 seconds and return to the resting position on the floor. Repeat three times. Rest for 30-60 seconds between repetitions. Perform one set only.

Opposite Arm and Leg Raise

This exercise fortifies core and the lower back muscles which help you maintain a strong back. The back muscle development linked to core strength can improve your self-esteem by enabling you to feel enhanced stability.

Directions

1. Begin on your hands and knees. Place your hands under your shoulders and position your knees hip-width apart.
2. While inhaling, extend your right hand out in front of you while reaching straight out behind you with your left leg. Your arm, leg, shoulders, and hips should be parallel with the floor.
3. Hold for a few seconds and exhale as you return to the neutral position on your hands and knees.
4. Repeat the same exercise 10 times with the left hand and the right leg. Rest for 30 seconds between sets. Perform three sets.

Side Squat With Knee Lift

This combination exercise focuses on your oblique and gluteal muscles and has the potential to be an aerobic workout. A set on each side during the day can serve as an energizer. You can perform a set in one to two minutes.

Directions

1. Start by standing with your feet together and your hands at your sides.
2. Step to the left, bend your knees, and lower your buttocks as if sitting. Clasp your hands together in front of you.
3. Exhale as you come out of the squat, bringing your left foot up as you return your arms to the side.
4. Repeat 10 times. Rest for 30 seconds between sets. Perform three sets with the left leg. Then do the same with the right side.

Full-Body Stretch

As you age, you tend to lose your overall flexibility and body suppleness. The activity enables you to stretch out your body, including your shoulders and spine, and represents a nice way to complete a workout. You can feel grounded and peaceful as you elongate your body on a mat, towel, blanket, or exercise ball.

Directions

1. To stretch without an exercise ball begin by lying on your back with your arms at your sides and your feet placed below the buttocks at hip-width, flat on the floor.

2. While inhaling, simultaneously lift your arms up toward the ceiling and place them above your head flat on the floor, all the while moving your feet away from your buttocks until they too are flat on the floor.

3. Hold for ten seconds and then exhale as you return to the starting position.

4. Repeat four times. No recovery time is needed. Perform one set only. Alternately, you can place an exercise ball under your lower back (see figure), all the while protecting your stability by keeping the feet placed below the buttocks and spread apart wider than your shoulders. This enables you to stretch your spine over the exercise ball providing an even deeper stretch.

Stretching for Flexibility

Stretching improves joint range of motion. Mindful stretching is similar to yoga, and evidence substantiates the health benefits of yoga (Büssing et al. 2012). Breathing mindfully into each stretch transforms it into a meditative practice.

The stretches illustrated in figure 6.3 are well known and easy to follow. Perform three sets of each stretch, which should be held for 10 to 30 seconds. Take a few minutes following every workout to stretch the targeted muscles. After working out, your joints work better. Your muscles, tendons, and ligaments are warmer and more pliable, and your joints are better lubricated. You will be able to achieve a better range of motion for each stretch. By contrast, if you are planning ballistic physical activity, involving jumping and fast starts and stops, such as in softball, basketball, or tennis, you should warm up in advance, as it will decrease subsequent muscle soreness (Law and Herbert 2007). Do some light jogging and then stretch before starting your workout.

Quadriceps stretch. Make sure to hold the top of the foot and stretch up and away from the buttocks, rather than holding the tip of the toes and stretching up and in toward the buttocks, which could cause injury to your ankle or knee.

Hip flexor straddle stretch. Many have tight hips. Begin by lying on your back with your knees bent to 90 degrees and your feet flat on the floor. Bring the right foot to the top of the left knee. Grasp the thigh of the left leg with both hands and gently pull the leg toward you until you feel a comfortable stretch in your hips and upper legs. Do not push past the point of discomfort. Hold for 10 to 30 seconds. Return to the starting position and repeat with the opposite leg.

Modified hurdle stretch. Always turn the bent leg so that the foot rests by the knee of the straight leg, not out and away from the body, which could cause injury to your knee.

Triceps stretch.

Cross-chest stretch.

Pectorals stretch.

FIGURE 6.3 Stretching can increase flexibility and decrease muscle soreness.

MAINTAINING A HEALTHY, ACTIVE LIFESTYLE

As you begin to understand the benefits of being active, barriers begin to disappear. You become more motivated as you learn. The American Heart Association (www.heart.org/HEARTORG/) and the American College of Sports Medicine (www.exerciseismedicine.org/) are excellent sources of information and materials. In addition, commentaries on TV, radio, newspapers, magazines, or the Internet can be good sources of information. You can learn a surprisingly large amount from the popular press (we recommend the health sections of well-known newspapers and media outlets that subscribe to journalistic standards of objectivity), but you should remain skeptical if someone is trying to sell something. Consider reading, clipping, filing, and rereading the print clips. Online video and media such as YouTube illustrate these exercises and offer a fascinating source of information about the health benefits of being active. (Again, use your discernment when watching YouTube videos. Determine the qualifications of the person or group presenting the information.)

Motivation is the key. If you have a *why*, you can find a *how*. If you see good reasons to do something, you are more likely to do it. Small, intermittent, positive steps are an ideal way to get used to a new idea or behavior. The initial steps may be mental ones. There is a discussion of the **stages of change** in chapter 9. Starting before you are ready can become a problem and might predispose you to failure. Work on enhancing your motivational readiness first.

No matter what you choose, follow a routine that is congruent with your lifestyle. Choose activities that fit your body and your values. A structured program such as a fun, social aerobic dance group at the fitness center can help, but the schedule of the classes may not always match your schedule. Don't let a fitness center class schedule stand in the way of your getting regular physical activity.

Each exercise session should include the four following phases:

- Warm-up: Gradually build up your heart rate. For example, when walking or even jogging, the first three or four minutes should be at a modest pace. By the end of five minutes, you should be right at your chosen intensity or pace.
- Moderate- to high-intensity exercise: Perform aerobic activities, muscle- and bone-strengthening activities, or both, for as long as you feel comfortable and as time permits. You will naturally select moderate intensity when walking to a destination.

- Cool-down: Toward the end of the activity, decrease the pace and begin a cool-down phase. For example, if you are walking briskly, such as at 3.5 miles (5.6 km) per hour, decrease the speed to 3.0 miles (4.8 km) per hour and then to 2.5 miles (4.0 km) per hour.
- Stretching: As you age and as you become more fit, your muscles tighten and you lose your range of motion if you do not stretch. At the end of the cool-down, you can begin stretching.

Whatever you don't use, you lose. Move it or lose it! A significant part of the physical deterioration that people experience as they age results from lack of regular physical activity. Taking time to move your body, keeping yourself motivated, getting outside, enjoying the sunshine, and enjoying the enhanced quality of life that physical activity provides are all part of the good health equation.

Adequate Hydration

Drink at least 4 ounces (120 ml) of fluid (preferably water) for every 20 minutes you are physically active, regardless of the weather. Hot weather makes it even more crucial to stay hydrated. Drinking water before and after completion of your physical activity is important when the duration is more than an hour. Consuming sugary sports drinks with electrolytes is unnecessary unless you are exercising for more than 90 minutes and sweating extensively. You do not need the extra calories and electrolytes for a short workout.

Rules of the Road

Physical activity outdoors is wonderful. You can walk, jog, and bicycle in public open spaces in parks, along trails, and along roadways. You always need to obey the laws and local ordinances. Walkers and joggers should cross at crosswalks and keep facing traffic, when possible. You should make every effort to walk in areas that have a generous sidewalk with a buffer zone between travelling vehicles and the sidewalk. Bright and reflective clothing is always in order.

Bicycling on sidewalks is illegal in many communities across the United States. Bicyclists need to wear helmets and avoid cycling between dusk and dawn, if possible. We recommend that bicyclists wear reflective clothing and red flashing lights if cycling on roadways, even during the day. In addition, bicycles are vehicles, and cyclists must therefore obey the rules of the road. Bicyclists should travel with the traffic and follow rules for stoplights and stop signs. Low-cost courses are available to help you cycle safely in traffic. Be extra careful when interfacing with motorized vehicular

Haslyn was not a particularly regimented person, but he continued integrating physical activity into his everyday life. Besides walking for transportation, he began to jog three days per week for 25 minutes. He said that jogging made him feel even better. He also continued his weightlifting, which he did at his apartment during breaks from studying. Haslyn used 15-pound (6.8 kg) dumbbells for his biceps curls and overhead triceps extensions. He located a discarded weight bench on which he performed bench presses using 25-pound (11.3 kg) dumbbells. He performed lunges using 15-pound dumbbells. Haslyn also joined the municipal pedestrian safety board to help promote a better walking infrastructure in the community. The board meeting takes only an hour per month. Haslyn finds civic engagement to be a way of giving back to the community and keeping himself motivated.

traffic while or after biking on a trail. It is possible that the safety of the trail might lull you into complacency about safety issues and the rules of the road.

Advocate and Engage

Some American cities have excellent infrastructure for walking and bicycling, but most do not. You have an opportunity to make a difference. You can contact local city council members, county commissioners, state and federal legislators, and your state department of transportation about the need for infrastructure to support active transport. Walking and biking are forms of active transportation. If you have better infrastructure, you may be less likely to drive. Less driving means less traffic congestion, fewer vehicular crashes, and reduced air pollution. The comments of residents can make a difference. Do your part! Speak up. In addition, wellness benefits are associated with engaging your community and contributing to social capital.

Fit or Fat

If you want to lose and sustain weight loss, restricting your food calorie intake without increasing your physical activity is ineffective (Catenacci et al. 2010). Dieting alone does not work in the long term. For more information on types of food to eat for optimal health and diet benefits, see chapter 7. You can do a lot of training at the dinner table.

People who consciously restrict their food intake might succeed in achieving a temporary weight loss, but most fail to see any net weight reduction at the end of one year. Aggressive dieting usually results in a reduction in metabolic rate even when fat-free mass is preserved (Johannsen et al. 2012). The consequence is that weight and body fat is regained. In the absence of exercise, the weight is regained as fat. Combining calorie restriction with at least 30 minutes (preferably 60 to 90 minutes) of daily physical activity results in more permanent weight loss (*Physical Activity Guidelines for Americans* 2008). Remember that what you eat and how much you exercise are not the only issues here. More important, you need to address what is "eating" (influencing) you.

SUMMARY

Although few question the value of regular physical activity, most Americans are still not active enough to improve their health. *Physical Activity Guidelines for Americans* (2008) suggests 150 to 300 minutes of moderate or 75 to 150 minutes of vigorous aerobic physical activity over the course of a week, preferably in at least three bouts. Muscle and bone strengthening and flexibility training twice a week are recommended. The FITT principle (frequency, intensity, time, and type) remains relevant. For most of us, walking remains the most convenient and effective type of physical activity to reach the aerobic recommendation, because walking is easily integrated into most lifestyles.

Muscle and bone strengthening should address the seven major muscle groups in the body. Give attention to proper form to avoid injury and maximize the benefits. You can also focus on core strength to improve overall health and physical performance.

Every workout should be followed by stretching the targeted muscle groups, which can enhance range of motion and flexibility. Hold each stretch from 10 to 30 seconds and perform three sets of each activity.

Physical activity is safe for most young adults. Obtaining medical clearance before beginning is not necessary, unless you have reason for concern, such as chest pain. Start gradually, use common sense, and drink adequate water. Most important, make your physical activity fun and convenient.

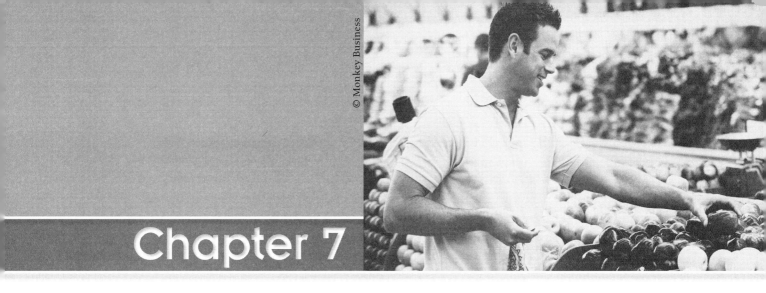

Chapter 7

Nutrition

Objectives

After reading this chapter, you will be able to
- list 10 foods basic to the wellness food plan,
- describe the recommendations of *Dietary Guidelines for Americans, 2010* (2011) for sodium, fiber, sugar, saturated fat and trans fat,
- describe strategies for eating in an all-you-can-eat cafeteria,
- identify four recommended foods to include on a shopping list,
- list four major classes of food that stimulate the appetite, causing us to overeat,
- identify four health problems associated with sugar,
- explain the process of food addiction, and
- design a one-week wellness food intake plan.

Wanda filled her plate to the brim at most meals, all of which she quickly consumed. She *always* finished her meals with a sweet dessert. She knew that she was overweight and needed to cut back but felt deprived whenever she tried various low-calorie diets. Eating sweets gave her a sense of comfort. But the price of her sweet tooth included persistent fatigue, afternoon drowsiness, and a poor self-image.

Things began to change, she noted, after a wellness course demonstration of mindful raisin eating. During the course, she spent 10 minutes eating a single raisin, swallowing it only after fully savoring its flavor. The session also demonstrated that appetite represents the psychological (perceived) desire for food, whereas hunger is more closely associated with the physical need for food.

Thereafter, she began to think more about her eating and slowed down the process. During a course-related potluck dinner, Wanda served herself an 800-calorie plate of sumptuous food. She ate mindfully, savoring her food slowly. Partway through the meal she realized that she was satisfied and no longer hungry. Rather than eat every morsel from her plate and then go for a dessert, as she was

105

accustomed to doing, Wanda left the table feeling wonderful. She had not unconsciously devoured an unneeded 500 calories.

Eating is an immensely pleasurable aspect of life. Along with this pleasure comes the challenge of eating well. The tastes, textures, and fragrances of food provide much pleasure. Without adequate calories, you could not survive. Delicious, attractive, and healthful foods provide ample energy, good health, and protection against disease. A balanced food intake, however, is necessary to maintain an ideal body weight.

If you are struggling with excess weight, sluggishness, high blood pressure, or diabetes, then implementing a wellness eating plan may be the ticket to good health (White, Horwath, and Conner 2013). The more **whole foods** you consume, especially vegetables, fruits, legumes, and whole grains, the better you will look and feel. Dietary improvement, not perfection, will make a substantive difference. As motivation increases, taking further steps toward wellness becomes progressively easier.

Eating is the most powerful contact you have with your physical environment. Think about the significance of consuming foods that travel vast distances by truck, train, and ship and then pass through your mouth, into your esophagus, stomach, and intestine, all of which is how food nourishes and helps create your physical body. This transformation is a sacred act. You would do well to treat eating with respect, even reverence. Certainly, you need to exercise care about the macro- and micronutrients that enter your body during the 21 or more opportunities you eat during any given week. Mindful eating is a huge first step toward dietary transformation.

Food can take on a life of its own, in terms of human psychology. **Compulsive overeating** is a major societal problem. Food can assume the role of friend when you are feeling blue or lonely. Eating can make a person feel short-term elation, no matter how unhealthy a particular food item might be. As with alcohol, however, the long-term consequences of dependence can be anything but pleasant.

This chapter addresses the physical, mental, emotional, and addictive aspects of eating, along with basic nutrition facts, concepts, and skills. It provides a recipe for a wholesome food journey.

OPTIMAL WELLNESS FOOD PLAN

Whole plant foods are the centerpiece of your wellness food plan. Colorful vegetables, tasty fruits, and an array of nutritious whole grains, such as brown rice, quinoa (pronounced keen-wah), beans, peas, and lentils, provide all necessary calories, protein, vitamins, and minerals. Whole plant foods, the fundamental building blocks for vitality and good health, also have fewer calories than most processed and packaged products.

Whole plant foods are low on the food chain; that is, they grow abundantly in nature and can be used immediately as human food, providing direct nutrition without any animal intermediary. Plants are good for the planet because they require less energy and water to produce than animal products. Plant products can feed far more people at less expense than animal products. Note that it takes 18 pounds (8.2 kg) of grain to make a single pound (.45 kg) of beef.

Most plant foods have low caloric density (Rolls 2007). **Low caloric density** means that each bite (or ounce of food) has few calories. An ounce (28 g) of steamed carrots, for example, has 11 calories. In comparison, a 1-ounce serving of cheddar cheese has more than 100 calories. Eating foods with low caloric density permits people to eat more food without contributing to excess body fat. The volume of food is filling in and of itself (Rolls 2007). There is less need to count calories when primarily eating foods of low caloric density.

Similarly, you need to be alert to nutrient density. According to *Dietary Guidelines for Americans, 2010* (2011), a **nutrient-dense food** is one with a high ratio of vitamins, mineral, fiber, and other important dietary components to the amount of calories. A nutrient-dense food provides essential dietary components.

The typical U.S. diet includes an excess of calories, **saturated fats**, trans-fatty acids (**trans fats**), sodium, and sugar (Flock and Kris-Etherton 2011). American meals focus on beef, cheese, pork, fish, and fowl. Americans daily consume only 1.6 servings of fruits, 3.2 servings of vegetables, and .8 servings of whole grains, along with a whopping 31 grams of saturated fat (Johnson et al. 2009) and 3,400 milligrams of sodium (*Dietary Guidelines for Americans* 2010). Our diets contain too few fruits and vegetables and too much fat and salt (Moss 2013)!

Overall, current U.S. daily caloric intake is 1,877 calories for women and 2,618 calories for men (*What We Eat in America* 2010). This is clearly far more calories than are needed for current physical activity levels. Between 1999 and 2010, American men experienced a

"Freshman 15"

Most incoming college students know about the risk of gaining 15 pounds (6.8 kg) during their freshman year. In fact, only 12 percent of students gain the "Freshman 15"; the average weight gained is 3 to 4 pounds (1.4 to 1.8 kg), gained between the first and third semesters at college (Gillen and Lefkowitz 2011). Although this problem is not as dire as people think it is, it is still serious. The weight gain continues through undergraduate and graduate education, albeit at a slower rate.

Most college and university campuses provide advice about how to avoid weight gain. Unquestionably, eating on a full meal plan poses a challenge, because unfettered access to a vast array of food is a recipe for disaster. Observing several simple guidelines can preserve your health and appearance.

- Mindful eating is always in order. Enjoy your food like never before. Select your food enthusiastically, chew it, savor it, and be present with what you are putting into your mouth. Paradoxically, this extra focus on your food may enable you to eat less while enjoying it more.

- Remember that *all-you-can-eat* buffet does not mean that you have to "stuff" yourself full with the available food just because it is "free."

- Approximately 15 to 20 minutes is required for your body's appetite regulatory mechanism to signal that you are full. Exercise discretion. Stop eating when you realize that you are full. Remember, you do not have to clean your plate.

- Food selection is critically important. Eat a balanced meal. Choose your vegetables, fruits, whole grains, and low-fat protein first.

- Portion size is a major challenge. Selecting a smaller plate alone has been shown to reduce portion size and caloric intake (Wansink, Van Ittersum, and Payne 2014).

- People may eat more just because they think something is healthy.

- You likely did not have a dessert during every meal at home. Consider not eating dessert, eating fruit, or going very light on the cake and ice cream.

- Be mindful and be aware while eating.

linear increase in **body mass index (BMI)** representing 1 to 4 pounds (.45 to 1.8 kg) of weight gain per year, but no significant change was observed for women (Flegal et al. 2012). Since 2010, obesity levels have plateaued in the United States (Flegal et al. 2012) and elsewhere (Eriksson et al. 2011). Unfortunately, however, obesity continues at unacceptably high levels.

Dietary change does not have to be difficult. When you eat a diet consisting mainly of vegetables and fruits, you feel better, will be closer to your ideal weight, and will likely have better mental health (White, Horwath, and Conner 2013). All these benefits are mutually reinforcing. Initially, shopping for and preparing meals might take a bit longer because you are shopping for fresh produce and less-processed foods. After you have your pantry stocked with the right foods and have learned to cook with better ingredients, no extra time is required. Investing a few minutes in educating yourself now can yield benefits that last a lifetime.

All of your recommended wellness foods are available in supermarkets. Many can also be purchased at local farmers' markets, convenience stores, and restaurants. These shopping practices promote community

vitality and social capital because you are supporting the local food economy.

MAJOR FOOD GROUPS

Eating well is perhaps the most important step you can make toward good physical health. The optimal wellness food plan described in this chapter includes foods from each of the major food groups. Make sure that every plate includes a generous portion (one to two cups) of vegetables, a serving or more of fruit, and at least one serving of whole grains. A wide array of protein foods are available, but caution is in order because meats and cheeses are high not only in calories but also often high in saturated fat. A good guide to eating well is to prepare a colorful plate (Kushner and Ognar 2006). Different colors offer different benefits to the body.

Dietary Guidelines for Americans, 2010 (2011) references MyPlate, which illustrates the recommendations for healthy eating (see figure 7.1). Note that half the plate is made up of vegetables and fruits, which are loaded with nutrients and flavor.

Check With Your Doctor

A person who is ill or on medication should consult a health professional knowledgeable about nutrition before making substantial dietary changes. This recommendation is particularly important when taking medication for such conditions as high blood pressure and diabetes, which can be positively affected by eating whole plant foods (Sacks et al. 2001). The need for medications may be reduced on a plant-based diet (Fung et al. 2004). Your doctor may even have to lower your blood pressure medications if you are on a healthy diet to prevent blood pressure from getting too low and causing dizziness! Remember that your body will begin to return to its normal healthy state of balance (homeostasis) through your improved lifestyle. Hence, you may need fewer medications.

FIGURE 7.1   USDA MyPlate.

USDA's Center for Nutrition Policy and Promotion.

Vegetables and Fruits

Eat vegetables and fruits to your heart's delight. Both are excellent sources of vitamins, minerals, and dietary fiber and are naturally low in calories. Fresh vegetables and fruits are best, but frozen and canned are fine too. Be wary of the added salt in canned vegetables and added sugar in canned fruits. Try to purchase low-sodium or no-salt-added vegetables and fruits canned in 100 percent fruit juice. Locally grown vegetables and fruits are an even better selection. They are readily available in farmers markets and have special flavor because they are ripened on the vine. In addition, being a "locavore" (a person who eats local produce) promotes local economies and benefits the environment because storage and long-distance shipping are less necessary (Lee et al. 2010). Purchasing precut, ready-to-eat produce can increase the cost, but the added convenience may be worth the investment.

When you shop for fruits and vegetables, take a shopping list to reduce impulse buying. Be open to products on sale. If you have apples on your list but pears are on sale, you might decide to purchase pears instead. Buy small quantities of fresh produce because

of its short shelf life. Purchasing frozen or canned produce eliminates most concerns about spoilage.

Vegetables are the edible and colorful part of a plant. They are rich in vitamins, minerals, and dietary fiber. Unless they are cooked in or coated with fat, sugar, salt, and oil, eating too many vegetables is difficult because they are generally low in calories and sodium. According to calculations by the **Center for Science in the Public Interest**, publisher of the **Nutrition Action Healthletter**, the most nutritious vegetables are swiss chard, kale, spinach, collard greens, brussels sprouts, pumpkin, broccoli, sweet potatoes, red and green peppers, and carrots (Liebman and Hurley 2007). These rankings involve an algorithm of caloric and nutritional density. Eat green leafy and highly colored vegetables on a daily basis.

Dietary Guidelines for Americans, 2010 (2011) recommends consuming 2 1/2 to 3 cups of vegetables daily, although actual need depends on your physical size, sex, age, and physical activity level. If that quantity seems like too much, start with one cup of veggies for lunch and dinner, that is, two cups or four servings daily. This amount is not as much food as it seems because vegetables have few calories. For example, a cup (two servings) of broccoli contains 40 calories, a cup of green peppers has 25 calories, a cup of cauliflower has 25 calories, and a cup of carrots has 52 calories.

The key to eating more vegetables is to prepare them so that they taste good. Doing this is not rocket science, but it does require experimentation to find cooked and uncooked foods that you find irresistible. You can start by identifying which vegetables and seasonings you most prefer. Fresh ginger shredded into a vegetable stir-fry adds zest. Adding toasted sesame oil increases flavor. A tablespoon of parmesan cheese, 25 calories, can be sprinkled on top of an onion, kale, and spinach stir-fry to enhance the taste.

You can use other strategies to eat more vegetables. Consider including vegetables in smoothies. A cup of carrots is unrecognizable in a milk and frozen fruit smoothie. Try experimenting. Green leafy vegetables in a smoothie may not look great because of the greenish tint, but they taste wonderful, especially if fresh lemon is added. Smoothies are like a milkshake and make a great treat. Smoothies can be an entire meal or a tasty liquid dessert, and they are certainly an adventure with wholesome foods. Vegetable soups also represent a quick and easy way of preparing low-cost meals. Water-soluble vitamins and fat-soluble vitamins may be lost if you use too much oil or water while cooking; nutrients are often lost in the cooking fluid and discarded. Soups reduce nutrient loss during cooking because you consume the entire product.

Fruits are the sweet and seedy part of plants, which are naturally low in calories and high in dietary fiber. Fruits provide flavor, fragrance, texture, and color to meals. *Dietary Guidelines for Americans, 2010* (2011) recommends that both men and women with food intake of 2000 calories consume at least two cups or four servings per day. A serving is one fruit, such as a medium apple, orange, or pear; one half cup of fresh, frozen, and canned fruits, such as grapes, berries, or diced pineapple; and one quarter cup of dried fruit, such as raisins or prunes. *Nutrition Action Healthletter* (Liebman and Hurley 2007) ranks watermelon, grapefruit, papaya, cantaloupe, apricots, oranges, strawberries, and peaches as among the most nutritious fruit selections. Although people with diabetes

Recipe

Thai Carrot Soup

Prep time: 30 minutes maximum

3 onions, chopped

3 stalks celery

3 cloves garlic, finely chopped

4 cups water

2 pounds (.9 kg) carrots, peeled and chopped

1 1/2 inches (3.8 cm) fresh ginger cut up and placed in the blender with 1/4 cup water (Alternatives: powdered ginger or fresh ginger in a jar)

3/4 teaspoon red pepper flakes

1 tablespoon fresh lime juice

4 tablespoons low-sodium peanut butter

1 tablespoon sesame oil

Fresh ground pepper to taste

1. Steam onions, celery, and garlic in 1 cup water until soft.
2. Add remaining water, carrots, ginger, and red-pepper flakes. Bring this carrot mixture to a boil and then simmer covered until carrots are tender (20 minutes).
3. Scoop the cooked water, carrots, onions, celery, ginger, and red-pepper flake mixture into a blender.
4. Add lime juice, peanut butter, and sesame oil.
5. Puree and serve hot or cold.

More Information

- This one-pot meal makes approximately 5 cups (serving size is 1 cup).
- Calories: 190 per cup, which counts as two servings of vegetables.
- The recipe can easily be doubled. Store in an airtight container in a refrigerator at 40 degrees Fahrenheit (4.4 degrees Celsius) or frozen.
- Serve hot or cold. Avoid danger-zone temperatures. To lessen the risk of bacterial contamination, serve hot at 140 degrees Fahrenheit (60 degrees Celsius) or hotter or serve cold at 40 degrees Fahrenheit (4.4 degrees Celsius) or colder.

Recipe

Fruit Veggie Smoothie

Prep time: 3 minutes maximum

1/2 cup fruit juice of your choice (orange, apple, and so on) or low-fat milk, soymilk, or low-fat yogurt

1 peeled fresh banana or frozen banana

1/2 cup frozen strawberries

3/4 cup frozen blueberries

1 cup carrots or baked sweet potato

Other ingredient options:

Almost any vegetable (spinach, celery, zucchini or squash, broccoli, cauliflower)

Almost any fruit (mango, pineapple, pears, peaches, cantaloupe, watermelon)

1. Be creative. Use what is on hand.
2. Put all ingredients in a blender.
3. Blend until you have a great-tasting smoothie.

More Information

- The recipe makes approximately 5 cups (this is not too much for a healthful breakfast).
- It can serve as a make-and-eat-now breakfast or snack.
- Contains 250 to 300 calories, depending on fruits and vegetables used. A smoothie has lots of flavor and fiber, many minerals and vitamins, and no saturated fat.
- Can be stored up to three hours (blended food oxidizes quickly). Make only as much as you want to eat.
- Pour over a cup of bite-size shredded wheat for a more filling breakfast.

---

might limit themselves to no more than two sweet fruits per day, all others should consider their meals incomplete without fruit.

Whole Grains

To be considered a **whole-grain** product, all the naturally occurring essential components of grain (germ, endosperm, and bran) must still be present (Liebman 2006). Most processed grains contain only the starchy endosperm. Unfortunately, Americans eat less than one serving of whole grains per day, or approximately 20 percent of the recommended level (*What We Eat in America* 2010). The current recommendation is to eat at least five servings of whole grains daily. Whole grains are nutritionally superior to refined white wheat. Other than the five nutrients that are added back into refined wheat flour, whole wheat is superior (see figure 7.2).

You can choose from among many tasty whole-grain selections. You might eat mini wheat or bran flakes for breakfast, stir-fried vegetables over brown rice for lunch, and pasta primavera with whole-wheat noodles for dinner. Whole-wheat bread or pita can accompany all meals.

When shopping, check the nutrition label on the package. Avoid breads that have high fructose corn syrup added. The ingredients are listed on the nutrition label in descending order. Many bread selections have healthful-appearing labeling such as "whole grain" or "wheat" on the packaging, but this labeling is cleverly designed to sell the product, not to promote your health. Many breads and breakfast cereals have high levels of sodium. Ezekiel 4:9 Low Sodium Whole Grain Bread (Food for Life), cooked oatmeal, and spoon-sized shredded wheat are tasty whole grains with zero sodium.

Most commonly available grains are processed, bleached, and enriched (Djoussé and Gaziano 2007), becoming part of the "killer whites" in the American diet. The term *killer whites* is a colloquial expression for those grains from which significant nutrients are removed by milling and bleaching. Enriching then returns some nutrients, but a nutritionally inferior product results compared with whole grains. Figure 7.2 illustrates the nutrients lost in processing whole grains to turn them into white-enriched flour.

Beware! Nutritionally inferior refined grains are

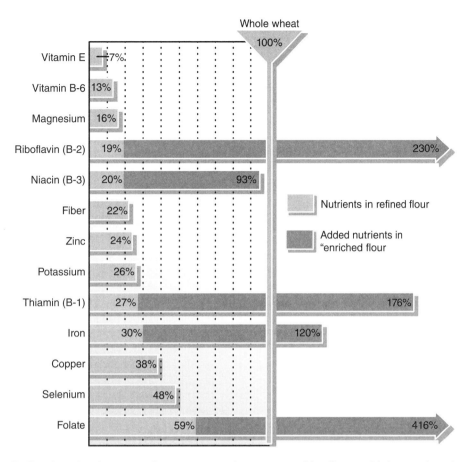

FIGURE 7.2 Refined grains have nutrients removed to create white flour, which can then be enriched to add some nutrients back in. Whole-wheat flour retains more nutrients.

Reprinted, by permission, from B. Liebman, 2014, "Whole grains: The inside story," *Nutrition Action Health Letter.* © Center for Science in Public Interest. Available: https://www.cspinet.org/nah/05_06/grains.pdf.

posing as whole wheat. These products have caramel coloring or molasses added to make them appear darker and thereby resemble whole-grain bread. Look for 100 percent whole wheat on the ingredients list. The *Subway US Product Ingredient* (2014) web page lists their available breads. All breads listed have enriched wheat flour as the first ingredient, including the nine-grain wheat.

Beware of such deceptive marketing practices. The food industry uses the token presence of a few whole grains in cookies, crackers, cakes, pies, and other pastries to promote the consumption of more food. Your body does not need excuses to take in extra calories, especially those that lack dietary fiber and a spectrum of vitamins and minerals.

Evidence for the health benefits of whole grains is strong (Fung et al. 2002). Studies have shown that people who regularly consume whole grains versus refined grains gain less weight (Halton and Hu 2004), experience a 20 to 35 percent reduction in heart dis-

ease (*Healthy People 2020*, 2010), a 30 percent reduction in stroke (Hu 2005), and a 26 percent reduction in type 2 diabetes (Ye et al. 2012). Whole grains also improve bowel function (McIntosh et al. 2003).

Disclaimer: No direct causal relationships have been demonstrated for these health benefits, but the association is strong. The evidence does not indicate that eating whole grains actually causes the earlier mentioned health benefits. Rather, people who eat them seem to experience better health. People who consume whole grains may also engage in other healthful activities, such as increased physical activity, or enjoy better social support networks, which could contribute to those benefits.

Protein

Americans have a romance with protein. The traditional American diet centers on animal protein. People often eat bacon and eggs for breakfast, a hamburger for lunch, and either fish, meatloaf, or chicken for dinner. You often hear parents urging their children to make sure to eat their meat. In fact, stark protein deficiencies rarely occur in the industrialized world when adequate calories are consumed (McDougall and McDougall 2012). The typical American diet provides sufficient protein, representing 12 to 15 percent of total calories (*Dietary Guidelines for Americans, 2010* (2011)).

A complete protein is composed of 22 different amino acids, although you do not need to consume that many on a daily basis (Campbell et al. 2008). Rather, adults can synthesize all amino acids from the eight essential ones, which are found in fruits, vegetables, whole grains, beans, peas, and lentils, not solely in animal or dairy products. For example, alternative sources of protein include the following (*National Nutrient Database for Standard Reference Release 26* 2010):

- Mushrooms—56 percent protein
- Spinach—50 percent protein
- Skim milk—41 percent protein
- Lentils—35 percent protein
- Whole-wheat bread—21 percent protein
- White potatoes—11 percent protein
- Honeydew melons—6 percent protein

- Oranges—8 percent protein

Unfortunately, although protein itself is good, most animal protein sources, such as beef, cheese, and high-fat milk, are linked with saturated fat. This fat clogs your arteries; is a dense source of calories; and promotes heart disease, stroke, diabetes, and several cancers. Americans are killing themselves by eating protein-based, high-saturated-fat meals 14 to 21 times per week (Meyer et al. 2000). A trip to almost any restaurant will demonstrate the pervasiveness of gargantuan-sized animal-based meals.

Protein has been shown to make people feel full longer (Halton and Hu 2004) and can help control blood glucose levels, an important consideration for people with diabetes and those who are insulin resistant. Fish, chicken, turkey, lean cuts of beef and pork (such as tenderloin), low-fat dairy products, and legumes are excellent sources of protein that are low in saturated fat. Alternative leaner meat sources include deer, buffalo, and elk.

Although fish and chicken are healthier than red meat, be sure to limit their consumption as well. The recommended serving size for fish, fowl, beef and pork is the size of a deck of cards, which is quite small. Removing the skin from chicken eliminates fat

Recipe

Chicken on the Run

Preparation time: 3 minutes

    4 boneless skinless chicken breasts

    1 tablespoon seasoning to taste (for example, garlic, pepper, thyme, rosemary, or lemon)

    1/8 cup water

    Optional ingredient: if possible, vegetables of choice added to the slow cooker, along with another 1/8 cup water 1 hour before serving

1. Place water and chicken breasts in a slow cooker (crock pot) on low heat for 8 to 10 hours or on high heat for 3 to 4 hours.
2. Place seasonings on the top of the chicken breasts.
3. Add optional ingredients, such as the vegetables of your choice along with another 1/8 cup water 1 hour before serving.
4. Remove from the slow cooker when ready to eat.

More Information

- This recipe makes four servings, depending on the size of the chicken breasts.
- Serving size of a cooked chicken breast is 67 grams.
- A serving contains 69 calories, .3 grams of saturated fat, 66 milligrams of sodium, and .1 grams of fiber.

Reprinted by permission from Bria Vossen.

and calories. Baking rather than frying dramatically reduces calories and fat. Butter used during preparation adds unnecessary fat.

Some skinless poultry options can be healthy. A skinless turkey breast contains only 114 calories, 1.5 grams of total fat, .3 grams of saturated fat, and 23.7 grams of protein; a skinless chicken breast has 120 calories, 2.6 grams of total fat, .6 grams of saturated fat, and 22.5 grams of protein; and 93 percent lean ground turkey has 150 calories, 7.3 grams of total fat, 2.2 grams of saturated fat, and 18.7 grams of protein

(National Nutrient Database for Standard Reference Release 26 2010).

Legumes

Beans, peas, and lentils are a tasty but all too often neglected source of protein and dietary fiber. As the United States has become more culturally diverse, excellent legume-based meals are increasingly available. For example, Mexican Americans prepare a vast array of bean dishes, Cuban Americans contribute red and black beans, and Middle Easterners serve hummus, falafel, and savory lentils.

Recipe

Red Lentil Curry, by Kate Sherwood
Total time: 30 minutes.

1 cup red lentils

½ tsp. turmeric powder, optional

1 Tbs. unsalted butter

2 Tbs. canola oil

1 large onion, thinly sliced

1 inch piece ginger

1 Tbs. curry or chili powder

15 oz. can no-salt-added diced tomatoes

½ tsp. kosher salt

½ cup cilantro leaves

1. In a medium pot, combine the lentils and turmeric with 4 cups of water. Bring to a boil, then reduce the heat and simmer until tender, 15-20 minutes.
2. Meanwhile, in a large skillet over medium heat, melt the butter with the oil. Sauté the onion until browned, about 10 minutes.
3. Cut half of the ginger into fine matchsticks for garnish and grate the rest. Stir the grated ginger and the chili powder into the onions. Stir in the tomatoes and simmer until the lentils are done.
4. Stir the lentils into the skillet and simmer for 5 minutes. Season with up to ½ tsp. of salt and garnish with the ginger matchsticks and cilantro leaves.

Optional: *Try tossing a bag of baby spinach into the pot just before serving. Then top each bowl with a dollop of plain yogurt.*

More Information
- This makes four 1 cup servings
- Calories 270
- Sat Fat 2 grams
- Sodium 300
- Fiber 9

Soaking uncooked beans overnight provides the starting ingredients for a variety of wholesome, low-cost, and tasty spreads, soups, and entrees. Canned beans are easy but relatively expensive and usually have high sodium levels. Refried beans are often cooked with lard, making them an unhealthy alternative. Fortunately, vegetarian versions of refried beans are available at supermarkets, but tend to be high in sodium. Alternatively, you can refry your own beans for pennies per serving. First, rinse and then cook dried black or pinto beans until they are soft, but not mushy. You can do this in the slow cooker while you are in school or at work. After adding onion, garlic, chili pepper, and cumin, you can mash the bean mixture with a potato masher until they reach the desired consistency.

Nuts and Seeds

The flavor, texture, and health qualities of your recipes can be amplified by adding nuts and seeds (Ohr 2012). They are good sources of protein and omega-3 fats but be cautious about the calories. The serving size is generally 1/4 cup, or what can be held in the palm of your hand. Nuts and seeds are highly palatable and have a high caloric density (Rolls 2007). If you are trying to lose weight, judiciously add nuts to dishes and limit consumption to one or two times per week. By placing them out of sight in the home, you will be less tempted to use them as a daily snack.

Calcium

Because of extensive advertising, many people are led to believe that dairy products are the only source of dietary calcium. But plant foods also supply plenty of calcium, which contributes to endocrine activity, muscle function, and bone strength. In addition, the calcium from plants is better absorbed because it is associated with other vitamins and minerals. Here are some examples of calcium-rich foods (*National Nutrient Database for Standard Reference Release 26* 2010):

- Skim milk, 8-ounce (240 ml) cup—500 milligrams
- Soymilk, 8-ounce (250 g) cup (information from label)—450 milligrams
- Figs, 8-ounce (250 g) cup—241 milligrams
- Turnip greens, 8-ounce (250 g) cup—209 milligrams
- White beans, 8-ounce (250 g) cup—131 milligrams
- Kale, 8-ounce (250 g) cup—94 milligrams
- Orange (navel), 2 7/8 inches (7.3 cm) fruit—60 milligrams

Although vegetarians take in slightly less calcium than do people who consume dairy products, no

Skim milk is a good source for calcium, but it is not the only source. Branch out and try some of the many other foods that can provide a variety of minerals and nutrients along with calcium.

Recipe

One-Pot Kale and Quinoa Pilaf

2 cups water

1 cup quinoa

1 bunch kale, washed and chopped into 1-inch (2.5 cm) lengths, center stem removed

1 lemon, zested and juiced

2 scallions, minced

1 tablespoon toasted walnut oil

3 tablespoons toasted pine nuts

1/4 cup crumbled goat cheese

1/4 teaspoon salt

Pepper to taste

1. Bring the water to a boil in a covered pot. Add the quinoa, cover, and lower the heat until it is just enough to maintain a simmer. Let simmer for 10 minutes and then top with the kale and re-cover. Simmer another 5 minutes, turn off the heat, and allow to steam for 5 more minutes.

2. While the quinoa is cooking, take a large serving bowl and combine half of the lemon juice (reserving the other half), all of the lemon zest, scallions, walnut oil (you can substitute olive oil if you desire), pine nuts, and goat cheese.

3. Check the quinoa and kale when the cooking time has completed. The water should have been absorbed, the quinoa should be tender but firm, and the kale should be tender and bright green. If the quinoa still has a hard, white center, you can steam a bit longer (adding more water if needed).

4. When the quinoa and kale are done, fluff the pilaf and tip it into the waiting bowl with the remaining ingredients. As the hot quinoa hits the scallions and lemon, it should smell lovely. Toss to combine, seasoning with salt, pepper, and the remaining lemon juice if needed.

More Information

- This recipe makes three servings.
- The serving size is 344 grams, or approximately 11 ounces.
- A serving contains 320 calories, 2.0 grams of saturated fat, 170 milligrams of sodium, 605 milligrams of calcium, and 6 grams of fiber.

Reprinted, by permission, from Food52. Available: http://food52.com/recipes/2434-one-pot-kale-and-quinoa-pilaf

increased risk of osteoporosis is reported for vegetarians (*Dietary Guidelines for Americans, 2010* (2011). There is no evidence that dairy intake is necessary to protect against hip fractures, a sign of weak bones (Benetou et al. 2011). It has long been known that osteoporosis is more related to calcium retention than to calcium consumption (Willett 2005). Factors that contribute to osteoporosis include a sedentary lifestyle, lack of weight-bearing exercise (e.g., walking), smoking, and excess consumption of protein and alcohol.

Fiber

Vegetables, fruits, whole grains, and legumes are excellent sources of dietary fiber. This nondigestible plant portion offers protection against constipation, cancers of the colon and rectum, heart disease, diverticulitis, and many other diseases (Nedeltcheva et al. 2009). Two main types of fiber exist: insoluble and soluble. Insoluble fibers, such as wheat bran and cellulose, add bulk to the stool and speed the removal of toxic

Major Food Groups: Fantasy Fibers

A fiber free-for-all is going on across the United States (Liebman 2008). Major food industries are tripping all over themselves getting into the fad with fiber-fortified yogurt, ice cream, and juice. But not all fibers are created equal. The synthetic nondigestible fiber polydextrose and the polysaccharide food additive maltodextrin may have little value in enhancing regularity or preventing disease (Liebman 2008). But consuming foods rich in soluble and insoluble fibers, such as vegetables, fruits, whole grains, beans, peas, and lentils, will make a big difference in your health.

wastes from the colon (*Dietary Guidelines for Americans, 2010* (2011). The soluble dietary fibers found in fruits, legumes vegetables, pectin, and oat bran reduce blood cholesterol levels (Theuwissen and Mensink 2008). Soluble fiber attracts water and slows digestion.

The average American dietary fiber intake was 15.9 grams in 2007–2008 (King, Mainous, and Lambourne 2012), whereas the recommended level is between 25 and 38 grams per day, depending on physical size and activity level (*Healthy People 2020* [2010]). Dietary fiber is plentiful in a number of healthy foods, but not enough of them are consumed to meet recommendations.

An average-size baked white or sweet potato provides five grams of fiber; half of the available fiber is found in the skin. A 140-calorie serving of white potatoes has roughly three grams of fiber, 50 percent of the recommended vitamin C, and 20 percent of recommended potassium (Cotton et al. 2004).

White potatoes have a high glycemic index, contributing to a disproportionate increase in blood sugar. Because of this, they have the potential to contribute to diabetes and obesity. Although people with diabetes should be careful, potatoes fit well into a wellness meal plan for most Americans. Watch out for butter, sour cream, and deep frying, which often add unnecessary fat and calories. Potatoes can be tasty on their own or with herbal seasonings. Just bake them in your oven, slow cooker, or microwave and enjoy.

Other good sources of dietary fiber include bran breakfast cereals, legumes (beans, peas, and lentils), berries, peaches, nuts, seeds, and whole-wheat bread. Fiber is readily available in apples, which have six grams; oranges, which have five grams; and in brown rice or whole-wheat bread, which have two grams of dietary fiber per serving. *Dietary Guidelines for Americans, 2010* (2011) recommends that individual food items contain at least two grams of dietary fiber for every 100 calories. Thus, a person eating 1,500 calories per day should take in 30 grams of fiber.

NUTRIENTS TO AVOID

Eating a balanced healthy diet can be challenging. You should eat more of some things and avoid other things. Clearly, your diet would benefit from including vegetables, fruits, whole grains, nuts, and seeds, as well as low-fat sources of protein and calcium-rich foods. But what about all the foods you eat that contain unhealthy amounts of sodium, sugar, trans fat, and saturated fat? These items are found in many processed foods and pose a real threat to your health.

Sodium Chloride (Salt)

Salt serves to enhance the taste of food and helps prolong the shelf life of processed foods. Little wonder then that sodium is such a popular additive. Salt is

Recipe

Quick and Easy Trail Mix

1. Trail mix such as mixed nuts, sunflower seeds, raisins, and other dried fruits makes a tasty snack full of fiber and protein.
2. Because trail mix contains a lot of calories, aim to eat a reasonable amount only one or two days per week.
3. Make your own, because commercial products are generally high in sodium and salt.

Mindfulness exercises enabled Wanda to see her food differently, and she found it hard to believe how good her food tasted. After she experienced the raisin-eating exercise and the potluck meal in class, she began setting aside the first five minutes of every meal to be present and pay attention to her food. Her food was immensely more flavorful, and she lost her craving for dessert.

made up of sodium and chloride. Ninety percent of sodium intake comes from salt (*Dietary Reference Intakes for Water, Potassium, Sodium Chloride, and Sulfate* 2005). Some sodium is essential to muscle and nerve functioning and balancing fluid levels. Adequate intake levels for sodium are set at 1,500 milligrams, which is deemed safe for all, except "highly active individuals and workers exposed to extreme heat stress" (*Dietary Guidelines for Americans, 2010* (2011, p. 23). The upper limit for sodium intake was established by the Institute of Medicine at 2,300 milligrams (*Dietary Reference Intakes for Water, Potassium, Sodium, Chloride, and Sulfate* 2005), but the average sodium intake for American adults is 3,400 milligrams per day (*What We Eat in America* 2010). Although excess sodium is not much of a concern for those who eat fresh vegetables, fruits, and legumes, it is for those who eat restaurant, packaged, and canned foods. Unfortunately, most Americans fall into this second category.

Sodium is now recognized as one of the most harmful food ingredients. It contributes to high blood pressure, stroke, heart disease, kidney damage, and even male impotence (Henney, Taylor, and Boon 2010). Too much salt weakens the walls of blood vessels and arteries (Coxson et al. 2013). According to the National Academy of Science Institute of Medicine, as many as 150,000 cardiovascular deaths could be avoided annually if packaged and restaurant foods had their sodium reduced by half (Henney, Taylor, and Boon 2010). The issue is not primarily because of the salt that people add to their food. Approximately 80 percent of dietary sodium comes from canned, processed, and restaurant-prepared foods (Mattes and Donnelly 1991). Taste buds can adapt to a reduced salt intake in 10 to 14 days.

You can decrease sodium by eating restaurant food less frequently, by eliminating high-sodium canned and packaged foods, and by eating 8 to 11 servings of fresh vegetables and fruits per day (Sacks et al. 2001). Sodium-free breads such as Ezekiel 4:9 Low Sodium Whole Grain Bread are tasty (Food for Life). Cook with sodium-free spices, including Mrs. Dash salt-free blends, Jane's Krazy Mixed-Up Seasonings, Original Mixed-Up Pepper, as well as fresh and dried basil and other herbs. Use salt sparingly at the table and in food preparation. Lightly sprinkling salt on the surface of

the food immediately before eating maximizes flavor enhancement while reducing total salt intake. Another strategy for cutting down on salt intake at the table is to remove the shaker from the table! Many people shake before they taste.

Sugar

Americans consume lots of added sugar. In fact, as a nation we consume 10,000 tons of added sugar annually, some 23 teaspoons per person per day (*What*

FIGURE 7.3 Pepsi is one of many examples of sugar-sweetened soft drinks. According to the nutrition information label on a Pepsi can, 12 ounces (360 ml) of the drink contains 150 calories. All calories are from different forms of sugar. One soda a day for a year equals 15.6 pounds (7.1 kg) of weight (3,500 calories per pound; 365 days multiplied by 150 calories = 54,750 calories in a year; 54,750 divided by 3,500 = 15.6 pounds).

Class Discussion: Sugar Addiction

Sugar is by far the most socially accepted addictive substance. Its use is far less ridiculed by society than is the use of hard drugs, marijuana, or alcohol. Something does not need to be classified as a drug to be addictive. Perhaps that's one reason for its popularity.

1. But overall, which of these addictions is really the more deadly or costly, from both a personal and societal perspective? There are no right or wrong answers—just your opinion.
2. What is your personal experience? What is the experience of your friends?

We Eat in America 2010), representing a significant percentage of the total daily caloric intake for women and men (Marriott et al. 2010). Nearly one in five young adults consumes more than 25 percent of total caloric intake from added sugar. For this group, 60 percent of the added sugars come from sugar-sweetened beverages, such as soft drinks, also known as liquid candy (Marriott et al. 2010) (see figure 7.3). But sugar is also added to breakfast cereals, baked goods, candy bars, ice cream, ketchup, salad dressing, fast foods, pasta sauce, potato chips, pizza, toothpaste, mouthwash, chewing gum, and even cough suppressants. We are wolfing down sugar both consciously and unconsciously.

Sugar fuels every cell in the brain and influences brain chemicals. But in excess, sugar mediates enormous physiologic and behavioral problems. People who regularly consume sugar-sweetened beverages have higher levels of heart disease, stroke (de Koning et al. 2012), gout (Choi, Willett, and Curhan 2010), diabetes, obesity (Schulze et al. 2004), and an increased incidence of **metabolic syndrome** (Malik et al. 2010), compared with those who consume less. Metabolic syndrome is defined as having at least three out of the five following medical conditions: abdominal obesity, elevated blood pressure, elevated fasting blood sugar, high triglycerides (blood fats), and low HDL (healthy) cholesterol levels. In a word, added sugar and sugar-sweetened beverages are killing us.

High doses of sugar alter brain receptors and interfere with the mechanisms that regulate food cravings and the amount of food that you eat (Kelley et al. 2002). Scientists are not quite ready to lump sugar in with heroin, although they are currently advising treatment and prevention methods similar to those used for drug addictions (Gearhardt et al. 2011). More on this will be addressed in the chapter on addictions. Simply put, sugar is a powerful drug, and many of us are abusing it.

How much you should be eating is different from how much you are eating. The American Heart Association recommends that no more than 5 percent of total calories come from added sugar, that is, no more than 100 calories daily for women and 150 calories for men, or six to nine teaspoons, respectively (Johnson et al. 2009). Sugary treats should be reserved for special celebrations rather than being indulged in on a daily basis.

Eating a 100-calorie serving of cookies is a case in point. You can eat just one cookie or mindlessly gobble the whole snack pack of 15 cream-centered Oreos. You undoubtedly will still be hungry if you mindlessly devour the single 100-calorie cookie, but mindfully savoring this cookie as a treat can provide a satisfying experience. Your goal is to regain control of the eating process. Instead of eating while talking, reading, studying, working at the computer, or driving, begin to reclaim a pleasurable experience that can add quality to your life.

Liquid Candy

Sugary beverages or those containing high-fructose corn syrup add innumerable calories to the American diet, in part because people do not seem to be able to register and compensate for all those extra liquid calories; they fly under the radar, so to speak. To make matters worse, an insulin spike from all the sugar provokes a paradoxical drop in blood glucose, which may increase hunger. Fructose-containing beverages may not stimulate satiety, or the high palatability of the taste may override satiety (*CDC Guide to Strategies for Reducing the Consumption of Sugar-Sweetened Beverages* 2014). The result is that people gain weight when they regularly drink such liquid calories.

Pervasive Fat

The typical American diet is high in cholesterol, saturated fat, and trans fat. Fat can be solid at room temperature, such as animal fat, or liquid at room temperature, such as vegetable oil. An extra tablespoon of fat consumed on a daily basis represents 12.4 pounds (5.6 kg) of extra fat in a year! That figure may seem overstated, but look at the calories. A tablespoon of fat has 119 calories (*National Nutrient Database for Standard Reference Release* 26 2010). Multiply that by the number of days in a year (119 multiplied by 365 days = 43,435 calories; 43,435 divided by the number of calories in a pound of fat, which is 3,500 = 12.4 pounds). Fat contributes to appetite stimulation (Rolls 2007) and is the most concentrated form of energy that you eat, containing nine calories per gram. Saturated fat and cholesterol come primarily from animal and dairy products. Because fat is highly palatable and less expensive, it can easily become prevalent in the diet. Fat also stores toxins from the host. A bioaccumulation in fish can have a deleterious effect on the developing fetus in pregnant women.

Fat contributes significantly to taste, as many recognize, and if used judiciously it can heighten the taste of meals. Humans probably evolved to love fat because it helped people survive in times of food scarcity. Those who ate large quantities of fat in early times were more likely to survive a famine and propagate the species. But today your love of fat is endangering your survival by contributing to obesity. Extra fat calories can make you fat, and fat can be fatal.

For good health and weight management, keep total fat to less than 20 percent of total calories. Dr. Barbara Rolls (2007) at the University of Pennsylvania has demonstrated that reduced caloric density is associated with improved body-weight regulation. By eating foods with modest caloric density, you can actually eat a greater quantity of food. A simple memory aid is this: Foods should have two or fewer grams of fat per 100 calories. Keep in mind that fat intake can be achieved as an average across all food eaten in a day. Some foods might have 25 percent of their calories from fat, whereas others might have only 15 percent from fat.

Trans fat is the most dangerous fat of all. The current recommendation is to limit trans fat to two grams or less per day (*What We Eat in America* 2010). Trans fat has been chemically altered (partially hydrogenated) to add shelf life to a product. Products with partially hydrogenated vegetable oil on the label (like Crisco) contain trans fat. A new formulation of Crisco has less trans fats but still has questionable health values in that this new product has been shown to increase blood glucose and to reduce insulin (Brandeis University 2007). In spite of the available information about the ill effects, people still use Crisco with trans-fat and saturated-fat-dense lard for cooking (Shields 2010).

Trans fat is much more harmful than saturated fat

per gram (*Healthy People 2020*[2010]). A two percent increase in energy intake from trans fat represents a 23 percent increase in cardiovascular disease (Remig et al. 2010). Curiously, this partial hydrogenation shortens your life while adding to the shelf life of products. Not a good exchange! Hard margarines (solid at room temperature), baked goods, and candies are commonly made using trans fat. Fortunately, trans fat is now becoming less prevalent in the American diet.

Americans can reduce half of their average 31 grams of daily saturated fat intake by eliminating five artery-clogging foods from their diets, namely beef, cheese, whole and 2 percent milk, baked goods, and butter and margarine (Subar et al. 1998). Tasty, saturated-fat-free alternatives exist. Making these changes would reduce consumption of saturated fat to within the recommended daily allowances.

Fortunately, not all fat is created equal. Some fat is good. Monounsaturated oils, containing omega-3 fatty acids, commonly found in cold-water fish and flaxseed oil, have health-protective effects (Lloyd-Jones et al. 2010). A staple of the heart-healthy Mediterranean diet is **monounsaturated fat**, found in olive oil and canola oil. Use a flavorful extra-virgin olive oil in salads and in spreads, but avoid olive oil when preparing stir-fry because of its low flash point. Olive oil burns easily and loses its healthy properties. Canola oil contains omega-3 fatty acids and has a higher flash point, allowing it to be used more safely in stir-fry dishes.

Because of the omega-3 fat content of seafood, an American Heart Association Scientific Statement recommends eating two servings of fish, particularly fatty fish, weekly (Kris-Etherton, Harris, and Appel 2002). The evidence is reasonably solid that fatty cold-water fish, such as salmon, has many health benefits. Fish may help memory and mental function (Morris et al. 2005), act as an anti-inflammatory (Maroon and Bost 2006), and protect against heart disease (He et al. 2004), heart failure (Djoussé et al. 2012), cancer (Norat et al. 2005), and eye disease (San Giovanni et al. 200). The evidence is far less clear that omega-3 supplements will have the same benefits.

Cholesterol is technically not a fat, but it is found only in animal and dairy products, often associated with saturated fat. Cholesterol never occurs in plant-based foods. Your body makes all the cholesterol you will ever need, so you have no reason to consume cholesterol. Nevertheless, the intake of saturated fat and trans fat is what really elevates blood cholesterol levels. Many high-cholesterol foods, such as egg yolks and shrimp, are now thought to be safe to eat in moderation.

Finally, a word about low-fat processed foods. Unfortunately, food manufacturers have often substituted sugar or carbohydrate for fat to keep their products tasty. The description "low fat" is now used to advertise many products that will make you fat because they are loaded with sugar and calories. Thus, people consume ever more low-fat food, thinking that it is good for them when in fact it's not! Always read the label to see what is actually in the food.

SAVVY FOOD SHOPPING

Grocery shopping is one of your most important lifestyle tasks. Indeed, your survival may depend on it. Shopping for healthy foods and mindfully reading labels requires an initial time commitment. Changing the way that you shop is a worthwhile investment of your time, and once you are familiar with the selections, the time required diminishes. Remember that a few staples go a long way. Purchase foods without labels, because that omission suggests that the food has not been processed. Fresh fruits and vegetables can become the centerpiece of most meals. Whole grains, beans, peas, and lentils are available at supermarkets and in bulk at health food stores. Whole food and organically grown food selections are becoming increasingly available.

Remember that everything you place in your food-shopping cart will end up inside you. As university students, you are undoubtedly hard pressed for time. This section addresses some other potentially problematic choices such as liquid meal substitutes, heat-and-serve dinners, and the use of dietary supplements.

Label Reading

Food labels make the shopping process easier (see figure 7.4). Key items to read on the label are the number of servings per container, total calories per serving, grams of saturated fat and trans fat, milligrams of cholesterol, milligrams of sodium, grams of total carbohydrate, grams of dietary fiber, grams of sugar, and grams of protein. The total calorie intake posted on the labels, 2,000 and 2,500 calories, is probably higher than your caloric needs. With regard to total fat, saturated fat, sodium, and so on, lower values are better. Limit total fat to less than 20 percent of total calories, limit saturated fat to 10 grams per day (half of the USDA recommendation), and avoid all trans fat. Make sure that no partially hydrogenated oils are listed in the ingredients, because that ingredient is code for trans fat. Consume no more than 1 milligram of sodium per calorie consumed daily (1,500 milligrams daily) and aim for at least two grams of dietary fiber per 100 calories.

For a person consuming 1,500 calories in a day, this recommendation translates into 30 grams of total fat,

Nutrition Facts

8 servings per container

Serving size 2/3 cup (55g)

Amount per 2/3 cup

Calories 230

% DV*	
12%	**Total Fat** 8g
5%	Saturated Fat 1g
	Trans Fat 0g
0%	**Cholesterol** 0mg
7%	**Sodium** 160mg
12%	**Total Carbs** 37g
14%	Dietary Fiber 4g
	Sugars 1g
	Added Sugars 0g
	Protein 3g
10%	Vitamin D 2mcg
20%	Calcium 260mg
45%	Iron 8mg
5%	Potassium 235mg

* Footnote on Daily Values (DV) and calories reference to be inserted here.

FIGURE 7.4 The proposed updated FDA nutrition facts food label that may be adopted 2015.

From Nutrition Facts Label Programs & Materials. U.S. Food and Drug Administration. Available: http://www.fda.gov/Food/IngredientsPackagingLabeling/LabelingNutrition/ucm20026097.htm

10 grams of saturated fat, 0 grams of trans fat, 1,500 milligrams of sodium, and at least 30 grams of dietary fiber. These values are all consistent with *Dietary Guidelines for Americans, 2010* (2011). When evaluating a food, determine total fat as well as saturated fat and trans fat. Look for partially hydrogenated oils in the ingredients, which pose a significant risk for heart disease. Note that if the serving provides less than a half gram of trans fat, the label can legally read zero for trans fat! Thus, you may eat trans fat without realizing it, because the lower amount is not required to be on the label. This point isn't trivial. Because the threshold for trans-fat intake is less than 2 grams per day, if you were to consume six different foods with .4 grams of trans fat, you would have exceeded the recommended level for that day. Check the ingredients; if they include partially hydrogenated oils, trans fat is in the product.

You should eliminate as much fat from your diet as you can. Here are a few strategies. When baking cakes and cookies, substitute applesauce for oil. The applesauce provides moisture and has only a fraction of the calories. When preparing a stir-fry, experiment with sauteing in water. Herbs and spices go a long way in providing flavor. For any recipe requiring oil, consider using olive oil or canola oil. These monounsaturated oils will not raise LDL (bad) cholesterol and may raise the HDL (good) cholesterol. Grill or bake fish without adding butter.

Fresh Is Best

Luscious locally grown fruits and vegetables should be central to your wellness food plan, especially in summer. Local farms provide mouth-watering fresh produce. The colors, textures, and fragrance are an experience in and of themselves. Local fruit ripens on the vine, keeping food sweet and authentic tasting. Farmers' markets provide a vast array of beautiful and flavorful produce, and the costs to consumers can be less. One study demonstrated a 37 percent lower cost for locally grown fruits and vegetables available at farmers' markets as compared with supermarkets (Lee et al. 2010). But local produce may not always cost less than produce sold at the supermarket, which benefits from economies of scale.

Price is but one component of the total cost of any food. Farmers' markets stimulate the local economy, preserve farmland, promote local jobs, and are less burdensome to the physical environment. For example, food in the United States typically travels from 1,500 to 2,500 miles (2,400 to 4,000 km) from farm to the dinner table (Halweil 2002). Transportation uses energy for shipping and refrigeration. In contrast, locally grown produce reduces shipping cost and requires less fertilizer use. Local supermarket managers are often receptive to customer requests to stock local produce. Being a "locavore" sends a message to local farmers that you value their efforts and products. You can help small local farms in their struggle to survive.

The global food supply chain makes fresh vegetables and fruits readily available year round, but recognize that this convenience comes with a heavy environmental cost. Frozen and canned vegetables, fruits, and beans have fine nutritional properties and can stand in for more expensive imports. The only downside is that salt and sugar tend to be used in processing canned items. Both increase your appetite. Rinsing with water before use will reduce the sodium and calorie content.

Liquid Food

Solid foods are more satisfying than liquid foods (Mourao et al. 2007). Liquid meal replacements may seem like a good idea given their convenience and advertised nutrient content, but people tend to overconsume them. When people consume watermelon versus watermelon juice, cheese versus milk, or coconut meat versus coconut milk, they can better regulate their caloric intake. In fact, people consume 12 percent more calories with watermelon juice, 15 percent more with milk, and 19 percent more with coconut milk (Mourao et al. 2007). Likewise, whole fruit is more satisfying than fruit juice or fruit puree (Bolton, Heaton, and Burroughs 1981). When you consume liquids you simply need more calories to feel full. A fruit and vegetable smoothie is less harmful than a soda pop, but the calories of such beverages can add up. People consume fewer calories when drinking water or a calorie-free beverage with a meal, compared with having the meal with a caloric beverage (Dellavalle, Roe, and Rolls 2005). When you drink a 150-calorie soda pop with your dinner, you don't compensate for these liquid calories; that is, you eat all your normal calories in addition to the 150-calorie soft drink (Tate et al. 2012).

Supplements

A healthful diet is the preferred source for vitamins and minerals. Supplements never make up for a deficient diet. Industry marketing has an established record of touting the substantial benefits of vitamins and mineral supplements, without much evidence to support the claims (Neuhouser et al. 2009). In fact, increasing evidence shows that relying on vitamins and supplements for nutrition may increase mortality rather than decrease it (Mursu et al. 2011). But not all the literature agrees. For example, Gaziano et al. (2012) demonstrated a modest protective effect for cancer among older men who took a one-a-day multiple vitamin and mineral supplement.

The common wisdom is that a one-a-day supplement vitamin provides nutritional insurance for about 10 cents per day. But until the controversy associated with multivitamins is sorted out, you should try to achieve your nutrition through good food rather than trying to compensate through pills. People make various choices about whether to use supplements and which supplements to take. Certain situations such as pregnancy, strict vegan diets (in which B_{12} supplements are useful), vitamin D deficiency, or severe caloric restriction can justify the temporary use of supplements. Supplements are not regulated by the Food and Drug Administration, and nutrient competition may affect absorption. Supplements provide a false sense of security, which can inadvertently promote poor dietary habits.

To conclude, eating well is far more effective than

Activity

Refrigerator and Kitchen Pantry Self-Evaluation

After reading this section, examine your refrigerator and cupboard for 10 foods that you usually eat.

1. How many green leafy vegetables are in your refrigerator?

2. Examine the labels on canned and other packaged foods:

   • How much sodium and dietary fiber is in each serving?

   • What percentage of the total calories is from fat? The percentage from fat helps determine caloric density. A gram of fat contains nine calories.

   • How much saturated fat and trans fat are in the product? Remember that no trans fat is the goal.

   • Do any foods list zero grams of trans fat but include partially hydrogenated oil?

3. Write a 250-word summary of your findings and post it to your journal.

---

augmenting a mediocre diet with a supplement. Instead, you should supplement your diet with green leafy vegetables, broccoli, cauliflower, cabbage and other cruciferous vegetables, fruit, and whole-grain products. A healthy diet usually provides all the vitamins you need.

Eating healthy does not necessarily cost more. You can use more dried beans, legumes, and brown rice; purchase fruits and vegetables on sale; frozen and canned foods have a long shelf life (beware of the added sodium); plant a vegetable garden in the yard; or even grow tomatoes in a planter on the porch or in a south-facing window. Many communities now permit public gardens on underutilized community property. Growing your own produce provides better appreciation for wholesome, pesticide-free foods. If you are just starting a garden, try kale, leaf lettuce, and tomatoes, which are easy to grow.

MAKING A WELLNESS EATING PLAN WORK FOR YOU

Given the fast pace of life of the 21st century, you might think that eating well is going to be impossible, especially if you want to have a life and go to school. Admittedly, eating well will initially take a bit more time. You will need to alter certain habits. Looking at ingredients and reading labels will take more time, but using some shortcuts will make your life richer and easier. The next section reviews convenience, food preparation, flavor and taste, eating smaller amounts more often, healthy snacks, and selecting restaurant foods.

Convenience

You are more likely to engage in activities that are attractive and immediately available. Convenience appeals to everyone. If you can do something without going out of your way, you are likely to make it happen (Sallis, Owen, and Fisher 2008). By contrast, if you have to go out of your way to do something, it is less likely to occur.

Make healthy eating convenient by having healthy food choices available everywhere for snacks and meals. This way, you are less likely to grab unhealthy alternatives! Make a habit of placing cut-up vegetables and fruits in the refrigerator, on your desk at work, in your lunch box, and around the house. These convenience strategies increase the likelihood of consumption and decrease the likelihood of eating something that would be high in calories, like candy or chips.

Most supermarkets have plenty of attractive fruits and vegetables. You may need to pay a little extra for the convenience of prepared items and bagged salads. Celery sticks are great. You can cut up apples, pears, watermelon, and cantaloupe. Leave a salad base prepped and visible in a clear container in a prominent place in the refrigerator. If apples and baby carrots are located in the crisper drawer at the bottom of the refrigerator, you are less likely to see and grab them for a snack.

Meals prepared in advance can be warmed up later when you don't have time to cook. Similarly, the slow cooker is a forgotten wonder, right up there with the microwave oven. You can use a slow cooker to prepare soups and create one-pot meals.

Supermarkets now offer a wide variety of healthy frozen foods. Plenty of vegetables are typically avail-

Recipe

Baked Potatoes

1. Scrub russet or sweet potatoes well and remove any bad areas.
2. Puncture the skin of the potato to a depth of 1/4 inch (6 mm) with a fork or knife.
3. Place potatoes in the microwave or in a convection oven. Microwave cooking time varies from 6 to 15 minutes. Oven time at 450 degrees Fahrenheit (232 degrees Celsius) will be around an hour.

More Information

- Baking potatoes properly takes some experimentation because baking time varies depending on the size (for both microwave and convection ovens) and the number (for microwave ovens) of the potatoes.
- If you use a convection oven, you can use the waiting time to work out, relax, study, do a mindful body scan, take a nap (set an alarm), or work around the house.
- You should easily be able to penetrate a sweet potato with a fork when it is done.
- A russet potato should no longer be firm to a squeeze.
- A baked potato can be the foundation for a salad, chili, or a soup.
- Sweet potatoes may be kept in the refrigerator to include later in a smoothie.

---

able, some of which are already chopped up and ready to saute or bake with a little olive oil and seasoning. No chopping, no mess. Frozen whole fruit is convenient for smoothies. A wide array of low- or no-sodium canned and frozen vegetables and fruits are available. Vegetables frozen before shipping have been found to be even more nutritious than some fresh, nonfrozen choices.

Food Preparation

Cooking healthy foods often requires less time than traveling to a local fast-food restaurant. Wellness foods do not require any more preparation time than that required to cook fattening, unhealthy foods. For example, vegetable stir-fry dishes can be prepared quickly using fresh or frozen vegetables. Rice can be cooked and then frozen in zip-lock bags. Beans and legumes can be cooked during the weekend and then frozen and thawed as needed.

The optimal wellness food plan relies on herbs and spices for flavoring, as opposed to flavoring created by adding unnecessary calories from fat, sugar, and oil. Fresh garlic, celery, onion, herbs, ginger, and other spices are excellent flavor enhancers. Salt doesn't add calories, but it stimulates appetite so that you eat more (Moss 2013). Sauteing vegetables in water eliminates the need for oils. Using a cast-iron skillet slightly increases the amount of iron available to the body, although most people who eat red meat already have more than enough (de Oliveira et al. 2012).

If you are accustomed to meat as an ingredient in spaghetti sauce, cook the meat first and then rinse under water to eliminate unnecessary calories. This method helps to maintain both the appearance and the flavor of the spaghetti sauce. Remember that people eat with their eyes and their noses. Appetizing foods take the extra fat out, but leave the fancy in.

Rice cookers may be, as the saying goes, "the best thing since sliced bread!" They are inexpensive and make your life much easier. Place brown rice or quinoa in the cooker with one more cup of water than the number of cups of dry grain (three cups of water for two cups of rice or quinoa). After you turn on the rice cooker, you can go about whatever else you need to do. When the rice is finished, the cooker keeps it warm for hours.

Arsenic contamination has been a problem in American-grown rice, so you may want to consume fewer than one and a half servings of rice per week ("Arsenic in Your Food" 2012). Refer to the sidebar "Arsenic Contamination" for additional information. Quinoa is a safer alternative.

Flavor and Taste

Flavor is another important dimension of healthy eating. People won't change their eating habits for the better unless they have quick, easy, and flavorful options. Americans characteristically season their meals with salt, sugar, fat, and oil, all of which add

© Elke Dennis - Fotolia

Selecting wholesome and nutritious food is the first step. The second step is to prepare it in healthy ways to enhance flavor while still providing the healthy meal you envisioned.

unneeded calories, making the food less healthy and overstimulating the appetite.

People in many other cultures use herbs and spice as their primary sources of seasoning, and as a result they do not experience these ill effects. For best results, herbs and spices should be fresh. Place a date on dried spices when purchased and discard after 12 months, before they lose their flavor. When used to replace salt, herbs and spices should be increased by 25 percent or more. Finally, to maximize flavor, at least a fourth of the seasoning should be added within the last few minutes of cooking, particularly with long-cooking dishes.

Making a Wellness Eating Plan Work for You: Arsenic Contamination

Consumer Reports has published analyses of arsenic in juice ("Arsenic in Your Juice" 2012) and rice ("Arsenic in Your Food" 2012). Research has shown that arsenic is associated with cardiovascular disease as well as lung and bladder cancer (Yuan et al. 2007). Rice grown in the United States is likely contaminated by arsenic residual to the soil. Arsenic was used in cotton growing to control the boll weevil, and rice is now grown in those same soils. Adults who reported consuming one and two or more servings of rice on the day before testing had arsenic levels that were 44 percent and 70 percent higher, respectively, compared with those who did not consume rice ("Arsenic in Your Food" 2012).

Many express dismay about the arsenic contamination of rice. Although the contamination of this staple food is unacceptable, the good news is that future changes in food production may mitigate the problem. Remember that plant-based diets, including rice, even with some contaminants, are still more nutritious and less harmful than the more prevalent meat- and cheese-based American diet (McDougall and McDougall 2012). Insecticides, pesticides and other toxins are consumed by food animals and become concentrated in their fat. Animal and dairy products lack dietary fiber and are sources of saturated fat and cholesterol, which significantly contribute to cardiovascular disease and stroke, the major causes of death in the United States and elsewhere.

Eat Smaller Meals More Often

Skipping meals is a perceived strategy for weight loss and a by-product of America's fast-paced lifestyle. Twenty-four percent of young adults regularly skip breakfast (Deshmukh-Taskar et al. 2013), but people who regularly eat breakfast are significantly more likely to have normal blood pressure and a favorable cardiovascular lipid profile (Deshmukh-Taskar et al. 2013). The National Weight Loss Registry shows those who successfully maintained weight loss of 10% of their initial body weight were more likely to regularly eat breakfast (Wing and Phelan 2005). Skipping meals may make you more likely to gain weight (Farshchi, Taylor, and Macdonald 2005). The resultant hunger may trigger overeating at the next meal or the consumption of high-calorie snacks.

Grazing may be the best strategy. People who consume food throughout the day appear to have lower blood pressure, cholesterol, and weight, even when the composition and calories of the foods they eat are identical (Bhutani and Varady 2009). The challenge is to avoid overeating. You should not graze through the day in addition to eating your three regular meals! The health and weight-control benefits of grazing, indeed any food intake pattern, result from *not* increasing total caloric intake.

Healthy Snacks

Fruit is an excellent snack. It is sweet and can be eaten often. Vegetables cut up and kept on hand are also quick and easy. Other good snacks include air-popped popcorn, salt-free whole-grain pretzels and bagels, baked potatoes, and corn chips.

Processed sweets and treats can fit into a balanced diet, but they should be limited to three servings per week. Remember that a daily 250-calorie candy bar or soft drink represents 26 pounds (11.8 kg) of extra weight consumed in a year! (Calculation: 250 multiplied by 365 days = 91,250 calories. Divide by 3,500 calories in a pound of fat = 26.07 pounds). The average person would need to walk an extra 3 miles (4.8 kg) a day to burn that many extra calories. Of course, you may not gain 25 pounds by eating a daily candy bar because you may well compensate for the calories elsewhere. But for a 1,500-calorie diet, a single candy bar represents one-sixth of the daily caloric intake!

Depending on your health, sugar- or fat-containing treats in moderation are acceptable. A few bites of dark chocolate can be one of life's little pleasures. As long as the treat is calculated into your overall caloric intake, there is no problem. Still, you must exercise caution and consume treats sparingly.

Recipe

Kenyan Café Organic Beans and Kale

1 teaspoon olive oil

10 ounces (280 g) red onions, chopped

1 clove garlic, minced

8 ounces (230 g) mixed peppers, chopped

1 tomato diced

15-ounce (420 g) can organic black beans, washed and drained

16 ounces (450 g) kale, chopped (can use cabbage)

1 teaspoon curry powder

1. Heat oil in a stockpot over medium-high heat.

2. Add onion and garlic. Saute onions until translucent, about 4 minutes.

3. Add peppers, tomato, beans, kale, and curry powder. Cook 3 to 5 minutes or until kale is tender. Serve on a bed of cooked brown rice, ugali (cornmeal cooked to porridgelike consistency), quinoa, or bulgur wheat.

More Information

- This recipe makes six 2-cup servings.
- A serving contains 210 calories, 0 grams of saturated fat, 390 milligrams of sodium, and 11 grams of fiber.

Reprinted, by permission, from Kenyan Café, Morgantown, WV.

Activity

Food Logs

A good way to get in touch with your food consumption is to record what you eat and your relative level of mindfulness. Identifying a problem is difficult without data.

1. Enter into your daily calendar the type and quantity of food that you eat.
2. Give yourself a mindfulness score of 0 to 10 regarding your eating attentiveness, with 0 representing total distraction (such as watching television, reading the newspaper, driving, or studying) and 10 representing your highest level of mindfulness.
3. Keep track of your food intake for one week, giving you at least 21 data points for your food intake and mindfulness.
4. Keep track of your snacks.
5. In 250 words, summarize the experience for the week and post to your wellness journal. Did your pleasure quotient increase regarding your food intake?
6. Subjectively, did you eat the same as, more than, or less than normal?
7. Enter your food log and summary statement into your Chapter 7 journal.

The original participants in Dean Ornish's (1990) Lifestyle Trial had problems with the over consumption of fat-free cookies, cakes, and pastries. Treats marketed and labeled as healthy can have absolutely no fat or oil yet be loaded with calories from simple sugar.

In addition, new synthetic fats such as olestra have few if any calories, but research indicates they can leach precious fat-soluble vitamins and minerals from the intestines and, in excess, are likely to cause stomach cramping and diarrhea (Thomson, Hunt, and Zorich 1998). Procter & Gamble (P&G) markets olestra under the brand name Olean.

At least one research team concluded that the more favorable scientific reviews of olestra were written by researchers who had a financial relationship with P&G (Levine et al. 2003). Unfortunately, this kind of scientific bias is an all too common practice among industry consultants. Scientific journals now require scientists to disclose whether they have any competing interests that could influence their research.

Restaurant and Fast Food

Eating outside the home is fun and a big part of social life. It's rewarding and promotes camaraderie. But it's also an expensive way of satisfying your hunger. The other drawback is that dining out involves huge portions of unhealthy food. But you do not need to give up dining out. Instead, transform the experience by making it a special and less frequent event. In any community, you should be able to find two or three restaurants able to meet your nutritional needs. Patronize these establishments and establish client loyalty.

Your first contact with any restaurant is usually through the server, although you may also want to speak with the chef. Work with the staff to determine how the food is prepared, especially the use of salt, saturated fat, and trans fat. Explain your situation. Let the server and cook know that you are trying to eat healthfully. Working with management can be a way of solving your problems. Restaurants will offer any type of food on which they can make a profit.

You can order pasta primavera with a fat-free or reduced-fat dressing for the salad. The server may be able to make suggestions. Never assume anything! Tell the staff not to add any salt or sodium. When returning to the same restaurant, repeat your guidelines and order the tried-and-true choices.

Restaurants seem to be competing for clients by serving gargantuan portions. Large portions may appear to offer good value, but it's a problem for you if you eat it all. Remember that you are not required to eat everything. Just ask for a take-home bag and immediately set aside half the meal for lunch the next day. By so doing, the food is off your plate and the visual cue to overeat is gone.

You can also solve the problem of these enormous portions by sharing your meal with a friend or partner. One entree often feeds two people. Sharing food is acceptable in many cultures. You must make the best choices when it comes to your health.

Total reformation of your diet may seem like a daunting project. Remember the motivational stages of change. Progress by the yard is hard, but inch by inch it is a cinch! This cliche has some wisdom. As with any behavior change, start with manageable steps and build gradually.

Most of us already eat some healthy foods. Adding three or four wholesome food selections to your usual meals can transform your diet (unless you are particularly ill, in which case you may need to do more). Most people repeat a limited number of meal selections throughout the week. For instance, you may eat a particular breakfast cereal daily. You may follow this with a burger for lunch and perhaps a cheese pepperoni pizza for dinner. Substituting a healthier option for any of these can make a dramatic 33 percent improvement in your overall food intake for that day.

Eating better translates into more energy, better sleep, a clearer complexion, and just feeling better overall. Your whole body will feel lighter and respond favorably, both inside and out.

Acceptance and Food

Learning about acceptance in overeating is good for everyone. Fretting or condemning yourself about overeating is not helpful. Don't aggravate the situation by judging yourself and feeling depressed. Eat mindfully and purposively. Just as you need to accept yourself when distracted, you also need to accept yourself as heavy, short, tall, or predisposed to eat more calories than your body needs, if that is the case.

You waste a lot of time and energy by not accepting yourself as you are. The key point is that if you beat up on yourself, you are more likely to feel so overwhelmed that you overeat even more (Bybee et al. 1996). The less anxious and tense you are, the more likely you are to make correct decisions (Niemeier et al. 2012). Tension becomes part of a cascade of events, which predisposes you to defeat and mindless overeating. By contrast, acceptance can lead to better decision making as you grow in touch with the person you are (Forman et al. 2009).

Overeating and being overweight is associated not just with what you are eating but also what's "eating you" inside your mind and heart. This short section may well be the most important one of the chapter. Thich Nhat Hanh, the well-known contemporary Buddhist monk, wrote an entire volume, *Savor*, focused on mindful eating (Hanh and Cheung 2010). You want to eat with more pleasure and gusto, not to deny or accuse

© EastWest Imaging -Fotolia

Go ahead, enjoy your food! Yes, you should try to keep it healthy most of the time, but it is not the end of the world if you occasionally indulge in "sometimes" foods.

yourself. Try to savor each bite as if you were tasting that food for the first time. You need to be present in the moment, right here, right now, with your focus on the experience of eating.

This process has the potential to transform your meals into feasts, no matter what you are eating. Mindful eating can help you stop wolfing down meals or gorging (Albers 2011). You may realize that you are consuming your food mindlessly, not thinking about what you are eating or whether you are truly hungry. You grab something as you leave the house in the morning. You eat at your desk when at work or school. You eat in the car. You eat while watching television. You eat during meetings.

Activity

Mindful Eating

Many of us eat because of environmental cues, not because of an immediate need for food. Instead, try eating mindfully for just five minutes daily. This eating meditation will encompass the first five minutes of your next three meals.

1. After you have your food in front of you, take the first five minutes to be mindful.
2. Remember the STOP mindfulness strategy:
   - Stop.
   - Take three long, slow, deep breaths.
   - Observe what you are experiencing.
   - Proceed with the five-minute mindful eating.
3. Before placing a bite of food into your mouth, view it with all the nonjudgmental attention you can muster.
4. Can you notice new dimensions of the appearance or the aroma?
5. Mindfully move your utensil to your mouth so that you can feel and taste the food, as if for the first time.
6. Spend time with the first bite as if it is the only food that you have on a camping trip. If this were your only bite, imagine how you would focus on it.
7. Be patient. You typically move your food to your mouth and quickly dispatch it.
8. Patience, patience, patience! Stay with the bite of food in your mouth for a full minute, without looking at the clock.
9. You learn the subtleties of food only by spending time with it. Appreciate the food as if it is the best poem you have ever read, the best song you have ever heard, or the most brilliant sunset you have ever seen.
10. After you have done the five-minute mindful eating exercise, continue with your meal, remaining attentive throughout the eating process.

Mindful Eating Written Assignment

1. Express your three-meal mindful eating experience in 250 words.
2. Describe the many dimensions of the five-minute mindful eating exercise as well as what transpired as you ate the remaining food of the meal.
3. Did you enjoy the five-minute segment more than the rest of the meal? Was the rest of the meal different from other meals?
4. Share your written description with one other person.
5. Write a 100-word summary of how the two of you had similar or different experiences.
6. Enter both assignments into your wellness journal.

During a wellness course, Wanda grew in touch with how rapidly she ate. She believed that she was out of control, and she constantly struggled with a weight issue, even though she jogged for 25 minutes five days per week. She rarely took time to savor her food. As a 21-year-old undergraduate, she typically ate on the run and often grabbed a candy bar to stave off her hunger.

Wanda's life changed after she made mindful eating a regular practice. Previously, she had been an overeater. This began to change with the incremental progress she made during the semester and her ongoing commitment to live her life with a more mindful awareness. Now at age 30, she feels better than she has at any time of her life.

SUMMARY

Eating may be the most important component to your physical wellness. Eat mindfully. Taking time to appreciate the aromas, taste, and texture immeasurably enhances the pleasure of food. The optimal wellness food plan revolves around eating vegetables, fruits, whole grains, and plant protein. Cheese, chicken, beef, fish, and other meat should not be the centerpiece of the meal, but instead should be used to enhance it. Season foods with herbs and spices instead of fat, sugar, salt, and oil.

Dietary Guidelines for Americans, 2010 (2011) provides a sample plate to serve as a guide to your food intake for each meal. Vegetables and fruits should make up half the plate. Protein and grain foods make up the other half, and dairy products and a small dessert are on the side. The Omni health diet recommends 11 servings of vegetables and fruits daily.

Protein provides the building blocks (amino acids) for your body and has the ability to signal satiety. Focus on plant protein in the form of beans, peas, and lentils, and use the saturated-fat-laden animal and dairy products for flavoring, not for the center of the meal as is customary. Plant products are an overlooked source of protein.

Grains are bountiful and make up a significant percentage of calories in the American diet. Unfortunately, most of these grains are white, that is, bleached. Whole grains, such as whole-wheat bread, brown rice, and quinoa are far preferable, offering abundant vitamins, minerals, and fiber. They are digested slowly, helping to stabilize energy levels. Aim for five servings of whole grains daily.

Many myths surround the intake of calcium. Milk, preferably 1 percent or skim milk, is a good source of calcium, but so are soymilk, turnip greens, white beans, kale, and oranges. Calcium is essential for the functioning of the neural system and muscles and for bone strength.

Saturated fat, trans fat, sugar, and salt pose substantial threats to wellness. Arteries are clogged over time by excess intake of saturated fat and trans fat, leading to heart attacks and strokes. Your goal should be 0 percent trans fat (partially hydrogenated oils) in the diet.

Sugar contributes to obesity, heart disease, and diabetes. The American Heart Association recommends that sugar intake not exceed six teaspoons per day for women and nine for men. One regular 12-ounce (360 ml) soft drink alone has 10 teaspoons of sugar. Salt increases risk for high blood pressure and overeating.

You can take many actions to manage your wellness food plan. Make a grocery list and read the labels. Eat wisely in restaurants and avoid all-you-can-eat buffets.

Make dietary changes happen incrementally. If you are drinking whole or 2 percent milk, switch to 1 percent. After adjusting to that, changing to skim milk will be much easier. Your tastes adapt quickly. Food can be addictive. Living in balance can help you avoid attempting to fulfil your emotional needs by eating, which puts you at risk for **food addiction**. Be mindful and savor your life and your food.

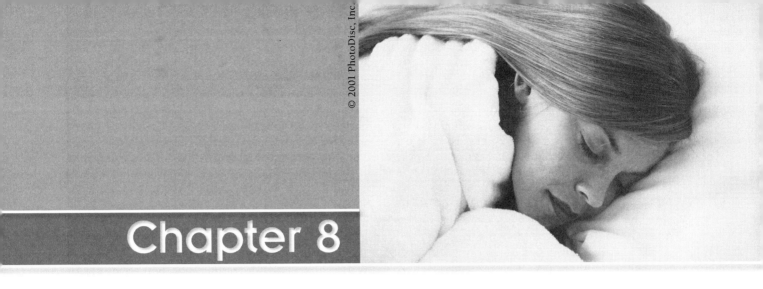

Chapter 8

Sleep Balance

Objectives

After reading this chapter, you will be able to

- define the outcomes of sufficient sleep,
- list two outcomes of sleep deprivation and irregular sleep patterns,
- list three causes of insomnia,
- develop two plans for improving sleep in their life,
- observe whether the implemented sleep practices improve the quality and quantity of their sleep, and
- modify sleep practices based on their own observations.

Sunjay enjoyed his tough academic career as an electrical engineering major. He worked hard and carried a 3.45 grade-point average at the end of his junior year. Although getting a good night of sleep had been a lifelong challenge, he managed.

Unfortunately, a strange convergence of events happened just before his final exams in the fall term. His relationship with his girlfriend deteriorated, and he was challenged in preparing for a particularly difficult exam. During the three days before the exam, his sleep became more fitful than ever. He attempted to study but was aware that the material was not registering. He could not remember what he had just reviewed. When he tried to sleep, he simply could not.

Although he did not usually consume caffeine, he drank coffee in an attempt to concentrate but became jittery. His four-hour final was a disaster. He was barely able to concentrate and earned a D. Before this exam, his lowest grade had been a B.

Adequate sleep keeps your life in balance. After a night's rest, you have more energy, think clearly, and feel at peace. Petty annoyances and the challenges of life are manageable. You are able to learn cognitive material and perform physical tasks well. You can concentrate on the task at hand, be that studying, listening to music, interacting with others, or going for a drive. Your mood improves. Relationships flow smoothly, and you are able to accept the perspectives and behaviors of others without judging.

Even when surrounded by an imperfect world, your perspective remains peaceful, compared with your outlook when you are sleep deprived. Sleep helps store memories. According to the National Sleep Foundation, your sleep is sufficient if it is "followed by a spontaneous awakening and leaves one feeling refreshed and alert for the day" (*How Much Sleep Do Adults Need?* 2014, p. 1).

More is known about sleep deprivation than sleep excess. Insufficient sleep makes you feel tired and unable to perform well. As many as 47 million Americans are sleep deprived (*Adult Sleep Habits* 2002). Substantial individual variation exists in the amount of sleep that people need. Even so, the National Sleep Foundation recommends a full seven to eight hours of sleep daily for most adults (*How Much Sleep Do We Really Need?* 2014).

This chapter explores the wellness implications for sleep, the consequences of insufficient sleep, the causes of sleep deprivation, and strategies to improve the quality and quantity of sleep. Sleep is a critically important but often overlooked component of wellness.

SLEEP PATTERNS

Adult sleep patterns change over time. Sleep quality and quantity gradually decline from age 19 to about age 60 (Vitiello 2012). After age 60, changes in sleep are modest. Circadian rhythms, that is, the physiologic pattern shifts within the 24-hour daily period, also change with age. Younger adults tend to go to sleep later and wake later, compared with older adults (Monk 2005).

In 2013, Americans reported sleeping 6 hours and 31 minutes on workdays and 7 hours and 22 minutes on weekends (*Sleep in the Bedroom Poll* 2013). Among those reporting not getting enough sleep, 59 percent believed that lack of sleep negatively affected their work, 78 percent their social life, 84 percent their mood, and 56 percent their intimate relationship. Forty-one percent worry about work stress when they go to bed, and 35 percent are concerned about financial stress.

College students have irregular sleep schedules. Most retire between 12 midnight and 2 a.m. (Taylor

and Bramoweth 2010). Observational data suggest that the later you fall asleep, the less well you perform academically (Curcio, Ferrara, and De Gennaro 2006). Although total sleep time for college students averages about 7 hours and 30 minutes per night, at least once per week more than 70 percent of students sleep less than six hours and 43 percent sleep less than five hours (Taylor and Bramoweth 2010).

Most young adults in the United States are devoted to using technology. In the hour before bedtime, 67 percent report using their cell phones, in contrast to 36 percent of middle-aged adults and 16 percent of older adults (Gradisar et al. 2013). The use of interactive electronic devices such as cell phones, computers, and video games was associated with more difficulty falling asleep and less restorative sleep (Gradisar et al. 2013).

SLEEP FUNCTIONS

Sleep is restorative and augments memory storage. You learn better if you can sleep after studying. In a sense, your brain is recharged by sleep just as your cell phone is recharged when you plug it in. Unfortunately, both acute and chronic stress negatively affect sleep function. Worry and chronic life stress are major causes of sleep loss. Many questions exist about why people sleep and what mechanisms are involved.

An improved understanding of how sleep restoration works was achieved by studying mice at the University of Rochester. Dr. Nedergaard (2013) demonstrated that waste products built up during waking hours are flushed from the brains of mice during sleep. Cerebrospinal fluid is moved through channels in the brain by a network of specialized cells called the glymphatic system (Nedergaard 2013). This system is the equivalent of the lymphatic system for the brain. The research team observed that this system helps with the elimination of beta-amyloid, a toxic protein that accumulates in the brains of Alzheimer patients. The implications of this finding are significant for human function and disease.

Watson (2014) studied how genetics and sleep influenced depression among 1,700 adult twins. Among those with normal sleep, genetic influence was just 27 percent versus 53 percent for those sleeping five hours and 49 percent for those sleeping 10 hours (Watson 2014). Too much or too little sleep seems to activate genetic mechanisms that predispose people to depression.

SLEEP CHALLENGES

A 2011 Centers for Disease Control and Prevention report identified insufficient sleep as a public health epidemic (McKnight-Eily et al. 2011). Approximately

Rest is just as important to your health as eating nutritious food and getting enough physical activity.

35 percent of survey respondents reported that insufficient sleep detracted from their quality of life (*How Much Sleep Do Adults Need?* 2014). Chronic lack of sleep presents a challenge to everyday life. For example, 22 percent of insomniacs rated their quality of life as bad, whereas only 3 percent rated it as good (Brown 2009). Lack of sleep impairs alertness, reasoning, cognitive performance, problem solving, and ability to recall details (Fulda and Shultz 2001).

Irregular sleep patterns and sleep deficits lead to an increased incidence of driving while drowsy, traffic accidents (Ohayon et al. 2003), use of alcohol and hypnotic drugs as sleep aids, and dependence on caffeine to stay awake. Caffeinated beverages are used by 43 percent of Americans to combat sleepiness (*Caffeine and Sleep* n.d.).

Seven to nine hours of daily sleep are associated with a lower prevalence of heart disease, diabetes, stroke, obesity, and mental health problems, compared with more or less sleep (Knutson and Turek 2006). Spiegel et al. (2002) observed that sleep-restricted young adults given a flu shot had half the antibody response compared with those who had normal sleep, suggesting that lack of sleep compromises immune function.

Total sleep deprivation has a profound effect on mood and performance. But a much more common experience is chronic partial sleep loss. Many students suffer prolonged sleep deprivation because of stress—studying for final exams, finishing work projects, or dealing with difficult problems at home. Five hours of sleep per night for seven days results in subjective and psychomotor deterioration in performance, which begins on day 1 (Dinges et al. 1997). The effects are cumulative across the entire seven-day period, and they negatively affect job performance, schoolwork, and interpersonal interactions.

Insomnia is provoked by many aspects of your life. Emotional, cognitive, and physiologic factors, leading to a state of hyperarousal, interfere with your ability to fall or stay asleep (Bonnet and Arand 1997). Hyperarousal is characterized by a state of increased psychological and physiological tension marked by reduced pain tolerance, anxiety, exaggeration of startle responses, insomnia, and irritability.

Ong et al. (2012) propose a two-level arousal model that emphasizes awareness of and reaction to sleep expectations. *Primary arousal* consists of worrisome thoughts and other mental activities occurring while trying to fall or remain asleep. *Secondary arousal* consists of reaction to all the factors that are preventing sleep. The strength of your secondary reactions to sleep-deprivation determines the relative degree of charge or valence related to your thoughts about your insomnia. You consciously or unconsciously project that the next day will bring disastrous consequences, such as poor job performance, inability to learn, and compromised interpersonal relationships. This kind of reactive thinking provokes a vicious cycle that arouses you even more and further prevents you from sleeping well.

The more rigidly you hold on to particular beliefs about not sleeping, the more you become mentally and emotionally stirred up or, in medical terms, hyperaroused (Ong, Ulmer, and Manber 2012). In other words, the more you strive or try to force yourself to sleep, the more difficult sleeping can be. Thinking more in terms of mindful nonstriving is better, particularly when it comes to sleep. Lie down in a comfortable place with the awareness of going to sleep, but avoid obsessing about it. Keep your mind calm and peaceful. Let go of the preoccupations for the day.

Additional Causes of Insomnia

Many factors can interfere with the quality and quantity of sleep. Some of the out-of-balance behavioral practices that arise from not sleeping further cause a person to sleep less well. Chemicals, namely alcohol, barbiturates, amphetamines, caffeine, and tobacco, have a negative effect on sleep and rest (Garcia-Rill et al. 2009). Alcohol may enhance falling asleep, but people then sleep less well, wake up prematurely, and are less able to return to sleep. So drinking or taking pills to fall sleep often results in a long-term vicious cycle. In addition, the soundness of sleep is negatively influenced by loud noises, high and low temperatures, and the time of sleep onset.

Sleeping Pills

According to Petersen (2011) in the *Wall Street Journal*, up to 10 percent of the U.S. adult population uses a psychoactive or hypnotic drug to assist with sleep. Our society is inclined toward pharmacologic solutions to life's problems, whether or not they are in fact the best solution. Americans are overprescribed and overmedicated (Greene and Watkins 2012). The pharmaceutical industry is predisposed to developing medical and pharmaceutical solutions for every human condition (Abramson 2004). The extraordinary revenue associated with these practices negatively affects public health. Insomnia is no exception.

Sleeping pills have long been recognized as a risk factor for premature death. Kripke et al. (1979) reanalyzed a 1960 American Cancer Society survey to reveal a 50 percent increase in mortality among those who reported often taking sleep pills. Similar results were observed among adults prescribed hypnotic sleeping pills in rural Pennsylvania during a two-and-a-half-year observation period (Kripke, Langer, and Kline 2012). Increased mortality risk is also seen for the newer sleeping pills, such as eszopiclone (Lunesta),

which were supposed to be safer than the older benzodiazepines (Kripke 1979; Kripke et al. 2012). The evidence suggests that newer "improved" sleeping pills also pose increased risk for premature mortality (Belleville 2010).

Other risks of sleeping pills include retrograde amnesia, residual sleepiness, tolerance, habituation, and cognitive impairment (Kripke et al. 2012). Kripke et al. (2012) recommend therapy as an alternative to sleeping medications. Although therapy certainly has the potential to discover and address underlying mental health issues, other helpful strategies are available, as will be discussed later.

DRIVING DROWSY

Driving drowsy is a serious public health problem that is just as dangerous as driving while drunk (*Alcohol-Impaired Drivers Involved in Fatal Crashes, by Gender and State, 2007–2008* [2009]). Nearly 7 percent of all car crashes involved a drowsy driver (Tefft 2010). Although 22 percent of deadly vehicular crashes involve alcohol (*Alcohol-Impaired Drivers Involved in Fatal Crashes, by Gender and State, 2007–2008* [2009]), 17 percent of all fatal crashes involve a drowsy driver (*Drowsy Driving* 2011; Tefft 2012).

Driving drowsy is especially problematic among young adults; 50 percent of 19- to 29-year-old respondents reporting driving drowsy within the past month (*Drowsy Driving* 2011). The irregular sleep patterns of young adults undoubtedly contribute to this problem.

Driving while drowsy is pervasive. Twenty-five percent of respondents to the *2010 Traffic Safety Culture Index Survey* (2010) by the American Automobile Association Foundation reported having had difficulty keeping their eyes open while driving within the past year. Thirty-seven percent of respondents to a National Sleep Foundation survey reported falling asleep at the wheel during the past year (*Drowsy Driving* 2011). **Microsleep** episodes, that is, when a person experiences temporary sleep lasting a fraction of a second to many seconds, are not uncommon (Poudel et al. 2014). Time of day is important. More single-vehicle crashes occur between 2 p.m. and 4 p.m. and between 1 a.m. and 4 a.m. than at any other time of day (Lowden et al. 2009).

Inexperience places you at risk for driving while drowsy (Asaoka et al. 2012). You may not appreciate how much sleep deprivation affects your ability to stay awake while driving. In addition, research indicates that human beings are quite incompetent at judging exactly how sleepy they are. Subjective and objective measures of sleepiness show little concordance (Tremaine et al. 2010). Thus, you may think that you are in control and a second later find yourself off the road or careening into another vehicle.

Paradoxically, some of the enhanced engineering features of 21st-century vehicles can contribute to driving drowsy. The driver's seat of a modern car is an ideal environment for falling asleep. Drivers are comfortably enclosed in a climate-controlled compartment with humming tires and soft engine noise, similar to the white noise prescribed for sleep. Automobile interiors have dim lighting and offer access to soothing music.

Highway travel is often boring, offering minimal distractions and few unanticipated stimuli. Merging vehicles from interchanges blend seamlessly into the established highway traffic at the prevalent speed. This environment can easily lull an inexperienced driver into complacency, inattention, and drowsiness. When something unanticipated happens, your drowsiness prevents you from taking evasive action.

Tips to Staying Awake While Driving

A variety of strategies can help you avoid drowsy driving. A cup of strong coffee or a caffeinated soda will help for a while. Caffeine consumption has been demonstrated to be effective almost immediately, and it continues to work for two hours (Mets et al. 2012). Taking a 20- to 30-minute nap also revitalizes people when they are sleep deprived and drowsy (*Napping* 2014; Moore-Ede 1994). Moore-Ede's research team demonstrated that people can continue to function effectively under periods of great sleep deprivation with this strategy. A study of truck drivers in Japan also demonstrated the usefulness of napping (Asaoka et al. 2012). If you are tired, pulling off the road into a safe place and taking a nap will be beneficial. If you are unable to sleep, 20 minutes of mindfulness practice can rejuvenate you (Tang et al. 2007).

Engaging in physical activity at least every two hours is another means of keeping yourself alert. Periodically stopping the vehicle at rest stops or public areas is best. Walking around, swinging your arms, and even patting your chest and head will help revive you. You should start slowly and then increase your activity level. Increasing your heart rate brings additional oxygen to a drowsy brain. Even brief physical activity increases your energy level and lifts your mood (Bonnet and Arand 2000). Some other common strategies are unsuccessful at counteracting sleepiness. Opening a window and/or listening to music didn't reliably mitigate drowsiness while driving (Schwarz et al. 2012).

Beginning a Trip

Begin long trips only when well-rested. Some times of day are riskier than others. Adequate planning can help you avoid driving when sleep-deprived or during the night when your circadian rhythm makes you the most sleepy. You can fall asleep at any time given these circumstances. Vehicular crashes between 11:00 p.m. and 6:59 a.m. are five times more likely to involve a drowsy driver, compared with crashes between 7 a.m. and 10:59 p.m. (Tefft 2012). Even with adequate sleep, you should realize that your energy levels are lowest in the early afternoon and early morning.

Remember that no matter how much you want to arrive at a destination, no trip is worth dying over. Try not to fight your normal circadian rhythm and sleep pattern because biology often trumps will power. When you are behind the wheel and feeling sleepy, take a break. Checking into a motel makes good sense, even in midafternoon. The paramount goal is to arrive safe and alive.

METHODS TO ATTAIN SOUND SLEEP

Sleep duration and quality have both genetic and environmental components. Your genetic heritage accounts for about 31 percent to 55 percent of your sleep pattern (Heath et al. 1990; Watson et al. 2012). Altering the environment through good sleep hygiene, however, can moderate this genetic influence or change how your genes express themselves. In terms of biology, **epigenetics** is the study of how gene expression occurs without necessitating changes in the gene's actual DNA sequence. But in developmental psychiatry, epigenetics relates to the bidirectional interchange between genetics and environment. Therefore, your genetic expression is not fixed, but it can be modified to some extent. Achieving sound and regular sleep is easier if you engage in mindfulness, regular physical activity, and judicious napping, and developing a normal sleep routine. Knowing your sleep preferences and creating an environment conducive to sleep are also important.

The National Sleep Foundation (*Healthy Sleep Tips* 2011) makes the following recommendations:

- Perform 30 minutes of daily physical activity.
- Retire at the same time every night, weekends included.
- Turn off your cell phone before retiring for the night.
- Avoid e-mailing and texting for one hour before going to bed.

Sunjay had struggled with insomnia since his youth. Every night was a source of anxiety as he was unsure whether he would be able to sleep and for how long he would sleep. Consequently, he had no established sleep hygiene. He went to bed at a different time every night. His bedroom was a mess of books, research articles, and unfinished projects.

After the wellness course, Sunjay undertook a major renovation of his schedule and his apartment. He cleaned out his study materials and relocated them to his office downstairs. He realized that his mental health and his career were at stake.

- Avoid caffeine for at least six hours before going to bed.
- Sleep in a comfortable, dark, and quiet environment.
- Employ white noise (a soft, rhythmic, constant sound) to block disrupting sounds and provide a soothing environment.

Mindfulness as a Sleep Aid

Mindfulness represents a means of bringing flexibility to your beliefs about sleep and can lessen secondary arousal. For example, if you choose to be mindful and nonjudgmental at bedtime, you lessen your tendency toward overthinking or worrying about what will happen tomorrow. Without mindfulness, you are vulnerable to the runaway or catastrophic thinking patterns that guarantee insomnia. Focusing on breathing and accepting your emotional and mental state without attachment or aversion can help you attain equanimity, the quality of feeling calm (Ong, Ulmer, and Manber 2012). This practice lessens the stress and anxiety that you experience while trying to go to sleep.

Jon Kabat-Zinn (2013) uses the example of preparing your parachute before jumping out of a plane. A person does not wait until it is time to jump before making sure the parachute is in order. Rather, one will have spent quite a bit of time in advance checking out the systems involved. Similarly, mindfulness should be practiced before it is needed. You obviously can't wait for a catastrophe to occur before getting such a critical skill right. Instead, you must commit yourself to practicing it in advance. Then, when a crisis arises, you can access your reserve capacity to address the problem. Twice-a-day mindfulness sessions of 20 minutes each can set the stage for greater awareness, equanimity, and peace of mind, which can contribute to better sleep.

Regular mindfulness establishes refined coping skills. A positive correlation exists between time spent in mindfulness and reductions in hyperarousal (Ong, Shapiro, and Manber 2008). The more you

practice mindfulness, the more your state of arousal decreases (inverse relationship). The more your arousal decreases, the easier it is for you to fall and remain asleep.

Research evaluating the efficacy of mindfulness processes and sleep is in the embryonic stage. Mindfulness promotes high-quality sleep, which then further mediates balance in your life (Howell, Digdon, and Buro 2010). Mindfulness also promotes improved sleep duration, which promotes the self-regulation of behavior (Brown and Ryan 2003). Better sleep improves your mood, and you are more likely to make healthy behavioral choices.

Getting a good night of sleep is a special challenge for people who are recovering from **substance abuse**. A multicomponent pilot program among adolescents in substance abuse recovery included mindfulness training sessions. Follow-up observations made at 12 months showed improved sleep and reduced substance abuse relapse among those who completed the program, compared with noncompleters (Bootzin and Stevens 2005).

Sleep problems encountered when undergoing treatment for breast cancer (and likely for any cancer) often persist for years afterward. Andersen et al. (2013) randomly assigned 336 women to an eight-week mindfulness-based stress reduction program or to treatment as usual. The research team looked at changes in sleep. Immediately after intervention, those with the most severe sleep problems reported better sleep compared with the control group, although this improvement disappeared 12 months later. In another study, improvements in sleep quality and overall quality of life were experienced among both breast and prostate cancer patients who practiced mindfulness for eight weeks (Carlson et al. 2004).

Improved sleep quality with mindfulness is not limited to self-report. In a small study, Gross et al. (2011) compared the practice of mindfulness to use of the sleeping pill eszopiclone (Lunesta), using diaries and electronic devices, called actigraphs, to monitor movement, quantity, and quality of sleep. Initially, no differ-

Concentration Exercise to Return to Sleep

When waking during the night, try the following concentration exercise as an aid to relax and return to sleep:

1. Try repeated breath counting as follows: Count 1 with the in breath, 2 with the out breath, 3 with the in breath, 4 with the out breath, 1 with the in breath, 2 with the out breath, and so on with each in and out breath. When you find yourself distracted, just focus on where your mind has wandered and return to the breath counting. This form of mindfulness and paying attention serves to clear your thoughts and permits your brain to relax.

2. Light reading or listening to the radio in dim light for 30 to 60 minutes during the night may enable you to return to sleep. As part of good sleep hygiene, you should move to another room and then return to your sleep room as you become sleepy (National Sleep Foundation 2014). Don't read in bed.

3. Trust yourself. If you find healthful patterns and techniques that have worked well, that help you relax your mind, fall asleep, and sleep well, then you should practice those techniques.

4. If you wake up during the night, the breath counting recommended earlier may go on for some time. But this form of mindfulness is intrinsically restful. Being nonstriving will result in rest for the body and mind, independent of sleep. If you accept yourself, don't fret about not sleeping, and trust in the mindfulness process, then you are more likely to fall asleep. Getting frustrated will only ensure your failure to sleep that night.

---

ences were observed between the two approaches, but in the long run, the mindfulness group demonstrated earlier sleep onset and longer total sleep times.

Mindfulness cultivates a nonjudgmental response to your primary and secondary insomnia arousal. By contrast, mindless reactions to insomnia exacerbate the situation (see figure 1.1, p. 5, stress-reaction cycle). Nonjudgmental awareness helps you view your insomnia more objectively. When you are falling asleep, you can be more peaceful when you let go of your concerns or at least when you don't overreact to your first-level concerns (Bonnet and Arand 1997). You also avoid elevating first-level thoughts to second-level status. For example, a second-level thought such as, "If I do not sleep seven hours, I will fail my test tomorrow," can become a monumental barrier to falling asleep.

The attitudinal foundations of mindfulness, as detailed in chapter 2, are processes that enable you to gain awareness of your thoughts within a nonjudging context. You are then less likely to exaggerate the first-level thoughts into catastrophic ones, which can further heighten your arousal.

Physical Activity and Sleep

Regular physical activity and exercise should be a part of everyone's daily life for many reasons, including its important contribution to a good night's sleep. The effects of exercise on sleep are consistent across stud-

ies (Youngstedt and Kline 2006). On average, people who exercise regularly tend to have less trouble falling asleep compared with those who do not (Brand et al. 2010). In addition to this, the quality of sleep for regular exercisers is usually much better (Passos et al. 2010).

The preliminary evidence is that physical activity and exercise are at least as good as hypnotic medications for the treatment of chronic insomnia. Exercise has the added benefit of having no side effects, which are commonly associated with pharmaceuticals (Passos et al. 2012).

The time of the exercise does not seem to matter in relation to sleep effects. Sixty-five percent of late-evening exercisers reported falling asleep more quickly, 62 percent sleeping deeper, and 60 percent waking feeling better (Vuori et al. 1988). The authors of this book and many of their students have found exercise one of the best remedies for insomnia.

Creating an Environment for Sleep

Although the lifestyle of the sleeper is important, so too is the sleeping environment. Living in a nocturnally noisy area, such as a dormitory, can reduce the amount and quality of your sleep (Muzet 2007). Loud music, partying neighbors, bright lights, and road noise will also rob you of sleep.

The standard advice is to sleep in a quiet, dark environment to avoid outside stimulation. Paradoxically, you typically fall asleep easier when it is warm but awaken more comfortably to a cooler environment (Pan, Lian, and Lan 2012). A white-noise machine or fan that generates constant background hum will block out other potentially sleep-disruptive noises (Zaharna and Guilleminault 2010). Sleep apps for smart phones are available to use in lieu of buying a sound machine.

Napping

Napping tends to be part of life for people of all ages (Campbell and Murphy 2007). Among the elderly, naps are associated with subsequent improved cognitive performance with only mild to moderate disturbance of nighttime sleep (Campbell, Murphy, and Stauble 2005). This finding is good news because it suggests that a nap can serve to make up for sleep deprivation without negatively affecting sleep during the following night. Napping should be avoided close to bedtime, however, because it will interfere with subsequent sleep efforts.

Know Your Sleep Preferences

People are divided into those who prefer working in the mornings ("larks") and those who prefer evenings ("owls"). Although these preferences can be lifelong, they can change as you grow older. All people benefit from a better understanding of their own circadian preferences. Core body temperature drops during the night (lowest temperatures are recorded at approximately 4 a.m.) and begins to increase back toward the baseline at about 7 or 8 a.m., which signals arousal.

Sleep-related problems can be caused by everyday occurrences, such as stress, anxiety, and depression. A daily routine, regular physical activity, healthy eating, and mindfulness can help restore personal lifestyle balance and reduce stress and anxiety. Consider meeting with a mental health professional if stress, anxiety, and depression persist. Physical issues may be causing sleep problems independent of your best efforts to sleep. Note that negative emotional and psychological states will erode your sleep and diminish your quality of life.

Normal Sleep Routine

Establishing a set, nightly sleep routine is an important and simple method of achieving high-quality sleep. During the hour or so before going to bed, you should follow a habitual pattern. Common recommended presleep activities include reading and mindfulness (Winbush, Gross, and Kreitzer 2007). You should also go to bed and wake up at approximately the same time every day of the week (*How Much Sleep*

© pixhunter.com – Fotolia

Take a nap! Our culture might seem to prize constant work, focus, or movement, but you have much to gain by allowing your mind and body to rest and recharge.

Activity

Test Your Sleep Sense

The National Center on Sleep Disorders Research (n.d.) web page provides excellent information, including a 10-item quiz titled *Test Your Sleep IQ* (www.nhlbi.nih.gov/about/ncsdr/patpub/patpub-a.htm). This quiz contains important insights about sleep issues.

Do the quiz results provide you any new information to help you sleep better?

Do Adults Need? 2014). Exceptions should not be made for weekends or holidays.

The National Sleep Foundation suggests eating heavy foods and drinking alcohol can, contrary to popular belief, make it much more difficult to fall or remain asleep (*Healthy Sleep Tips* 2011). Alcohol may help you fall asleep more quickly, but sleep later becomes disrupted in the second half of the night. The regular use of alcohol to fall asleep is a sign of alcohol abuse (Vinson et al. 2010). Generally, it is best to avoid drinking alcohol or coffee during the six hours before bedtime.

The electronic era offers the constant temptation to browse the Internet, channel surf, or check the cell phone immediately before retiring. But engaging in these activities in the hour or so leading up to bedtime can be detrimental to your sleeping. The artificial light of computer or television screens seem to disturb human circadian rhythms, making falling and staying asleep more difficult (Brunborg et al. 2011).

SUMMARY

The wellness benefits of sleep are myriad. With sufficient sleep, about seven to eight hours per night, people learn better and remember more. Their relationships are more satisfying, and life challenges are more manageable. Sleep deficits negatively affect physical and mental health, academic performance, and overall quality of life.

Many societal and personal factors work together to interfere with sleep quantity and quality. Caffeine, alcohol, and other chemicals have a negative effect. Obsessing about the inability to fall asleep provokes an arousal state that virtually guarantees insomnia. Sleeping pills are not a workable long-term solution. Attempting to solve the problem with pills or alcohol just makes things worse.

Driving drowsy is a major risk factor for injury or premature death, particularly among young adults. Gauging your level of impairment is hard, if not

---

Sunjay followed through with reestablishing order in his life and in his sleep patterns. He realized that he was out of control, and in a moment of desperation saw a mental health counselor. The counselor's advice was on target, and Sunjay committed to regular, ongoing mental health sessions. His future success with his schoolwork and even his future career were obviously jeopardized by his inability to sleep well. He needed to revise his sleep hygiene and his life priorities.

Sunjay realized he needed at least 7 hours of sleep to function well. He decided to remain in bed for 8 hours daily. In case he awoke during the night, he had a buffer. He scheduled a set-in-stone midnight to 8 a.m. sleep timetable, regardless of how he felt. Then he removed all his work clutter from his bedroom, leaving only his bed, a good reading light, and some light reading material.

Sunjay committed to mindfulness breath counting when he was unable to sleep. He began maintaining a sleep log and wore an actigraph activity monitor (actimetry sensor). The monitor showed that he was sleeping more than he realized. This finding removed some anxiety from his life, and he started feeling better. Sunjay was pleasantly surprised to see how much this change in perception improved his sense of well-being.

impossible, especially when you are chronically sleep deprived. In this way, driving drowsy is a lot like driving drunk. Caffeine, physical activity, and a 20-minute nap can help overcome the drowsiness. Better yet, you can just stop driving for the day.

Mindfulness in your daily life and in bed can assist with sleeping. Setting up an environment conducive to sleep should be a priority. Avoid the temptation to check the Internet, watch television, or work with your cell phone during the hour before going to bed.

© Cat London

Chapter 9

Health Care Advice to Live Well

Objectives

After reading this chapter, you will be able to

- describe how to relate to health professionals,
- describe a strategy for a visit with a general practitioner,
- describe the importance of a family history to a health professional,
- list two characteristics of cross-cultural communication,
- identify four different health care screenings for young adults,
- describe three issues related to elevated body mass index (BMI),
- describe how to apply the five stages of change to tobacco cessation,
- identify and describe two mental health issues, and
- identify intended goals for three complementary alternative medical practices.

Marcel, a 24-year-old graduate student from Paraguay, was seen for urethral discharge and burning that began one week after unprotected sex. He was initially uncomfortable with the student health doctor but did admit that he had been intoxicated one night and "forgot" to use a condom with a new partner. He was treated for urethritis with an injection of ceftriaxone and a week of oral doxycycline. His urethral symptoms went away. His test for chlamydia came back positive.

On Marcel's follow-up visit, it became clear that his alcohol use was problematic (he scored positive on the CAGE substance abuse screening test) and that he was moderately depressed (he scored 9 out of 14 on the Personal Health Questionnaire [PHQ-9]). He began to speak more freely with the doctor.

Marcel had arrived in the United States eight months earlier on a student visa. The excitement of the new life carried him through his first summer and the fall semester during which time he earned a 3.4 grade point average. Thereafter, he started to feel rootless and disconnected. He began drinking, got into some fights, and was soon placed on academic probation. He seldom had enough energy to go to morning classes and was unable to fall asleep at night without first drinking alcohol or smoking marijuana. He also drank yerba mate tea from Paraguay for hangover and fatigue.

A mental health evaluation was consistent with culture shock (an adjustment reaction with depressed mood) and alcohol abuse. Marcel was encouraged to begin walking and jogging for exercise, was started on sertraline, a serotonin reuptake inhibitor (SSRI) with trazodone, another antidepressant, for sleep. He also began counseling and agreed to stop all alcohol and drug use. He started playing soccer again and did not use his car for in-town commuting. Fortunately, as his mood improved, he drank less alcohol. His academic performance returned to his earlier level of excellence.

Living well involves a commitment to a healthy lifestyle, including eating a balanced diet, getting regular exercise and adequate sleep, living mindfully, and maintaining a sense of purpose or meaning in life. Access to good health care and regular screening for illness is also an important part of a commitment to health.

The U.S. health care delivery system is almost impossible to navigate without help. Although the U.S. medical system has the most sophisticated technology in the world, accessing that care can be a challenge, especially if you do not have lots of money or excellent health insurance. Lack of insurance is one of the principal barriers to obtaining care, although health care reform has made insurance coverage more affordable to young people. This chapter focuses on how you can optimize your health care experiences to live well and it will help you find your way through the labyrinth of the modern-day health care system.

YOUNG ADULTS AND MEDICAL CARE

The age range for young adults is usually considered to be 18 to 26, the typical college years in the United States, a period that follows the turbulence of adolescence but precedes the restrictive responsibilities of adulthood (characteristically marriage and launching a career). With graduate school or travel, the young adult years often extend to 30.

Although this age range is typically a healthy period of life, it is also fraught with special risks that are largely preventable. These perils include substance abuse, sexually transmitted disease acquisition, fatal accidents, mental health issues, suicide, and homicide.

Unfortunately, nearly 70 percent of visits to primary care providers by young adults lack any preventive counseling (Fortuna, Robbins, and Halterman 2009). The opportunity now exists to do much better. The

Affordable Health Care Act of 2010 extends coverage of dependents until age 26, effectively insuring an entire age group that otherwise might lack coverage—assuming, of course, that your parents have insurance (English 2012).

Remember that about 40 percent of your mortality risk is determined by lifestyle behaviors (McGinnis, Williams-Russo, and Knickman 2002). The United States is expected to spend approximately $3.13 trillion in 2014 for medical care (CMS 2013), yet the totality of that expenditure accounts for only about 10 percent of your risk of death. Social circumstances represent 15 percent, environmental exposures 5 percent, and genetics approximately 30 percent (McGinnis, Williams-Russo, and Knickman 2002).

As a young adult, you face a critical stage in life. You are becoming responsible for your own care. You need to navigate the health care system by making and keeping appointments and developing a long-term, trusting relationship with a care provider. Establishing trust is the critical first step to success. An ideal strategy is to establish a long-term **medical home** where you can go with all your future health concerns.

Partnerships in Health Care

Navigating the health care system is facilitated by establishing a friendly partnership with a health care provider in your medical home. This kind of collaboration may not always be possible, but most people are willing to share after they've developed a trusting relationship. The lack of good communication is the most significant area of patient discontent. Appointments can be stress-provoking, and medical terminology can be confusing. Many patients feel rushed or fear being treated in a condescending manner by health professionals. Taking a friend or family member to the appointment can help. The accompanying person can help by recording important points while you are engaged with the doctor.

Remember that good communication is a two-way street. You will always do better if you are well prepared, open, honest, and treat your provider with courtesy and respect. You should also make a list of your health concerns and symptoms before the visit. Never assume that the caregiver can read your mind. You must inform your doctor exactly what is going on with your health and how you want to be treated. Staying with the same health care provider for an extended period promotes good rapport.

You should begin addressing your concerns without much delay. You need to describe your symptoms adequately, ask your questions, and answer your doctor's questions as best you can. The average medical visit lasts only about 15 minutes. This time passes quickly, so it's easy to forget important items. Having prepared notes about your symptoms is helpful. When you are tense, a written record of your past symptoms will keep you on track. Be specific.

Medical terminology can be confusing. Of course, every profession has its jargon. Make a practice of clarifying what you think the health provider is saying so that you are sure you heard it correctly. You should feel free to ask for an explanation of anything you don't understand. Most health professionals will be glad to do so.

If medications or medical treatment is recommended, ask whether any alternative approaches are available. Would diet, exercise, or stress reduction make a difference? What are the common side effects of the medications? How much do the medications cost? Are lower-cost alternatives available? What happens if you miss a dose? *Consumer Reports Best Buy Drugs* is a useful resource (www.consumerreports.org/health/best-buy-drugs/index.htm) to review drug specifics. The materials are available in English and Spanish.

Well-intentioned medical preaching about smoking or alcohol cessation, the necessity of using condoms, and avoiding drugs usually falls on deaf ears. Likewise, some physicians show images of sexually transmitted infections or other dire consequences of ill-advised behavior. This evidence can be informative, but the desired reaction of shock has a short-lived effect. If you notice such communication patterns, you should respectfully share your concerns with your provider. You may prefer having a life coach type of caregiver, a professional who will provide guidance and options while not giving unsolicited or authoritarian directives. A paternal or confrontational approach will likely prove self-defeating because it threatens your hard-won independence.

Many young people are concerned about confidentiality. You may have fears that your confidence might

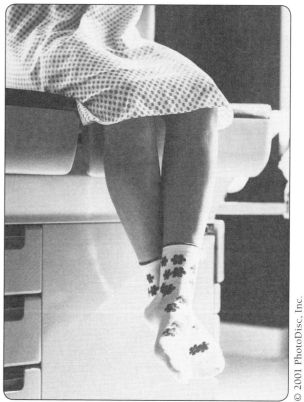

© 2001 PhotoDisc, Inc.

Take responsibility for your own health. Keep records, make appointments, and learn to talk openly with the people entrusted with your care.

be betrayed. This issue is generally not a problem, especially under new federal guidelines that seek to protect patient rights. Most state laws provide assurances of confidentiality in regard to issues involving birth control or sexual activity. You should understand that confidentiality has its limits in certain situations. Reporting to authorities is mandatory in cases of physical and sexual abuse, certain sexually transmitted infections (reported to health department only), and suicidal or homicidal behavior.

A classic characteristic of youth is the sense of invulnerability, which is both frustrating to older adults and yet necessary for your personal development. Many young adults see themselves as infallible, invincible, immortal, invulnerable, and infertile!

Acknowledging your vulnerability to sexually transmitted infections, injury, and unwanted pregnancy is a sign of maturity. Failure to engage in appropriate levels of risk may even equate with a failure to launch into adulthood. The challenge, of course, is managing this risk to maximize its potential benefits while minimizing potential harm.

GUIDE TO THE MEDICAL APPOINTMENT

You need to know what should take place during a medical encounter. Ideally, the interview should occur in a comfortable private setting. An accompanying partner, friend, or parent may be invited in at some point if you desire, but the more sensitive questions should be asked in private.

Sometimes discussing deeply personal issues during the appointment is embarrassing. A sensitive health care provider will begin with a little small talk at the start of the interview. This focuses on building trust, which is essential if honest sharing of confidential concerns is to take place. The interview usually focuses on identifying a chief complaint (the problem necessitating the visit), noting symptoms (and what makes symptoms better or worse), establishing a diagnosis, and making recommendations.

You should bring a log of your relevant symptoms pertaining to this visit, as well as a list of your medications and known vaccinations. For some people, the health care examination room can feel like an alien, intimidating environment. If you are experiencing any pain, you should rate it using a 1 to 10 pain scale, with 10 being the worst pain you can imagine. Pain is now considered the fifth vital sign, after blood pressure, pulse, respiration, and weight with height (Morone and Weiner 2013).

Past medical information, medications, allergies, and screening questions about major body systems (review of systems) will customarily be obtained. This review may include a body mass index (BMI). A social and family history is also useful. For the social history, the American Academy of Pediatrics' *Bright Futures* publication uses the mnemonic HEADSSS to represent questions about home, education, activities, drugs, sexuality (number of partners, condom use, and sexual orientation), suicide (and other mental health issues, like anxiety and eating disorders), and safety (seatbelt and helmet use) (Hagan, Shaw, and Duncan 2008). Be honest.

You should also share a family medical history with your doctor. If high blood pressure, high cholesterol, diabetes, or premature heart disease runs in your family, you may be predisposed to similar problems in the future. The family history will help guide your doctor in selecting the right tests and recommendations.

Health professionals should discuss their recommendations with minimal use of medical jargon and, if necessary, supplement their recommendations with handouts at the appropriate reading level. But realize that not all health professionals succeed in being as clear as they would like to be. It is your responsibility to ask for clarification if you don't understand something. Ask for literature and links to more information. Being engaged with your medical care is strongly corre-

Activity

Research Your Family Medical History

Researching your family's medical history can help you determine your future health risks.

1. Ask your parents and grandparents about their health problems. Find out what contributed to the deaths of any deceased relatives. If it was cancer, what type of cancer was it and when did it start? If they had a heart attack or stroke, how old were they when this happened?

2. Describe their lifestyles. Did they seem to have a sense of purpose in their lives? Were they physically active? Did they make a practice of regularly eating vegetables, fruits, whole grains, and legumes? Were they particularly stressed? Did they have good social support?

3. It helps to prepare a family tree diagram using squares to represent male relatives and circles for female relatives. Note pertinent medical conditions alongside each person's symbol. An example is available at http://www.genomics.health.wa.gov.au/images/diagram-fhh_pedigree.gif.

4. Place a diagonal line through the squares or circles representing deceased relatives and note their age and cause of death.

5. Knowing about these potential risks and sharing this diagram with your doctor may save your life if it can help in the detection of disease at an early, treatable stage.

6. Place your family tree diagram and the information you have collected in Chapter 9 of your wellness journal.

lated with your health (Donaldson, Csikszentmihalyi, and Nakamura 2011).

Many practitioners use a method called teach back, a review technique in which the doctor asks you to repeat back his or her instructions in your own words until it is clear that you understand everything (Kountz 2009). If your doctor does not provide this opportunity, take the initiative. Repeat what you heard and ask questions to ensure that you understand. Your visit needs to center on you.

Cross-Cultural Communication

In today's multicultural society, interacting with people from other countries or ethnic groups is nearly certain to occur. You and your doctor have a good chance of being from different backgrounds. Even the age difference represents a communication challenge. Cultural barriers, either real or perceived, could make your visit challenging. Expectations differ between cultures. Appropriate levels of sensitivity and respect for cultural issues can make a big difference in the success of your visit.

A useful mnemonic for the cross-cultural interview is LEARN (Berlin et al. 1983). Your health care provider should

listen to your story about the problem,

explain her or his understanding of your problem,

acknowledge any differences and similarities in viewpoints,

make recommendations, and

negotiate care.

If the provider lacks sensitivity to you and your needs, you might consider choosing another.

You should share information about whether you are using traditional medicines (such as herbs and teas) so that your provider will to know how to proceed. Make a list of your prescription medications, vitamins, dietary supplements, and herbs, or better yet bring everything in to your appointment in a paper bag.

The use of teach back is even more essential when trying to convey instructions in a cross-cultural context. Remember to restate what you understand is being said. Clear communication is a challenge in all aspects of life, but especially when there are differences in age and culture.

Socioeconomic status can also make a difference when you are seeking health care. The Institute of Medicine's 2002 report *Unequal Treatment: Confronting Racial/Ethnic Disparities in Health Care* (2002) cited over 175 studies that documented quality disparities. If you are from a poor or disadvantaged background, you will likely experience a cultural difference,

independent of your race or ethnicity. Your communication may be handicapped in ways you do not realize. Recent immigrants and ethnic minorities from specific urban areas, as well as poor people from rural areas, may be impoverished, less educated, and uninsured. Economic and social problems, coupled with illegal immigration status, create a "perfect storm." The result is that some people have difficulty gaining access to high-quality health care.

The Office of Minority Health (part of the U.S. Department of Health and Human Services) has published National Standards for Culturally and Linguistically Appropriate Services (CLAS) to deal with these discrepancies. These 14 standards fall into three main themes: culturally competent care, language access services, and organizational supports (National Standards for CLAS 2001). If you are a Medicaid or Medicare patient, these standards support your right to a free interpreter if you have limited English proficiency. You should know about these rights if you are a recent immigrant or belong to one of these disadvantaged minority groups.

The challenges of cross-cultural medical communication are magnified when you have limited English proficiency or a hearing impairment. In this situation the need for an interpreter is often met by a family member or friend, but you should be aware that such nonprofessional interpretation may be far from ideal and lack any guarantee of confidentiality.

Nonprofessional interpreters are often ill equipped to discuss medical issues. This situation may be a violation of the confidentiality mandates of the Health Insurance Portability and Accountability Act (HIPAA) and may lead to misunderstandings, poor outcomes, and increased liability.

CLAS standard 4 mandates that language assistance services, including interpreter services, must be offered at no additional cost during all hours of operation if you have limited English proficiency. You should check with your doctor in advance if an interpreter might be needed.

Ask your physician if she or he could provide you with a *free* medical interpreter. Many larger health networks employ professional interpreters for common languages such as Spanish and Chinese. If these are unavailable, then paid telephone interpreter services are the next best option (e.g., Language Line or Cyracom).

For those who are hearing impaired, interpretation through sign language may require a video phone or a communication access real-time translation, in which an instantaneous written script of the conversation is visually projected on a screen. A teletypewriter for the deaf may be used for telephone conversations, although this method is rapidly being replaced by the

Marcel performed well with teach back and was relieved to discover that his doctor could speak some Spanish. He enthusiastically reviewed everything that was said, taking pride in getting everything right. He said it all in his own words, but every detail was correct. When the appointment was complete, his doctor was convinced that Marcel understood.

convenience of simple cellular phone texting. These are your rights and the provider's responsibility. Do not hesitate to request help.

Interviews using an interpreter should be transparent, meaning that everything discussed should be interpreted sentence by sentence with no side conversations. The verbal exchange and eye contact should be between the interviewer and patient; the interpreter should be an inconspicuous, albeit essential, part of the encounter (Karliner et al. 2007). Interpretation refers to the spoken word, whereas translation applies to the written word. Translated educational materials and online links will help reinforce the interview instructions for you as needed.

SCREENING RECOMMENDATIONS

Regular health care screening for disease is an important aspect of care, but it is often difficult to know which screening tests are most worth doing. Although some tests can be lifesaving, others have been found to be harmful, either through creating needless anxiety or by subjecting the patient to unnecessary procedures.

The U.S. Preventive Services Task Force (USPSTF) identifies key screening recommendations for various age groups based on experimental evidence and rated by their effectiveness in improving outcomes. The USPSTF is a group of national experts in prevention and evidence-based medicine that makes recommendations about screenings, counseling services, and preventive medications.

An A rating indicates that the intervention is based on high-certainty evidence, and B ratings are based on moderate certainty. Grade C recommendations are based on expert opinion (as opposed to direct scientific research) and thus are lower priority. D recommendations lack evidence (or may be harmful) and should be discouraged. The I category indicates insufficient evidence to make a recommendation for or against an intervention. Table 9.1 lists recent recommendations for young adult patients.

There is currently a hodgepodge of different agency recommendations for different age ranges, rather than a single authoritative source for the young adult age group (Ozer et al. 2012). The U.S. Preventive Services Task Force, for example, provides only a barebones framework for evidence-based screening. The American Academy of Family Practice (AAFP, n.d.), American Academy of Pediatrics (AAP, n.d.), American Medical Association (AMA), and American Congress of Obstetricians and Gynecologists (ACOG, n.d.) have

Activity

Preparing for a Medical Interview to Aid Screening

The goal of this activity is to provide guidance and practice for a successful medical visit.

1. After reading the USPSTF and other recommendations, make a list of what screening tests you think you need based on your age and risk factors.
2. Make another list of any symptoms that concern you and list the names of your medications, including any over-the-counter medications, vitamins, and herbs that you are taking.
3. Alternatively, you can take all your medications and supplements to the visit.
4. Make an appointment with your doctor to schedule your screening.
5. Set up an appointment to discuss the results.
6. Place your medical interview preparation sheet into the Chapter 9 section of your wellness journal.

TABLE 9.1 USPSTF Recommendations (A and B Ratings) for Young Adult Conditions

Topic	Description	Grade	Date in effect
Alcohol misuse counseling	The USPSTF recommends screening and behavioral counseling interventions to reduce alcohol misuse by adults, including pregnant women, in primary care settings.	B	April 2004
Anemia screening: pregnant women	The USPSTF recommends routine screening for iron deficiency anemia in asymptomatic pregnant women.	B	May 2006
Bacteriuria screening: pregnant women	The USPSTF recommends screening for asymptomatic bacteriuria with urine culture for pregnant women at 12 to 16 weeks' gestation or at the first prenatal visit, if later.	A	July 2008
Blood pressure screening in adults	The USPSTF recommends screening for high blood pressure in adults aged 18 and older.	A	December 2007
BRCA screening, counseling about risk of ovarian or breast cancer if +BRCA	The USPSTF recommends that women whose family history is associated with an increased risk for deleterious mutations in BRCA1 or BRCA2 genes be referred for genetic counseling and evaluation for BRCA testing.	B	September 2005
Breastfeeding counseling	The USPSTF recommends interventions during pregnancy and after birth to promote and support breastfeeding.	B	October 2008
Cervical cancer screening	The USPSTF recommends screening for cervical cancer in women older than aged 21 who have a cervix. Pap smears may be performed every 3 years instead of annually.	A	March 2012
Chlamydial infection screening: nonpregnant women	The USPSTF recommends screening for chlamydial infection for all sexually active nonpregnant young women aged 24 and younger and for older nonpregnant women who are at increased risk.	A	June 2007
Chlamydial infection screening: pregnant women	The USPSTF recommends screening for chlamydial infection for all pregnant women aged 24 and younger and for older pregnant women who are at increased risk.	B	June 2007
Cholesterol abnormalities screening: men younger than 35	The USPSTF recommends screening men aged 20 to 35 for lipid disorders if they are at increased risk for coronary heart disease.	B	June 2008
Cholesterol abnormalities screening: women younger than 45	The USPSTF recommends screening women aged 20 to 45 for lipid disorders if they are at increased risk for coronary heart disease.	B	June 2008
Depression screening: adolescents	The USPSTF recommends screening of adolescents (12 to 18 years of age) for major depressive disorder when systems are in place to ensure accurate diagnosis, psychotherapy (cognitive-behavioral or interpersonal), and follow-up.	B	March 2009
Depression screening: adults	The USPSTF recommends screening adults for depression when staff-assisted depression care supports are in place to assure accurate diagnosis, effective treatment, and follow-up.	B	December 2009
Diabetes screening	The USPSTF recommends screening for type 2 diabetes in asymptomatic adults with sustained blood pressure (either treated or untreated) greater than 135/80 mm Hg.	B	June 2008
Folic acid supplementation	The USPSTF recommends that all women planning or capable of pregnancy take a daily supplement containing .4 to .8 milligrams (400 to 800 µg) of folic acid.	A	May 2009
Gonorrhea screening: women	The USPSTF recommends that clinicians screen all sexually active women, including those who are pregnant, for gonorrhea infection if they are at increased risk for infection (that is, if they are young or have other individual or population risk factors).	B	May 2005
Healthy diet counseling	The USPSTF recommends intensive behavioral dietary counseling for adult patients with hyperlipidemia and other known risk factors for cardiovascular and diet-related chronic disease. Intensive counseling can be delivered by primary care clinicians or by referral to other specialists, such as nutritionists or dietitians.	B	January 2003

(continued)

TABLE 9.1 *(continued)*

Topic	Description	Grade	Date in effect
Hepatitis B screening: pregnant women	The USPSTF strongly recommends screening for hepatitis B virus infection in pregnant women at their first prenatal visit.	A	June 2009
HIV screening	The USPSTF strongly recommends that clinicians screen for human immunodeficiency virus (HIV) all adolescents and adults at increased risk for HIV infection.	A	July 2005
Obesity screening and counseling: adults	The USPSTF recommends that clinicians screen all adult patients for obesity and offer intensive counseling and behavioral interventions to promote sustained weight loss for obese adults.	B	December 2003
Rh incompatibility screening: first pregnancy visit	The USPSTF strongly recommends Rh (D) blood typing and antibody testing for all pregnant women during their first visit for pregnancy-related care.	A	February 2004
Rh incompatibility screening: 24 to 28 weeks' gestation	The USPSTF recommends repeated Rh (D) antibody testing for all unsensitized Rh (D)-negative women at 24 to 28 weeks' gestation, unless the biological father is known to be Rh (D)-negative.	B	February 2004
STIs counseling	The USPSTF recommends high-intensity behavioral counseling to prevent sexually transmitted infections (STIs) for all sexually active adolescents and for adults at increased risk for STIs.	B	October 2008
Tobacco use counseling and interventions: nonpregnant adults	The USPSTF recommends that clinicians ask all adults about tobacco use and provide tobacco cessation interventions for those who use tobacco products.	A	April 2009

Adapted from USPSTF A and B Recommendations. August 2010. U.S. Preventive Services Task Force. www.uspreventiveservicestaskforce. org/uspstf/uspsabrecs.htm.

all published their own guidelines for various young adult age ranges which often, but not always, follow those of the U.S. Preventive Services Task Force.

Other major resources include the American Medical Association's *Guidelines for Adolescent Preventive Services* or *GAPS* (1994) and the American Academy of Pediatrics' *Bright Futures: Guidelines for Health Supervision of Infants, Children and Adolescents* (Elster and Kuznets 1994). *Bright Futures, Third Edition* (2008) now covers young adults up to age 21.

Vaccine recommendations are the purview of the Centers for Disease Control and Prevention's (CDC) Advisory Committee on Immunization Practices (ACIP 2010).

All these recommendations need to be summarized in a way that maximally protects your health. But remember that your own involvement in getting these screenings is crucial. Your health is at stake! Become educated in what is best and then seek the care that you need.

Gynecologic Screening

Recent recommendations from the U.S. Preventive Services Task Force (USPSTF) radically revise pelvic and Papanicolaou (pap) smear testing. The pap smear is a screen for cervical cancer, obtained by sampling cells from a woman's cervix. Cervical cancer is more common in women over the age of 30. The guidelines say that routine pap smears are no longer necessary under age 21 (even if sexually active) and that pap

smears need to be performed only every three years instead of annually.

Although many abnormalities are identified on pap smears before age 21, nearly all these resolve spontaneously in a few years, according to the USPSTF. The USPSTF found that aggressive treatment at this time in life damages the cervix and probably does more harm than good. Therefore, performing pap smears before age 21 has been given a D rating.

Nearly all cervical dysplasia (precancerous cervical cells) are caused by human papilloma virus (HPV) infection. Approximately 14 million new cases of HPV appear annually, and 75 percent of them occur among 15- to 24-year-olds (*Genital HPV Infection—Fact Sheet* n.d.). The good news is that two vaccines (Gardasil by Merck & Co. and Cervarix by GlaxoSmithKline) are now available to prevent HPV infection and cervical cancer if given before the start of sexual activity.

The Advisory Committee on Immunization Practices (ACIP) recommends human papilloma virus (HPV) vaccine for both genders, not just women, as early as 9 years of age, or more typically between 11 and 26 years of age. The HPV vaccine Gardasil protects against four common HPV strains, reducing the risk of cervical cancer in women and genital warts in both sexes.

Breast cancer is an important concern among women. An estimated one in eight women contracts the disease during their lifetime (*Breast Cancer Risk in Women* n.d.). Similarly, testicular cancer is the most common cancer among men ages 15 to 35 years (Testicular Cancer Society n.d.).

The USPSTF currently discourages breast self-exams and testicular self-exams. Although the evidence to support self-examination for risk reduction is insufficient, other organizations (e.g., ACOG) still promote them as having the potential to detect cancer.

Sexual Health: Sexually Transmitted Infection (STI) Prevention and Screening

Most young people in the United States now become sexually active in high school or college. Sexual activity includes oral, vaginal, or anal genital contact, not just vaginal intercourse. Multiple partners are common, although this often takes the form of serial monogamy in which a series of short-term exclusive dating relationships occur.

Risk of STI is high in new relationships (shorter than six months), but the riskiest encounters are "one-night stands," especially when condoms are not used. This particular risk can manifest itself in a sexually transmitted infection (STI), distinguished from a sexually transmitted disease (STD) in that the latter manifests symptoms. Estimates are that one in two sexually active young people will get an STI by age 25, although most will be unaware that they are infected because they lack symptoms (Cates et al. 2004).

Condoms, when used properly, have been shown to have an effective role in the prevention of chlamydia, gonorrhea, and HIV–AIDS. Condoms are less effective against herpes simplex virus (HSV) and human papilloma virus (HPV), because these infections can spread from any genital contact with genital skin not covered by a condom. Condom use is therefore considered to represent a certain level of safer sex, but not necessarily safe sex. People do not always show signs of active infection when they have a contagious STI.

The U.S. Preventive Services Task Force recommends annual screening for chlamydia infection for all sexually active women up through age 25. Gonorrhea screening is recommended for all higher risk males and females (two or more partners). Annual STI screening for sexually active males (per GAPS and AAP recommendations) is also recommended. In practice, chlamydia and gonorrhea screening are usually obtained together through urine nucleic acid amplification testing, which has replaced the need for an uncomfortable urethral swab. Table 9.2 compares various agency recommendations for STI screening for young women.

Sun Protection

The chief risk to young skin is excessive sun (ultraviolet light) exposure, which not only prematurely ages the skin but also increases the risk of skin cancers such as melanoma. Some vitamin D benefit is associated

Skin cancer is not fashionable. If you're going to spend time out in the sun, use sunscreen with at least an SPF 15 and be sure to reapply after two hours or if you swim or get sweaty.

TABLE 9.2   Comparison of STI Screening Recommendations for Sexually Active Nonpregnant Women

STI	USPSTF	CDC	AAFP	ACOG
Chlamydia	Screen women younger than 25 years old and others at increased risk (A)	Screen women 25 years old and younger and others at increased risk	Screen women 25 years old and younger and others at increased risk	Screen women 25 years old and younger and others at increased risk
Gonorrhea	Screen women younger than 25 years old and others at increased risk (B)	Screen women at increased risk	Screen women younger than 25 years old and others at increased risk	Screen adolescents and others at increased risk
Syphilis	Screen women at increased risk (A)	Screen women exposed to syphilis	Screen women at increased risk	Screen women at increased risk
HIV	Screen women at increased risk (A)	Screen all	Screen women at increased risk	Screen women at increased risk
Hepatitis B	Do not screen general population (D)	Provide prevaccination screening for women at increased risk	Do not screen general population	No specific recommendation
Hepatitis C	Do not screen (I) general population; insufficient evidence to recommend for or against screening women at increased risk	Screen women at increased risk	Do not screen general population; insufficient evidence to recommend for or against screening women at increased risk	Screen women at increased risk
HSV	Do not screen (D)	Do not screen general population	Do not screen	Screen if sexual partner has HSV
HPV*	Insufficient evidence to use as primary screening test for cervical cancer (I)	Do not screen for subclinical infection	Insufficient evidence to use as primary screening test for cervical cancer	Testing with a pap smear is an option for women older than 30 years old

STI = sexually transmitted infection; USPSTF = U.S. Preventive Services Task Force; CDC = Centers for Disease Control and Prevention; AAFP = American Academy of Family Physicians; ACOG = American College of Obstetricians and Gynecologists; HIV = human immunodeficiency virus; HSV = herpes simplex virus; HPV = human papillomavirus; pap = Papanicolaou.

*No treatment available; currently used to stratify risk of cervical neoplasia.

Reprinted from D. Meyers et al., 2008, "Recommendations for STI screening," *American Family Physician* 77: 819-824.

with reasonable sun exposure, but excessive tanning and sunburns can cause cancer.

Tanning beds, which generate ultraviolet A (UVA) light, only add to the problem. Tans are considered fashionable but they have long-term consequences. Skin cancer is the most common of all human cancers in the United States, and one in five people will get skin cancer in their lifetime (*Skin Cancer Information* n.d.). Between 30 percent and 60 percent of college students reported using a tanning bed within the past year; the highest prevalence was among females (Bagdasarov et al. 2008; Hillhouse, Turrisi, and Shields 2007).

Obesity

Obesity is the leading health problem among young adults because it increases the risk of cardiovascular disease, cancer, and diabetes (Preston and Stokes 2011). More than one third (35 percent) of U.S. adults

are now obese. Many of these are young adults, teens, and children. An overweight teenager has an 80 percent chance of becoming an overweight adult. African American teens have twice the prevalence of obesity of white teens (Strasburger et al. 2006).

Obesity raises the risk of high blood pressure (five- to sixfold), diabetes mellitus (threefold), sleep apnea, high cholesterol and triglycerides (**hyperlipidemia**), as well as certain cancers, including pancreatic cancer. Mental health issues such as low self-esteem are also associated with obesity (Serdar et al. 2011).

People should not be considered at fault for being overweight or obese. This problem has societal causes. You live in a toxic, **obesogenic** society. Becoming overweight is easier than not. Staying thin often means swimming against the tide, always making a special effort to keep weight off. It may not be your fault if you are obese. But if you are obese, you will endure many additional health problems, including increased risk of high blood pressure and diabetes.

Because obesity is so prevalent, the USPSTF recommends that all young adults be screened using the BMI or body mass index (USPSTF, AAFP). Normal body mass index is 18.5 to 24.9, overweight is 25 to 29.9, and obese is defined as over 30. Of course, an overweight or obese person can be physically fit, and this fitness conveys a protective effect. However, BMI works well in categorizing most of the population, although some will have a high BMI because of extensive muscle development.

But you are not your BMI. Too many obsess over weight when overall wellness is your goal. Being mindful, eating well, being regularly physically active, and promoting positive emotions are far more important than being concerned about your BMI. If you have an elevated BMI, this is an opportunity to be nonjudgmental and accept yourself.

Intensive dietary counseling is also recommended for all adult patients with high blood **lipids** (total cholesterol greater than 200 milligrams per deciliter, LDL cholesterol above 100 milligrams per deciliter, triglycerides above 150 milligrams per deciliter, and HDL cholesterol less than 40 milligrams per deciliter) and other known risk factors for cardiovascular and diet-related chronic disease.

Diet (caloric restriction) and exercise can temporarily reduce weight, but unfortunately people usually regain this weight when they cease dieting or exercising (Rolls 2007). What works is a progressive, long-term lifestyle change. Permanently stopping the consumption of sodas and fast food and limiting meal portions pays off with permanent weight loss (Rolls 2007). A regular exercise program also works, but only if it is maintained (*Physical Activity Guidelines for Americans* 2008). Too much time in front of the TV or computer is also associated with obesity (Boulos et al. 2012).

Old habits are difficult to break. Changes are not likely to happen at once. The stages of change (or transtheoretical) model of behavior states that most behavioral change occurs in a stepwise fashion, progressing through a series of five predictable stages (Prochaska and DiClemente 1983). Not everyone is ready to make sustained behavioral changes. You are likely to progress through a series of motivational stages, as follows:

1. Precontemplation (the "not ready" stage) describes the state of being unready or unable to change your lifestyle, or perhaps even lacking awareness that a problem exists. You have no motivation to change anything.

2. Contemplation (the "getting ready" stage) follows after you recognize the problem and decide to make a change—a process that can take quite a while.

3. Preparation is planning this change in the immediate future ("I definitely must do this!").

4. Action is making the change happen. Although you have made the change, you are still vulnerable to relapse.

5. After action, you enter the maintenance stage (with a lessened risk of relapse). With practice, the new behavior becomes so well established that relapse is unlikely.

Hypertension, Diabetes Mellitus, and Metabolic Syndrome

The USPSTF recommends screening for high blood pressure: (a) in adults over 18 years old, and (b) for those who have type 2 diabetes as well as sustained blood pressure (treated or untreated) greater than 135/80 mm Hg, even if there are no other symptoms (USPSTF 2012). Type 2 diabetes used to be known as adult onset diabetes, but the prevalence of overweight and obesity among youth have made this label inaccurate.

A combination of obesity with elevated blood pressure, glucose intolerance (prediabetes or diabetes), and hyperlipidemia is called **metabolic syndrome**, or syndrome X. This condition is not only common (up to 25 percent of the U.S. population) but also associated with premature death from stroke and heart attack (Ford, Giles, and Dietz 2002). The key underlying feature of metabolic syndrome is obesity with insulin resistance, which weight loss can reverse.

Hyperlipidemia

High blood fats or hyperlipidemia, defined as high levels of low-density lipoprotein (LDL) cholesterol (colloquially known as "bad" cholesterol), high triglycerides, or low levels of protective high-density lipoprotein (HDL) cholesterol ("good" cholesterol), leads to coronary artery disease (CAD) and increased risk of premature death. These circulating fats are called lipids. Your health professional can assess your status by means of a lipid panel blood test, customarily conducted after a 9- to 12-hour fast.

Some doctors explain LDL as "lousy" cholesterol and HDL as 'healthy' cholesterol to make the distinction clearer. Young adults should ideally know their lipid status and, if lipids are high, seek treatment for it. Usually increasing physical activity; eating more vegetables, fruits, and whole grains; and cutting out saturated fat, trans fat (partially hydrogenated vegetable oils), and sugar from the diet will correct the problem. But sometimes medication is needed, especially if a heritable lipid disorder is present. The USPSTF recommends routine screening for males age 20 to 35 and females age 20 to 45 if they have another risk factor for heart disease (B rating). There is no recommendation for or against screening in young adults lacking a known risk factor (C rating).

Substance Abuse and Dependence

Young people usually start smoking (inhaling addictive nicotine) and using other drugs, including alcohol, for social reasons, but what begins as a recreational activity can soon turn into a life-long addiction with profound health consequences. Psychiatric distress such as a mood or anxiety disorder also contributes to substance abuse. Tremendous psychological damage can result from physical, sexual, or psychological abuse in childhood (as well as adulthood); intimate partner violence; and other social problems. Alcohol or other drugs are often used in an attempt to self-medicate severe underlying psychological and emotional conditions, but such self-treatment can also turn into a vicious cycle of chemical dependency.

Most smoking begins in adolescence. Picking up the habit after age 19 is unusual. The younger the age at which a person starts smoking, the more likely it is that she or he will continue smoking through life. The USPSTF recommends that all patients be asked about tobacco use and that tobacco cessation interventions be provided for anyone using tobacco products (A rating).

You can expect your health professional to be proactive about tobacco use. Stopping the use of tobacco is probably the single most important physical behavioral change you can make. Typically, they will follow the five major steps to intervention (the five A's) for smoking (Schroeder 2005):

1. Asking about tobacco use
2. Advising to quit
3. Assessing willingness to quit
4. Assisting with the quit attempt
5. Arranging follow-up

The USPSTF also recommends that all patients be screened for alcohol abuse. The four CAGE questions are often used to screen for **alcoholism**. Two or more positive responses indicate the need for further investigation (Ewing 1984). The CAGE questions are the following:

1. Have you ever felt that you needed to *cut* down on your drinking?
2. Have people *annoyed* you by criticizing your drinking?
3. Have you ever felt *guilty* about drinking?
4. Have you ever felt you needed a drink first thing in the morning (an *eye*-opener) to steady your nerves or to get rid of a hangover?

The stages of change model applies to smoking or alcohol cessation just as well as it does to diet modification and exercise. Indeed, this model was originally proposed for smoking cessation. If someone is currently in the precontemplation phase, trying to convince him or her to stop smoking right away is futile. Instead, get the person to move into contemplation by discussing why smoking is problematic. Only after change is seriously contemplated will it be possible to act and keep a quit date.

Mental Health Issues

Depression, anxiety, eating disorders, and panic attacks are common in the young adult years. Suicide is the third-leading cause of death among 15- to- 24-year-olds (Strasburger, Brown and Braverman 2006). By the end of adolescence, up to 20 percent of people have experienced a major depressive episode (Strasburger, Brown, and Braverman 2006). Most of these episodes go untreated. Anxiety, especially social phobia, is even more common than depression, and anxiety symptoms often precede depressed mood. As mentioned before, many sufferers self-medicate with alcohol or drugs, eventually leading to substance abuse as a secondary problem.

The USPSTF advises screening for depression in adolescents and adults if resources are available for its accurate diagnosis, treatment, and follow-up. The Patient Health Questionnaire, or PHQ-9, screening test (table 9.3) and the Beck Depression Inventory are two standard screening tests for depression. In the PHQ-9 screen, nine questions are asked about how things have been going over the past two weeks. Each question is scored from 0 (not at all) to 3 (nearly every day). The final tally determines the severity of depression. Scores of 5, 10, 15, and 20 represent mild, moderate, moderately severe, and severe depression, respectively (Kroenke, Spitzer, and Williams 2001).

Women are twice as likely as men are to report depression and anxiety (Sachs, Ni, and Caron 2014). Depression frequently presents with anhedonia (the loss of ability to experience pleasure), rather than classic sadness. Because symptoms develop gradually, those with anhedonia (often men) may not even be aware they are depressed, despite suffering from

TABLE 9.3 PHQ-9 Screening Test for Depression

Over the last two weeks, how often have you been bothered by any of the following problems?	0 Not at all	1 Several days	2 More than half the days	3 Nearly every day
1. Little interest or pleasure in doing things				
2. Feeling down, depressed, or hopeless				
3. Trouble falling or staying asleep, or sleeping too much				
4. Feeling tired or having little energy				
5. Poor appetite or overeating				
6. Feeling bad about yourself—or that you are a failure or have let yourself or your family down				
7. Trouble concentrating on things, such as reading the newspaper or watching television				
8. Moving or speaking so slowly that other people could have noticed, or the opposite—being so fidgety or restless that you have been moving around a lot more than usual				
9. Thoughts that you would be better off dead, or of hurting yourself in some way				
If you checked off any problems, how difficult have these problems made it for you to do your work, take care of things at home, or get along with other people?	1 Not difficult at all	2 Some-what difficult	3 Very difficult	4 Extremely difficult

PHQ-9 scores of 5, 10, 15, and 20 represent mild, moderate, moderately severe, and severe depression, respectively

Springer and the original publisher, *Journal of General Internal Medicine*, 16(9), 2001, pgs. 606-613, "The PHQ-9: validity of a brief depression severity measure," K. Kroenke, L. Spitzer, and J. B. Williams, © Springer: With kind permission from Springer Science and Business Media.

insomnia, fatigue, and social withdrawal. In cross-cultural settings, depression frequently presents with somatic symptoms (headache, insomnia, stomach upset) rather than as a mood disorder. Screening exams like the PHQ-9 not only diagnose depression but also help monitor treatment success over time.

Suicide is a major problem in the adolescent and young adult population. Rates in men and women decreased from 1991 to 2000 but have been increasing since then (Suicide Trends Among Youth and Young Adults 2007). Suicide has become a critical problem for the military in general and the U.S. Army in particular; 38 Army soldiers were lost to suicide in July 2012 alone. More recently, between 70 and 80 suicides occur per 100,000 Army enlisted during their first year of deployment (Gilman et al. 2014). Suicide risk and substance abuse are also elevated in gay, lesbian, bisexual, transgender, and questioning (GLBTQ) youth (McKay 2011). The National Suicide Prevention Line is 800-273-8255. The Veterans Crisis Line is obtained by using the same number and pressing 1. Preliminary evidence has demonstrated the efficacy of positive psychology (Huffman et al. 2014) and mindfulness practices (Le and Gobert 2013) as deterrents to suicide.

Eating Disorders

Eating disorders are a critical mental health concern that primarily affects young women, although 5 to 10 percent of cases occur in males (Strasburger, Brown, and Braverman 2006). The two main types of eating disorders are anorexia nervosa and the much more common bulimia (in which binging is followed by either purging or excesses of fasting or exercise). Culture plays a contributing role because these conditions typically occur in countries where being thin is associated with being attractive.

Anorexia frequently results in dramatic weight loss, is challenging to treat, and has a significant risk of mortality or even suicide. Compared with those who have anorexia, women who have bulimia have a better prognosis, are often normal weight, and usually lack overt symptoms. Many eating disorders of lesser severity don't meet all the criteria for either condition and are called eating disorders not otherwise specified (EDNOS).

A team approach to treatment of anorexia with medication, intensive counseling, dietary therapy, and lifestyle change is most effective. Even so, only half of those with anorexia recover fully, and the mortality rate is 5 percent (Strasburger, Brown, and Braverman 2006). The USPSTF found that dieting among overweight or obese adults does not usually lead to problems in psychological functioning or eating disorders and has no specific screening recommendations.

VACCINATION RECOMMENDATIONS

The Advisory Committee on Immunization Practices (ACIP) recommended routine vaccinations include tetanus vaccine (given either as Tdap vaccine, consisting of tetanus, diphtheria, and acellular pertussis, or as Td injections, lacking pertussis), hepatitis A (routine for infants since 2005), hepatitis B, MMR (measles, mumps, and rubella), haemophilus influenzae type B (Hib), pneumococcal vaccine, influenza or "flu" vaccine, inactivated polio vaccine (IPV), varicella (chickenpox), and meningitis vaccine.

Most of these vaccinations are completed in infancy, although tetanus should be boosted every 10 years through life. Pertussis (whooping cough) vaccine has been added to the Tdap shot because immunity from the current acellular pertussis vaccine wanes within just 5 years of finishing childhood immunizations (Klein et al. 2012). Influenza shots are recommended by the CDC to all age groups before the onset of each winter flu season. Meningitis vaccine should be given to 11- and 12-year-olds, previously unvaccinated 15-year-olds, and all students before entering college. Meningitis boosters are recommended every 5 years while still at risk (living in crowded conditions such as dorm rooms).

Human papilloma virus (HPV) quadrivalent vaccine should be given to both genders starting at age 11, ideally before onset of sexual activity (ACIP). Despite controversy within some communities, recent research shows that receiving the HPV vaccine does not increase sexual activity in young women (Liddon, Leichliter, and Markowitz 2012).

Alternative Primary Care Providers

Before discussing the main domains of complementary and **alternative medicine**, we want to address the scarcity of primary care providers in the United States, which occurs especially in rural areas (Ricketts 2005). These are typically family practice physicians, internal medicine doctors, pediatricians, and obstetricians and gynecologists. These providers are your first line of contact for an undiagnosed health problem and ongoing care. Although young adults do not yet need as much medical treatment as they will need later in life, everyone should have a primary care medical home.

Nurse practitioners, physician assistants, and other health practitioners are filling in for and extending physician care. These medical professionals receive extensive training in primary care. Research demonstrates no difference in outcomes between physicians and nurse practitioners (Horricks, Anderson, and Salisbury 2002). Midlevel health practitioners will likely be replacing medical doctors as primary care givers during your life. We anticipate that this trend will improve access to primary care.

COMPLEMENTARY ALTERNATIVE, OR INTEGRATIVE, MEDICINE (CAM)

Alternative medicine is popular with young adults, but it should be conceived of as an approach that complements rather than replaces conventional care—hence the title **complementary alternative medicine (CAM)**. Various therapies that are not taught in U.S. medical schools are still popular outside the scientific medical community (Eisenberg et al. 1993).

The newest incarnation of CAM is integrative medicine, because it ideally integrates the best available options in conventional and alternative care. An integrative approach for migraine headaches might entail conventional pain medication augmented with mindfulness, relaxation, and breathing exercises. Another example of an integrated approach would be the use of the herbal therapy, butterbur, to replace a seizure medicine, topiramate (Topamax by Janssen Pharmaceuticals, Inc.), for migraine prevention in some patients (Holland et al. 2012), particularly if the side effects of topiramate became problematic. Similarly, conventional back pain therapy with muscle relaxants could be integrated with acupuncture, chiropractic care, and yoga exercises (Williams et al. 2005). Although CAM treatments usually lack the extensive evidence base of conventional therapies, a small but growing body of evidence supports the effectiveness and safety of some of these therapies.

CAM therapies fall into five domains or categories. These include alternative medical systems, mind–body interventions, biological-based treatments, manipulative methods, and energy therapies. Alternative medical systems such as traditional Chinese medicine and Ayurvedic medicine (India) are based on ancient healing traditions that remain popular today. Traditional Chinese medicine views the body as an energy system,

Complementary Alternative Medicine (CAM) Websites

- Ask Dr. Weil—www.drweil.com/drw/ecs/ask_dr_weil/index.html
- Cancer Guide—http://cancerguide.org/alternative.html
- Herbal Remedies World—www.herbalremediesworld.com/Mexican-herbs.html
- National Cancer Institute Office of Cancer Complementary Alternative Medicine (OCCAM)—www.cancer.gov/cam/health_camaz.htm
- National Center for Complementary and Alternative Medicine (NCCAM) Homepage—http://nccam.nih.gov/
- NCCAM on PubMed—www.nlm.nih.gov/nccam/camonpubmed.html
- Natural Medicines Comprehensive Database—(subscription required) http://naturaldatabaseconsumer.therapeuticresearch.com
- Stanford Health Library CAM Therapies and Modalities—http://healthlibrary.stanford.edu/resources/treatment/treatment_cam2.html
- Quackwatch (points out CAM problems, not benefits)—www.quackwatch.com

rather than as a machine, in which the life force *chi* (*qi*) flows through various channels, or meridians. Acupuncture is based on regulating this flow of energy through the body by inserting needles at specific sites.

Nearly all these alternative systems, whether from Asia, Africa, or South America, emphasize the need to balance opposing forces within the body, variously labeled as *yin* and *yang* or *cold* and *hot*. Many ancient traditions recognize this inherent need for balance in life.

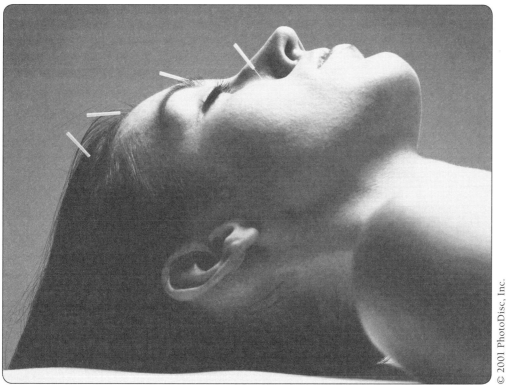

© 2001 PhotoDisc, Inc.

Alternative medicine therapies should complement rather than completely replace traditional medicine.

Marcel's doctor was pleased with his progress. He noted that Marcel was initially somewhat depressed in his new cultural environment, even to the point where he began to self-medicate with alcohol and then treat his hangovers with yerba mate tea. Initially, Marcel did not like or trust his doctor, but he grew more at ease over time. He liked that his doctor asked for his opinion and feedback. His doctor even looked up yerba mate and discussed it with him. He was pleased that his doctor discussed how he could change his life for the better rather than just recommending more medications. Marcel had been physically active playing soccer in Paraguay before coming to the States. He began to feel much better after he resumed regular physical activity.

The mind–body domain includes meditation techniques, such as mindfulness, which have been demonstrated to alter physiologic responses previously thought to be involuntary (Campbell et al. 2012). For example, Indian yogis can control their breathing, heart rate, body temperature, and even pain threshold through meditation.

An example of therapies that involve manipulating body parts (known as manipulative methods) is chiropractic care, in which spinal adjustment is believed not only to relieve back pain but also to reduce many other symptoms. The Feldenkrais method of somatic education is another manipulative approach that focuses on postural and movement retraining.

Energy therapy practices, the final CAM domain, involve auras or channeling energy to the patient by the laying on of hands. Reiki is a popular example, in which the healer places his or her hands over the patient to send healing energy. Additionally, a number of religious and spiritual denominations practice the laying on of hands.

Discernment is needed in adapting complementary alternative medicine. Just because a therapy is natural doesn't necessarily mean it is safe. Some herbs and therapies can be toxic (digitalis) or of questionable effectiveness (*Echinacea*, a genus of herbs in the daisy family, for colds). A series of recent clinical trials has discounted the benefits of many antioxidants and vitamin therapies. Some regimens, like high-dose synthetic vitamin E, may even be harmful, possibly increasing the risk of prostate cancer (Klein et al. 2011). Currently, the USPSTF recommends against routine use of vitamins to prevent cancer and cardiovascular disease. As with all medical interventions, researching what works should precede investing time and money. Check *Consumer Reports* and *Nutrition Action HealthLetter*. Eating well is preferable to taking supplements.

As a rule, the higher the stakes involved, the more important it is to use a proven approach. Conditions such as life-threatening cancer, infections, or trauma should be treated with conventional, well-established therapies. For example, conventional medicine does a good job of treating bacterial pneumonia, myocardial infarction (heart attack), abdominal trauma, and diabetes. Complementary alternative medicine may be more useful in managing chronic pain or fatigue, conditions for which conventional treatments often fall short.

Many advantages may result from adopting a holistic, whole-person, approach to care. Conventional medicine usually treats the human body as a malfunctioning physical machine. Its worldview is reductionist: seeing the human body, or even the entire person, as nothing but the sum of its component parts. In contrast, most holistic healers view the patient as much more than this.

SUMMARY

Honest two-way communication with your health care provider is a great starting point for a good therapeutic relationship. Find a doctor (medical home) that you can trust and visit whenever necessary. Know how the medical interview works and become more knowledgeable about your medical and family history. Remember that at least half of your health is determined by your lifestyle choices. Invest in your health by making the right choices now rather than postponing them. Time invested in a healthy diet, good exercise habits, and stress reduction can provide vast benefits in health promotion.

The U.S. Preventive Services Task Force (USPSTF) screening recommendations provide useful guidance about which screening tests are the most cost effective for young adults. Find out which ones apply to you. These tests can spot problems and bad habits early, while they can be more easily dealt with. Keeping up with your recommended screenings and vaccinations keeps you well.

Health care should be about more than just taking the right medications when you get sick. That approach is "illness care." Real health care involves optimizing your health and preventing illness before it even starts. Holistic approaches to health, which integrate the best complementary alternative practices with conventional care, keep the focus on wellness, not illness.

Complementary alternative, or integrative, medicine (CAM) offers a variety of popular health services. Some have demonstrated excellent results, but many of the practices are not effective. You are encouraged to remain open to the possible efficacy of some methods, but make every effort to determine their potential benefits or harms. Integrating the best complementary alternative practices with more conventional care offers young adults a comprehensive, holistic approach to health care.

Part III

Strategies for a Higher Level of Wellness

Chapter 10

Understanding Addictions

Objectives

After reading this chapter, you will be able to
- explain how compulsions and addictions occur in life,
- identify four factors that contribute to addiction,
- describe the addictions circuitry in the human brain,
- distinguish between passions and addictions, and
- create three strategies to enhance control over addictive tendencies.

Aiden is 24 years old and has been out of college for 2 years. He lives with his girlfriend and holds a steady job. While in college he drank alcoholic beverages most nights of the week and lived in "the party house." Typically, he shared a 30-pack of beer with a fraternity friend. He figured that his drinking would slow down after he left college.

Aiden comes home after work and sits in front of the TV drinking beer. He typically drinks a six-pack. He and his girlfriend drink to pass the time. Aiden thinks it is fun that they go to the bars together.

Although Aiden's job requires him to be active, he keeps gaining weight and often feels tired and irritable. One night he woke up vomiting with intense pain in his upper abdomen. This incident led to an emergency department visit and admission to the hospital. Aiden found out that he had pancreatitis. After being in the hospital for a week, he was released with the instruction to never drink again.

Addiction is engaging in **compulsive behavior**. In the journey of life, people have successes and pitfalls, and few make it through without occasionally slipping. Nakken (1990) characterized addiction as searching for happiness, wholeness, and peace by means of a persistent special relationship with an object, behavior, or event. This circumstance occurs for most of us.

The American Psychiatric Association's *Diagnostic and Statistical Manual* (2013), also known as *DSM-5*, has a chapter on substance use disorders and addictive disorders. Specifically, the manual describes 11 possible individual criteria, which are tallied by clinicians to determine the relative degree of disorder severity as follows: 0 to 1, no disorder; 2 to 3, mild; 4 to 5, moderate; 6 or more, severe.

For the purpose of this volume, **addiction** is the compulsive use of a mind-altering substance or repeated behavior in spite of negative consequences. The wellness characterization of addiction is broader than that used by *DSM-5* or other professional societies. This text is a wellness manual, not a technical manual.

The drug of preference for most people in the United States, including young adults, is alcohol, partly because of its widespread availability and legal nature. Many people begin drinking when they are young. Approximately 70 percent of young adults reported alcohol consumption, and 20 percent reported using marijuana, cocaine, psychotherapeutics, and hallucinogens in 2011 (*Results From the 2011 National Survey on Drug Use and Health* 2012). An estimated 22 million Americans have a formal alcohol problem or other drug problem, but fewer than 5 percent are aware or willing to admit that they have a problem (*Healthy People 2020* 2010). This circumstance represents a public health catastrophe of epic proportions. No other major public health problem exists in which 95 percent of those affected fail to recognize that the problem exists.

The practice of mindfulness and the application of the attitudinal foundations can enable people to overcome their dysfunctional behaviors. To be well is to live with mindful awareness in a supportive environment. To be well is to live a life of balance. To be well is to be nonjudging with self and others. To be well is to live your life with acceptance.

This information is intended to provide insights, tools, techniques, and strategies to help young adults live more fully, with more control, with more choices, and more satisfaction. By recognizing the spawning grounds for addictive and dependency patterns, you can take steps to improve your lifestyle.

Changing any behavior is hard, but changing established habitual behaviors is a particular challenge.

For example, 50 percent of heart attack victims do not stop smoking after their heart attack (Huang et al. 2012). Many tobacco users spend years attempting to quit before becoming tobacco free. Habitual behaviors can have a deep-seated hold. For compulsive and addictive behaviors, the hold is even more deeply established. Humans have an amazing ability to suppress conscious awareness of the ill effects of habitual destructive behavior that might otherwise motivate them to change.

The more people are aware of being at risk, the more negative consequences they experience, the more motivated they are to change their behaviors (Garland et al. 2014). Losing yourself to addictions can cause you to lose opportunities and happiness because you are unable to manage your life in the most effective way.

The overarching goal for this chapter is to understand personal substance use, as well as compulsive, addictive, and dependent behaviors. Redirecting your energies toward more productive pursuits represents a transformation into improved positive psychological well-being. Recognizing the lifestyle, policy, system, and environmental barriers to overcoming addictions can help chart a course to well-being.

SPECTRUM OF ADDICTIONS

Challenges exist at every turn in life, and many involve stress. Work, relationships, school, family, and coping with physical pain tax people's resources. There are countless ways (some good, some bad) to cope with pain and self-regulate. Many involve immediate gratification, quick fixes, and avoidance behaviors. Solutions can involve legal and illegal substances, such as alcohol and cocaine, "shopaholism" (overconsumption of consumer goods), excessive exercise, and avoidance behaviors such as such busyness and "**workaholism**" (working too much). If all is not well at home, you may spend more time at work, where the rewards are more visible. If you feel unappreciated, you can compulsively work at your studies to earn A's, which demonstrate your value.

Many of these behaviors are innocent of themselves, and the patterns evolve unconsciously. There is nothing wrong with working hard at school or work. There is nothing wrong with taking a pill to alleviate bodily pain. There is nothing wrong with drinking socially. The problems come from predisposition, from excess, from the social consequences of engaging in the repeated patterns, and from the physiologic responses established by the **dopamine** reward pathway in the brain.

First, know that emotional, spiritual, psychological, and physical ill effects or harms are associated with addictions. They hurt people. Note that people use drugs for various reasons and that some drugs resonate for some people more than they do for others. People who tend to be anxious self-medicate with marijuana or alcohol to calm themselves, whereas people who struggle with depression and fatigue may be more likely to abuse cocaine to increase their energy level. Self-medication, the kind that turns into full-blown addiction, doesn't work long term, despite its perceived effects as a coping mechanism. The actual effects, both physical and psychological, can be pernicious and long lasting.

You are all familiar with the horror stories of lives driven by **drug addiction**—poor, hopeless, wretched, and helpless people, living for the next fix, and in miserable physical conditions. Substance use, addiction, and dependency exist on a spectrum. Those with addictions are not just the stereotypic heroin user shooting up in the back alley or the homeless man drinking cheap wine out of a brown paper bag under the railroad bridge. Although notable, these are worst-case scenarios. Rather, everyone has dysfunctional behavior patterns, which given the appropriate conditions, could evolve into full-blown abuse, addiction, and dependency. Alcoholics commonly progress rapidly, in steps, from casual recreational use to full-blown dependency.

You may commonly think of people being addicted to substances such as alcohol, tobacco, heroin, crack cocaine, and amphetamines (Cami and Farre 2003). Imbalances also manifest in the realm of other compulsive behaviors such as gambling (*DSM-5* 2013), food (Meule and Kübler 2012), television watching (McIlwraith et al. 1991), sex (Carnes 1983), relationships (Peele and Brodsky 1975), videogame playing, Internet use, work (Griffiths 2005), tobacco, and exercise (Terry, Szabo, and Griffiths 2004).

Many people have underlying issues in their lives that make them vulnerable to addiction. These issues may stem from a lack of emotional coping capacity or a past misfortune or traumatic event. This explanation is most obvious in the case of a returning military veteran with post-traumatic stress disorder (PTSD). Many others have less stark traumas in their lives.

Compulsive behavior permits a person to function, at least superficially, without ever having to cope with these issues. Many people have unrecognized emotional and psychological pain that the drug or behavior serves to anesthetize. A compulsive behavior can mute the pain, even if the pain was never consciously recognized.

You can become addicted to almost any substance or behavior. These physical, psychological, and social addictive patterns have potential negative effects on quality of life. Some can even be life threatening. Nev-

© crazymuzzle

Self-medicating with drugs or alcohol may feel like a solution at the beginning, or even like a way to have fun, but it can quickly spiral out of control, sometimes with horrible consequences not only for you but also for everyone around you.

ertheless, the dysfunctional behaviors continue in spite of the victim's best efforts to quell them.

Persistently drinking three to six alcoholic beverages per day or watching 40 to 70 hours of television per week are common examples. Behavior patterns and reliance on substances to cope can inadvertently become major addiction problems.

FINE LINE BETWEEN PASSIONS AND ADDICTIONS

The lives of young adults are often supercharged, and passions can take on a life of their own. Many in the United States have access to a rich array of opportunities that includes satisfying relationships, delicious food, stimulating education, wholesome friends, fine wines, good music, and more-than-adequate shelter. Under the best of circumstances, life offers wonderful places to visit and intriguing people with whom to interact. Look around. Many people have fine goals, healthy relationships, and a hopeful future. Enjoying the presence of others in a world that includes but also transcends the material is part of a wellness lifestyle.

But a fine line may exist between passions and addictions. Your passions provide an interesting texture to your experiences. Why live if you can't enthusiastically enjoy what you are doing? Passions are intense, powerful emotional responses. As humans, we are naturally attracted to what gives pleasure and seek to avoid what causes discomfort. Our life journey is most engaging when our motivation levels are high. We innately want to be stimulated, to learn, and to feel good, and those drives can serve us well. Sport, sex, art, work, eating well, money, music, friends, social events, academic achievement, dancing, and even fitness serve as major focal points of our attention and energies. Dancing the night away and drinking a few beers with friends after a long day are normal.

You have satisfactions, challenges, and, of course, frustrations. In the 21st century, you are living at a fast pace; working on getting ahead; and perhaps focusing on money, achievement, image management, and social status. You may be aware of the ill effects of your passion but repeat the behavior in spite of negative consequences. After a while, the passionate, obsessive, or distracting behavior loses its original value, meaning, and purpose. What has happened? It no longer serves as a means to an end; it has become an end in itself. The process takes on a life of its own; the behavior becomes the high (Nakken 1990).

When you live out of balance, you can easily become engrossed in otherwise benign dimensions of life that become harmful. You may perceive immediate positive effects, such as the relaxation associated with alcohol consumption, or the stimulation that occurs when you elevate your blood nicotine levels through smoking cigarettes, or the sheer distraction of social media on the Internet.

Many develop an addictive pattern, which can progress through stages of dysfunction mediated by the frequency and intensity of the stimuli. Repeated thoughts, attitudes, and behaviors train the brain and nervous system to reactive patterns. The first stages involve curiosity, trying something out, such as a substance, object, or behavior, to see how well it might meet a need (Cami and Farre 2003). This activity might represent a coping mechanism in certain circumstances. If the results are pleasurable, you repeat the behavior. This action may not be a problem, although negative consequences may occur. The repetition may then progress through sporadic to habitual, abusive, and dysfunctional, and finally to addictive use and behaviors (Cami and Farre 2003).

Your thoughts help fix behavior patterns in place. It's not just what you do but also what is going on in your mind during these times that enables a seemingly innocuous activity to become a dependency or addiction. Being passionate about work can be a positive and desirable attribute. But working compulsively may be keeping you out of touch with dysfunctional parts of your life. Instead of addressing interpersonal issues with your spouse or romantic partner, for example, you may retreat to work, where you receive praise for your contributions. People love workaholics. They become go-to people in an organization. They get things done. Associates count on workaholics to make things happen. Instead of dealing with the isolation, work accomplishments can calm the mind or, to put it another way, anesthetize psychological pain.

Addicts often speak of the excitement in their lives. Following the straight and narrow is perceived as no fun. Living on the edge of catastrophe can be exhilarating. Many love to tempt fate, perhaps by having four to eight drinks and then getting into a bar fight, by driving 70 miles per hour (113 km/h) in a 25-mile-per-hour (40 km/h) downtown zone, or by consuming another chemical. This rush can feel like an overwhelming, albeit counterproductive, adrenaline high!

Addictions are insidious. Most people do not even realize a problem exists, at least initially. Addictive behaviors are shown to diminish awareness and rational thought (Childress et al. 2008). Sigmund Freud (1900) recognized this more than 100 years ago. Problems become more dominant when out-of-control behaviors control you. You become that way of life. Many resort to their substance of choice when having a good time, stressed, bored, or in crisis. The setting does not matter; the effects of addiction are the same. When this happens, you have slipped to the other side. You are no longer having these experiences. Rather, the experiences are having you!

Repeated behaviors can serve to provide an artificial buffer from an unpleasant aspect of life and can progress to **dependence** for coping with everyday life events. When this happens, you are addicted. Your addictive substance of choice inhibits mental, emotional, and spiritual growth (Adams, Tull, and Gratz 2012). You are no longer able to live with what Jon Kabat-Zinn (2013) refers to as "the full catastrophe," which are the normal challenges, feelings of pain, discomfort and frustration—the full spectrum of life. The texture of life is diminished. When your self-awareness is compromised, you may become even more compulsive, more driven to prove yourself, which brings on more stress and more use of mind-altering substances.

You transition from true living to a life of craving

Activity

Passions in Your Day-to-Day Life

We have little excuse for living a dull life, but keeping life in balance at the same time is the ultimate challenge. This activity involves identifying and reflecting on compelling facets of your life.

1. List 10 interests and activities in your life that involve considerable time or energy. These may involve earning an education, working to support yourself, watching television, playing soccer, hanging out with friends, helping others, and so on.
2. Describe the circumstances that surround these interests and activities. When do you do them? How often?
3. What are the consequences in terms of wellness of each interest and activity?
4. What are the benefits? Do they promote health?
5. Are there potential risks or associated dangers?
6. Describe how you would feel if you could not do them.
7. What activities could you do in their stead? How would those make you feel?
8. Enter your responses to this activity into your wellness journal.

and obsessing, consciously and subconsciously feeling that you need ever more. After years of living a life of compulsive use and addiction, a 30-year-old person may act as if she or he were 15. Emotional and spiritual growth stops when people start using addictively (*Alcoholics Anonymous* 2001).

Compulsive forces limit your choices, dominate your time, and rob you of free choice. Think about the time you spend drinking alcohol, smoking, and watching television that you might have more profitably spent otherwise. Perhaps you are being controlled by, rather than being in control of, what is happening. Repeated use and addictions are precursors of dependency and breakdown.

STRESS

Stress is pervasive. Many are stressed during the entire semester or the entire year. You may find yourself feeling insecure about upcoming tests, sitting in traffic gripping the steering wheel as you wait impatiently for the traffic light to change, wondering how your job is working out or whether your romantic relationship will go anywhere, or fretting about everyday demands of life.

Long-lasting stress contributes to chronic muscle tension, a rise in blood pressure, tension headaches, constriction of arteries, stomach problems, and other symptoms. People respond to stress differently depending on their coping capacity, but high levels of stress make almost everything worse and compromise deci-

sion-making capacity (Heatherton and Wagner 2011).

The effect of chronic stress on your mind and body is enormous. Stress can put you into a high-octane but self-defeating state of productivity. For example, you may drink caffeine to be more alert. If a little is good, more must be better. What about a 20-ounce (600 ml) Starbucks with over 400 milligrams of caffeine? You need to recognize an escalating cycle of behavior and take steps to counteract falling into pernicious patterns, which, in reality, further increase your stress burden.

Understanding Reacting and Responding Pathways

Figure 1.1 (see p. 5) segments behavior into two pathways—reacting pathways and responding pathways. This figure aids in understanding addictions, which are dysfunctional behaviors.

The reacting pathway, described on the left side of figure 1.1, is often unconscious. External life events can lead to a physiologic stress reaction. Here, heart rate and breathing increase along with overall arousal and alertness. Assuming that work, school, and relationships are chronic sources of stress, the fight-or-flight response is not appropriate. Rather, the stress reaction is inhibited. This pattern of internalization and inhibition of stress leads to ill health, which might include chronic hyperarousal, sleep disorders, chronic headaches, anxiety, and inflammation (Kabat-Zinn 2013). Maladaptive coping behaviors might involve drugs, alcohol, pornography, overworking, generalized busyness, **binge drinking**, overeating, smoking cigarettes, and gambling. All these can serve as anesthetics and provide perceived relief, albeit for just a while. The substances or behaviors keep you out of touch with what is being suppressed.

These reactive behaviors lead to a downward spiral of addiction. It may take the form of alcoholism, compulsive overeating, unprotected sex, gambling, or drug abuse. It can end with depression, a heart attack, or stroke. Addictive reactions are usually unconscious. Nobody makes mindful choices to be miserable. People evolve into out-of-control patterns. Continued pursuit of the behavior leads to overload, breakdown, life-threatening illness, and even premature death.

The responding pathway provides access to inner resources (Kabat-Zinn 2013). Mindfulness practices facilitate the development of healthy coping patterns and allow for a person to live with more nonjudgmental awareness. By practicing the seven attitudinal foundations in your mindful sittings, body scans, yoga, walking, and social interactions, you will have learned how to respond successfully to challenges.

Mindful practices present opportunities to deal with bodily discomfort, pain, and strong emotions. With mindfulness, you become aware and let go; you learn to trust yourself. Distractions and discomfort are part of any serious practice; they do not detract from it. Dealing with them patiently develops the strength to live effectively with challenges. You can then employ these same coping tools when additional stressors occur in everyday life.

Regular mindfulness practice helps you master the skills that enable you to buy time to respond. Given a noxious stimulus, you may just have a millisecond to decide to stay calm. This moment of awareness introduces new perspectives.

The heightened consciousness associated with the new perspectives enables you to experience your problems, associated fears, tensions, and emotions. You do not need to run or hide. You do not have to react unconsciously. Rather, you can recruit the skills and strategies that now contribute to an expanded perspective (Kabat-Zinn 2013). Your regular practice will have developed your mindfulness coping muscles, which enable you to maintain your equilibrium in the midst of what might otherwise be a trigger for substance use, abuse, and maladaptive coping behaviors.

We do not mean to suggest that by practicing mindfulness alone you will be able to recover from alcoholism or drug abuse. But mindfulness can be an important component of responding appropriately (Garland et al. 2014).

An example of overeating can illustrate the responding pathway. While studying in your apart-ment, you become bored and go to the refrigerator for a snack. You are not truly hungry because you just had lunch the previous hour. The attractive food inside the fridge can stimulate either a reaction or a response. As you look at the food, you think about mindlessly grabbing a cupcake.

Instead, however, you pause and become aware of your breath. You relax and become nonjudgmentally aware. You now can respond by (1) choosing the cupcake, (2) choosing an apple, or (3) closing the refrigerator door. You calmly close the door of the refrigerator and take a two-minute mindful walking break. Your awareness helps you recognize that you are bored, not hungry. You return to your studying relaxed, rejuvenated, and motivated to go another hour with your books, without having mindlessly consumed an extra 300 calories of sugar and fat.

MECHANISM FOR ADDICTIONS

Addictive responses are related to stress, environmental cues, developmental trajectories, and genetic makeup (Volkow et al. 2012). Any two people can respond quite differently to the same situation. Cigarette smoke becomes suffocating to one person and a source of euphoria to another.

Addictions are linked to physiologic and biochemical responses. Certain people are predisposed to the cascade of brain chemicals that naturally reward certain behaviors, and thus respond with a higher degree of sensitivity (Volkow et al. 2012). The addiction process appears to be mediated by dopamine responses in the brain. Dopamine is a neurotransmitter that plays a key role in the pleasure response in the brain, thus reinforcing addiction. Repeated exposure to the addictive stimuli develops the dopamine pathway, and a surge of dopamine rewards the behavior. Common neurobiological pathways are associated with a host of addictions (Nestler 2005).

Alcohol and other drugs, highly palatable food, sex, exercise, and shopping, for example, can cause an uptake of dopamine from transmitting nerve cells to receiving nerve cells in the brain (Volkow et al. 2012). This transmission provides pleasure, satisfaction, and relief as the dopamine flows and soothes the body and mind. Paradoxically, as the behaviors are repeated, the dopamine response diminishes. The person then frantically attempts to regain the pleasure (see figure 10.1).

The reduced dopamine receptor sites in the brain also signal a reduction of cerebral density and cerebral capacity. Your decision-making ability is physically impaired by overstimulation of the dopamine cycle (Goldstein et al. 2009). You fail to recognize how your

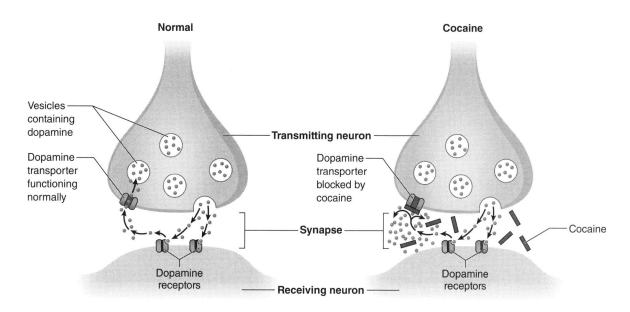

Normal / **Cocaine**

Vesicles containing dopamine

Dopamine transporter functioning normally

Transmitting neuron

Dopamine transporter blocked by cocaine

Synapse

Cocaine

Dopamine receptors

Dopamine receptors

Receiving neuron

FIGURE 10.1 Dopamine transmission cycle. When cocaine, for example, enters the brain, it blocks the dopamine transporter from pumping dopamine back into the transmitting neuron, flooding the synapse with dopamine. This action intensifies and prolongs the stimulation of receiving neurons in the brain's pleasure circuits, causing a cocaine high.

Adapted from NIDA Teens, 2005, *Teacher's guide: Effect of drugs of abuse on the brain* (Bethesda, MD: National Institute of Health and Human Services), 5.

sense of pleasure diminishes in spite of redoubling your efforts to maintain it. Using ever more, you receive ever less reward—and the costs of using keep mounting. This path leads you out of balance, out of control, and out of happiness.

In this vicious cycle, your addiction to a chemical substance becomes your primary relationship, not your mental health, job, possessions, friends, loved ones, or spiritual path. Many of us have seen addicts and alcoholics ignore their spouses and children to continue their drinking. Every year, scores of students drop out of school because of substance abuse.

The addiction takes on an almost mystical role. Repeating the addictive behavior no longer provides any true pleasure, but images and other substance cues can stimulate a dopamine-mediated response that continues to drive the addictive behavior (Childress et al. 2008). The cues can be longstanding. Even after long-term abstinence, running into a drinking colleague, seeing drug paraphernalia and pictures on a dessert menu, or taking in the scent of secondhand cigarette smoke can all open the doors to resumed compulsive use.

Through prolonged indulgence, neural pathways are wired to associate these distractions with pleasure, even though they no longer do so. Further, undesirable consequences occur in the short term and deep-seated addiction is the result in the long term. Behaviors can

become emotions, emotions become passions, passions become compulsions, compulsions become physical addictions, and addictions become dependencies.

An inordinate dependency on behaviors, substances, and people can take control of your life. You no longer have the choices that accompany a vibrant, fulfilling life; control of your life is outside you. Your addictions now define who and what you are. In other words, you are no longer having the experience; the experience is having you.

SUBSTANCE ABUSE

The spectrum of addiction is large. We limit our discussion to alcohol, other drugs, food, prescription drugs, tobacco, and busyness. In fact, anything can become a source of physical, mental, emotional, and spiritual imbalance and addiction.

Alcohol and Other Drugs

Because alcohol is intrinsic to our culture, many do not see it as a drug. It's not taken seriously and is often laughed off. You often hear, "Yeah, I drink a lot of beer, but I am all right." Yet if you drink a lot of beer, you drink a lot of alcohol! On campus, some brag about their overconsumption of alcohol. Among certain groups, the norm appears to be (1) drink heavy,

(2) drink often, and (3) everything is better with alcohol. Although the perception can be that alcohol overuse is the norm, this is not the case. Less than 30 percent of the college student population binge drink or are heavy users (*Results From the 2011 National Survey on Drug Use and Health* 2012).

According to *Dietary Guidelines for Americans, 2010* (2011), about half of adults in the United States regularly drink alcohol, 29 percent report binge drinking, and 9 percent of men and 4 percent of women are heavy drinkers. Alcohol is often a large part of the social scene among young adults. It is the most abused drug in the United States (Merikangas and McClair 2012).

Alcohol has an enormously destructive impact. An estimated 80,000 deaths occur annually in the United States because of consumption of alcohol (*Alcohol-Related Disease Impact* 2010). The threshold for problem drinking is much lower than many realize. The Centers for Disease Control and Prevention defines heavy drinking as habitually consuming more than 14 drinks per week for men and 7 drinks for women (*Alcohol and Public Health* 2014). One standard drink is 0.6 ounces (18 ml) of pure alcohol, which is what is contained in a 12-ounce (360 ml) beer, an 8-ounce (240 ml) malt liquor, a 5-ounce (150 ml) glass of wine, or a 1.5-ounce (45 ml) shot of 80-proof distilled liquor, such as whiskey, gin, rum, or vodka (*Alcohol and Public Health* 2014).

Binge drinking is classified as drinking more than four drinks for women and five drinks for men during a two-hour period (*Binge Drinking* 2014). Such use compromises judgment, leading to more drinking and devastating effects on the body. The result can be dependence, which further leads to personal, academic, social, health, and legal problems.

Some insist that alcohol or drug consumption is a "college thing," something that will not persist after graduation. Alcohol use does tend to decrease slightly with age, but the reduction is modest. The introductory story of Aiden indicates that he continued with his usual behavior, which resulted in a life-threatening health crisis. After graduation, you are not magically transformed into a non-substance-using member of society.

Alcohol use for health promotion purposes is paradoxical. Very moderate alcohol consumption does produce some cardiovascular health benefits (O'Flaherty, Buchan, and Capewell 2013). A daily glass of red wine may reduce the risk of heart disease. But 30 percent of cancer deaths are associated with drinking less than one and a half drinks per day (*Alcohol-Related Disease Impact* 2010). Increasing alcohol consumption beyond this amount soon counteracts any health benefits, and the risk may just not be worth it.

Certainly, anyone not currently drinking alcohol should not start for health purposes. The net effect of alcohol consumption is a negative one. The premature death rate among active alcoholics is two to three times higher than that for the remainder of the population (Vaillant 1995).

Research with laboratory rats demonstrated brain damage associated with moderate alcohol intake. The animals were given a level of alcohol daily that would elevate their blood alcohol content to the equivalent of .08 in humans (Anderson et al. 2012). After two weeks of this daily alcohol intake, the data indicated a 40 percent reduction in the number of cells regenerated in a part of the hippocampus, even though no perceptible decrease occurred in motor skills or learning in the short term.

Recovery from alcohol and other drug abuse is challenging. The founders of Alcoholics Anonymous (AA) found that all other treatment modalities were ineffectual. Most medical providers saw alcoholics as beyond help (*Alcoholics Anonymous* 2001).

Almost every city in the United States has an active fellowship of AA and Al-Anon, a support group for the friends and family of addicts. AA and Al-Anon have no rules, dues, or fees. The only requirement for AA membership is a desire to stop drinking. The only requirement for Al-Anon membership is having a relative or friend who is affected by addictions. These fellowships are free and open to the public.

The AA program is primarily delivered through meetings, and there is no paid staff on the local level. The structure of the meetings is varied. Typically, each fellowship group has a meeting weekly. Volunteers rotate through the role of meeting chair. At most meetings, there is a reading of the 12 steps and 12 traditions. Anonymity is a foundation for these spiritual recovery programs. People are introduced by their first name only. Some of the meetings are closed; that is, only people who have a problem with alcohol are welcome. Other meetings are open. Attendance at an open AA meeting does not indicate that a person is an alcoholic.

Many alcoholics may need to be detoxified at a treat-

Aiden reported to his therapist that he had no idea that six or more beers per day were a problem. His friends all drank that much. He did fine in college and was not missing work because of hangovers.

Substance Abuse: Twelve Steps of Alcoholics Anonymous

1. We admitted we were powerless over alcohol—that our lives had become unmanageable.
2. Came to believe that a Power greater than ourselves could restore us to sanity.
3. Made a decision to turn our will and our lives over to the care of God as we understood Him.
4. Made a searching and fearless moral inventory of ourselves.
5. Admitted to God, to ourselves, and to another human being the exact nature of our wrongs.
6. Were entirely ready to have God remove all these defects of character.
7. Humbly asked Him to remove our shortcomings.
8. Made a list of all persons we had harmed, and became willing to make amends to them all.
9. Made direct amends to such people wherever possible, except when to do so would injure them or others.
10. Continued to take personal inventory and when we were wrong promptly admitted it.
11. Sought through prayer and meditation to improve our conscious contact with God, as we understood Him, praying only for knowledge of His will for us and the power to carry that out.
12. Having had a spiritual awakening as the result of these Steps, we tried to carry this message to alcoholics, and to practice these principles in all our affairs.

ment facility for several days to a week. All are encouraged to have a sponsor, who guides them through their recovery. This person acts as a mentor. Newcomers are often encouraged to attend 90 meetings in the first 90 days in recovery as one way of breaking themselves from the bondage of alcoholic obsession.

An axiom heard around the fellowship is that "Meeting makers make it." Consistent with the directives of positive psychology, meetings are a way to become involved in a meaningful community. Regular attendance at AA meetings can serve as a positive focus for people who were accustomed to spending time drinking (Vaillant 2013). People are encouraged to become actively involved by arriving at the meeting early to help set up and to stay afterward to straighten up. The more a person is involved, the more social support and social capital he or she can experience.

Attendance at a meeting is a simultaneous incompatible behavior with drinking, that is, a person cannot be drinking during the hour of the meeting. Early in recovery particularly, a person has to live sober one minute, one hour, one day at a time. AA emphasizes that a person only has to stay sober today (*Alcoholics Anonymous* 2001). This strategy works for many, as making a commitment to never ever drink again may be overwhelming.

Listings of meeting times and locations customarily are available online. Telephone directories have toll-free numbers to obtain more information. Excellent inpatient and outpatient treatment programs are housed in many hospitals and as stand-alone facilities.

Other Drugs

Cocaine, marijuana, amphetamines, tranquilizers, heroin, MDMA (3,4-methylenedioxy-N-methylamphetamine, commonly known as ecstasy), and lysergic acid diethylamide (LSD, commonly known as acid) are popular on college campuses (Johnston et al. 2009). Heroin was used by 620,000 Americans in 2011 (*Health Statistics* 2014). These drugs are associated with problems that are similar to alcohol misuse. Marijuana is the most popular illegal drug; 7 percent of Americans used it in 2011 (*Health Statistics* 2014). The marijuana landscape is rapidly changing throughout the United States as the drug becomes legal for medical or recreational use.

Many who smoke marijuana think they will never start to use heavier drugs like cocaine, heroin, or LSD. Eventually, however, marijuana or benzodiazepines (prescription drugs like Xanax) may not be sufficient to achieve the desired effect. Addictive behaviors seem to run in packs. A dependency on one substance easily translates into other dependencies. So when other substances, like crack cocaine, become available, they may also be tried. If crack has a desirable effect, it will be used again. Typically, the wonderful feeling achieved the first several times diminishes with subsequent use. But users try it repeatedly, hoping to replicate the wonderful sensations of their first use.

Prescription Drug Abuse

Prescription drug use for nonmedical purposes in the United States represents a complex and serious issue (Biondo and Chilcoat 2014). Rates dropped by 14 percent from 2 million to 1.7 million between 2010 and 2011 among adults aged 18 to 25 years (*Prescription Drug Abuse* 2014), but abuse rates continue to be high, especially in rural areas. No change in the prescription drug abuse rate was observed for adolescents and adults 26 years old and older.

Medications are necessary at times to assist during physical illness and to control pain. Many people, however, rely on drugs as a solution for all life's problems. Our society is geared to the quick fix. Prescription and over-the-counter drugs seem to do just that. Prescription drugs are carefully designed with the latest in modern technology to effect an alteration to our physical, mental, and emotional symptoms. These medications are often started for pain control but are then continued "just to get through a rough day." Many people use them to help cope with life, which for many is difficult and devoid of meaning. This use quickly leads to addiction and dependency. Unfortunately, addiction to prescription drugs is sometimes exacerbated by well-meaning medical practitioners who over prescribe painkillers. Patients demand more medication, stating, "I just need this pill!" long after the original pain is gone.

The origin of the prescription drug abuse problem is at least twofold: (1) Patients are prescribed substances that they then become addicted to, and (2) patients seek out medical providers to provide them with more medication. For example, people may be prescribed opiate-based pain reducers, such as oxycodone. Taking such powerful drugs for even a short period can lead into full-blown addiction. Direct-to-consumer pharmaceutical advertising suggests prescription drugs as the first line of approach for a wide array of conditions (Abramson 2004).

Most drugs focus on symptom reduction. But patients can become dependent on drugs instead of first examining what they personally can do otherwise to address the problem, such as making lifestyle changes. Most health problems do not require highly technical pharmacologic solutions. Frankly, many such problems result from lifestyle imbalances that are amenable to other solutions.

Health-related change is always difficult, but the medical and pharmacologic industries profit from dispensing pills. Patients often feel satisfied if they are given a prescription, and the drug industry profits enormously from this transaction. The profit motive both corrupts and perpetuates the system, and there is little incentive to change.

People know that opiates have little beneficial long-term effect on nerve pain (Viguier et al. 2012). That is, taking opiates seems to exacerbate nerve pain because they actually increase sensitivity to pain as the drug wears off. Yet opiates are dispensed daily in the form of Vicodin (acetaminophen and hydrocodone) and other similar pills, such as fentanyl, butorphanol (known by the brand name Stadol), meperidine hydrochloride (Demerol), morphine sulfate (MS-Contin), acetaminophen and oxycodone (Percocet, Lorcet), and plain oxycodone (Oxycontin).

Compulsive Overeating

A study by Gearhardt et al. (2009) suggested that at least 11 percent of all young adults are compulsive overeaters. Unknowingly, people may become addicted to certain foods. The biochemical and neural pathways for food addiction are similar to those for other addictions in both animals (Geiger et al. 2009) and humans (Volkow et al. 2001). Our brains may respond to certain foods as cocaine addicts respond to their drug of choice (see figure 10.1). Cravings are stimulated by overeating sugar, fat, a fat and sugar combination, calorie-dense foods, food deprivation, an all-you-can-eat buffet, and images of highly palatable foods (Corsica and Pelchat 2010; Liebman 2012).

Restaurants, food manufacturers, and food chemists are in the business of making foods highly pleasurable. Food marketing specialists know how to promote sales. Effective marketing is part of their business plan. Increased sales mean more profits.

The euphoria associated with certain foods is much more pronounced after a period of caloric restriction, a cruel trick of nature (Corwin, Avena, and Boggiano 2011). Think about what happens when you skip breakfast. You might compensate by binge eating during your next meal. Cutting back on caloric intake to lose weight initially results in an augmented dopamine response. People repeat the eating behavior with the high-stimulus foods, anticipating a similar euphoric response. Such repetitive behaviors turn predisposed people into compulsive eaters. The response creates a subconscious craving that leads to repeated consumption. Compulsive eaters no longer like to eat that food;

Activity

Combating Food Addictions

Read and then practice the following control strategies for various food situations over the next seven days, whether or not you see yourself as having issues with food.

- Mindfulness. When eating, just eat. Stay focused on and present to your food. Have a high level of awareness of the pleasurable appearance, flavors, aromas, and textures of the foods. Make the decision not to eat while (a) watching television, (b) using electronic media, (c) in the car, and (d) while reading.

- Cues. Marketers create demand. Images of highly palatable foods create cravings. But alternatives are available, such as the tools of mindfulness. In addition, resolve to walk past the candy counter in the movie theater (Liebman 2012), not to bring highly palatable unhealthy foods into the home, and to avoid smorgasbords. Being proactive is a good strategy. Ask your workplace manager and colleagues to keep candy and cookies out of sight.

- Triggers. Certain foods set off bingeing. Identify and record what creates problems. Keep those foods out of your home and work environment.

- Healthy foods. Foods that are repeatedly consumed become more palatable over time (Methven, Langreney, and Prescott 2012). Make a daily practice of eating at least five vegetables, two fruits, four whole grains, and at least one legume. Identify which ones are more acceptable. You do not need to like all vegetables.

- Counterconditioning. Instead of gravitating to the refrigerator when bored, take a brief walk. Having a repertoire of alternative responses helps.

- HALT. Dysfunctional behaviors become a source of relief when hurried, angry, lonely, or tired. Adequate sleep and solid ongoing social support serve as antidotes.

- Exercise. Regular physical activity increases capacity for making correct decisions about food.

- Meditate: Take a three-minute sitting, walking, or mindful yoga break. If the urge to eat something is still present, do so mindfully, paying full attention to each bite.

No one is required to change all at once. Grow more conscious of the association between imbalance, lack of attention, and compulsive eating behaviors. Mindfulness can be a first step in addressing dysfunction. Change customarily occurs incrementally as you move through various stages of motivational readiness (Prochaska, Norcross, and DiClemente 1994).

---

they can't stop themselves from eating it. Preferences have been replaced by cravings.

Of course, there are antidotes for food obsession, but none are easy to implement. Compulsive eating must be treated as an addiction. Highly palatable foods (cookies, ice cream, candy, sugar-sweetened beverages) must be removed from the house. No food should be eaten while watching television (Boulos et al. 2012). Committing to mindfulness and mindful eating is also a critical part of treatment.

Overeaters Anonymous, another 12-step program, meets in most communities. This program emphasizes living in balance and working through the 12 recovery steps, even more than they discuss food (Bill 1981). Overeaters Anonymous meetings are free and open to the public. Times and locations are posted online or in phone directories.

By not paying attention to how much and how often you eat, you are likely to eat more food, and doing so can have a negative effect on health. If you are bored in class and decide to get some chips from the vending machine, you will consume many extra calories that can lead to weight gain and excess fat. All this results from trying to entertain yourself during a boring class. This eating pattern transfers over to eating while bored at home, work, or social functions, which is why it can have such detrimental effects on health. Be aware that when you finish a satisfying meal at a restaurant, the waitperson is instructed to present a menu with pictures of highly palatable desserts. The visual cue signals a stronger brain dopamine response than actually eating the dessert (Liebman 2012).

Tobacco

Tobacco contains nicotine and other psychoactive addictive substances. Many believe that these products are among the most addictive of anything used by humans. Each year, 85 percent of tobacco users would like to quit using but are unable to do so (National Institute on Drug Abuse 2010). Seventy-five to 80 percent of people who stop smoking relapse within six months (National Institute on Drug Abuse 2010), but those quitting need to realize that relapse is not necessary. Every day thousands of people quit for good.

Use of cigarettes has decreased by approximately 2 percent per year since 2000 (Connolly and Alpert 2008), even though 3,500 additional young people begin smoking every day (Centers for Disease Control and Prevention 2014c). These new smokers largely replace the number of older smokers who die daily. The established decrease in the prevalence of smoking is now being offset by increased use of nontraditional tobacco products, such as e-cigarettes, which are being marketed aggressively (Connolly and Alpert 2008). When the use of all tobacco products is considered, the United States has not done well. Since 2009, use of cigarettes, cigars, and roll-your-own cigarettes has remained stable at 25 to 26 percent (*The Health Consequences of Smoking—50 Years of Progress* 2014).

Given the seriousness of this addictive behavior, the best approach is primary prevention, which is never to begin any use of tobacco in the first place. Tobacco represents the number one cause of death and disability in the United States; more than 400,000 people die annually (Mokdad et al. 2004). Tragically, most established tobacco users begin before age 21, and the vast majority begin before age 18 (*Preventing Tobacco Use Among Youth and Young Adults* 2014).

Few start the habit later in life. In 2011 approximately 30 percent more teenage girls were smoking compared with 10 years earlier. Each year, the tobacco industry kills off roughly half a million of its best customers. This number is more than die from AIDS, alcohol abuse, drug abuse, motor vehicle crashes, murder, and suicide combined (Mokdad et al. 2004)! In addition, hundreds of thousands of people have their health problems exacerbated from tobacco use. Tobacco is a legal product that has no safe level of use. Any amount in any form is dangerous.

Use of tobacco, as with use of other addictive substances, begins for many reasons. Often, tobacco use starts as an experiment. Nicotine can induce a sense of pleasure. Many smokers report that smoking makes them feel calm, despite the fact that nicotine is a stimulant and actually causes them to become nervous and jittery, particularly when in withdrawal. The craving to smoke is provoked by nicotine withdrawal, so the drug is only relieving withdrawal-induced anxiety. Smoking can also cause people to feel as if they fit in. For example, if you are at a party and everyone seems to be smoking, you may join in out of insecurity.

Some people believe that smoking will help them lose weight, but this is simply not true (*The Health Consequences of Smoking—50 Years of Progress* 2014). Smokers generally tend to be leaner than nonsmokers. But many people who smoke are also overweight or obese. Smoking tobacco and being overweight cause tremendous strain on the heart and arteries.

Individual smokers and society pay a high price for the use of tobacco products. Smoking alters appearance, ages the skin, and fouls the smoker's breath and clothing. Second-hand smoke poses a risk to everyone around the smoker as well. But the long-term internal risks (heart disease and cancer and death) and associated costs are what make quitting imperative. Tobacco use in any form is a self-destructive act incompatible with wellness.

Quitting tobacco is possible, and the current U.S. success rate for tobacco cessation is admirable (Connolly and Alpert 2008). You may need help to quit and a deep commitment never to give up trying, even if you backslide. Mark Twain once said, "Quitting smoking is easy. I've done it thousands of times!" But Drs. James Prochaska, Norcross, and DiClemente (1994) points out that a lapse is not a relapse. Usually, it takes several attempts to quit successfully.

Most important, do not beat yourself up if you backslide. Continue with your commitment to quit. The tendency to judge yourself is a major barrier to tobacco cessation efforts (Adams et al. 2012). Consistent with the balance theme of this book, people can regain control over their lives by addressing the psychosocial factors that contribute to tobacco addiction.

Hyperactivity

Few treatises on addictions address being overbusy. Dr. Jon Kabat-Zinn (2013) states, "Filling up you time with busyness is another self-destructive avoidance behavior" (p. 326). Many of us maintain a frenetic pace, independent of having an attention-deficit disorder.

Americans tend to work hard, and our society respects and rewards hard work. Important things always need to be done. But you should realize that if you work too much, your life will fall out of balance and you will have no time left for yourself and your loved ones. Few people say on their deathbeds, "I wish I had spent more time at the office." Such activity eliminates the opportunity for being mindfully aware and for nondoing (Kabat-Zinn 2013).

BATTLING ADDICTION

The environments you create and the behaviors you engage in during your teens and 20s set up behavior patterns that last long into the future. Most addiction patterns are established during adolescence and early adulthood (*Results From the 2011 National Survey on Drug Use and Health* 2012). These patterns set up the vicious cycle of use, abuse, obsession, dependence, unhappiness, further use, and disregulation.

The wellness and public health focus should be on primary prevention, on not starting the habit. Rehabilitation is a struggle after addictive behaviors become entrenched. Try to reduce the risk factors for addiction while promoting the protective factors in your life. By learning a more proactive wellness-oriented lifestyle, you have the opportunity to reverse the dire prediction that your life expectancy will be shorter than that of your parents (Olshansky et al. 2005).

Remember that addictions may be a symptom of your lack of inner peace. Your compulsions and addictions are often a manifestation of what is going on emotionally and psychologically. Awareness is an important step toward attaining a wellness lifestyle.

One way to gain awareness is through honest self-reflection. A good test for alcohol addiction is available at the following link: www.ncadd.org/index.php/learn-about-alcohol/alcohol-abuse-self-test. Go to that link and take the test now. If you are dealing with other issues, take the same test but substitute your own issue for alcohol.

Confronting Addiction With a Nonjudging Attitude

A nonjudging attitude is an effective antidote to being out of touch with your dysfunctional behaviors (Adams et al. 2012). Seeing the true cost of your behaviors is difficult when you are living on automatic pilot. Most people are unaware of just how damaging the consequences of their compulsions and addictions really are.

A widespread but erroneous belief is that addicted people are totally dysfunctional. On the contrary, most of the 22 million addicted people in the United States live their lives in a way that appears normal, at least on the surface. But their friends, family, and loved ones report that they are often unavailable, insensitive,

© PicturenetCorp-Fotolia

Take an honest look at yourself and your emotions. Are things that are troubling you starting to manifest in some form of addiction? Reach out for help as early as you can so that you can start to feel better sooner.

Activity

Nonjudgmental Observation of Your Addictions

When you are alone, engaging in a three-minute mindful sitting may be helpful. Find a comfortable place, close your eyes, and relax.

1. Be aware of your breath as it flows all the way in and all the way out. Stay with the breath for three minutes.
2. At the end of the three minutes, remain in your seated posture and reflect on any possible dysfunctional and compulsive behavioral patterns. If you have come to recognize your dysfunction, then acknowledge the possible addiction.
3. Remain nonjudgmental about yourself.
4. Picture how the dysfunctional behavioral pattern began.
5. Follow the path of the behavior. Think of times you've tried to change your behaviors, but do not judge or beat yourself up about these attempts. Remember that you are like everyone else, on a journey.
6. Think of who you could talk to about your dysfunctional behavioral pattern or addiction, a person who would be knowledgeable and nonjudgmental about it.

---

self-absorbed, or even out of control. Do you feel irritable all the time and often get into stupid disagreements? Perhaps you miss a deadline at work because you are not on your A game after being out late a few nights in a row. Such incidents could be warning signs of an evolving problem. The situations can become ever more severe. Waller et al. (2013) reports that intimate partner violence often follows drinking.

Being depressed, angry, and frustrated with self serves little purpose in gaining control. Such self-condemnation can even result in suppression of the memory of the event. A strategy is needed to overcome these values, attitudes, and behaviors. Consider making impartial observations, being nonjudging, and permitting these memories to come into your consciousness. Once brought into consciousness, you may be able to deal with them personally, chat with a friend about them, consult with a therapist, or attend an AA meeting.

Engaging in Social Liberation to Change

Dealing with compulsions, addictions, and dependencies can be a springboard to high-level wellness. Your most serious challenges can become your greatest assets. Societal resources are available today to enable you to live your life well, to be liberated from the cognitive, attitudinal, behavioral, and neurobiological situations that keep you locked in a state of struggle. According to Prochaska, Norcross, and DiClemente (1994), **social liberation** is a process of change that involves any "alternatives that the external environment can give you to begin or continue your change effort" (p. 28).

For some, this change effort will be through the fellowship of Alcoholics Anonymous (AA), the most widely used method for alcohol addiction recovery. As of 2012 more than 100,000 AA groups served an estimated 2,000,000 alcoholics worldwide (AA Fact File 2012). The heaviest concentration is in the United States. The AA program provides members with social and emotional support and avenues for spiritual growth and recovery from addiction. The emphasis of the program is on living well and living in balance, rather than on just not drinking. In fact, only the first half of the first step addresses alcohol. All other steps address how to live in a positive and proactive manner. Personal responsibility and social support are significant parts of the recovery process. AA members make themselves available to each other 24/7 for support and crisis management.

The AA program model has been adapted, using related names, to serve people with many addictive behaviors. These fellowships open up new forms of unconditional positive regard, a nonjudging atmosphere for living with more awareness one day at a time. All these 12-step programs are compatible with the nonstriving approach to wellness. *Twelve Steps and Twelve Traditions* (1981) guides recovery, and the daily meetings provide the social support that can help you gain control over your life (see figure 10.2).

Almost nothing will disrupt a family more than addiction to alcohol and other drugs. The toll that addiction takes on a family is one of the major crises of society. For those who have been so affected, we recommend attending meetings of Al-Anon or Adult Children of Alcoholics. These programs exist to provide understanding and support to the families and friends of alcoholics and addicts.

Mental health professions can be of assistance. Workplaces often have an employee assistance program, a free counseling service that employees can go to for three free confidential counseling sessions. Supervisors are able to encourage, but not mandate, employees who are not acting or working appropriately to seek help through the employee assistance program. After the sessions, an employee may continue counseling with a referred agency or counselor. College and university campuses often have excellent student assistance programs. Students can self-refer, or faculty and staff who observe what appears to be a problem student can recommend the services of the student assistance program.

Other holistic recovery programs for chronic diseases exist to address some of the many breakdown issues that people experience. The Dean Ornish Program to Reverse Heart Disease (Ornish 1990) and the Commonweal Cancer Help Program (2014) promote a mindful balance of thought, social support, attitude, and other healthy behaviors. These programs promote the principles of positive psychology, the seven attitudinal foundations, and mindfulness.

The Dean Ornish Program for Reversing Heart Disease promotes mindful hatha yoga and letting go. Ornish (1990) admonishes participants to "remind yourself that the feeling of greater peace didn't come from anywhere outside you, it was there already" (p. 133). The social support helps Ornish participants accept where they are with their health status and trust themselves to resolve it in a nonstriving manner.

SUMMARY

Stereotypical images of addicts are of people who are totally dysfunctional. You might envision them drinking out of a brown paper bag under the railroad bridge. But compulsion and addictive behaviors affect many of

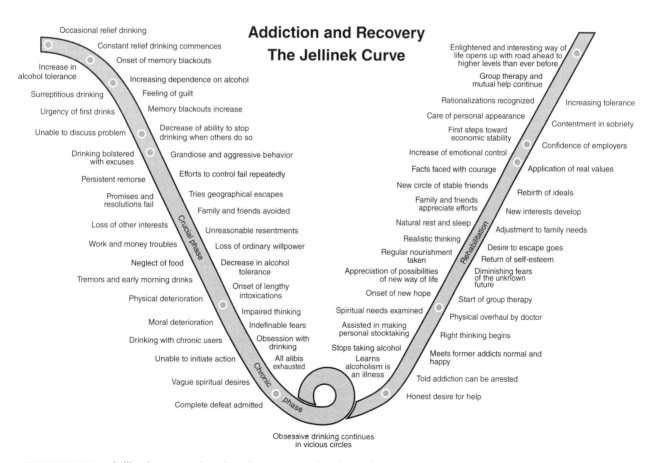

FIGURE 10.2   Jellinek curve showing the progression into alcoholism and then recovery.

Reprinted from http://www.in.gov/judiciary/ijlap/jellinek.pdf.

Aiden's diagnosis of acute pancreatitis in the hospital was enough for him to begin addressing his alcohol abuse. Fortunately, his girlfriend was incredibly accommodating. Even though they were accustomed to drinking together, Aiden came to realize that she was not drinking a fraction of the alcohol that he was. She supported him. As he began to attend Alcoholics Anonymous, she joined Al-Anon. Their circle of friends changed. They now have nondrinking friends with whom they have a wonderful time. He believes these friends are far more loyal than his former drinking buddies, whose interactions were always mediated by alcohol.

you and your friends. We say this to convince you that many people have dysfunctional characteristics. You may be compulsively overeating, working too many hours, studying through the night, or drinking more than is healthful.

Compulsive behaviors, obsessions, dependencies, and addictions are functional on a certain level in that they can help people cope with an unpleasant reality, even when that reality is subconscious. But, over time, compulsive behaviors become less manageable and can derail your best interests.

Science is clarifying common pathways for many addictive behaviors, which are mediated through a dopamine response in the brain. For example, eating a highly palatable substance might evoke a strong dopamine response in the brain. People who are pre-disposed are more likely to repeat that behavior to try to reexperience the original feelings of euphoria. Unfortunately, the neural pathway changes so that the number of receptor sites decreases. Increasing the intensity and frequency of the behavior or substance does not evoke the same pleasure. Addiction is occurring.

Mindful evaluation of your life every now and then ensures that you are doing what best promotes your well-being to fulfill unrealized personal potential. Our proposed antidote to addiction is the practice of mindfulness and the application of the attitudinal foundations to all your affairs. Mindfulness does not make your mental, emotional, physical, spiritual, and environmental problems go away. Rather, you have more inner resilience to address the issues.

© Andrew Penner

Chapter 11

Sustaining Environmental Health

Objectives

After reading this chapter, you will be able to

- define sustainable development,
- describe methods to promote sustainability,
- identify four reasons that people are not focused on sustainability in the United States,
- list five changes to enhance personal lifestyle sustainably,
- describe how an environment in balance will benefit our personal balance,
- list three methods of studying the environment, and
- list five actions to live local and promote a local economy.

Amy recently went to South America during a school break. Although she had a lot of fun, she was disturbed by the multinational agribusiness corporate practices she witnessed. They were engaged in practices that seemed grossly unethical. She saw indigenous people living in poverty while their way of life was threatened. Land was being seized and clear-cut, and the local people ended up working their former land for minimal wages. The reckless practice of massive clear-cutting of the forests led to increased flooding of local homes. She felt uncomfortable with what she saw and vowed to change her life and to raise awareness of poverty issues when she returned home.

Amy has since started an activist group at her school to discuss the effect of multinational corporations on populations around the world. To help in decreasing her impact on the planet, she decided to eat more locally, not to use nonbiodegradable products such as Styrofoam cups, and to avoid plastics when possible. She found that taking these steps helped her feel more in tune with what her body needs. Taking these actions has also helped Amy connect with what she can do to help the world around her.

Sustainability refers to the ability of humanity to accommodate present needs without compromising the ability of future populations to meet their needs (World Commission on Environment and Development 1987). This concept also applies to the other species on planet earth, but few represent a better model for sustainability than do ants, the pervasive and mighty creatures that are seemingly everywhere.

According to William McDonnough and Michael Braungart (2002), ants on planet earth have a biomass greater than that of humans. Composed of more than 8,000 different species, these creatures have been industrious and productive for millennia. Their efforts have resulted in improved soil, enriched plants, and healthier animals in a host of environments throughout the world (Hoyt 1996). In contrast, humans have focused on industrial production for only the past 200 years, causing degradation of most biological systems during that time. The sanctity of the planet is being desecrated (Feinberg and Willer 2013).

As you examine your relationship with the planet, you need to consider how you can individually and systematically sustain your environment. Much of the ongoing contamination may appear to be beyond the reach of individuals. Most consumption and production of resources are by industry and agriculture. But you should not underestimate the possible global role of individuals in this electronic age. This chapter examines how humans are adversely affecting the physical environment and some of the ways that your day-to-day lives are undesirably affected. We also propose mindfulness strategies that are intended to increase your consciousness and your relationship with earth.

PROTECTING OURSELVES, ASSAULTING THE PLANET

Humans have labored to protect themselves from external threats. As the human species evolved, the major risks were temperature extremes, predatory animals, lack of food, droughts, and inadequate drinking water (Diamond 1997). As a result, early humans organized communities to maximize life and well-being, consistent with the Maslow hierarchy of human needs (1954).

In the 1800s manufacturing began to address the needs of larger populations and the desire for higher standards of living (Keitsch 2010). In so doing, humans became the principal threat to their own continued survival. Although you no longer need to be as concerned about predatory wild animals as people were 200 to 300 years ago, socioeconomic policies and systems and the built environment have created innumer-

able challenges. Application of industrialization and technology has resulted in heightened manufactured risks (Yan 2012).

Manufactured items go to landfills when they are no longer needed or wanted. The production involves natural resources, energy, a product, distribution, and use. After use, when a product is no longer functional or goes out of style, it is discarded. Billions of such products end up in landfills on a daily basis, often **leaching** toxic by-products into the soil, air, and water.

Humans recklessly consume natural resources and create toxic by-products. For example, the average house size doubled between 1950 and 2005 in the United States (Wilson and Boehland 2005), requiring more than twice the construction, heating, and air-conditioning resources (Fuller and de Jong 2011). Although the planet has an innate capacity to restore itself, the current ongoing physical demands are exceeding the capacity of planet earth to heal.

According to the Environmental Protection Agency *Indoor Air: Report on the Environment* (2013), Americans, on average, spend 90 percent of their time indoors, cut off from the reality of planet earth. We have climate-controlled homes and transportation for the cold of winter and the heat of summer. Momentous quantities of fossil fuels are used to maintain comfort. It is almost as if we are living in a bubble without knowledge of or regard for the sustaining role of the planet in our lives. Greenhouse gases, particularly carbon dioxide and methane, are accumulating in the atmosphere. The resulting impacts are taking a toll that will persist for many decades.

Here are other examples of the effects of our lifestyle: Frederick, Maryland, created a $150 million flood control project in the 1970s to keep water out of the city and a multi-million dollar system to bring the Potomac River back into the city for drinking water. The oceans are increasingly acidic (Hönisch et al. 2012). Overfishing is depleting seafood supplies (Foley 2013). Agricultural lands are contaminated with many chemical substances including arsenic ("Arsenic in Your Food" 2012). Air quality has deteriorated because of contamination from smoke, smog, and particulates and the depletion of the protective stratospheric ozone layer (*Stratospheric Ozone and Surface Ultraviolet Radiation* 2010). In addition, freshwater supplies are endangered by agricultural fertilizers, insecticides, and pesticides (King et al. 2012).

KLEENEX CULTURE

More than two centuries ago, in 1798, Thomas Malthus, a conservative English cleric, made dire predictions about the environment and population.

Creature comforts such as cars and large air-conditioned houses have become more popular at the cost of pumping more greenhouse gases into the atmosphere and using up more natural resources to keep them running. What can you do to help reduce your personal consumption of resources and shrink your **carbon footprint?**

Malthus believed that England was approaching its maximal **carrying capacity**. He suggested that the global population was reaching a **tipping point** where starvation would limit further population expansion (Gilbert 1999).

But at about the same time, production efficiencies created by the Industrial Revolution changed the environment, solving some problems and creating others. Industrialization, including mechanized agriculture,

improved productivity, increased food availability, and accelerated waste generation. The common worker received low wages, toiled long hours in deplorable conditions, and lived in the filth associated with dense housing and inadequate infrastructure. By contrast, those who owned the means of production maximized profits, their possessions, and their quality of life.

Overconsumption and excessive production are by-products of the Industrial Revolution. A **Kleenex**

Activity

Using Freecycling in a Kleenex Culture

The Internet and social media are developing innovative ways to provide items a new home. The Freecycle program is working to repurpose items.

1. Go to www.freecycle.org to determine whether a group is operating in your area.
2. Join the freecycle.org group that is closest to your home.
3. Identify at least one item in your apartment or home that you are no longer using.
4. Work with the Freecycle group to give your item to someone else.

Write a 200-word journal entry that describes the experience. How did you feel about giving something to another who had use for it? Were you surprised that someone was interested in your item? Are you likely to do this again?

Library of Congress LC-USZ62-45868

Trash piled up in the streets of New York City in 1911 made it obvious that sufficient infrastructure was not in place to handle the effects of a growing population. Cities must continuously examine the best policies and methods for handling waste.

culture developed. Items are produced, used, and then thrown away, although there is no "away." Everything stays here on planet earth. Little emphasis is given to reusing or recycling materials. This mentality represents an accelerated use of natural resources and an unprecedented rate of environmental contamination.

The issues of a throwaway society were not perceived as a serious problem when the global population was less than one billion. Over the next 200 years, world population increased 10-fold and personal wealth increased 6-fold (Lucas 2002). These dramatic increases led to more severe environmental problems.

Many people viewed the by-products of the production cycle, such as surface, air, and groundwater contamination, as the inevitable results of prosperity. Even into the 1950s, there always seemed to be somewhere else to discard the unwanted items. The industrial processes and the new standard of living spewed smoke, particulates, and carbon dioxide into the air, and the wind carried it "away." This notion was especially true from the perspective of the richer nations, which used the air, water, and landmass of the planet as trash dumps.

In the short term, huge societal problems developed. The larger American cities were open dumps and sewers. The first septic tanks were not introduced for sewage treatment until 1895 (McKenzie, Pinger, and Kotecki 2012). In 1900, the average life expectancy in the United States was 47 years, and in New York City, where population was dense and water, air, and solid waste pollution were pervasive, life expectancy was only 19 years (Rosen 1975). The inadequacy of the infrastructure (such as sanitation services) to accommodate the quickly growing population contributed substantially to the limited life expectancy in New York City.

Modern regular trash collection and sewage infrastructure were developed as antidotes to the squalor of the cities. These services hid the more serious dimensions of waste disposal. People do what the environment enables and reinforces. When centralized landfills and curbside pickup were developed, the problem seemed to have been addressed. The physical environment seemed to be endlessly forgiving, and the throwaway culture continued unabated. The squalor of our major cities was made manageable, thereby enabling Americans to generate an increased amount of trash and other pollutants.

Products were and are produced without regard to their reuse or disposal. In fact, many manufactured items now have both a planned and a perceived obsolescence. The majority of what you use ends up in landfills, waterways, and in the air we breathe. Products wear out, break, or go out of style. According to the Product Policy Institute (2014), 75 percent of waste is composed of throwaway products and packaging. Since 1960, even with increased recycling, the total amount of municipal solid waste being generated has nearly tripled and the per capita waste load has increased by 60 percent (see figure 11.1).

The United States represents approximately 5 percent of the global population, but those people use roughly 25 percent of the natural resources being consumed annually. As this rate of consumption begins to

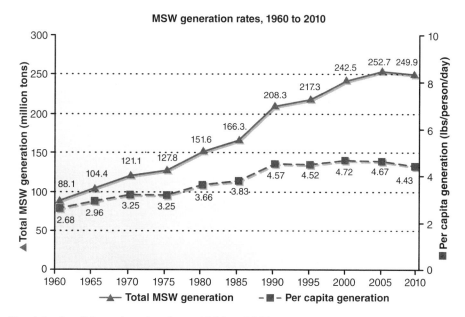

FIGURE 11.1   Municipal solid waste rates from 1960 to 2010.

Reprinted from EPA, 2011, *Municipal solid waste generation, recycling, and disposal in the United States: Facts and figures for 2010.* Available: http://www.epa.gov/epawaste/nonhaz/municipal/pubs/msw_2010_rev_factsheet.pdf

be approached by people in far more populous China and India, major impacts loom for our planet. These latter countries seek to have and deserve to have a lifestyle similar to that of more developed countries, but the same level of natural resource depletion is simply not sustainable.

Chemicals in the Environment

The ecological challenges in the United States spawned an environmental movement that began with the publication of natural history journalist Rachel Carson's *Silent Spring* (1962). This volume described the extensive use of DDT (dichloro-diphenyl-trichloroethane) as an insecticide for controlling agricultural pests and mosquitoes. DDT had the unintended consequence of killing birds. Carson presented evidence that the practices of agribusiness and the chemical industry were unsustainable. Her *Silent Spring* theme vividly depicted a world with no bird songs to welcome the spring.

President John F. Kennedy appointed a special science panel to examine the issues. Opposition to the themes of *Silent Spring* by the U.S. Department of Agriculture and the chemical industry called further attention to the issue among the public at large. The conclusion of the science panel was that Ms. Carson's contention was indeed valid. This book, the surrounding controversy, and the science panel recommendations were vital steps toward the regulation of DDT, which occurred about a decade later.

More recent analysis has demonstrated that U.S. agricultural practices still result in a reduction in species (Geiger et al. 2010). Land used by low-intensity agriculture, which uses fewer chemicals, has been found to have approximately three times the number of native species present compared with high-intensity agricultural land (Koellner and Stolz 2008). Many species serve useful agricultural purposes, such as bees that pollinate plants and ants that make the soil more nutrient rich.

The Endocrine Disruptor Exchange (2014), founded by zoology professor Theo Colborn, is a nonprofit organization dedicated to compiling and distributing the scientific evidence on the health and environmental problems caused by low-level exposure to chemicals that interfere with human embryo development and human body functions. She calls these chemicals **endocrine disruptors**.

Professor Colborn's focus has included pesticides and the diverse chemicals used in shale gas drilling and **fracking**. Much is known and more remains to be learned about such chemicals, and awareness is now available to everyone. The manufacturers of commercial and industrial chemicals are required by federal law to prepare material safety data sheets for each chemical product and make these available to the users. The material safety data sheets, which are generally available on the Internet, summarize the physical and chemical properties of the chemical and present the known hazard and toxic data.

Hazmat placards (EnvironmentalChemistry.com 2014) are diamond-shaped information signs required on chemical materials that are being transported on public roads or rivers. On the placards are internationally recognized four-digit UN numbers. The UN number identifies the substance and includes the category of its hazardous nature—class 1 for explosives, class 2 for compressed gases, class 3 for flammable liquids, class 6 for poisons, class 7 for radioactive materials, and class 8 for corrosive liquids. For example, sodium hydroxide (lye), in class 8, is an extremely corrosive chemical product in household use as a drain cleaner. It must be used with great care. The placards serve to alert community and government officials about what is travelling through their communities.

An increasingly large numbers of groups within the nation are helping with the issues of chemicals in our environment. Apps for phones and computers can decipher and summarize the impacts of the diverse products that we may encounter. *Consumer Reports* and the Center for Science in the Public Interest are committed to providing clear and unbiased information about various products. They take no advertising and accept no government support, offering a model for disseminating unbiased information.

Sustainability

Donella Meadows and the Club of Rome published *Limits to Growth* in 1972, using three computer models to examine Malthusian concerns. The computer models examined world population, industrialization, pollution, food production, and resource depletion. The models explored how exponential population growth interacts with finite resources, a process that inevitably leads to economic and social collapse. Although the original timetable for the impending catastrophe has not materialized, a 30-year update of the original publication (Meadows et al. 2004) suggested that the prediction of a 21st-century economic and societal collapse is still valid.

The problems today are more serious than ever before, even though much has occurred to limit the environmental harm. The United Nations formed the World Commission on Environment and Development (1987) (also known as the Brundtland Commission) in 1983 to address growing concerns about the global degradation of the natural environment. This commission, first chaired by G.H. Brundtland, former prime minister of Norway, focused on uniting countries to develop sustainable development strategies.

Sustainability has a two-way interaction. The physical environment can sustain humans only with the resources that remain. Remember that the major societal threats are now manufactured ones (Yan 2012).

If humans poison the air, water, and soil, then three of the major human interactions with the environment are toxic, not health promoting. The physical environment can help only if we treat it with respect and dignity.

All the things about this world and your life are interconnected. Indeed, the physical, political, social, economic, cultural, and spiritual environments interact. The systems of one environment influence all the others. For example, if prevailing political and economic norms call for economic growth at any price, the physical environment is almost necessarily compromised. The perception of a lack of connection between humans and the physical environment permits economic tunnel vision to persist.

The Fifth Assessment Report of the United Nations' expert Intergovernmental Panel on Climate Change (2014) reiterates the overwhelming scientific consensus that the world is warming, largely due to human activities. There is a need for immediate action. As reported by Tompkins and Levin (2014), four major conclusions are: (1) Climate change now affects every part of the planet. (2) Climate change will increase the frequency and severity of extreme weather. (3) Meeting the scale of the challenge requires adaptation and mitigation. (4) Rapid and steep reductions in greenhouse gas emissions can reduce risks and costs—and the timing matters. This Fifth Assessment Report warns what is done (or not done) to reduce emissions today will have an impact for decades to come and throughout the 21st century. If rapid reductions are not undertaken now, we will commit ourselves to levels of warming that will require radical and costly changes in the future to manage devastating impacts.

Triple Bottom Line

The environmental debate of the past 50 years has led to a more balanced **triple bottom line** approach involving people, planet, and profit. Full-cost accounting is crucial for this procedure to function and for people to survive in a living planet. Historically, **single bottom line** calculations exaggerated profits by using short-term accounting. The effects on people and the planet are minimized or neglected. If we are to be sustainable, we must include direct and indirect costs in all calculations (Leverkus et al. 2012).

The retail price of gasoline in the United States can serve as an example of the absence of full-cost accounting. The price of gasoline at the pump largely represents the costs related to research, exploration, drilling, refining, marketing, delivery, sale, and return on investment. But this at-the-pump price per gallon does not account for the whole cost. The whole cost includes the release of carbon dioxide into the atmo-

Amy encountered squalor in the South American villages that she visited. Instead of living in the bush as they did formerly, concentrated villages were put together without regard for solid or sewage waste disposal. Illness among children was rampant.

Amy noticed that plantation farmers were exposed to a wide array of agricultural chemicals. No breathing or clothing protection was provided, and it was clear that there was little regard for the chemicals leaching into the soil or local water. The farming practices that Amy observed seemed to disregard the people and the land. Workers were continually prodded to work faster, regardless of conditions.

sphere, the subsequent increase in global temperature because of greenhouse gases, the cost of the safe disposal of refining by-products, the cost of environmental remediation when petroleum catastrophes occur (such the 2010 Deepwater Horizon oil spill in the Gulf of Mexico), and the depletion of petroleum reserves for future generations. Societal single bottom line accounting practices are still widespread. Serious consequences are likely to occur because not enough thought is given to the total and hidden costs.

This triple bottom line, as illustrated in figure 11.2, represents the mainstream idea of sustainable development. When profit, planet, and people overlap, sustainability can occur for an undefined period. The sustainable portion is reflected in the small segment of overlap. This popular graphic has the unintended consequence of discouraging stakeholders from attempting to make changes because the area representing

possible success is small. Large areas of each sphere do not overlap and are seemingly to be addressed as separate issues.

We suggest that the U.S. federal General Services Administration Office of Governmentwide Policy approach (figure 11.3) might be a better idea for sustainable development. The economy and society are key components, but neither is viable without a healthy environment, which is fundamental to both. Note that neither the economy nor society can function without the environment. Mismanagement of earth's resources results in a reduction of the capacity for further economic development (Hall and Day 2009) and a reduced carrying capacity for planet earth. The maximum population that a geographic area can support for an indefinite period (Daily and Ehrlich 1992) is reduced.

There are no universally agreed-upon time frames for achieving sustainability. Currently, the global

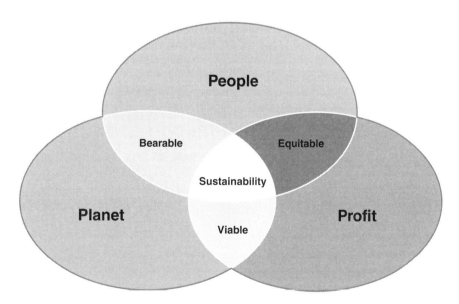

FIGURE 11.2 Triple bottom line combines aspects of people, planet, and profit in order to find a balanced sustainability.

Adapted from Dreamstime. Available: www.dreamstime.com/photos-images/3bl.html

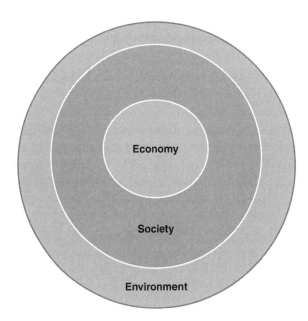

FIGURE 11.3 Triple bottom line. Note that the economy and society are within the context of the environment.

Adapted from U.S. General Services Administration, 2009, *The new sustainable frontier: Principles of sustainable development*, pg. 19. Available: www.gsa.gov/graphics/ogp/2009_New_Sustainable_Frontier_Complete_Guide.pdf

temperature has risen approximately 1.3 degrees Fahrenheit (.7 degrees Celsius) during the past century and is projected to increase another 2 to 7 degrees Fahrenheit (1.1 to 3.9 degrees Celsius) before 2100 (Intergovernmental Panel on Climate Change 2007). Climate cycles have occurred throughout recorded history. Portions of the presently observed temperature increase may be a cyclical planetary change, but the evidence suggests that the majority is directly caused by the emission of greenhouse gases, which for 2010 included 84 percent carbon dioxide (CO_2) 10 percent methane (CH_4), 4 percent nitrous oxide (N_2O), and 2 percent fluorinated gases (*Greenhouse Gas Overview* 2010). We have never observed temperatures similar to our 21st-century levels, and these warmer readings are closely associated with a well-defined carbon increase in the atmosphere. (Carbon dioxide levels are now over 400 parts per million.)

Rising temperatures are causing the polar ice caps and glaciers worldwide to melt, bringing about a change in sea levels. These changes in sea levels are imperiling coastal communities throughout the world. The very existence of reef islands is threatened. The Republic of the Marshall Islands, which has an average elevation of one to two meters above sea level, is an illustration of what may happen because of this impending catastrophe (Nicholls and Cazenave 2010). The average increase in sea level is not equally distributed across the globe (Rudiak-Gould 2012). Rather, evidence suggests that the area of the Western Pacific and the Marshalls will be disproportionately affected by the rises in sea level (Nicholls and Cazenave 2010). The projected increase in sea level in that area by the year 2100 is estimated to be up to two meters, which could cause total inundation of the Marshall Island chain (Nicholls and Cazenave 2010).

The absence of global outrage about the possibility of this kind of precipitous change in sea level is curious. For almost every possible catastrophe, people purchase insurance. In this case, world decision makers and economic powers are for the most part allowing greenhouse gas emissions to continue unabated with their single bottom line systems, policies, and practices. Their focus is primarily on profits and jobs. Little is being done to protect present or future coastal populations.

Carbon Emissions

Carbon footprint refers to the global warming that results directly and indirectly from gas emissions. According to Wright et al. (2011), carbon footprint is "a measure of the total amount of carbon dioxide (CO_2) and methane (CH_4) emissions of a defined population, system or activity, considering all relevant sources, sinks and storage within the spatial and temporal boundary of the population, system or activity of interest" (p. 61). This concept includes but supersedes individuals (SustainAbility.com 2014). Comparisons among states or countries can be made, but individuals must take responsibility and action to make a difference.

Activity

Individual and Household Carbon Footprint Calculator

The University of California at Berkeley provides an individual and household carbon footprint calculator at http://coolclimate.berkeley.edu/carboncalculator.

1. Pause for five minutes to work through the six dimensions of the calculator for your own personal life and household.

2. Write a 250-word summary in your chapter 11 journal section about the information generated. Were you surprised by the size of your carbon footprint?

The goal for each person is to be below average in carbon use. After you know your carbon footprint, you can take steps to reduce excess use, if necessary. You need to be aware of your impact. If you can measure it, you can change it. The goal is to contribute as little as possible to overall global warming through your behaviors and lifestyle choices.

This book focuses on living in balance, including balance with our planet earth's resources. The more you practice paying attention to your life, the more mindful you will be of your wasteful consumption. For example, you might grow in awareness of the many things you do automatically, such as driving to destinations closer than 1 mile (1.6 km) away. Depending on your fitness level, you can walk that distance in 15 to 25 minutes. Walking and biking reduce use

of carbon-based fuels, positively affect your health by reducing obesity, and promote fitness.

Carbon accounting is a methodology proposed for business and industry to determine relative carbon footprint. Accounting for greenhouse gas emissions is a sound business practice. The less such chemicals are emitted, the lower the expenditures will be. Applying this system might even result in improved profits. The United Kingdom now requires its largest 1,100 private corporations to track and publicize their carbon accounting data (Clegg 2012). Deputy Prime Minister Clegg maintains that stockholders and the nation have a right to know the environmental impact of the private sector.

Another measure of our environmental burden on the planet is the **ecological footprint** (Agostinho and

Biking or walking to school, work, or the market can help the environment *and* your waistline.

© Fancy/Veer / age fotostock

✓

Activity

Five-Minute Outdoor Meditation

Americans are known for their conspicuous consumption. We often purchase items only because we can or because we are unconsciously looking to complete ourselves with a material possession. The more comfortable we are with ourselves, the less we will strive to complete ourselves through the acquisition of material products.

1. Stand at a window where at least a tree or other plant is visible, or take a seat outdoors.
2. Take three long, slow, deep breaths, holding momentarily after the in breath and then letting go.
3. Feel the relaxation with each out breath.
4. Then breathe normally but mindfully, being attentive to the full in breath, the pause between breaths, and the full out breath.
5. Now, focus your attention on the tree or other plant. Use this opportunity to be with the plant while breathing in and out. As your mind wanders, bring your attention back to the breath and the plant.

At the end of the five minutes, resolve to bring similar awareness to every interaction with nature in your life.

Pereira 2013). This footprint measures the human demand on the planet's ecosystems, expressed in terms of the biologically productive land and sea area necessary to absorb the associated waste of human activities (Hall and Day 2009). As might be expected, the current ecological footprint for Americans is large and unsustainable (Global Footprint Network 2014). This concept can be applied to smaller regions as well (Hopton and White 2012).

LIFE-CYCLE ANALYSIS

The rule of thumb for the business community for the past century has been that 'cheaper' is better. A new mantra seems to be evolving that holds 'sustainable' as better, healthier, and more humane. Goleman (2009) contends that "Green is a process, not a status—we need to think of 'green' as a verb, not an adjective. This is more than a semantic shift that can help us focus better on greening" (p. 28). One aspect of what Goleman calls radical transparency is achieved by life-cycle analysis.

Life-cycle analysis is an analysis methodology that specifies production details, such as the energy and materials used as well as the pollutants generated. This tool represents a step toward controlling wasteful discarding of items without regard to the value lost. This analysis tool was created by industrial engineers, physicists, chemists, and biologists to detail inputs and outputs of manufacturing processes.

One of the first uses of life-cycle assessment was by a major soft drink company in the late 1960s to deter-

mine whether plastic or glass bottles contributed more toward environmental degradation and to ascertain the relative benefits of recycling (Hunt and Franklin 1996). Such quantification informs the manufacturing processes to maximize profits, enhance product utility, and contain pollution. Taking the sustainable approach is not always more expensive.

Manufacturing glass, for example, requires 659 ingredient inputs, including carcinogenic volatile organic compounds (Goleman 2009). Eight percent of the cancer-causing impacts are released during construction and maintenance of the glass manufacturing plant. Another 16 percent of the cancer-causing agents are associated with the natural gas used in the heating furnaces, and 31 percent is involved in producing high-density polyethylene for shipping glass. Approximately 60 percent of glass jars are recycled, resulting in a reduction of 500 gallons (1,900 L) of water and 20 pounds (9.1 kg) of CO_2 per ton (910 kg) of glass produced (Hunt and Franklin 1996).

Plastics are made from hydrocarbons which come from oil or natural gas. The manufacturing processes are energy consumers that generate greenhouse gases. In addition, it is becoming more widely known that rejected plastic products are polluting creeks, rivers, and oceans. The study of the extent and effects of this pollution are active areas of research (Law and Thompson 2014).

Other products, such as a new sport utility vehicle, include hundreds of thousands of individual life-cycle processes. Thousands of life cycles are involved in the production of the dashboard alone! The company may and often does choose the less expensive alternative, even though it will bring about long-term degradation of the environment (see figure 11.4).

As this book is being written, countless manmade environmental disasters are occurring. Many of these could have been avoided if we humans lived simpler lives. Our insatiable quest for energy, water, and food is creating a perfect storm of demands on planet earth.

The life-cycle analysis illuminates the cost–benefit of the various alternatives. The catastrophic 2010 Deepwater Horizon oil spill is one example. If we were not running out of oil in easy-to-drill places, we would not have events like that one. By pushing the limits of nature we are putting ourselves in harm's way. The oil and chemical dispersants used after the spill affected the ocean, wildlife, coastal residents, salvage workers, and health professionals (Diaz 2011; Moore and Burns 2011).

In 2014 approximately 10,000 gallons (38,000 L) of the coal-cleaning agent MCHM (4-methyl-cyclo-hexane-methanol) leaked from a large storage tank into the Elk River at Charleston, West Virginia, near the inlet for the public water supply of some 300,000 people. A nine-county area suffered without safe water for weeks. Sufficient funds had not been budgeted by the owner of the MCHM for adequate storage tank maintenance and safety protection, and the company is now bankrupt.

Citizens in the affected area now realize the need to press legislators and regulators to improve storage tank specifications and do inspections on a regular basis. Other sources of potential chemical pollution in this area have now been identified (Hansen et al. 2014). Public attention is on the state and federal government, and public input is needed, to avoid further contamination of the drinking water (Chang and Yang 2012).

In the Southwest region of the United States and increasingly throughout the world, clean, fresh water is scarce. But people still water their lawns, fill their swimming pools, and use water without a thought. Rivers have run dry. The mighty Colorado River is simply a trickle after it enters Mexico, and in most years it dries up completely before reaching the Gulf of California between Baja California and Sonora. Water is becoming scarce in tributaries like the Gila River in Arizona. Water wars occur, and some states take water from other areas to irrigate land that is too dry to farm normally. Diversion channels often lose significant water to evaporation (Clemmens 2008). Groundwater is contaminated by agribusiness and other industrial practices. Water tables are dropping.

The United States Green Building Council (2012) estimates a 3,700 billion gallon (14,000 billion L) annual water deficit in the United States. The Ogallala aquifer, which provides 30 percent of irrigation water and 80 percent of drinking water in the Great Plains

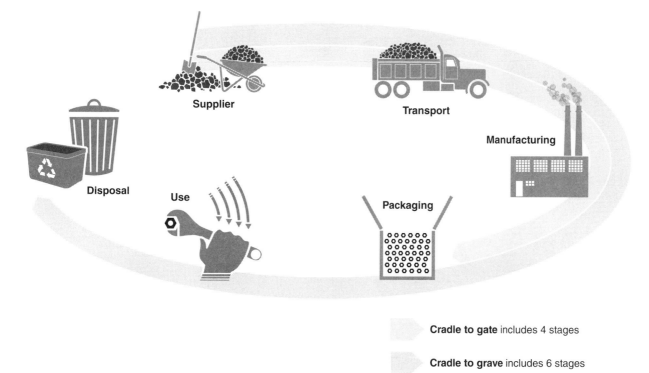

Cradle to gate includes 4 stages

Cradle to grave includes 6 stages

FIGURE 11.4 Six-stage structure of the life-cycle analysis, from supplier to disposal.

Based on TecEco Pty. Ltd, *Life cycle analysis.* Available: www.tececo.com/sustainability.life_cycle_analysis.php

and surrounding region, is being depleted (Dennehy 2000). Some view this situation as necessary for the United States to be able to eat and maintain its quality of life, but there has to be another way (Fereres and Soriano 2007).

SUSTAINABILITY CHALLENGE

"In our every deliberation, we must consider the impact of our decisions on the next seven generations" (**Great Law of the Iroquois Confederacy**). Indigenous cultures around the world have strong beliefs regarding our connection with nature. This perspective is seen with the Iroquois, an indigenous people of North America. The Iroquois Great Law provides a seven-generation time frame for sustainability. What will be available for our children, and their children? Rarely do contemporary Americans have a similar long-term vista. American businesses tend to think about the return-on-investment results of the next fiscal quarter.

Environmentalist Aldo Leopold initially set out to eradicate wolves in the American Southwest, thinking that fewer predators would mean greater yields during deer-hunting season (Aldo Leopold Foundation 2011). By the end of his life he grew to appreciate the error in his thinking, realizing that greater deer populations lead to the disruption of forests, increased soil erosion, and deer starvation.

Taking Action

So what exactly is living in harmony with nature, and how would we accomplish this in the modern world? This question has many different responses. It could mean living off the electrical grid far from population concentrations. Or it could mean changing aspects of our daily lives, like planting more food in our yards. And it could be anything in the middle. The remainder of this chapter addresses how we can make choices to live in a more sustainable manner.

Eating locally grown food is one way that we can start to live in balance with nature and improve our own personal balance (Halweil 2002). Food travels a long distance to our plate. Produce must be picked well in advance of being ripe so that it can be shipped safely. This process diminishes the taste as well as nutritional qualities.

Packaging and shipping use fossil fuels and other natural resources. Supermarket foods are then stored and displayed with the aid of 24-hour lighting and refrigeration, all of which use further resources. The economics of eating local are not always as favorable as

© bilderbox

You can find locally grown food at farmers' markets. These events can take on a fairlike quality with their booths of fresh vegetables, meats, breads, honey, and nonedibles like flowers and arts and crafts. Other resources include local butchers who may have meats that were locally raised, outdoor vegetable and fruit markets, and grocery stores that provide small selections of locally grown and locally manufactured items.

Activity

Taking Action by Decreasing Consumer Waste

Identify and describe which of the following nine action items you have done within the past month. Write a 200-word summary of your experience in decreasing your own consumer waste.

- Repurpose old items.
- Trade unwanted items with friends.
- Have a clothing swap with people of similar size.
- Shop at garage sales and thrift stores.
- Consider why you really want an item before buying it.
- Do not buy an item immediately. Instead, think about it for a few hours or overnight.
- Buy items that are well built and made to last (check *Consumer Reports*). There is often no correlation between price and quality. When you purchase a quality product, you will save money and resources by not having to replace broken or expended products.
- Purchase quality items that are well made in a sustainable manner and that can be upcycled.
- Check out clothing made by Patagonia, Inc. and other companies that have a commitment to sustainability.

---

we might expect. Eating locally grown food may cost the consumer more because of the economies of scale that supermarkets realize. But buying and eating local is good for building social capital and the local economy.

An important aspect of eating local is that we can speak with the people who grow our food. We can visit farms and observe the vegetables, trees, and livestock animals. Those with whom we have a personal relationship may be less likely to sell us what they themselves would not eat. And if for some reason we get a bad apple that makes us sick, we can immediately notify the grower. This possibility prevents nationwide recalls and widespread contamination. Why is this important? We have faced frequent food recalls, from meat, peanut butter, and spinach infected with Escherichia coli (E. coli) as well as tainted eggs (Jay-Russell 2013; McEntire 2013).

Food recalls can be the result of processing—how animals are contained while alive and then how their carcasses are handled. Most of us do not live near a concentrated animal-feeding operation where livestock essentially live head to rear, standing up to their knees in their own waste. Those who live near factory farms smell the manure lagoons, although the public is rarely permitted to see the animals covered in waste (Pollan 2006). There is ample reason that you sometimes have tainted meat. In contrast, when the food is produced locally, you are not exposed to this torpid mess, and you have more individual power to promote positive practices.

Ecosystem Services

Our discussion about ecological footprint addressed the ability of the planet to recover, to regenerate, and to heal, if given time. This has been defined by the United Nations as **ecosystem services** ("Ecosystems and Human Well-Being" 2005). These services are the many benefits that humans can receive from planet earth. Intact watersheds, clean air, healthy soil, and the like have a distinct value, but we have taken them for granted. With life-cycle analysis methodologies, we are better able to place a legitimate and data-driven value on these services. An example can illustrate the value of ecosystem services in our lives.

The New York City watershed was being compromised by runoff pollution from development in the region. The estimated cost for a new filtration system for the New York City watershed was $6 billion, and the annual operating cost was projected to be $300 million (Blaine, Sweeney, and Arscott 2006). By reaching a compromise with the municipalities within the watershed, local runoff was controlled. Thus, the ecosystem services were preserved and enhanced. No new industrialized filtration system was needed.

The dollar value of ecosystem services is enormous. Because of life-cycle analysis, we can specify their financial value and begin to hold them up against other dollar-motivated arguments, such as whether a tree is worth more as a log or as a living tree. It is also known that improved interpersonal security for individuals actually decreases the value they put on possessions (Clark et al. 2011).

By reducing consumerism, you will not only help the environment but also be living within your means. This means asking yourself why you want to purchase something and whether you really need it. Often times you think that you need something because it will make your life easier. Ask whether you already have something that could do this. Approaching your purchases with beginner's mind can help you avoid being swayed by advertisements for the product. In fact, you may not be at all conscious of why you are motivated to purchase a product. Also, you can check with *Consumer Reports*, which reliably tests the quality of products. You do not want to buy items that will stop working and shortly end up in a landfill.

Another way to decrease consumerism is to be thankful for what you already have. Having an attitude of gratitude can be helpful to your happiness and can quell your desires to augment yourself by the purchase of superfluous products (Ryff and Singer 2008). Being mindful is a helpful exercise. Each time you use an item, take a moment to appreciate what it does for you. Do not judge items as old, banal, or unexciting. Rather, learn from your choices to be mindful and let them influence you in the future.

Individuals and Society in Balance

Society and community are composed of individuals. Depending on your worldview, the collective comes first or the individual comes first. By constantly thinking on an individual level, society can be hurt. For instance, the environment is often sacrificed so that people can make money or gain immediate aggrandizement, such as by bulldozing a natural landscape for a new McMansion, a strip mall, a solid waste landfill, or a Marcellus shale gas well pad (Kenworthy et al. 2011). People often think only about what is best for them right here and right now, not how their action conflicts with what others want or the toll it takes on the planet (see figure 11.5).

Conflict is unnecessary when people are living in balance. By understanding how your needs and desires affect the world, you can make decisions that will benefit all involved. Of course, you will have difficult decisions to make. When the world is in balance, when you have homeostasis, then you as a human being will more likely fall into balance and happiness as well. Thus, the change begins with you. You need to establish your priorities and take time to find personal balance.

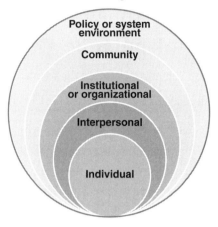

Social or Ecological Model

FIGURE 11.5 The social ecological model illustrates interconnected relationships. Everything for individuals, groups, institutions, organizations, and community depends on policy, systems, and the environment. If the environment is foul, nothing else works well.

Transportation Systems and the Future

Americans have a hopeless love affair with their private vehicles. According to the World Bank Institute (2013), there are 797 vehicles for every 1,000 people in the United States. Although mass transit may take more time and be less convenient at times, taking the train or bus is an energy-efficient means of travelling without risking your life and limb and the life and limbs of others. Consider that although taking a bus may initially take a bit more time (though not always), that expense can be compensated for by the reduced stress of driving and better safety (buses are generally constructed with greater safety considerations). The costs and benefits are not always immediately obvious, but we can look for ways to move from place to place that are less stressful and better for the environment. Unfortunately, train travel was largely dismantled in the United States starting in the 1950s, but a resurgence of train travel is evident, as illustrated in figure 11.6.

Will society require high-speed trains that can travel at more than 100 miles (160 km) per hour for routine travel? Planners are examining magnetic levitation techniques to propel trains at speed over long distances. Will four- and six-lane expressways require additional lanes and higher speed limits?

The importance of living local is obvious. The significance of energy conservation and energy efficiency can also be appreciated regarding modes of travel. The air pollution from gasoline, diesel fuel, and electric-

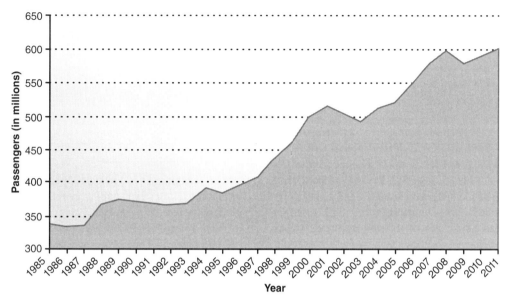

FIGURE 11.6   The number of train passengers nearly doubled between 1985 and 2010.

Reprinted, by permission, from S. Jackson, 2010, "Travel trends: Train travel in the USA," *Gadling.* Available: www.gadling.com/2010/05/27/train-travel-in-the-usa

ity production is also important to consider. Personal choices and public planning agencies are the key to the future in this regard.

Factory, Office, and Home

We can significantly enhance the future through careful consideration and planning. Leadership in Energy and Environmental Design (**LEED**) is transforming the thinking of society about how buildings and communities are designed, constructed, maintained, and operated. LEED is the green building tool that considers the entire building life cycle, using best-in-class strategies (Leitch et al. 2013). LEED can reduce operating costs and increase asset values; conserve energy, water, and other resources; be healthier and safer for occupants; and qualify for money-saving incentives like tax rebates and zoning allowances. Although methodologies are in place for the future, you still have to make a change toward sustainability in your choices, your lifestyle, and your interactions with your neighbors and society.

SUMMARY

The most significant threats to the environment are human-made because people have worked to protect themselves against all eventualities. Manufacturing and other basic industries represent the major activities that consume natural resources and generate environmental contamination.

There is no such place as "away." You cannot throw things away; rather, you need to plan for the use, reuse, and recycling or upcycling of products. You need to consider sustainability for a long period, something like seven generations, as recommended by the Great Law of the Iroquois Confederacy.

Rachel Carson's popular book *Silent Spring* recounted what happened because of the widespread use of DDT. This book marked the beginning of environmental consciousness on a wide scale. Material safety data sheets are available to chemical users and the public to provide safety information about the chemicals we encounter in our lives. Hazardous materials (HazMat) placards are displayed on trucks, railroad cars, and with other transport modes that move hazardous materials.

Triple bottom line accounting more accurately includes all components in a way that protects the environment. Society and profit are considered within the context of the environment.

People can monitor their carbon footprint as a measure of their impact on the earth due to greenhouse gases and live simply so that others may simply live. The ecological footprint of companies and countries is studied to determine the overall impact of these entities on the global environment. The United States and humanity as a whole are exceeding their means, exceeding earth's capacity to sustain the population in the long term.

Our society now has the methodology to help bring

A my has now finished her master's degree and is working for an agency in a rural state that promotes sustainable agriculture. The agency is funded by grant money, so her job may not be secure, but she is having a wonderful time helping farmers take their crops to the local farmers markets. The people who live in the region are thrilled to have a wide variety of locally grown produce, and the farmers are pleased to have an outlet where they can recover the costs of their investment.

about what Daniel Goleman (2009) calls radical transparency. Consumers have a right to know the results of life-cycle analyses. The information is increasingly available. Every negative value is an opportunity for suppliers to improve. The economy needs to focus on maximizing the best use of commercial products. We are talking about shifting purchasing behavior by meaningfully analyzing our needs, not our created wants.

Chapter 12

Spiritual Foundation

Objectives

After reading this chapter, you will be able to

- identify differences between spirituality and religion,
- define spirituality in the context of unique personal attributes,
- identify three approaches to promote personal spirituality,
- evaluate your own actions within a spiritual context,
- identify how spirituality is associated with improved well-being,
- apply spiritual principles to your own life, and
- distinguish between Buddhist mindfulness and psychological mindfulness.

Jill, a 24-year-old nursing student, remembers thinking that she was quite healthy, spiritual, and in balance. Although she no longer attended church, she felt spiritually in touch as she studied hard, exercised daily, ate a vegetarian diet, and took pride in being a good person. One day, the bottom fell out of her life as she experienced an acute bout of severe anxiety. She went to student health, where a therapist recommended that she slow down.

"Yeah, right!" Jill reacted. "I'm a full-time student, caring for patients 20-plus hours each week at the university hospital, and I must work out every day! With all I have to do, how am I supposed to slow down?"

Throughout the semester, Jill's anxiety grew. Finally, out of desperation, she attended a yoga class. Yoga was not something she had ever contemplated. It seemed weird to her. But her instructor was warm, calm, and serene. Jill experienced peace during the class.

Jill had another dramatic experience one day when biking along the Mississippi River. She realized that her mind was full of negative thoughts. It was a beautiful day, yet her thoughts were making her anxious, miserable, and depressed.

Jill's yoga teacher recommended that she join a mindfulness group. She made an initial commitment to attend weekly for at least six weeks, worked through a phase of boredom, and persisted with the practice. Six months after her bout of anxiety, Jill's life was more peaceful, although she still had many of the same life demands. She felt a deeper connection with her life, work, environment, friends, and family.

We began this book with the image of an iceberg (p. ix) to represent wellness. We have discussed mindfulness, positive psychology, social connections, physical fitness, nutrition, and more. Now it is time to go deeper, to examine how all these interrelate to inform spirituality.

Your fundamental attitudes and beliefs determine who you are and how you relate to others. What is driving you forward? What is holding you back? Might there be more to reality than what you see and feel? When do you feel most alive and well?

For many, difficulties arise from the seemingly disparate perspectives of life and human nature. Some traditions hold that people are incorrigibly bad. Others believe that people are out to take advantage, and therefore you must always be on guard. Still other traditions see all humans as wholesome and sharing in oneness. Your life may be richer and more peaceful if you view others as intrinsically good, as opposed to focusing on their less desirable attributes (Seligman 2006).

How does spirituality affect your balance in being and promote wellness? Mindfully paying attention provides an avenue for enhanced well-being, not just for self but also for other people, plants, animals, and planet earth. You can begin the work of further incorporating spiritual wellness into your life right now, a year from now, or much later. The journey is yours.

Everyone has his or her own spiritual concepts.

Some believe in a personal God, while others refer to a higher power or identify themselves as atheist or agnostic. There are believers and nonbelievers. No recommendation is being made here regarding any particular belief, value, or religion. The goal of this chapter is to help you develop a spiritual connection that will increase your inner strength and improve the quality of your wellness and the wellness of your community.

Read this chapter with an open mind. Some concepts will be new. No matter how you relate to these concepts, try to view the content nonjudgmentally. Your thoughts, beliefs, feelings, and ideas are yours, and our goal with this chapter is to share tools that will help you more mindfully accept yourself, others, and your journey.

SPIRITUALITY AND RELIGION

Students are often asked in wellness courses to provide a word or phrase they would use to describe spirituality. The following terms have appeared over the years: love, union, hope, connectedness, compassion, divine being, higher self, force within, intelligence beyond self, gratitude, guidance, and eternal peace, among others. The descriptions include beliefs about transcendence, identity, purpose in life, and the way in which you relate to others and the sacred.

Activity

Spirituality Is . . .

This 10- to 15-minute exercise helps you explore the various attributes of spirituality. Although the concept hasn't yet been defined, you should try to get in touch with what you believe about spirituality.

1. Write "Spirituality is" 10 times, one below another, leaving a blank space to complete the phrase.
2. Take three minutes to be quiet. Get in touch with the breath. Follow your breath all the way in and out. Increase your awareness right here, right now.
3. During five minutes, mindfully complete each of the 10 phrases. For example, "Spirituality is being nice to other people."
4. When you finish, sit mindfully, being attentive to your breath.
5. Take another three minutes to continue with your mindfulness.

You might see your notions of spirituality overlap with your notions of organized religion, cultural, or other experiences. There are no right or wrong answers. Enter a description of this experience into your journal.

Many misconstrue "spirituality" as being synonymous with "religion." Instead spirituality is a mixture of ideas and emotions, including love.

When students are asked to complete the same exercise with religion, the answers are more cognitive and institutional. Common words are the following: God, dogma, sin, churches, services, service, ritual, rules to live by, theology, mosques, the one and only way, grace, forgiveness, prayer, meditation, peace, and so on. Note some overlap between the two lists. But because religions are a social manifestation of spirituality, they are more focused toward institutions, rules, and rituals, which differ widely from each other (Abeysekara 2010). Historian and writer Jon Krakauer (2004) noted that there are perhaps 10,000 different faiths in the world and that they tend to be exclusive, rarely accepting the perspectives of any of the others. For the sake of this volume, spirituality will be viewed as a means of uniting rather than dividing people. But because religion can be a powerful expression of your spirituality, you are free to understand this discussion in terms of your own religious background.

DEFINING SPIRITUALITY

Spirituality refers to a sense of connectedness with something greater than yourself, and it often engenders a sense of oneness and purpose in life. Spirituality also helps you experience and share in the common values of others without regard to individual differences (*State of the World's Indigenous Populations* 2009). So spirituality provides a sense of belonging to both a

higher power and to each other.

As defined by Dr. George Vaillant (2013) of Harvard, spirituality is "the amalgam of the eight positive emotions that bind us to other human beings—and to our experience of 'God' as we may understand her/him" (p. 591). Vaillant (2008) identifies the positive emotions as love, hope, joy, forgiveness, compassion, faith, awe, and gratitude. All these virtues overlap with those of positive psychology, as discussed in chapter 1, the attitudinal foundations of mindfulness, as discussed in chapter 2, and the 12 steps of Alcoholics Anonymous, as discussed in chapter 10.

Positive emotions and spirituality reside in the "feeling" brain, the limbic system (Vaillant 2013). Spirituality is an internal dimension of who you are and does not necessarily involve institutions and ritual (Larson and Koenig 2000). You are hard wired to interact with your world in this manner. It is part of who you are as a human. These positive emotions are a culturally free denominator for the world (Vaillant 2013).

Spirituality may be contrasted with religion, which is an institutionalized, learned system of worship involving a spiritual community. Both spirituality and religion have their advantages, but you don't need to be religious to be spiritual. The thinking brain is the seat of religious practices and beliefs, whereas spirituality resides in the feeling brain. Obviously, the two brain functions are interrelated, but they sometimes

✓

Activity

Exploring Positive Emotions for Spiritual Development

This 15-minute exercise can help you better understand the eight positive emotions.

1. Write down each of the following positive emotions, leaving enough space to write two or three lines for each: love, hope, joy, forgiveness, compassion, faith, awe, and gratitude.

2. Prepare for the exercise by taking three minutes to be mindful. You can do this mindfulness exercise wherever and however you like, whether you sit, stand, walk, or whatever.

3. In your own words, describe what each of these words means to you and how you might incorporate it into your life.

4. Locate another person who has done the exercise to discuss your descriptions.

Although you were working with ideas, did you have any emotions during the time of the writing or discussion? Can you identify with any of these positive emotions in your day-to-day life?

---

seem to work in opposition to each other. Through the practice of mindfulness, however, you can bring these two aspects of the brain into more correspondence so that you can think and act more deliberately.

Spiritual development involves expressing what is best about you while connecting with the eight positive emotions. These provide a moral compass directing you to live in a more enlightened way and to serve others (Lindholm 2013). Just as there are many religions, there are many expressions of individual spirituality.

Analogies can help clarify spiritual perspectives. Two people looking up from opposite sides of a great mountain will have different opinions about it. Although they are looking at the same mountain, one person notices its massive cliffs whereas the other reports a vast forest. Neither is wrong; they just have different perspectives. The second example comes from the old story about the six blind men and the elephant. Each of the six uses his hands to explore the body of an elephant. The first man, feeling the elephant's trunk, indicated that the elephant was like a huge snake. The second, standing by the elephant's leg, compared it to a tree trunk. The others vehemently disagreed; the elephant was clearly a spear (its tusk) or a whisk broom (its tail), and so on. Each of these opinions was an accurate but partial description, but no one was able to see the big picture. Your perceptions and beliefs reflect where you stand but do not make your understanding any less true.

The concept of a force greater than yourself is important to any discussion of spirituality. Within monotheistic traditions such as Islam and Christianity, God is looked on as the one omnipresent and all-pow-

erful creator of the universe. Hindus believe in many different gods or manifestations of the divine. The Alcoholics Anonymous tradition describes a "Higher Power," or "God of my understanding." Sociologically, many people perceive their "God" as similar to their father (Hood, Hill, and Spilka 2009). This viewpoint is not surprising, given that in the New Testament, Christ refers to God as "Abba," an Aramaic word meaning "daddy" or "papa." This discussion could go on. As Krakauer (2004) reminded us, each of the thousands of religious sects has its own beliefs.

In contrast, some people do not exactly have a God or a divine being as part of their belief system or spirituality. To these people, "force greater than yourself" may represent the universe or nature. Humanists, for example, place priority on a belief in the ability of humanity to shape our destiny. Skeptics or agnostics place importance on the value of asking questions; they question the existence of a divinity or divinities (some may say they don't know whether a divine presence exists). Those who identify as atheists or nonbelievers do not believe in a divinity, but only in natural systems. Atheists and agnostics often believe in family, love, and a sense of community (Vail, Arndt, and Abdollahi 2012). As you can see, the range of thought regarding religion and spirituality is vast. Within this spectrum are numerous ways of thinking and various understandings of life.

In the 18th century, the deism religious concept developed primarily in Europe as a belief that God created the universe and abides without further direct involvement. The universe was set into motion and continues to change because of natural forces, called the laws of nature. Many of the founding fathers embraced much of the deist philosophy about the earth and life in it. But the spirituality concept is more general than any of these defined religions, representing personal thoughts, feelings, and actions on a minute-by-minute basis as we live our lives, as compared with acts of tribute to a God or other concepts.

Spiritual Nature

How do you wake up from living on auto-pilot to become meaningfully and spiritually engaged? Do you customarily define your reality only in terms of the temporal? Your materialistic, egotistical self is not you. You can easily be, and often are, your own worst enemy. By spending much of your time obsessing with the material world, you are blinded to your best interests.

Pierre Teillard de Chardin (1955), a prominent 20th century theologian and philosopher, wrote that "we are not human beings having spiritual experiences; rather we are spiritual beings having human experiences." Entertain for now this thought of yourself as a spiritual being, an extension of the oneness of eternity. Viewing your spiritual nature in this manner provides a basis for trusting in yourself to engage positively in life with others.

Recognize that, at your core, you have potential for great good. You are love, meaning that you should learn to love yourself and others in the best way you can. Some call this unconditional love or spiritual love. A common human longing is to love and be loved. Your journey is to recognize that love, hope, forgiveness, compassion, and gratitude are part of your lifelong commitment to living fully.

Viewing spirituality as an evolving process should come as a relief. Your life is unfolding as you express positive emotions. This idea takes the pressure off behaving perfectly. With unconditional self-acceptance, your life becomes immensely better. Whatever you give, you give to yourself. You are a spiritual being who shares in infinite goodness and oneness.

Your life purpose, self-concept, and inner peace reflect your spirituality. Spirituality may include a belief in a personal God, an impersonal higher power, or even no God at all. The spiritual spectrum is wide and variously defined. Spilka et al. (2003) proposed that the deep beliefs of theists and nontheists are not as dissimilar as they might first appear. Your words and the way in which you portray yourself to others often differ from your deepest commitments, underlying values, and higher self. What you are in your heart is far more important than the words that surround your beliefs.

Spirituality and Health

We would be remiss not to address the relationship of spirituality to physical, psychological, mental, and emotional well-being. From the previous discussion, you can see that spirituality has value in and of itself. Travis and Ryan's image of an iceberg illustrates the positive influence of spiritual beliefs on health (p. ix). Physical health is depicted as existing above the waterline, whereas most of your health lies below the surface. Lifestyle beliefs, attitudes, motivations, and behaviors are important determinants of health, but at the very base of the iceberg rest spiritual truths, which act as a foundation. These truths profoundly affect everything about us.

A spiritual quest is associated with improved health in several domains. Religious and spiritual practices improve quality of life and increase life expectancy (Hummer et al. 1999). These outcomes seem to be mediated through improved health behaviors, enhanced social support, and different psychological profiles (Oman and Thoresen 2002). Regular mindfulness practices are enhanced significantly by a religious or spiritual focus (Pargament 2008). Many

Activity

Finding Your Spiritual Nature Through Gratitude

In your journal, list three experiences in your life from the past week for which you are grateful (Bridges, Harnish, and Sillman 2012). Write about the three experiences separately, describing the circumstances of each.

1. What specifically is responsible for your gratitude?
2. What did you feel when the event occurred?
3. Did you express your gratitude to anyone?

Did writing about these experiences provide you with any additional positive emotions?

of the health benefits of regular mindfulness appear manifested through improved concentration.

A sense of coherence in life, profound beliefs that enable people to make sense of it all (Antonovsky 1993), gives greater control over behaviors and even over disease. Spiritual people are more likely to be successful in school and tend to be less obese and less likely to participate in high-risk sexual behaviors (Doswell et al. 2003). Spirituality helps create community connectedness (Krause 2008) and eases the transition to a normal balanced life for those addicted to alcohol and drugs (Turner-Musa and Lipscomb 2007). A positive link has been demonstrated between spirituality and decreased stress, anxiety (Anastasi 2008), depression, heart disease, and breast cancer (Feher and Maly 1999). Spirituality helps make suffering more meaningful and therefore reduces stress (Murphy, Johnson, and Lohan 2003).

An appreciation of the spirituality of friends and colleagues provides a protective effect against hostility and antagonism (Jager 1997). Negative life events are moderated by spiritual beliefs (Young, Cashwell, and Sheherbakova 2000). Depending on your belief structure, you seem to do better when you make decisions in collaboration with a higher power of your understanding (Yangarber-Hicks 2004). And, in fact, a positive-dose relationship seems to operate; that is, the deeper your commitment is to religious and spiritual values, the better you do (Hays et al. 2001).

PROCESSES OF CHANGE

How do you wake up from living reactively to becoming meaningfully engaged? How do you transition to being fully alive, awake, vibrant, and self-aware? We all evolve through stages of moral development. Jean Piaget described the stages for children, from being totally self-absorbed to being more social and considerate of others (Piaget 1974). Lawrence Kohlberg (1973) continued with the description of the adult stages of moral development up through the abstract and the spiritual. Ideally, your life experiences predispose you to express positive emotions and move to higher levels of functioning. Your good choices enable you to evolve further.

Nothing happens that doesn't affect your spiritual development. Do you live with a conscious awareness of the positive emotions, such as joy, forgiveness, compassion, and awe, or are you focused on accumulating material possessions? You are probably somewhere in between. Remember that after your basic needs are met, happiness is not increased by accumulating ever more material assets (Maslow 1961). Materialistic preoccupation is not your friend! It is an appetite that

Aspects of people who tend to be more spiritual, such as increased mindfulness and a sense of community connectedness, can help you feel healthier in other aspects of your life as well.

can never be satisfied by more acquisitions.

What and where you are in life matters less than how you journey. Life throws good and bad things your way. Boredom, physical illness, great sunsets, relationship challenges, a day at the beach, business success, a car crash, meeting the love of your life, job changes, and a walk in the woods are all events that can remind you of the presence of love, no matter how different they seem to be at the time. A Zen parable illustrates this point. In ancient China, a young man was thrown from his horse, and he broke his leg. Everyone in the village expressed their sorrow at this accident. But the next day, the emperor's army passed through, conscripting all the young men of the village to fight in his wars, except for the one with the broken leg. None of them ever returned. So what initially appeared to be a great tragedy turned into a blessing for this man. He just didn't know it at the time. So-called good and bad experiences are in reality opportunities for nonjudgmental awareness and awe. These insights can provide joy, solace, and hope in the midst of troubled times. You are continually presented with opportunities to accept, learn, and grow.

The spiritual journey can lead to recognition of

your inner qualities and your relationship to all that is around you. Historically, a spiritual journey was thought to be an excursion that each person took at a particular time, the "right" time in his or her life, such as going to Africa to serve as a missionary or opening an orphanage for children with AIDS. Although many embark on such excursions and learn from them, the physical location is irrelevant. The spiritual journey, not the physical one, is what matters. As your life progresses, you can see glimpses of an inner spiritual journey that guides your behaviors. Nonjudgmental awareness can transform your experience of life and the lives of others.

Quiet Realization

Your spiritual life is augmented when you live in the present. Appreciating the present moment is a relatively new concept for many Westerners, who are culturally accustomed to working toward goals. This striving leads to evaluating personal worth in terms of matter, time, and productivity.

The real question becomes this: How much of life are you missing when you are obsessed with lists, schedules, and incessant ruminations about the past and the future? Your life exists in the present moment. Your lists may well help you accomplish tasks, and doing so is commendable. Problems arise, however, when you identify with the lists, accumulations, and schedules. Problems arise when you see happiness in stuff that is outside you. Problems arise when you ignore the basic nature and needs of yourself and others.

How can you reconcile the seemingly opposing forces of the attitudinal foundations, the 12 steps of AA, and the eight positive emotions to your actual here-and-now life? If you focus all your energy outside yourself, you cannot be in tune within. Spiritual life, like your physical life, requires balance. Without quiet awareness, your thoughts "think you" and dictate who and what you are. Balance, homeostasis, and equanimity result from choosing your higher mind, your higher self, and what is best about you. Theorist George Pransky's (2003) *Prevention From the Inside-Out* proposes that your inner wisdom is always present to draw on.

Spirituality comes through quiet (Kornfield 2011). Claude Debussy once said, "Great music is the silence between the notes" (Koomey 2001, p 96), and so it is with your life. Quiet is the fundamental building block

Activity

Quiet Mindfulness Outdoors

Mindfulness is a practice to be implemented, not simply a thought to be understood. The more time you spend experiencing being here and now, which incorporates the attitudinal foundations, the more likely you are to be skilled in your practice.

1. Find a quiet place outside. You can stand, sit in a chair or on the ground, or even lie on a comfortable mat. You can do this in a park, the woods, or even in your own backyard. Just find a place where you are unlikely to be disturbed for 10 minutes.

2. Keep your eyes open and become aware of your breath. You do not need to change the way you breathe.

3. Follow the breath all the way in and all the way out for five minutes. This activity will bring you into the present moment.

4. Experience your breath as if for the first time. Notice even the pause between breaths. Remember that this exercise is about awareness, not thinking.

5. Continue with this process. As thoughts or other distractions come into your consciousness, invite them into the mindfulness process by identifying them and then returning to the breath.

6. Let go. Your distractions are part of mindfulness. Your goal is not to be distraction free, but to bring awareness of distractions into your practice.

7. Quiet awareness transforms all your experiences.

As the mindfulness session comes to an end, avoid the temptation to jump up and begin your next activity. Instead, slowly and mindfully make the transition, all the while bringing this mindful experience into every aspect of your life.

connecting your infinite love with your day-to-day experiences. This idea appears in several scriptures. The Hindu Bhagavad Gita refers to "the stillness of divine union." The Old Testament reminds us to "Be still and know that I am God" (Psalm 46:10). The Islamic Qur'an advises, "And stay quietly in your houses, and make not a dazzling display" (Surat Al-'Ahzab, chapter 33, verse 33). Quiet can be found in the natural world, no matter what your faith. Tibetan Buddhist nun Pema Chodron (2012) stated that the world looks different from a quiet space. Quiet provides an avenue to experience your true self. As an embodiment of unconditional love, quiet does not require you to do or say anything.

Trust

An important component of spirituality is having the faith to trust yourself (Ventres and Dharamsi 2013). When you trust your intrinsic love, you set the stage to manifest kindness, gentleness, forgiveness, and sensitivity. In this state of mind, you do not need to spend as much physical or psychic energy being defensive. Rather, you are able to reach out selflessly.

Paradoxically, the more secure you feel, the less self-centered you can be and the more likely you may be to include others in your life. Your love can be extended to everyone and everything. Being kind is an expression of your higher self.

Trust is a precondition to inner peace. Self-trust, however, is an experience, not just a cognitive insight. When you keep love in your heart, when you accept others unconditionally, your love flows far and wide. Mindfulness practice enables you to remain centered. In the quiet of everyday awareness are answers to many of your questions about life. In mindfulness you can better understand your goodness.

Mindfulness practice is one path for accepting yourself and others. With the foundation of that appreciation, you can then make your life more about your family, neighbors, animals, plants, and the planet that surrounds us. In each minute of every day, you have opportunities to invite love in. Give up the notion that you always know the best outcome in any situation. Rather, the better you feel about yourself, the more you can extend love to others. This kind of love is the gift of balance in being.

Nonjudging Love of Self and Others

Judging seems as natural to life as breathing. But making assessments along your path is quite different from making condemnations, which serve no one. You decrease the burden of life by being nonjudgmental, that is, by experiencing life impartially, without indictments or condemnation. How can you judge people without walking in their shoes? Ordinary day-to-day life has its ups, downs, and almost endless challenges. A nonjudgmental lifestyle provides deeper understanding and new spiritual insights.

When you critically judge the life path of anyone, you are suggesting that you know how things work. To judge others is to attest that you know everything about them and understand what is best for them. Obviously, such an exercise serves neither them nor you. When you unequivocally accept events and other people, you experience oneness and less strain. A historical example may help.

Abraham Lincoln's journey to the White House represents an example of being nonjudging. Born in poverty, Lincoln lost 8 out of 10 elections, twice failed in business, and suffered a nervous breakdown before becoming one of the greatest U.S. presidents. He could have quit many times, but he did not. He remained engaged. After a loss in one U.S. Senate race, Lincoln said, "The path was worn and slippery. My foot slipped from under me, knocking the other out of the way, but I recovered and said to myself, 'It's a slip and not a fall' " (Thomas 1952). Lincoln's statement reflected his perseverance, self-acceptance, and nonjudgmental attitude.

Learning occurs with patience and successive approximations. You may experience temporary setbacks, but those events are not failures. A positive attitude influences how you choose to experience your life, actions, and realities. You evolve spiritually through the process of trials, seeming errors, and acceptance. Experiences simply are. Life events may be deemed catastrophic, but these are equally as valuable as your successes. Be with and learn from them.

If the only reality is eternal, your day-to-day world serves as a spiritual classroom. You do well to withhold judgment. By focusing on a spiritual context, you are no longer as preoccupied with all that is happening in the physical world. When you judge someone who clashes with your values, you miss out on their intrinsic goodness, what you might share with them, and their awesome qualities. When you experience differences that you cannot understand, you should try to be mindful, not judgmental. This focus on positive regard for yourself and others represents unconditional love.

Be aware of traps that may appear to be spiritual but are actually nonproductive ways of thinking that you have inadvertently fallen into. Perhaps you have simply followed a tradition taught to you without ever thinking deeply about it. Even when saying, "I forgive you," it is all too easy to feel superior to the one you are forgiving. People will recognize when you are not being genuine. This condescending attitude is

Jill was pleased with her yoga. She found herself with like-minded young women, which was not what she expected. As she became friends with the women and the instructor, she experienced the commonality of their various religions and spiritual beliefs. People shared perspectives and accepted each other. The practice engrossed her. She relaxed into each pose. She focused on her practice, her breath, her body, and her friends. She was awed by the connection. Everything else disappeared.

a form of judgment and separation. A deeper level of forgiveness is linked with acceptance and feelings of oneness with others. You no longer see their interests as separate from your own.

To examine this example further, the customary use of forgiveness is not always done out of kindness. Consider the following perspective: "Although you have insulted me with your statement about my personal integrity, I forgive you." On face value, this seems praiseworthy. But the statement is judgmental and implies that the forgiving person is superior. She or he has concluded that it is in her or his power to decide whether the other person is worthy of pardon. If you truly forgive another, you accept that person. You are recognizing that the person's actions do not constitute her or his true identity. The harm that comes to you from judging is the disruption of your own inner peace. Instead, try to follow the counsel of Philo (20 BCE–50 BCE): "Be kind, for everyone you meet is fighting a hard battle."

None of this is to suggest that you be without standards or allow other people to take advantage of you. Your journey is one of consciousness, engagement with others, and recognition of risk. A typical college student, for example, must make many decisions each day, including which friends to trust, which coworkers to pick, and even whether a classmate plagiarized her or his work. These responsibilities include academic, behavioral, and leadership roles. When in such a situation, you can take action on a plagiarized term paper without condemning the colleague.

Your egotistical self can easily perceive an act of plagiarism as a personal attack or affront, as if the fellow student was out to get you. With love in your heart, you realize that while plagiarism is unacceptable, the fellow student is to be accepted as a fellow human being. You mindfully take the appropriate action. Similarly, when you see someone snatching a purse, the common sense action is to call the police but to do so without hating the perpetrator or seeking revenge. To be nonjudging here is to exhibit love of the highest order.

Efficacy of Connecting With Your Higher Power

To connect is to be in touch with your higher self or what you view as most important. This notion is a component of building your spirituality. This connection can be facilitated through prayer as practiced by different faiths, through quiet meditation, through conversation, through singing, as well as by viewing art, listening to music, and engaging in other forms of expression (Guilherme 2012).

To connect with your higher self is to perform an act of faith. If you or others make a mistake, accept it lovingly and move forward. This acceptance of falling short, of not having lived up to lofty aspirations is a divine act equal to anything else you do spiritually. Whatever is going on will be made better with love. This is a form of prayer (Jones 2012). To practice loving kindness and extend kind thoughts toward another asks for the best spiritual outcome, although you do not know what that outcome should be.

You might wonder if prayer works. For people who ask for specific items in their prayers, the answer is yes and no. From the material standpoint, the jury is still out. Some studies demonstrate the efficacy of prayer, and others do not (Hodge 2007). The most important dimension of prayer, however, addresses the universal and eternal, such as life after death, which is beyond direct physical observation.

Dr. Dorothy Jones (2012) encourages people to ask for higher guidance using whatever form is most comfortable. When you ask for this guidance, you are acknowledging that your world is bigger than you may perceive. Thus, you are humbly joining with the power of the universe to do something with genuine love, as opposed to self-centered love.

Whenever you are upset, you can choose to remain above the conflict. You can go to that place of peace in your mind. You may choose to look for answers or help within your own experience or within your concept of a higher power. If you don't believe in a higher power or that answers will be revealed to you, then trust in yourself or seek help from your friends and neighbors.

© 2001 PhotoDisc, Inc.

Your communications with a higher power can take whatever form is comfortable for you. Focus your thoughts on discovering how to view situations differently and how to approach life with loving kindness.

You can also go to that place of peace in your mind and ask for help in looking at the situation differently. Your prayer or request then becomes, "Please help me to see this differently." Often the problem with your prayers is that you are not asking for too much, but too little (*A Course in Miracles* 1972). You may remain myopic and ask for temporal solutions instead of infinite love.

Pray first and then live your life normally. This may mean watering the garden during a drought or calling the fire department when the garage is on fire. Never forget that you are living in a physical body. If you do forget, life will ultimately remind you! Remember also, however, that you are more than a physical body. People do best when they see themselves in a partnership with their higher power (Oman 2011). Spiritual growth has many paths and requires trust in yourself and the spiritual processes in which you are engaged.

Relationships Are Life

You first learned love while bonding with parents during infancy (Feldman 2007). You exhibit and further develop this love by relating to siblings, classmates, romantic partners, strangers in the market, animals, or others outside your immediate circle. In addition, the attitude that you adopt toward others is the same one that you will use to view yourself. This concept may be new and challenging, but remember that you are a spiritual being having a physical experience.

Anything that you can give and have less of is material, fleeting, and ultimately of marginal importance. Whatever you give with love is returned, with interest. When you selflessly think a loving thought about another, you extend that love to yourself as well. Giving and receiving are the same (Savundranayagam 2014; *A Course in Miracles* 1972).

Spiritual growth is often mediated through interpersonal relationships. These associations are among the most rewarding and challenging aspects of life (Schultz et al. 2014). Relationships provide opportunities to become aware of strengths and limitations, and they provide crucial feedback. Victor Hugo (1862) remarked that you can see the face of God by loving another person. How you interact reflects your spiritual values (Tolle 2005).

Developing a healthy relationship in today's world is a prospect of the highest order. It involves nothing less than undertaking a journey in search of your own self. Dr. Karl Menninger (1963) wrote that love cures both the giver and receiver. Discovering that you can help yourself and others at the same time is a refreshing, esteem-boosting experience. Genuine empathy radiates out to others.

Likewise, you often project your own qualities onto others. If you are self-critical, you are likely to find fault in someone else (Jones 2012). Although it may be the case that a relationship starts with selfish motives ("How can this person help me get what I want?"), it doesn't have to stay that way. All relationships can change into a vehicle for increased consciousness, empathy, and love.

Deep interpersonal relationships often represent amplified spiritual classrooms. Think about how loved ones can upset us. Nobody seems to affect your feelings as much as a family member or loved ones. Your loved ones know you best. They know consciously and unconsciously which buttons to push. You can experience endless love or endless challenges. How you handle the situation determines your growth and your inner peace. Do you practice patience or react with outrage?

People who want to explore the deeper meaning of life sometimes embark on a pilgrimage to a shrine, holy place, mountaintop, forest, or someplace where they might pray, meditate, or practice asceticism. Some enter a monastery or hermitage. A time of retreat can be beneficial, but it also isolates the seeker from family, everyday responsibilities, and her or his relationships in the world. If you live and work by yourself, you may be less aware of your own annoying habits. Your patience isn't tested by the necessity of dealing with other people. Being "saintly" under such conditions may be easier! Interpersonal relationships keep you in touch with events happening outside your own head.

Living with others may increase your awareness. The reactions of a loved one to your attitudes, words, and behavior can be difficult to ignore. Patience is put to the test when living together, undoubtedly more so than when living alone. Even something as mundane as dirty dishes left in the sink can be an exercise in patience, letting go, and acceptance. A morally developed person is able to be present with and see the implications of deep-seated attitudes and thus grow in consciousness.

Patience Matters

Impatience usually results from preoccupation with the impermanent; you want things to be accomplished right now and in accord with your expectations! Remember that expectations can be premeditated resentments. To be patient is to permit things to evolve in their own way and in their own time. The book *A Course in Miracles* (2007) identifies patience as one of the characteristics of advanced teachers. Being patient with others is easier when you recognize your commonalities with your sisters and brothers.

There is no need to worry about ultimate outcomes. Nothing can disturb your peace, even if someone has 16 items in a shopping cart in the 10-item checkout line. Consider that most material situations will not matter in the longer term. What will this concern look like 6 months, 1 year, or 10 years from now? The reason that you become upset is because you have decided to let something outside affect how you are inside. You can decide to see peace instead (*A Course in Miracles* 2007). You can apply patience to every situation.

Patience enables you to see clearly. Ask yourself what you most value in your connection with another. What are the moments you value most? You might answer, "When I feel loved," "When I am giving love," "When I feel heard and understood," or "When I feel safe and secure." What is really happening in such moments is that you can taste the richness of your being (Welwood 1991). At such times you no longer need to prove yourself. You can relax. Your usual worries and distractions fade. You feel more awake, alive, and at peace.

LOVE AND FEAR

Humans have two basic drives, namely, love and fear (Wapnick 2011). Societal forces are frequently aligned with materialistic, fear-based values that keep us preoccupied. The mass media present evidence 24/7 that people take advantage of each other. Your materialistic mind is focused on scarcity, competition, and fear (Christopher and Schlenker 2004). The message is clear: Keep on guard. Even Sigmund Freud (1922) believed that the innately aggressive nature of man was the reason that utopian societies could never work.

From the perspective of fear, you are in competition for scarce material resources. This scarcity keeps you mired in physical preoccupations and causes you to think about how to achieve an advantage over others. You move from one fixation to another.

How can you escape from your ego fear-based world? In the midst of this fragmented, violent, and competitive world, accessing your loving mind is difficult. Your loving (or higher) mind is linked to what is best about you. Love is the only way out, although your interpretation of the actions of others often dictates your response (Covey 1997).

When wronged, you can see this action either as an attack or as a call for love, and the interpretation takes place in a millisecond. This fact has powerful implications for your life. For example, when you witness a child misbehaving, can you see that he or she

✓

Activity

Learning to Lead With Love and Compassionate Understanding

This activity requires 20 minutes. Imagine that between classes you walk to the student union for lunch. After you pick up your food, you go to a table to enjoy your salad.

1. You notice that next to you is a man, presumably a father, with three unruly young boys. The boys are under 10 years of age and are creating quite a disturbance. The father seems to be doing nothing, even though everyone around seems annoyed.

2. You too are annoyed and finally muster the courage to say something to the man. He seems unresponsive but finally mutters that they just returned from the university hospital, where their mother passed away earlier that morning.

3. Your annoyance turns to empathy and compassion. You express your sympathy and ask if there anything you can do. You offer to stay with the boys and help.

4. Notice how a better understanding changed your entire demeanor.

5. Did you notice how your body felt before receiving the information and how it felt afterward?

Record these reactions in your journal.

---

is simply afraid? Can you see that he or she is calling out for love through misbehavior? When you see a fear reaction in a child as a call for love, you can accept him or her and offer comfort or support. Can you let yourself see this with adults?

Stephen Covey (1989) advises that in troublesome (problematic) situations, you must seek first to understand and then to be understood. When you are willing to look at the world this way, through the eyes of compassionate understanding, you are more likely to respond positively. That love may be either acceptance or tough love, a kind of love that requires direct action or honest dialogue. Whatever form it takes, loving acceptance can be its foundation.

Prominent spiritual traditions, such as *A Course in Miracles*, Buddhism, and the Hindu Vedanta, suggest that your perceived material life is an illusion or dream (Wapnick 1989). Your spiritual journey is to awaken from that state. In fact, most spiritual traditions inform us that the only things that matter are the eternal things.

Your day-to-day life is a classroom that can enhance or distract your spiritual self. *A Course in Miracles* contends that your obsession with worldly matters is because of your fear of love (Wapnick 2011). Pure love can be frightening in that there are no separate interests. You no longer exist with the same individuality (Tolle 2005). This perspective is radically different.

It is not always clear, even to yourself, whether you are motivated by love or fear. For example, if you help a frail person across the street, are you doing act this out of love? It would appear to be so, but you may be doing it to feel good or to win the approval of those who might be observing. Actually, multiple motivations may lead to the performance of good deeds.

If at your essence you are pure love, you could lose your individuality to that love. What you want no longer matters much. You could theoretically become so absorbed in the oneness of existence, in love, truth, and justice, that your individual self becomes less relevant. Some people have apparently moved toward this state. Can you think of people, either historical figures or those you know in your everyday life, who have consciously chosen a selflessly loving path?

Fortunately, truly wholesome spiritual folks are much more common than you would think. But few seem to be in that state 100 percent of the time. People move in and out of this deep spirituality. They spiritually evolve beyond having concern just for their own interests and become engrossed in the greater good of others.

Finding Meaning

You do well to establish goals (such as pursuing loving kindness and compassion) and then simply live your life with whatever is happening. You do not need to accumulate merits because of your kind deeds. The deeds are their own reward. Reaching out consciously and selflessly becomes your way of life.

© DAJ

Learn to relish the feeling of contentment and satisfaction that you have lived your life in loving kindness, rather than expecting some kind of extrinsic reward in return.

Activity

Finding Meaning Everyday

Your life may seem like an endless cascade of meaningless phenomena. You attend class during the day, study between classes, work in the evening, and catch an occasional exercise session at the student recreation center. According to Dr. Martin Seligman (2011), "The meaningful life consists in belonging to and serving something that you believe is bigger than the self" (p. 13). As an activity to help you find what is most meaningful to you in your everyday life, the following steps are suggested:

1. Every day for the next six days, use one of your signature strengths to help another person. You will want to do this with a person you know well (perhaps a neighbor who might need a hand around the house) and who is likely to want something you have to offer.

2. First, talk to the other person to engage him or her in the process. Tell the person that you are doing the exercise as a learning experience and let the other person know what your strengths are. Then ask the person whether you can do something that engages one of your strengths. Do this selflessly and don't look for praise or anything in return. Focus only on the act of helping. Remember that "kindness . . . consists in total engagement and in the loss of self-consciousness" (Seligman 2002, p. 9).

3. Keep a daily 10-minute log for the six days that addresses how your acts of kindness made you feel.

4. Were you absorbed in doing the act for the other person (making it about them), or were you concentrating on performing the assigned exercise? Did you have second thoughts?

5. Did you experience serving something that is bigger than yourself? Why or why not?

This behavior is particularly manifest in the non-striving aspect of your mindful sitting practice, when you may not appear to be doing anything. But by so doing, you are actually doing everything. For example, regular mindfulness has been demonstrated to promote personal calm and serenity, but if you obsess about your inner peace during mindfulness, you are thinking, not practicing mindfulness (Kabat-Zinn 2013). Your inner peace will not be positively affected. Committing to a process without regard to the outcome is an important step because you open up the process that permits life to flow. The goal remains, but your obsession disappears.

Your life and spiritual experiences are one. Thérèse of Lisieux (1957), a 19th-century French nun, popularized the spirituality of the householder, which made every mundane deed an act of loving prayer. She did not work long tireless hours with the poor or demonstrate great educational charisma. Rather, her everyday cleaning and gardening tasks were transformed by her prayerful awareness. When you are quiet and mindful, you can access the inner wisdom and love that resides within.

Heroic stories depict the incredible spiritual strength of prisoners in Nazi concentration camps. Physical survival is facilitated if your life has a purpose. Neuropsychiatrist Viktor Frankl (1959) survived the German concentration camps by using willpower to keep his mind free. In the midst of ignominious experiments performed by his captors, Frankl determined that they would never be able to control his mind and that the last of all human freedoms is the ability to choose. He chose peace and freedom from hate. With this deep conviction and commitment, Frankl did not hate the captors but held on to love, hope, and inner peace (Frankl 1959).

Other studies have focused on the survival of concentration camp prisoners during World War II. These captives survived the Holocaust because they had a sense of coherence and profound convictions that everything would be fine in spite of the seeming hopelessness (Antonovsky 1993). Even in the most trying circumstances, these people felt a sense of inner peace and control.

If you are able to cope or even make sense of your experiences and put them into a broader perspective, you will gain control. For Thérèse of Lisieux (1957), the act of serving through menial household tasks became her prayer. For Viktor Frankl (1959), being able to keep his mind free of resentments provided coherence and the inner strength to survive. Other Nazi concentration camp survivors found ways to maintain their convictions. Many different strategies can be successful.

A one-dimensional existence can remove us from the present. Walking for health alone can result in missing the total experience of the sunrise, the light glistening on flowers, and the tranquility of the forest path. Sobel and Ornstein (1989) suggest that pleasurable experiences are naturally healthy. But you rob yourself of pleasure by focusing only on the outcome. The alternative proposed here is that you can appreciate everything for its intrinsic, moment-to-moment value. The context becomes spiritual, transforming the experience into an event with greater meaning.

Of course, a paradox is part of all of this. On one hand, experiences have intrinsic worth, yet their value is further enhanced by a sense of coherence (Antonovsky 1987). In fact, both coexist. At times, pain cannot be avoided. A death in a family will bring psychological and emotional pain. But if you understand death as part of life, your pain will be muted by the context. Thus, you may be less devastated. Your sense of control is enhanced because the experience has meaning. Reflect on the concept of flow as defined by Dr. Michaly Csikszentmihalyi (1990), which involves meaningful engagement and using your skills within a challenging arena.

These characteristics can help you move along on the journey toward quiet and balance. Every interaction, indeed every experience, becomes an act of the spirit when you consciously perform it. Making time for nonstriving quiet awareness in your life opens the doors to what you might call the real world, as opposed to the one that advertisers have painted around us (Sirgy et al. 2012). Pursuing a life of materialism, spending, consumption, and a never-ending seeking for more ends in dissatisfaction or heartbreak. This thirst can never be satiated.

LEARNING TO ACCEPT LIFE

Living with spiritual motivation changes every life experience. If you share in the transcendence of eternity, would it not change how you react? You are bombarded daily, if not hourly, by perceived affronts. Remember that the actions of others cannot have a negative spiritual effect on your eternal self. A seemingly offensive act can remind you of your spiritual nature.

The choice is yours. You might customarily react defensively to a comment because of being preoccupied with how you look. When you have an accepting disposition, however, an outside behavior exists, and that is all. Spiritually speaking, what the other person does just is. It is neither injurious nor helpful. Your focus is inward, and your life is more stable.

When you accept your oneness with others, you

During her college days Jill was critical of her personal values, attitudes, and behaviors. Her counselor reminded her that life was better viewed as a workshop for evolving people than as a museum for saints. Although never a particularly religious person, Jill learned to seek help for herself to overcome negative thinking. Change took place slowly. When Jill succeeded at letting go of her negative thoughts, she noticed how peaceful she felt. Her total outlook on life began to change with this attitude adjustment.

will act with greater wisdom. You can purposefully move toward justice without vindictiveness, hate, or thoughts of revenge. Such a response takes much less of a toll than reacting with outrage.

Nakamura and Csíkszentmihályi (2001) identify six factors that define the positive psychology experience of flow, namely, focused concentration, merging of action and awareness, loss of self-consciousness, sense of control, loss of subjective time, and performing an intrinsically rewarding activity. Living a spiritual life is an open path to achieving flow.

TRADITIONS OF MINDFULNESS

Some students have asked whether practicing mindfulness means that a person has to become Buddhist. Not at all! People of any faith can practice mindfulness, and traditions of mindfulness can be found in most of the world's religions. An alternative way to understand this is in terms of two distinct traditions of mindfulness, in both historical Buddhism and in its modern psychological context.

Certainly, the long-established mindfulness practice is a part of Buddhism, which has roots going back nearly 2,500 years to the work of Siddhārtha Gautama, the Buddha, in India. A more recent psychological iteration was started in the United States by Dr. Jon Kabat-Zinn (2013). The health implications for mindfulness are significant.

More than one million people in the United States now self-identify as religious Buddhists. Mindfulness within Buddhism historically focused on becoming awake and growing in awareness to the impermanence of reality. Mindfulness was an important tool that the Buddha practiced and taught to his disciples. Enlightenment resulted from a long, arduous mindfulness practice that overcame greed, hatred, and delusion. A power of clear discernment was achieved through regular meditation. Current Buddhist practice aims at promoting present awareness, calmness, trust, a sense of connection and facilitating spiritual advancement

(Brazier 2013). Buddhists see no individual self separate from the universe (Keown 2013).

Jon Kabat-Zinn established mindfulness as the foundation of the Mindfulness-Based Stress Reduction Program at the University of Massachusetts Medical Center. This practice has since been labelled psychological mindfulness (Grossman et al. 2004), and benefitting from it does not require a person to become a Buddhist. Research has documented many psychological and physical benefits from participation in both high- and low-intensity mindfulness interventions (Cavanagh et al. 2014).

Paying attention is at the heart of experiencing life fully. Mindfulness enables you to live right here, right now. This approach is an effective therapeutic application for people who suffer from mental, emotional, and physical pain. It has also reduced anxiety, depression, and stress in community settings (Szekeres and Wertheim 2014). The practice has relevance to all facets of life and living, as is evidenced by this wellness volume.

Obviously, the practice of mindfulness is also a strategy to become more nonjudgmentally aware. Mindfulness can be a spiritual act which helps you escape from materialism and negative thinking. Mindful awareness is transformative. What dwells in your heart transforms your journey. Either Buddhist or psychological mindfulness opens doors to living fully, with meaning, pleasure, and peace.

The following 10 words capture the essence of living a spiritual life: Show up, be present, be yourself, don't judge, let go.

SUMMARY

Spirituality undergirds wellness. Life is a classroom. It is easy to become sidetracked, because the material world is alluring. You have a choice to be mindfully aware. You may not yet recognize your own worth, the worth of others, and the meaning of your journey.

Do you choose to see yourself and others as good or as evil? Choosing love as your guide enables you to live your life with satisfaction and less strain. Spirituality is appreciating a level of meaning that transcends your immediate physical, mental, and emotional world. Peace of mind emerges with deepening spirituality as your life context enlarges.

The concepts of religion and spirituality overlap. Both focus on the eternal. Religions deal more with the social aspects of connecting with a higher power, emphasizing ritual, doctrine, regulations, and membership. Spirituality provides a broader perspective that places more emphasis on the internal dimensions of love and connectedness. Many people are both religious and spiritual.

Teillard de Chardin suggests that we are spiritual beings having a physical experience. In quiet, you can appreciate your true nature. Everyone is spiritual and evolves through stages of moral consciousness. At your essence, you are love. Your journey is to gain better appreciation of that fundamental state for yourself and for others.

Trusting yourself enables you to grow into a better appreciation of your oneness with others. When you believe in yourself, you can see your self-love as an extension of your oneness with others.

Hope is a means of connecting with divinity and your higher self. When you hope for something, remember that you do not yet know what is in anyone's best interest. True use of faith in your life is to ask to understand and accept the meaning of existence.

A meaningful life is a spiritual life. Bringing love to any arena transforms the experience. You are not expected to do great things, but to do ordinary things with great love.

Overall, spiritual people have better health and better health practices. Whether those benefits result from an eternal perspective that intrinsically reduces stress and anxiety, or whether they stem from a more healthful lifestyle may not be that important.

Living your everyday spiritual life is experiencing flow with your world. You can find extraordinary satisfaction in the process of life that you know through love. You can lose track of time and find your life intrinsically rewarding. You can decide to invite love into your life wherever you are and whatever your circumstances.

Jon Kabat-Zinn translated the Buddhist practice of mindfulness to a secular clinical setting. Mindfulness practice brings quietness and focus to your everyday activities, thereby giving you ownership and self-control through nonjudgmental awareness.

GLOSSARY

acceptance—"Realizing how things are and finding ways to be in wise relationship with them. And then to act, as appropriate, out of that clarity of vision" (Kabat-Zinn 2012, p. 130).

addiction—The compulsive use of a mind-altering substance or repeated behaviors in spite of negative consequences.

Alcoholics Anonymous (AA)—Fellowship of recovering alcoholics whose purpose is to stay sober and help others recover from alcoholism. There are no dues or fees for AA membership or meeting attendance.

alcoholism—Excessive consumption of alcohol that results in social, emotional, and behavioral problems associated with everyday living. According to the CDC, problem drinking is consuming an average of more than 2 drinks per day (more than 14 drinks over the course of a week) for men and an average of more than 1 drink per day (more than 7 drinks per week) for women.

alternative medicine—Therapies often not taught in conventional medical schools of the Western world. Some of these therapies are becoming increasingly more mainstream, such as chiropractic, naturopathy, homeopathy, acupuncture, stress management, and exercise.

anaerobic physical activity—Exercising at an intensity that exceeds the ability of the body to metabolize oxygen. This level of intensity generally is greater than 85 percent of a person's maximal heart rate.

attitudes—Established beliefs that guide thinking, behaviors, and responses.

attitudinal foundations—These seven, namely, nonjudging, patience, beginner's mind, trust, nonstriving, acceptance, and letting go, represent guiding principles for the practice of mindfulness, whether that be mindful sitting, body scan, walking, eating, or everyday living.

beginner's mind—Enables us to see objects afresh, as if for the first time.

binge drinking—Reaching a blood alcohol content of .08, which typically results when men consume five or more drinks and women consume four or more drinks within two hours.

body mass index (BMI)—A measure of body fat calculated by dividing weight (in kilograms) by the square of the height (in meters). Normal BMI 18.5 to 24.9; overweight is 25 to 29.9; obese is greater than or equal to 30.

body scan—An opportunity to experience full-body awareness, segment by segment. Calling attention to each body part serves to purify it incrementally of tension and stress.

carbon accounting—Methodology proposed for business and industry to determine their relative carbon footprint.

carbon footprint—The greenhouse gases, especially carbon dioxide (CO_2) and methane (CH_4), that contribute to global warming and are produced by a system, organization, or individual

carrying capacity—The amount of life that planet earth can maintain given its finite resources.

Center for Science in the Public Interest (CSPI)—Structured similar to Consumers Union, the organization that publishes *Consumer Reports*, CSPI takes no advertising or government funding. By so doing, they are able to provide unbiased information about food and health.

cholesterol—A sterol found in most tissues of the human body. High concentrations in the blood are associated with heart disease and stroke.

coherence—The ability to find meaning in every aspect of life, no matter how seemingly absurd or disconnected.

complementary alternative medicine (CAM)—Refers to less conventional therapies that can be used either as an alternative or as an addition (complement) to conventional medical care. Some of these therapies are becoming increasingly more mainstream, such as chiropractic, naturopathy, homeopathy, acupuncture, stress management, and exercise.

compulsive behavior—Consistently and repetitively performing an act that does not lead to positive outcomes.

compulsive overeating—Overconsumption of food without regard to the effect on health and well-being. Overeating is as addictive as tobacco, alcohol, and other drugs.

Consumer Reports—Magazine published monthly by Consumers Union, a not-for-profit organization that expertly tests consumer products in an objective manner. By not taking advertising or governmental support, the organization offers reports that are not influenced by outside entities, so its recommendations about products are unbiased.

dependence—A state of being whereby a person is psychologically or physiologically dependent on a substance or other outside stimulus.

dietary guidelines—Published every five years by the United States Department of Agriculture, these guidelines provide an overview and detailed recommendations regarding food intake among Americans.

dopamine—A brain neurotransmitter that serves as a chemical messenger.

drug addiction—Dependence on (or compulsive need for) a drug or medication, often characterized by intense craving, which persists in spite of the negative consequences of using the drug.

ecological footprint—The measure of human demand on the earth's ecosystems, expressed in terms of the biologically productive land and sea area necessary to absorb the associated waste of human activities (Hall and Day 2009).

ecosystem services—The ability of an ecosystem to self-regulate, thereby providing humankind with processes and resources not otherwise available. New York City drinking water purification has been augmented by restricting building in the nearby watershed, thereby enabling the environment to preserve the quality of the water.

endocrine disruptors—Chemicals which even at low levels cause interference with human embryo development and human body functions.

epigenetics—Public health tool to quantify the relative contribution of various stressors on the health outcomes of people. In terms of biology, epigenetics includes study of how external environments affect genes and influence disease.

exercise—Bodily movement done repetitively and purposely to promote fitness, such as aerobics, Zumba, swimming, jogging, brisk walking, and lifting weights.

fight-or-flight reaction—First described by Harvard physiologist Walter Bradford Cannon, MD, in the 1920s, this physiologic reaction occurs in the presence of a highly charged physical, mental, or emotional experience.

fitness—The ability to perform physical work. Fitness improves with regular physical activity or exercise.

flexibility exercise—Working to elongate the muscle groups and improve range of motion in the joints addressed in aerobic and strengthening work, usually performed two or more days per week.

flow—A construct of positive psychology that represents being immersed in a challenging and rewarding endeavor without distraction, sense of time, or self-consciousness, and feeling one with and having control over the outcome (Donaldson, Csikszentmilhalyi, and Nakamura 2011).

food addiction—Compulsive overeating, often manifested by binge eating, that persists in spite of negative health consequences, such as weight gain. Binge eating is often followed by feelings of shame and depression.

fracking—The industrial process used to access oil and natural gas reserves that requires drilling down 1 to 2 miles (1.6 to 3.2 km) and then drilling another 5 to 10 miles (8 to 16 km) horizontally. Water and chemicals are pumped into the ground to break up rock in order to extract the gas within.

Great Law of the Iroquois Confederacy—In our every deliberation, we must consider the impact of our decisions on the next seven generations.

health—Customarily defined as the absence of disease. The World Health Organization (1986), however, defines health as "the state of complete mental, physical, and social well-being; not merely the absence of disease or infirmity" (p. 1).

hierarchy of needs—Abraham Maslow's psychological theory indicated that human development is predicated on having physiological and safety needs met. Thereafter, a person can address social connections, self-esteem, and self-actualization.

high-density lipoprotein (HDL) cholesterol—Good, or healthy, cholesterol that protects against heart disease.

high-intensity interval training (HIIT)—Performing repeated bouts of vigorous or maximal physical activity for short periods followed by a longer recovery period of light- or moderate-intensity activity.

hyperlipidemia—High blood fats, that is, high levels of low-density lipoprotein (LDL) cholesterol (colloquially known as bad cholesterol), high triglycerides, or low levels of protective high-density lipoprotein (HDL) cholesterol (good cholesterol). These conditions lead to coronary artery disease (CAD), including stroke, male impotence, and increased risk of premature death.

Kleenex culture—The wasteful practice in American society and elsewhere in which material products are used once and then discarded, not unlike Kleenex tissues. This culture is also referred to as the consumer culture or consumption society.

leaching—When the soluble portions of solids are dissolved by water (or other solvent).

learned optimism—The cultivated skills that permit a person to be able to see and experience joy, happiness, and well-being.

LEED—A program to achieve green buildings underway nationwide, namely Leadership in Energy and Environmental Design.

letting go—The ability to let be, to relinquish attachment, to be nonattached to outcomes, and not to cling to what we hate or detest (Kabat-Zinn 2012).

life-cycle analysis (LCA)—Tool created by industrial engineers, physicists, chemists, and biologists to detail inputs and outputs of the manufacturing processes. The goal is to control wasteful discarding of items without regard to the value lost.

lipids—A class of compounds, including fats and triglycerides, that are insoluble in water. Lipids are composed of saturated, monounsaturated, and polyunsaturated fats.

low caloric density foods—Foods having a relatively small number of calories per ounce. For example, a potato has .6 calories per gram. In contrast, beef and cheese have a caloric density of approximately 4.0 calories per gram.

low-density lipoprotein (LDL) cholesterol—Bad, or lousy, cholesterol that is a major contributor to atherosclerosis, hardening of the arteries, heart disease, and stroke.

medical home—Family practice physicians, internal medicine doctors, obstetricians, gynecologists, nurse practitioners, and physician assistants serve as primary care physicians. These people are the first contact for an undiagnosed health problem, ongoing care, and referral to specialty care.

medicalize—A health condition that is defined in such a manner as to be treated with a pharmaceutical or surgical solution.

mental health—The state of psychological, emotional, and social well-being that enables a person to perform activities of daily living without difficulty.

metabolic syndrome (syndrome X)—An unhealthy but common combination of obesity, elevated blood pressure, high cholesterol, and glucose intolerance that results in a fivefold increased risk of developing diabetes mellitus and heart disease.

microsleep—Sleep episodes that last fraction of a second to many seconds. These events are particularly dangerous when driving.

mindfulness—"The awareness that emerges through paying attention on purpose, in the present moment, and nonjudgmentally to the unfolding of experience moment by moment" (Kabat-Zinn, 2003, p. 145).

moderate-intensity physical activity—Physical exertion level that is 3 to 5.9 times the amount of energy being expended at rest, such as walking at greater than 3 miles (4.8 km) per hour but less than 4 miles (6.4 km) per hour, depending on fitness.

monounsaturated fat—The healthiest type of dietary fat. This fat remains stable at higher temperatures and is therefore better for cooking because it is less likely to hydrogenate or become saturated.

muscle- and bone-strengthening activity—Includes resistance training and weightlifting, which cause muscles and bones to work against an applied force or weight (*Physical Activity Guidelines for Americans* 2008). An example of a strengthening activity would be biceps curls using a resistance band.

nonjudging—The mindful ability to see and experience impartially, without labels or indictments.

nonstriving—Being present with whatever is happening, without the need for goals, objectives, or outcomes to justify the process.

nutrient dense food—A food with a high ratio of vitamins, minerals, fiber, and other important dietary components to the amount of calories.

Nutrition Action Healthletter—With nearly a million subscriptions, this monthly science-based publication takes no advertising or government support and represents the best interests of consumers.

obesity—Officially classified as a disease by the American Medical Association in 2013, obesity for adults is having a body mass index of 30 or higher.

obesogenic—An environment that contributes to obesity, such as a place that doesn't promote walking or other physical activity and has a preponderance of fast-food outlets.

optimism—Expecting the best possible outcome.

patience—Permits everything to evolve in its own time.

physical activity—Any bodily movement that produces an increase in heart rate and respiration, such as gardening; washing the car; swimming; jogging; and walking for health, to the bus stop, to work, to class, or in the woods.

positive emotions—Composed of trust, compassion, gratitude, awe, forgiveness, joy, hope, and love (Vaillant 2013).

positive psychology—The branch of psychology that focuses on identifying and promoting people's genius and talents.

prayer—An act of connecting with a power greater than yourself. Most prayer is intercessory, that is, asking for something.

prevention—Measures taken to forestall the effects of illness and disease. Three levels exist.

primary prevention—Measures taken to forestall an illness or injury from occurring.

quality of life—Subjective measure of happiness that is an important component in many decisions; factors include mental health, cultural environment, financial security, job satisfaction, family life, health, and safety.

saturated fat—Unhealthy fat consisting of fatty acids naturally saturated with hydrogen atoms, such as found in cheeses, butter, and lard; a fatty acid chain that cannot accept additional hydrogen atoms and that is often solid at room temperature, although palm and coconut oil are saturated fats that are liquid at room temperature.

secondary prevention—Measures taken to detect a disease or injury early or to treat the condition promptly after it is detected.

single bottom line—Considering the only value to be the financial one, that is, the costs.

social capital—The informal values or norms shared among members of a community that enhance cooperation. Social capital can be enhanced by cooperative community actions.

social liberation—Changes to social systems that enable health-promoting behaviors, such as no-smoking policies at the workplace.

social network—The available social resource contacts within a community. The potential of social media has accelerated such connections through web-based groups.

social support—The perception that we are cared for, that assistance is available, and that we are part of a supportive social network.

spirituality—A fusion of eight positive emotions that unite people to other human beings and to the God of their understanding (Valliant 2013). The important emotions include love, hope, joy, forgiveness, compassion, faith, awe, and gratitude (Valliant 2008). These universal positive emotions guide people to look beyond apparent differences and help them to recognize common values.

stages of change or transtheoretical model of behavior change—Prochaska et al. (1990) suggested that behavioral change occurs in a stepwise fashion, instead of all at once.

substance abuse—A pattern of misuse of any substance for mood-altering purposes.

sustainability—The ability to accommodate the present needs of a population without compromising the ability of future populations to meet their needs (World Commission on Environment and Development 1987).

telomeres—Specialized ends of chromosome structures that provide constancy to DNA molecules and enable them to replicate safely.

tertiary prevention—Measures taken to retrain, reeducate, and rehabilitate a diseased, injured, or impaired person.

tipping point—The critical point beyond which a significant and often unstoppable effect takes place.

total cholesterol—The total amount of cholesterol in the blood, usually determined by means of a lipid analysis.

trans fat—Unhealthy chemically altered (partially hydrogenated) fat used to add shelf life to a product. Trans fat is best avoided altogether, and the recommendation is to consume no more than two grams per day.

triple bottom line—An economic approach that takes into account people, the planet, and profit. The intersection of these goals is where sustainability occurs.

trust—Represents confidence in self.

vigorous-intensity physical activity—Physical activity of sufficient intensity that speaking or carrying on a conversation is difficult.

wellness—"The integration of body, mind, and spirit—the appreciation that everything you do, think, feel, and believe has an impact on your state of health and the health of the world" (Travis and Ryan 2004, p. xvi).

whole foods—Foods grown in nature and that require no processing to be eaten, such as carrots and apples.

whole grains—Grains that retain the germ (embryo), bran (husk), and endosperm (starch-containing part of the seed) as opposed to refined grains, which contain only the endosperm.

workaholism—An addiction or compulsion to work excessive hours in spite of the cost to health and relationships.

yoga—A series of practices aimed at bringing tranquility, peace, calm, and insight to the mind of the practitioner. **Hatha yoga** emphasizes specific body postures (asanas) and awareness of breathing (pranayama).

young adults—Usually considered ages 18 through 26, typically the college years in the United States. With graduate school and travel, the young adult years often extend to age 30.

REFERENCES AND RESOURCES

Introduction

Abramson, J. 2004. *Overdosed America: The Broken Promise of American Medicine*. New York City: HarperCollins.

Anderson, O., R. Davis, G.B. Hanna, and C.A. Vincent. 2013. "Surgical Adverse Events: A Systematic Review." *American Journal of Surgery* 206 (2): 253–262.

Assadourian, Eric, and Tom Prugh (Eds). 2013. *Is Sustainability Still Possible? The Worldwatch Institute State of the World*. Washington, DC: Island Press.

Boehm, J.K., L.L. Vie, and L.D. Kubzansky. 2012. "The Promise of Well-Being Interventions for Improving Health Risk Behaviors." *Current Cardiovascular Risk Reports* 6: 511–519.

Brill, S. 2013. "Bitter Pill: Why Medical Bills Are Killing Us." *Time* 181 (8): 16–55.

Daubenmier, J., J. Lin, E. Blackburn, F.M. Hecht, J. Kristeller, N. Maninger, M. Kuwata, P. Bacchetti, P.J. Havel, and E. Epel. 2012. "Changes in Stress, Eating, and Metabolic Factors Are Related to Changes in Telomerase Activity in a Randomized Mindfulness Intervention Pilot Study." *Psychoneuroendocrinology* 37 (7): 917–928.

Donaldson, Stewart, Mihaly Csikszentmihalyi, and Jeanne Nakamura. 2011. *Applied Positive Psychology: Improving Everyday Life, Health, Schools, Work, and Society* (Applied Psychology Series). New York: Routledge.

Ferhman, C. 2013, February 20. "New Era for Coach, Team and Region." *New York Times*. www.nytimes.com/2013/02/21/sports/after-50-years-at-connecticut-high-school-coach-vito-montelli-lets-go.html?pagewanted=all&_r=3&

Horton, M., and P. Freire. 1990. *We Make the Road by Walking: Conversations on Education and Social Change*. Eds. Brenda Bell, John Gaventa, and John Peters. Philadelphia: Temple University Press.

Kabat-Zinn, J. 1994. *Wherever You Go There You Are*. New York: Hyperion.

Kabat-Zinn, J. 2003. "Mindfulness-Based Interventions in Context: Past, Present, and Future." *Clinical Psychology: Science and Practice* 10 (2): 144–156.

Kabat-Zinn, J. 2005. *Coming to Our Senses*. New York: Hyperion.

Kabat-Zinn J. 2012. *Mindfulness for Beginners*. Boulder, CO: Sounds True.

Kabat-Zinn, J. 2013. *Full Catastrophe Living: Using the Wisdom of Your Body and Mind to Face Stress, Pain, and Illness*. New York: Bantam.

Kohlberg, L. 1973. "The Claim to Moral Adequacy of a Highest Stage of Moral Judgment." *Journal of Philosophy* 70 (18): 630–646.

Meditation, *American Cancer Society*, 2014, www.cancer.org/treatment/treatmentsandsideeffects/complementaryandalternativemedicine/mindbodyandspirit/meditation.

Mokdad, A.H., J.S. Marks, D.F. Stroup, and J.L. Gerberding. 2004. "Actual Causes of Death in the United States, 2000." *Journal of the American Medical Association* 291 (10): 1238–1245.

Moss, Michael. 2013. *Salt Sugar Fat: How the Food Giants Hooked Us*. New York: Random House.

Piaget, J. 1965. *The Moral Judgment of the Child*. New York: The Free Press.

Seligman, M.E.P., and M. Csikszentmihalyi. 2000. "Positive Psychology: An Introduction." *American Psychologist* 55 (1): 5–14.

Siegel, Ronald (ed.). 2013. *Positive Psychology: Harnessing the Power of Happiness, Mindfulness, and Inner Strength*. Boston: Harvard Health.

Travis, John W., and Regina S. Ryan. 2004. *Wellness Workbook: How to Achieve Enduring Health and Vitality* (3rd ed). Berkeley, CA: Celestial Arts.

Chapter 1

Abramson, J. 2004. *Overdosed America: The Broken Promise of American Medicine*. New York City: HarperCollins.

Ardell, Donald B. 1986. *High Level Wellness: An Alternative to Doctors, Drugs, and Disease*. Berkeley, CA: Ten Speed Press.

Assadourian, Eric, and Tom Prugh. 2013. *.Is Sustainability Still Possible? The Worldwatch Institute State of the World 2013*. Washington, DC: Island Press.

Baruth, M., D.-C Lee, X. Sui, T.S. Church, B.H. Marcus, S. Wilcox, and S.N. Blair. 2011. "Emotional Outlook on Life Predicts Increases in Physical Activity Among Initially Inactive Men." *Health Education and Behavior* 38 (2): 150–158.

Berra, Yogi, and David Kaplan. 2001. *When You Come to a Fork in the Road, Take It*. New York: Hyperion Press.

Biegler, K.A., A.K.L. Anderson, L.B. Wenzel, K. Osann, and E.L. Nelson. 2012. "Longitudinal Change in Telomere Length and the Chronic Stress Response in a Randomized Pilot Biobehavioral Clinical Study: Implications for Cancer Prevention." *Cancer Prevention Research* 5 (10): 1173–1182.

Blanchflower, D.G., A.J. Oswald, and S. Stewart-Brown. 2013. "Is Psychological Well-Being Linked to the Consumption of Fruit and Vegetables?" *Social Indicators Research* 114 (3): 785–801.

Blank, L. 2006. "Medical Professionalism in the New Millennium: A Physicians' Charter." *Radiology* 238 (2): 383–386.

Boehm, J.K., L.L. Vie, and L.D. Kubzansky. 2012. "The Promise of Well-Being Interventions for Improving Health Risk Behaviors." *Current Cardiovascular Risk Reports* 6: 511–519.

Boesten, D.M.P.H.J., J.M.J. De Vos-Houben, L. Timmermans, G.J.M. Den Hartog, A. Bast, and G J. Hageman. 2013. "Accelerated Aging During Chronic Oxidative Stress: A Role for PARP-1." *Oxidative Medicine and Cellular Longevity*. Article ID 680414, 10 pages. http://dx.doi.org/10.1155/2013/680414

Borgonovi, F. 2008. "Doing Well by Doing Good: The Relationship Between Formal Volunteering and Self-Reported Health and Happiness." *Social Science and Medicine* 66 (11): 2321–2334.

Brill, S. 2013. "Bitter Pill: Why Medical Bills Are Killing Us." *Time* 181 (8): 16–55.

Chida, Y., and A. Steptoe. 2008. "Positive Psychology and Mortality: A Quantitative Review of Prospective Observational Studies." *Psychosomatic Medicine* 20: 741–756.

Coffey, D.S. 2001. "Similarities of Prostate and Breast Cancer: Evolution, Diet, and Estrogens." *Urology* 57 (4): 31–38.

Covey, Stephen R. 1995. *First Things First*. New York: Fireside.

Daniels, S.R. 2006. "The Consequences of Childhood Overweight and Obesity." *Future of Children* 16 (1): 47–67.

Danhauer, S.C., L.D. Case, R. Tedeschi, G. Russell, T. Vishnevsky, K. Triplett, E.H. Ip, and N.E. Avis. 2013. "Predictors of Posttraumatic Growth in Women With Breast Cancer." *Psychooncology* 22 (12): 2676–2683.

Daubenmier, J., J. Lin, E. Blackburn, F.M. Hecht, J. Kristeller, N. Maninger, M. Kuwata, P. Bacchetti, P.J. Havel, and E. Epel. 2012. "Changes in Stress, Eating, and Metabolic Factors Are Related to Changes in Telomerase Activity in a Randomized Mindfulness Intervention Pilot Study." *Psychoneuroendocrinology* 37 (7): 917–928.

Diamond, Jared. 1997. *Why Is Sex Fun?* New York: Basic Books.

Diekmann, K.A., A.E. Tenbrunsel, and A.D. Galinsky. 2003. "From Self-Prediction to Self-Defeat: Behavioral Forecasting, Self-Fulfilling Prophecies, and the Effect of Competitive Expectations." *Journal of Personality and Social Psychology* 85 (4): 672–683.

Donaldson, Stewart, Mihaly Csikszentmihalyi, and Jeanne Nakamura. 2011. *Applied Positive Psychology: Improving Everyday Life, Health, Schools, Work, and Society* (Applied Psychology Series). New York: Routledge.

Donate, L.E., and M.A. Blasco. 2011. "Telomeres in Cancer and Ageing." *Philosophical Transactions of the Royal Society B: Biological Sciences* 366: 76–84.

Emmons, R.A., and M.E. McCullough. 2003. "Counting Blessings Versus Burdens: An Experimental Investigation of Gratitude and Subjective Well-Being in Daily Life." *Journal of Personality and Social Psychology* 84 (2): 377–389.

Emmons, R.A., and R. Stern. 2013. "Gratitude as a Psychotherapeutic Intervention." *Journal of Clinical Psychology* 69 (8): 846–855.

Epel, E. 2012. "How 'Reversible' Is Telomeric Aging?" *Cancer Prevention Research* 5 (10): 1163–1168.

Fordyce, M.W. 1977. "Development of a Program to Increase Personal Happiness." *Journal of Counseling Psychology* 24 (6): 511–521.

Fordyce, M.W. 1983. "A Program to Increase Happiness: Further Studies." *Journal of Counseling Psychology* 30 (4): 483–498.

Georgin-Lavialle, S., D.S. Moura, J. Bruneau, J.-C. Chauvet-Gélinier, G. Damaj, E. Soucie, S. Barete, et al. 2014. "Leukocyte Telomere Length in Mastocytosis: Correlations With Depression and Perceived Stress." *Brain, Behavior, and Immunity* 35: 51–57.

Greenland, P. 2001. "Beating High Blood Pressure With Low-Sodium DASH." *New England Journal of Medicine* 344 (1): 53–4.

Haythorn, M.R., and R.J. Ablin. 2011. "Prostate-Specific Antigen Testing Across the Spectrum of Prostate Cancer." *Biomarkers in Medicine* 5 (4): 515–526.

Kabat-Zinn, Jon. 2013. *Full Catastrophe Living: Using the Wisdom of Your Body and Mind to Face Stress, Pain, and Illness*. New York: Dell.

Kaiser Health News. 2012, June 12. http://capsules.kaiserhealthnews.org/index.php/2012/06/report-health-spending-will-climb-to-nearly-one-fifth-of-gdp/

Killingsworth, M.A., and D.T. Gilbert. 2010. "A Wandering Mind Is an Unhappy Mind." *Science* 330 (6006): 932.

Lee, Bruce. 1975. *Tao of Jeet Kune Do*. Valencia, CA: Black Belt Communications.

Mackey, M.C., S.H. McKinney, and A. Tavakoli. 2008. "Factors Related to Smoking in College Women." *Journal of Community Health Nursing* 25 (2): 106–121.

McFarland, Robert. 2007. *Now That I Have Cancer I Am Whole*. Kansas City, MO: Andrews McMeel.

Mian, S.M., S. Lazorick, K.L. Simeonsson, H.F. Afanador, C.L. Stowe, and L.F. Novick. 2013. "Prevention Screening and Counseling: Strategy for Integration into Medical Education and Practice." *American Journal of Preventive Medicine* 44 (6): 666–671.

Mokdad, A H., J.S. Marks, D.F. Stroup, and J.L. Gerberding. 2004. "Actual Causes of Death in the United States, 2000." *Journal of the American Medical Association* 291 (10): 1238–1245.

Moses III, H., D.H.M. Matheson, E.R. Dorsey, B.P. George, D. Sadoff, and S. Yoshimura. 2013. "The Anatomy of Health Care in the United States." *Journal of the American Medical Association* 310 (18): 1947–1963.

Moss, Michael. 2013. *Salt, Sugar, Fat*. New York: Random House.

Mulley, C., R. Tyson, P. McCue, C. Rissel, and C. Munro. 2013. "Valuing Active Travel: Including the Health Benefits of Sustainable Transport in Transportation Appraisal Frameworks." *Research in Transportation Business and Management* 7: 27–34.

National Health Expenditure Data. 2014. Center for Medicare and Medicaid Services. www.cms.gov/Research-Statistics-Data-and -Systems/Statistics-Trends-and-Reports /NationalHealthExpendData/index.html

Occupational Employment Statistics. 2013. U.S. Department of Labor. www.bls.gov/oes/home.htm

Ornish, D. 2011. "And the Only Side-Effects are Good Ones." *The Lancet Oncology* 12 (10): 924–925.

Ornish, Dean. 2007. *The Spectrum: A Scientifically Proven Program to Feel Better, Live Longer, Lose Weight, Gain Health*. New York: Ballantine Books.

Ornstein, Robert, and David Sobel. 1989. *Healthy Pleasures*. Woburn, MA: Addison-Wesley.

Otake, K., S. Shimai, J. Tanaka-Matsumi, K. Otsui, and B.L. Fredrickson. 2006. "Happy People Become Happier Through Kindness: A Counting Kindnesses Intervention." *Journal of Happiness Studies* 7 (3): 361–375.

Physical Activity Guidelines for Americans. 2008. U.S. Department of Health and Human Services. Rockville, MD: United States Department of Health and Human Services.

Pischke, C.R., S. Frenda, D. Ornish, and G. Weidner. 2010. "Lifestyle Changes Are Related to Reductions in Depression in Persons With Elevated Coronary Risk Factors." *Psychology and Health* 25 (9): 1077–1100.

Pransky, Jack. 2003. *Prevention From the Inside-Out*. First Book Library.

Prostate-Specific Antigen Test. National Cancer Institute. 2013. www.cancer.gov/cancertopics/factsheet/detection/PSA

Preston, C.M., and M. Alexander. 2010. "Prevention in the United States Affordable Care Act." *Journal of Preventive Medicine and Public Health* 43 (6): 455–458.

Reichard, R.J., J.B. Avey, S. Lopez, and M. Dollwet. 2013. "Having the Will and Finding the Way: A Review and Meta-Analysis of Hope at Work." *Journal of Positive Psychology* 8 (4): 292–304.

Schwarz, M., and F. Strack. 1999. "Reports of Subjective Well-Being: Judgmental Processes and Their Methodological Implications," in *Foundations of Hedonistic Psychology: Scientific Perspectives on Enjoyment and Suffering*, eds. D. Kahneman, E. Diener, and N. Schwarz. New York: Russell Sage Foundation.

Sclafani, A., and K. Ackroff. 2012. "Role of Gut Nutrient Sensing in Stimulating Appetite and Conditioning Food Preferences." *American Journal of Physiology—Regulatory Integrative and Comparative Physiology* 302 (10): R1119–R1133.

Seligman, Martin. 2011. *Flourish: A Visionary New Understanding of Happiness and Well-Being*. New York: Free Press.

Seligman, M.E., and M. Csikszentmihalyi. 2000. "Positive Psychology: An Introduction." *American Psychologist* 55 (1): 5–14.

Seligman, M.E.P. 2006. *Learning Optimism*. New York: Vintage Books.

Seligman, M.E.P., T. Rashid, and A.C. Parks. 2006. "Positive Psychotherapy." *American Psychologist* 61 (8): 774–788.

Seligman, M.E., T.A. Steen, N. Park, and C. Peterson. 2005. "Positive Psychology Progress: Empirical Validation of Interventions." *American Psychologist* 60 (5): 410–421.

Sheldon, K., B. Frederickson, K. Rathunde, M. Csikszentmihalyi, and J. Haidt. 2014. *Positive Psychology Center*. www.ppc.sas.upenn.edu/akumalmanifesto.htm

Siegel, Ronald (ed.). 2013. *Positive Psychology: Harnessing the Power of Happiness, Mindfulness, and Inner Strength*. Boston: Harvard Health.

Starr, Paul. 1982. *Social Transformation of American Medicine*. New York: Basic Books.

Steger, M.F., Y. Shim, J. Barenz, and J.Y. Shin. 2013. "Through the Windows of the Soul: A Pilot Study Using Photography to Enhance Meaning in Life." *Journal of Contextual Behavioral Science*.

Swain, J.F., P.B. McCarron, E.F. Hamilton, F.M. Sacks, and L J. Appel. 2008. "Characteristics of the Diet Patterns Tested in the Optimal Macronutrient Intake Trial to Prevent Heart Disease (OmniHeart): Options for a Heart-Healthy Diet." *Journal of the American Dietetic Association* 108 (2): 257–265.

Tindle, H.A., Y.-F. Chang, L.H. Kuller, J.E. Manson, J.G. Robinson, M.C. Rosal, G.J. Siegle, and K.A. Matthews. 2009. "Optimism, Cynical Hostility, and Incident Coronary Heart Disease and Mortality in the Women's Health Initiative." *Circulation* 120 (8): 656–662.

Travis, John W., and Regina S. Ryan. 2004. *Wellness Workbook: How to Achieve Enduring Health and Vitality*. Berkeley, CA: Celestial Arts.

Tummers, N. 2013. *Stress Management: A Wellness Approach*. Champaign, IL: Human Kinetics.

U.S. Department of Transportation Budget Highlights. 2013. www.dot.gov/sites/dot.gov/files/docs/dot_budget_highlights_fy_2013_5MB.pdf

United Nations World Population Prospects Report. 2011. Department of Economic and Social Affairs. www.un.org/esa/population/unpop.htm

Vaillant, G.E. 2013. Psychiatry, Religion, Positive Emotions and Spirituality. *Asian Journal of Psychiatry* 6 (6): 590–594.

Values in Action Program Institute on Character. 2014. *Inventory of Signature Strengths Survey*. www.viacharacter.org

World Health Organization (WHO). 1947. *Constitution of the World Health Organization*. Chronicle of the World Health Organization 1. Geneva, Switzerland.

Chapter 2

Bordenhauser, G.V., L.A. Shephard, and G.P. Kramer. 1994. "Negative Affect and Social Judgment: The Differential Impact of Anger and Sadness." *European Journal of Social Psychology* 24: 45–62.

Borysenko, Joan. 2007. *Minding the Body, Mending the Mind*. Philadelphia: De Capo Press.

Cohen, S., D. Janicki-Deverts, W.J. Doyle, G.E. Miller, E. Frank, B.S. Rabin, and R.B. Turner. 2012. "Chronic Stress, Glucocorticoid Receptor Resistance, Inflammation, and Disease Risk." *Proceedings of the National Academy of Sciences of the United States of America* 109 (16): 5995–5999.

Covey, Stephen R. 1989. *The Seven Habits of Highly Effective People*. New York: Free Press.

Csikszentmihalyi, M. 2000. "Happiness, Flow, and Economic Equality." *American Psychologist* 55 (10): 1163–1164.

Dalen, J., B.W. Smith, B.M. Shelley, A.L. Sloan, L. Leahigh, and D. Begay. 2010. "Pilot Study: Mindful Eating and Living (MEAL): Weight, Eating Behavior, and Psychological Outcomes Associated With a Mindfulness-Based Intervention for People With Obesity." *Complementary Therapies in Medicine* 18 (6): 260–264.

Dumontheil, I., S.J. Gilbert, C.D. Frith, and P.W. Burgess. 2010. "Recruitment of Lateral Rostral Prefrontal Cortex in Spontaneous and Task-Related Thoughts." *Quarterly Journal of Experimental Psychology* 63 (9): 1740–1756.

Ellis, Albert. 2006. "Rational Emotive Behavior Therapy and Mindfulness Based Stress Reduction Training of Jon Kabat-Zinn." *Journal of Rational-Emotive and Cognitive-Behavior Therapy* 24: 63–78.

Emmons, R.A., and M.E. McCullough. 2003. "Counting Blessings Versus Burdens: An Experimental Investigation of Gratitude and Subjective Well-Being in Daily Life." *Journal of Personality and Social Psychology* 84 (2): 377–389.

Forgeard, M.J.C., and M.E.P. Seligman. 2012. "Seeing the Glass Half Full: A Review of the Causes and Consequences of Optimism." *Pratiques Psychologiques* 18 (2): 107–120.

Forster, S., and N. Lavie. 2014. "Distracted by Your Mind? Individual Differences in Distractibility Predict Mind Wandering." *Journal of Experimental Psychology: Learning Memory and Cognition* 40 (1): 251–260.

Goldberg, L.S. 2008. "Embodied Trust Within the Perinatal Nursing Relationship." *Midwifery* 24 (1): 74–82.

Kabat-Zinn, Jon. 2012. *Mindfulness for Beginners: Reclaiming the Present Moment—and Your Life*. Boulder, CO: Sounds True.

Kabat-Zinn, Jon. 2013. *Full Catastrophe Living: Using the Wisdom of Your Body and Mind to Face Stress, Pain, and Illness*. New York: Dell.

Kemeny, M.E., C. Foltz, J.F. Cavanagh, M. Cullen, J. Giese-Davis, P. Jennings, E.L. Rosenberg, et al. 2012. "Contemplative/Emotion Training Reduces Negative Emotional Behavior and Promotes Prosocial Responses." *Emotion* 12 (2): 338–350.

Killingsworth, M.A., and D.T. Gilbert. 2010. "A Wandering Mind Is an Unhappy Mind." *Science* 330 (6006): 932.

Kornfield, J. 2000. *After the Ecstasy, the Laundry: How the Heart Grows Wise on the Spiritual Path*. New York: Bantam Books.

Kornfield, J. 2011. *The Wise Heart: A Guide to the Universal Teachings of Buddhist Psychology*. New York: Bantam Books.

Ornish, Dean. 2007. *The Spectrum: A Scientifically Proven Program to Feel Better, Live Longer, Lose Weight, Gain Health*. New York: Ballantine Books.

Pert, C.B. 1997. *Molecules of Emotion. Touchstone: The Science Behind Mind-Body Medicine.* New York: Touchstone.

Seligman, Martin. 2011. *Flourish: A Visionary New Understanding of Happiness and Well-Being.* New York: Free Press.

Williams, K., M. Kolar, B. Reger, and J. Pearson. 2001. "Evaluation of a Wellness-Based Mindfulness Stress Reduction Intervention: A Controlled Trial." *American Journal of Health Promotion.* July/August, 16 (6): 422–432.

Wubbolding, R. 2002. *Reality Therapy for the 21st Century.* Bridgeport, NJ: Buchanon.

Chapter 3

Barnes, P.M., B. Bloom, and R.L. Nahin. 2008. *Complementary and Alternative Medicine use Among Adults and Children: United States, 2007.* National Health Statistics Reports.

Bem, Darryl J. 1971. *Beliefs, Attitudes, and Human Affairs.* Basic Concepts in Psychology Series.

Bos, E.H., R. Merea, E. van den Brink, R. Sanderman, and A.A. Bartels-Velthuis. 2014. "Mindfulness Training in a Heterogeneous Psychiatric Sample: Outcome Evaluation and Comparison of Different Diagnostic Groups." *Journal of Clinical Psychology* 70 (1): 60–71.

Brefczynski-Lewis, J. A., A. Lutz, H. S. Schaefer, D. B. Levinson, and R. J. Davidson. 2007. "Neural Correlates of Attentional Expertise in Long-Term Meditation Practitioners." *Proceedings of the National Academy of Sciences of the United States of America* 104 (27): 11483-11488.

Chin, R. 1995. *The Energy Within: The Science Behind Eastern Healing Techniques.* New York: Marlowe.

Csikszentmihalyi, M. 1990. *Flow: The Psychology of Optimal Experience.* New York: Harper Perennial.

Dacci, P., S. Amadio, S. Gerevini, L. Moiola, U. Del Carro, M. Radaelli, G. Figlia, V. Martinelli, G. Comi, and R. Fazio. 2013. "Practice of Yoga May Cause Damage of Both Sciatic Nerves: A Case Report." *Neurological Sciences* 34 (3): 393–6.

Dalen, J., B.W. Smith, B.M. Shelley, A.L. Sloan, L. Leahigh, and D. Begay. 2010. "Pilot Study: Mindful Eating and Living (MEAL): Weight, Eating Behavior, and Psychological Outcomes Associated With a Mindfulness-Based Intervention for People With Obesity." *Complementary Therapies in Medicine* 18 (6): 260–264.

Davis, D.M., and J.A. Hayes. 2011. "What Are the Benefits of Mindfulness? A Practice Review of Psychotherapy-Related Research." *Psychotherapy* 48 (2): 198–208

Grossman, P., L. Niemann, S. Schmidt, and H. Walach. 2004. "Mindfulness-Based Stress Reduction and Health Benefits: A Meta-Analysis." *Journal of Psychosomatic Research* 57 (1): 35–43.

Kabat-Zinn, Jon. 2013. *Full Catastrophe Living: Using the Wisdom of Your Body and Mind to Face Stress, Pain, and Illness.* New York: Bantam Books.

Knox, Sarah. 2010. *Science, God, and the Nature of Reality.* Boca Raton, FL: Brown Walker Press.

Oman, D. 2011. "Spiritual Practice, Health Promotion, and the Elusive Soul: Perspectives From Public Health." *Pastoral Psychology* 60 (6): 897–906.

Pbert, L., J.M. Madison, S. Druker, N. Olendzki, R. Magner, G. Reed, J. Allison, and J. Carmody. 2012. "Effect of Mindfulness Training on Asthma Quality of Life and Lung Function: A Randomised Controlled Trial." *Thorax* 67 (9): 769–776.

Siegel, Ronald (ed.). 2013. *Positive Psychology: Harnessing the Power of Happiness, Mindfulness, and Inner Strength.* Boston: Harvard Health.

Suzuki, S. 1992. *Zen Mind, Beginner's Mind.* Ed. T. Dixon. New York: Weatherhill.

Tummers, N.E. 2011. *Teaching Stress Management: Activities for Children and Young Adults.* Champaign, IL: Human Kinetics.

Vedral, V. 2011. "Living in a Quantum World." *Scientific American* 304 (6): 20–25.

Chapter 4

Alcoholics Anonymous (4th ed.). 2001. New York: Alcoholics Anonymous World Service.

Astrup, A., M.W.L. Bovy, K. Nackenhorst, and A.E. Popova. 2006. "Food for Thought or Thought for Food?—A Stakeholder Dialogue Around the Role of the Snacking Industry in Addressing the Obesity Epidemic." *Obesity Reviews* 7 (3): 303–312.

Banks, S. 1998. *The Missing Link: Reflections on Philosophy and Spirit.* Manitoba, Canada: International Human Relations Consultants.

Bazinger, C., and A. Kühberger. 2012. "Is Social Projection Based on Simulation or Theory? Why New Methods are Needed for Differentiating." *New Ideas in Psychology* 30 (3): 328–335.

Beacham, A.O., B.A. Stetson, K.C. Braekkan, C.L. Rothschild, A.G. Herbst, and K. Linfield. 2011. "Causal Attributions Regarding Personal Exercise Goal Attainment in Exerciser Schematics and Aschematics." *International Journal of Sport and Exercise Psychology* 9 (1): 48–63.

Beckmann, N., R.E. Wood, A. Minbashian, and C. Tabernero. 2012. "Small Group Learning: Do Group Members' Implicit Theories of Ability Make a Difference?" *Learning and Individual Differences* 22 (5): 624–631.

Boehm, J.K., L.L. Vie, and L.D. Kubzansky. 2012. "The Promise of Well-Being Interventions for Improving Health Risk Behaviors." *Current Cardiovascular Risk Reports* 6: 511–519.

Cannon, W.B. 1932. *The Wisdom of the Body.* New York: Norton.

Choi, J.C., Chung, M. I. and Y.D. Lee. 2012. "Modulation of pain sensation by stress-related testosterone and cortisol." *Anaesthesia,* 67: 1146–1151.

Courage to Change. 1992. Al-Anon Family Group Headquarters.

Cousins, Norman. 1989. *Head First: The Biology of Hope and the Healing Power of the Human Spirit.* New York: Dutton.

Darling, C.A., McWey, L.M., Howard, S.N., and Olmstead, S.B. 2007. "College Student Stress: The Influence of Interpersonal Relationships on Sense of Coherence." *Stress and Health* 23: 215–229.

Edelman, G. 2001. *Consciousness: The Remembered Present.* Annals of the New York Academy of Sciences. Vol. 929, 111-122.

Gerin, W., M.J. Zawadzki, J.F. Brosschot, J.F. Thayer, N.J.S. Christenfeld, T.S. Campbell, and J.M. Smyth. 2012. "Rumination as a Mediator of Chronic Stress Effects on Hypertension: A Causal Model." *International Journal of Hypertension.*

Haukkala, A., H. Konttinen, T. Laatikainen, I. Kawachi, and A. Uutela. 2010. "Hostility, Anger Control and Anger Expression as Predictors of Cardiovascular Disease." *Psychosomatic Medicine* 72 (6): 556–562.

Heikkinen, T. and A. Järvinen. 2003. "The Common Cold." *Lancet* 361 (9351): 51-59.

Holmes, T.H., and R.H. Rahe. 1967. "The Social Readjustment Rating Scale." *Journal of Psychosomatic Research* 11 (2): 213–8.

Jampolsky, Gerald G. 2011. *Love Is Letting Go of Fear.* New York: Random House.

Jung, Carl G. 1958. "Psychotherapists or the Clergy." In Vol. 11, *Psychology and Religion: West and East of Collected Works.* Trans. R.F.C. Hull. New York: Pantheon.

Kabat-Zinn, Jon. 1994. *Wherever You Go There You Are: Mindfulness Meditation in Everyday Life.* New York: Hyperion.

Knox, Sarah. 2010. *Science, God, and the Nature of Reality.* Boca Raton, FL: Brown Walker Press.

Kovácsová, N., E. Rošková, and T. Lajunen. 2014. "Forgivingness, Anger, and Hostility in Aggressive Driving." *Accident Analysis and Prevention* 62: 303–308.

Lewis, F.M., and L.H. Daltroy. 1990. "How Causal Explanations Influence Health Behavior: Attribution Theory." In K. Glanz, F.M. Lewis, and B.K. Rimer (Eds.), *Health Behavior and Health Education: Theory, Research and Practice*, pp. 92–114. San Francisco: Jossey-Bass.

Lowe, F. 2013. "The August 2011 Riots: Them and Us." *Psychodynamic Practice* 19 (3): 279–295.

Maslow, Abraham H. 1954. *Motivation and Personality.* New York: HarperCollins.

Opree, S.J., M. Buijzen, and P.M. Valkenburg. 2012. "Lower Life Satisfaction Related to Materialism in Children Frequently Exposed to Advertising." *Pediatrics* 30 (3): e486–e491.

Perrone-Bertolotti, M., L. Rapin, J.-P Lachaux, M. Baciu, and H. Lœvenbruck. 2014. "What Is That Little Voice Inside My Head? Inner Speech Phenomenology, Its Role in Cognitive Performance, and Its Relation to Self-Monitoring." *Behavioural Brain Research* 261: 220–239.

Pert, C.B. 2006. *Everything We Need to Know to Feel Go(o)d.* Carlsbad, CA: Hay House.

Pert, C.B., H.E. Dreher, and M.R. Ruff. 1998. "The Psychosomatic Network: Foundations of Mind-Body Medicine." *Alternative Therapy Health Medicine* 4 (4): 30–41.

Pransky, J. 2003. *Prevention From the Inside-Out.* First Book Library.

Pransky, J. 2007. *Modello: A Story of Hope for the Inner City and Beyond* (2nd ed.). New York: Strategic Book.

Prazak, M., J. Critelli, L. Martin, V. Miranda, M. Purdum, and C. Powers. 2012. "Mindfulness and its Role in Physical and Psychological Health." *Applied Psychology: Health and Well-being* 4 (1): 91-105.

Richardson, C.G., and P.A. Ratner. 2005. "Sense of Coherence as a Moderator of the Effects of Stressful Life Events on Health." *Journal of Epidemiology and Community Health* 59 (11): 979–984.

Sallis, J.F., N. Owen, and E.B. Fisher. 2008. "Ecological Models of Health Behavior" in K. Glanz, B.K. Rimer, and K. Viswanath (Eds.), *Health Behavior and Health Education: Theory, Research, and Practice*, 4th ed., 465–485. San Francisco, CA: Jossey-Bass.

Seligman, M.E.P. 2006. *Learning Optimism.* New York: Vintage Books.

Seligman, M.E.P. 2011. *Flourish.* New York: Free Press.

Talbot, N.L., B. Chapman, Y. Conwell, K. McCollumn, N. Franus, S. Cotescu, and P.R. Duberstein. 2009. "Childhood Sexual Abuse Is Associated With Physical Illness Burden and Functioning in Psychiatric Patients 50 Years of Age and Older." *Psychosomatic Medicine* 71 (4): 417–22.

Tarlaci, A. 2013. "What Should a Consciousness Mind-Brain Theory Be Like? Reducing the Secret of the Rainbow to the Colours of a Prism." *NeuroQuantology* 11 (2): 360–377.

Uchino, B.N. 2006. "Social Support and Health: A Review of Physiological Processes Potentially Underlying Links to Disease Outcomes." *Journal of Behavioral Medicine* 29 (4): 377–387.

Williams, R. 1989. *The Trusting Heart: Great News About Type A Behavior.* New York: Times Books.

Yerkes, R.M., and J.D. Dodson. 1908. "The Relation of Strength of Stimulus to Rapidity of Habit-Formation." *Journal of Comparative Neurology and Psychology* 18: 459–482.

Chapter 5

Alcoholics Anonymous (4th ed.). 2001. New York: Alcoholics Anonymous World Service.

Bandura, A. 1988. "Organizational Application of Social Cognitive Theory." *Australian Journal of Management* 13 (2): 275–302.

Bandura, A. 1991. Social Cognitive Theory of Moral Thought and Action. In *Handbook of Moral Behavior and Development,* vol. 1, ed. Kurtines and Gewirtz, pp. 45–103. Hillsdale, NJ: Lawrence Erlbaum.

Bandura, A. 2011. *Psychotherapy as a Learning Process.* www.all.about-psychology.com. Kindle edition.

Banerjee, P.M. 2013. "Sustainable Human Capital: Product Innovation and Employee Partnerships in Technology Firms." *Cross Cultural Management* 20 (2): 216–234.

Benson, Herbert. 1987. *Your Maximum Mind.* New York: Random House.

Berkman, L. F., T. Glass, I. Brissette, and T. E. Seeman. 2000. "From Social Integration to Health: Durkheim in the New Millennium." *Social Science and Medicine* 51 (6): 843-857.

Boman IV, J. H., M. D. Krohn, C. L. Gibson, and J. M. Stogner. 2012. "Investigating Friendship Quality: An Exploration of Self-Control and Social Control Theories' Friendship Hypotheses." *Journal of Youth and Adolescence* 41 (11): 1526-1540.

Briscoe, C., and F. Aboud. 2012. "Behaviour Change Communication Targeting Four Health Behaviours in Developing Countries: A Review of Change Techniques." *Social Science and Medicine* 75 (4): 612–621.

Centola, D. 2011. "An Experimental Study of Homophily in the Adoption of Health Behavior." *Science* 334 (6060): 1269-1272.

Chou, W.-Y.S., Y.M. Hunt, E.B. Beckjord, R.P. Moser, and B.W. Hesse. 2009. "Social Media Use in the United States: Implications for Health Communication." *Journal of Medical Internet Research* 11 (4).

Christakis, N.A., and P.D. Allison. 2006. "Mortality After the Hospitalization of a Spouse." *New England Journal of Medicine* 354 (7): 719-730.

Custers, A. F. J., G. J. Westerhof, Y. Kuin, and M. Riksen-Walraven. 2010. "Need Fulfillment in Caring Relationships: Its Relation with Well-being of Residents in Somatic Nursing Homes." *Aging and Mental Health* 14 (6): 731-739.

Dagaz, M.C. 2012. "Learning From the Band: Trust, Acceptance and Self-Confidence." *Journal of Contemporary Ethnography* 41 (4): 432–461.

Donaldson, Stewart, Mihaly Csikszentmihalyi, and Jeanne Nakamura. 2011. *Applied Positive Psychology: Improving Everyday Life, Health, Schools, Work, and Society* (Applied Psychology Series). New York: Routledge.

Donovan, D.M., M.H. Ingalsbe, J. Benbow, and D.C. Daley. 2013. "12-Step Interventions and Mutual Support Programs for Substance Use Disorders: An Overview." *Social Work in Public Health* 28 (3–4): 313–332.

Dyer, J. 2007. "How Does Spirituality Affect Physical Health? A Conceptual Review." *Holistic Nursing Practice* 21 (6): 324–328.

Egolf, B., J. Lasker, S. Wolf, and L. Potvin. 1992. "The Roseto Effect: A 50-Year Comparison of Mortality Rates." *American Journal of Public Health* 82 (8): 1089-1092.

El-Guebaly, N. 2012. "The Meanings of Recovery From Addiction Evolution and Promises." *Journal of Addiction Medicine* 6 (1): 1–9.

Elwert, F. and N. A. Christakis. 2006. "Widowhood and Race." *American Sociological Review* 71 (1): 16-41.

Fawzy, F. I., N. W. Fawzy, C. S. Hyun, R. Elashoff, D. Guthrie, J. L. Fahey, and D. L. Morton. 1993. "Malignant Melanoma: Effects of an Early Structured Psychiatric Intervention, Coping, and Affective State on Recurrence and Survival 6 Years Later." *Archives of General Psychiatry* 50 (9): 681-689.

Ferguson, T., and the E–Patients Scholars Work Group. 2007. *E-Patients: How They Can Help Us Heal Healthcare.* Robert Wood Johnson Foundation White Paper. San Francisco: Creative Commons.

Ferlander, S. 2007. "The Importance of Different Forms of Social Capital for Health." *Acta Sociologica* 50 (2): 115–128.

Fraser, M.R. 2013. "Bringing It All Together: Effective Maternal and Child Health Practice as a Means to Improve Public Health." *Maternal and Child Health Journal* 17 (5): 767–75.

Gottman, J.M. 1998. *Psychology and the Study of Marital Processes.* Annual Review of Psychology. Vol. 49.

Guilley, E., S. Pin, D. Spini, C.L. D'Epinay, F. Herrmann, and J.-P Michel. 2005. "Association Between Social Relationships and Survival of Swiss Octogenarians. A Five-Year Prospective Population-Based Study." *Aging Clinical and Experimental Research* 17 (5): 419–425.

Hanibuchi, T., Y. Murata, Y. Ichida, H. Hirai, I. Kawachi, and K. Kondo. 2012. "Place-Specific Constructs of Social Capital and Their Possible Associations to Health: A Japanese Case Study." *Social Science and Medicine* 75 (1): 225–232.

Headey, B., F. Na, and R. Zheng. 2008. "Pet Dogs Benefit Owners' Health: A 'Natural Experiment' in China." *Social Indicators Research* 87 (3): 481-493.

Heaney, C.A., and B.A. Israel. 2008. "Social Networks and Social Support." In K. Glanz, B.K. Rimer and K. Viswanath (Eds.), *Health Behavior and Health Education: Theory, Research and Practice* (4th ed.), 169–188. San Francisco: Jossey-Bass.

Hether, H. J., S. T. Murphy, and T. W. Valente. 2014. "It's Better to Give than to Receive: The Role of Social Support, Trust, and Participation on Health-Related Social Networking Sites." *Journal of Health Communication.* In press.

Holt-Lunstad, J., T.B. Smith, and J.B Layton. 2010. "Social Relationships and Mortality Risk: A Meta-Analytic Review." *PLoS Medicine* 7 (7).

House, J.S. 1981. *Work Stress and Social Support.* Reading, Mass.: Addison-Wesley.

Hu, Y. and N. Goldman. 1990. "Mortality Differentials by Marital Status: An International Comparison." *Demography* 27 (2): 233-250.

Humphreys, K., and R.H. Moos. 2001. "Can Encouraging Substance Abuse Patients to Participate in Self-Help Groups Reduce Demand for Health Care? A Quasi-Experimental Study." *Alcoholism: Clinical and Experimental Research* 25: 711–716.

Humphreys, K., and R.H. Moos. 2007. "Encouraging Posttreatment Self-Help Group Involvement to Reduce Demand for Continuing Care Services: Two-Year Clinical and Utilization Outcomes." *Alcoholism: Clinical and Experimental Research* 31: 64–68.

Hutcherson, C. A., E. M. Seppala, and J. J. Gross. 2008. "Loving-Kindness Meditation Increases Social Connectedness." *Emotion* 8 (5): 720-724.

Ji, J., D. Brooks, R.P. Barth, and H. Kim. 2010. "Beyond Preadoptive Risk: The Impact of Adoptive Family Environment on Adopted Youth's Psychosocial Adjustment." *American Journal of Orthopsychiatry* 80 (3): 432–442.

Kabat-Zinn, Jon. 2013. *Full Catastrophe Living.* New York: Dell Bantam.

Kernes, J.L., and R.T. Kinnier. 2005. "Psychologists' Search for the Good Life." *Journal of Humanistic Psychology* 45 (1): 82–105.

Kim, S., and G. Kochanska. 2012. "Child Temperament Moderates Effects of Parent-Child Mutuality on Self-Regulation: A Relationship-Based Path for Emotionally Negative Infants." *Child Development* 83 (4): 1275–1289.

Kozlowski, A. 2013. "Mindful Mating: Exploring the Connection Between Mindfulness and Relationship Satisfaction." *Sexual and Relationship Therapy* 28 (1–2): 92–104.

Lammintausta, A., J.K.E. Airaksinen, P. Immonen-Ra¨iha, J. Torppa, A.Y. Kesa¨niemi, M. Ketonen, H. Koukkunen, P.¨ ivi Ka¨rja¨-Koskenkari, S. Lehto, V. Salomaa, and FINAMI Study Group. 2013. "Prognosis of Acute Coronary Events Is Worse in Patients Living Alone: The FINAMI Myocardial Infarction Register." *European Journal of Preventive Cardiology* 0 (00) 1–8.

Leana, C. R. and H. J. Van Buren III. 1999. "Organizational Social Capital and Employment Practices." *Academy of Management Review* 24 (3): 538-555.

Leifheit-Limson, E.C., K.J. Reid, S.V. Kasl, H. Lin, P.G. Jones, D.M. Buchanan, S. Parashar, P.N. Peterson, J.A. Spertus, and J.H. Lichtman. 2010. "The Role of Social Support in Health Status and Depressive Symptoms After Acute Myocardial Infarction Evidence for a Stronger Relationship Among Women." *Circulation: Cardiovascular Quality and Outcomes* 3 (2): 143–150.

Mahon, N.E., A. Yarcheski, and T.J. Yarcheski. 2004. "Social Support and Positive Health Practices in Early Adolescents: A Test of Mediating Variables." *Clinical Nursing Research* 13 (3): 216–236.

Marmot, M.G., and S.L. Syme. 1976. "Acculturation and Coronary Heart Disease in Japanese Americans." *American Journal of Epidemiology* 104 (3): 225–247.

Marmot, M.G., S.L. Syme, and A. Kagan. 1975. "Epidemiologic Studies of Coronary Heart Disease and Stroke in Japanese Men Living in Japan, Hawaii and California: Prevalence of Coronary and Hypertensive Heart Disease and Associated Risk Factors." *American Journal of Epidemiology* 102 (6): 514–525.

McClelland, D.C. 1989. "Motivational Factors in Health and Disease." *American Psychologist* 44 (4): 675–683.

Medalie, J.H., K.C. Stange, S.J. Zyzanski, and U. Goldbourt. 1992. "The Importance of Biopsychosocial Factors in the Development of Duodenal Ulcer in a Cohort of Middle-Aged Men." *American Journal of Epidemiology* 136 (10): 1280–1287.

Mentoring Partnership of Southwestern Pennsylvania. 2014. www.mentoringpittsburgh.org

Mundt, M.P., S. Parthasarathyb, F.W. Chib, S. Sterling, and C.I. Campbell. 2012. "12-Step Participation Reduces Medical Use Costs Among Adolescents With a History of Alcohol and Other Drug Treatment." *Drug and Alcohol Dependence* 126: 124–130.

Nakhaie, R. and R. Arnold. 2010. "A Four Year (1996-2000) Analysis of Social Capital and Health Status of Canadians: The Difference that Love Makes." *Social Science and Medicine* 71 (5): 1037-1044.

Papageorgiou, D.E., I. Mpolioudaki, E. Papala, P. Stamataki, and M. Kagialari. 2011. "Investigation of Factors that Influence the Development of Emotional Intelligence in Nurses." *Nosileftiki* 50 (2): 185–193.

Pinquart, M., and P.R. Duberstein. 2010. "Associations of Social Networks With Cancer Mortality: A Meta-Analysis." *Critical Reviews in Oncology/Hematology* 75 (2): 122–137.

Pléh, C. 2012. "The History of the Nature/Nurture Issue." *Behavioral and Brain Sciences* 35 (5): 376–377.

Prochaska, J. O., J.C. Norcross, and C.C. DiClemente. 1994. *Changing for Good.* New York: William Morrow.

Proulx, C.M., and L.A. Snyder-Rivas. 2013. "The Longitudinal Associations Between Marital Happiness, Problems, and Self-Rated Health." *Journal of Family Psychology* 27 (2): 194–202.

Putnam, Robert. 2000. *Bowling Alone: The Collapse and Revival of the American Community.* New York: Simon and Shuster.

Reger-Nash, B., A. Bauman, L. Cooper, T. Chey, and K. Simon. 2006. "Evaluating Communitywide Walking Interventions." *Evaluation and Program Planning* 29: 251–259.

Rendall, M.S., M.M. Weden, M.M. Favreault, and H. Waldron. 2011. "The Protective Effect of Marriage for Survival: A Review and Update." *Demography* 48 (2): 481–506.

Repper, J., and T. Carter. 2011. "A Review of the Literature on Peer Support in Mental Health Services." *Journal of Mental Health* 20 (4): 392–411.

Russek, L. G. and G. E. Schwartz. 1997. "Feelings of Parental Caring Predict Health Status in Midlife: A 35-Year Follow-Up of the Harvard Mastery of Stress Study." *Journal of Behavioral Medicine* 20 (1): 1-13.

Sallis, J.F., N. Owen, and E.B. Fisher. 2008. "Ecological Models of Health Behavior," in K. Glanz, B.K. Rimer, and K. Viswanath (Eds.), *Health Behavior and Health Education: Theory, Research and Practice* (4th ed.), 465–485. San Francisco: Jossey-Bass.

Shibata, H. 2004. "Implications of Research Findings Obtained From Centenarians." *Japan Medical Association Journal* 47 (7): 338–343.

Slater, L.Z., L. Moneyham, D.E. Vance, J.L. Raper, M.J. Mugavero, and G. Childs. 2012. "Support, Stigma, Health, Coping, and Quality of Life in Older Gay Men With HIV." *Journal of the Association of Nurses in AIDS Care.*

Smith, K.P., and N.A. Christakis. 2008. "Social Networks and Health." *Annual Review of Sociology* 34: 405–29.

Social Life of Health Information. 2011. *Pew Internet and American Life Project.* Washington, DC: Pew Research Center. http://pewinternet.org/Reports/2011/Social-Life-of-Health-Info.aspx

Spiegel, D., J.R. Bloom, H.C. Kraemer, and E. Gottheil. 1989. "Effect of Psychosocial Treatment on Survival of Patients With Metastatic Breast Cancer." *Lancet* 2 (8668): 888–891.

Subrahmanyam, K. and P. M. Greenfield. 2008. "Virtual Worlds in Development: Implications of Social Networking Sites." *Journal of Applied Developmental Psychology* 29 (6): 417-419.

Thoits, P.A. 1992. "Identity Structures and Psychological Well-Being: Gender and Marital Status Comparisons." *Social Psychology Quarterly* 55:236–256.

Thoits, P.A. 1995. "Stress, Coping, and Social Support Processes: Where Are We? What Next?" *Journal of Health and Social Behavior* Extra issue: 53–79.

Thoits, P.A. 2011. "Mechanisms Linking Social Ties and Support to Physical and Mental Health." *Journal of Health and Social Behavior* 52 (2): 145–161.

Thoits, P.A., and L.N. Hewitt. 2001. "Volunteer Work and Well-Being." *Journal of Health and Social Behavior* 42 (2): 115–131.

Tocqueville, Alexis de. [1835] 2003. *Democracy in America.* New York: Penguin Putnam.

Tolle, E. 2005. *A New Earth: Awakening to Your Life's Purpose.* New York: Plume.

Tudoroiu, T. 2014. "Social Media and Revolutionary Waves: The Case of the Arab Spring." *New Political Science.* In Press.

Volunteers: A Valuable Resource. 1982. President's Task Force on Private Sector Initiatives. Washington, DC.

Widmer, E.D., N. Kempf, M. Sapin, and G. Galli-Carminati. 2013. "Family Beyond Parents? An Exploration of Family Configurations and Psychological Adjustment in Young Adults With Intellectual Disabilities." *Research in Developmental Disabilities* 34 (1): 207–217.

Williams, R.B., J.C. Barefoot, R.M. Califf, T.L. Haney, W.B. Saunders, D.B. Pryor, M.A. Hlatky, I.C. Siegler, and D.B. Mark. 1992. "Prognostic Importance of Social and Economic Resources Among Medically Treated Patients With Angiographically Documented Coronary Artery Disease." *Journal of the American Medical Association* 267 (4): 520–524.

Wing, R. R. and R. W. Jeffery. 1999. "Benefits of Recruiting Participants with Friends and Increasing Social Support for Weight Loss and Maintenance." *Journal of Consulting and Clinical Psychology* 67 (1): 132-138.

Wolf, S. 1992. "Predictors of Myocardial Infarction Over a Span of 30 Years in Roseto, Pennsylvania." *Integrative Physiological and Behavioral Science* 27 (3): 246–257.

Wray-Lake, L., and C.A. Flanagan. 2012. "Parenting Practices and the Development of Adolescents' Social Trust." *Journal of Adolescence* 35 (3): 549–560.

Chapter 6

Akers, J.D., R.A. Cornett, J.S. Savla, K.P. Davy, and B.M. Davy. 2012. "Daily Self-Monitoring of Body Weight, Step Count, Fruit/Vegetable Intake, and Water Consumption: A Feasible and Effective Long-Term Weight Loss Maintenance Approach." *Journal of the Academy of Nutrition and Dietetics* 112 (5): 685–692.

Akuthota, V., and S.F. Nadler. 2004. "Core Strengthening." *Archives of Physical Medicine and Rehabilitation* 85 (3 Suppl 1): S86–92.

American College of Sports Medicine. 1986. *ACSM's Guidelines for Exercise Testing and Prescription* (5th ed.).

Bharakhada, N., T. Yates, M.J. Davies, E.G. Wilmot, C. Edwardson, J. Henson, D. Webb, and K. Khunti. 2012. "Association of Sitting Time and Physical Activity With CKD: A Cross-Sectional Study in Family Practices." *American Journal of Kidney Diseases* 60 (4): 583–590.

Bliss, L.S., and P. Teeple. 2005. "Core Stability: The Centerpiece of Any Training Program." *Current Sports Medicine Reports* 4 (3): 179–183.

Büssing, A., A. Michalsen, S.B.S. Khalsa, S. Telles, and K.J. Sherman. 2012. "Effects of Yoga on Mental and Physical Health: A Short Summary of Reviews." *Evidence-Based Complementary and Alternative Medicine.*

Byberg, L., H. Melhus, R. Gedeborg, J. Sundström, A. Ahlbom, B. Zethelius, L.G. Berglund, A. Wolk, and K. Michaëlsson. 2009. "Total Mortality After Changes in Leisure Time Physical Activity in 50 Year Old Men: 35 Year Follow-Up of Population Based Cohort." *British Journal of Sports Medicine* 43 (7): 482.

Catenacci, V.A., G.K. Grunwald, J.P. Ingebrigtsen, J.M. Jakicic, M.D. McDermott, S. Phelan, R.R. Wing, J.O. Hill, and H.R. Wyatt. 2011. "Physical Activity Patterns Using Accelerometry in the National Weight Control Registry." *Obesity* 19 (6): 1163–1170.

Centers for Disease Control and Prevention (CDC). 2011. *Behavioral Risk Factor Surveillance System Survey Data.* Atlanta, GA: U.S. Department of Health and Human Services, Centers for Disease Control and Prevention.

Chambliss, H.O., R.C. Huber, C.E. Finley, S.O. McDoniel, H. Kitzman-Ulrich, and W.J. Wilkinson. 2011. "Computerized Self-Monitoring and Technology-Assisted Feedback for Weight Loss With and Without an Enhanced Behavioral Component." *Patient Education and Counseling* 85 (3): 375–382.

Chau, J.Y., H.P. van der Ploeg, D. Merom, T. Chey, and A.E. Bauman. 2012. "Cross-Sectional Associations Between Occupational and Leisure-Time Sitting, Physical Activity and Obesity in Working Adults." *Preventive Medicine* 54 (3–4): 195–200.

Colbert, L.H., J.M. Hootman, and C.A. Macera. 2000. "Physical Activity-Related Injuries in Walkers and Runners in the Aerobics Center Longitudinal Study." *Clinical Journal of Sport Medicine* 10 (4): 259–263.

Coleman, S., C.J. Berg, and N.J. Thompson. 2014. "Social Support, Nutrition Intake, and Physical Activity in Cancer Survivors." *American Journal of Health Behavior* 38 (3): 414–419.

Conn, V.S. 2010. "Depressive Symptom Outcomes of Physical Activity Interventions: Meta-Analysis Findings." *Annals of Behavioral Medicine* 39 (2): 128–138.

Cooper, K.H. 1970. *The New Aerobics.* New York: Bantam Books.

Cortright, J. 2008. Driven to the Brink: How the Gas Price Spike Popped the Housing Bubble and Devalued the Suburbs. White Paper, Boston: CEOs for Cities.

Deslandes, A., H. Moraes, C. Ferreira, H. Veiga, H. Silveira, R. Mouta, F.A. Pompeu, E.S. Coutinho, and J. Laks. 2009 "Exercise and mental health: many reasons to move." *Neuropsychobiology* 59(4):191–198.

Donahoo, W.T., J.A. Levine, and E.L. Melanson. 2004. "Variability in Energy Expenditure and Its Components." *Current Opinion in Clinical Nutrition and Metabolic Care* 7: 599–605.

Dresler, M., A. Sandberg, K. Ohla, C. Bublitz, C. Trenado, A. Mroczko-Wasowicz, S. Kühn, and D. Repantis. 2013. "Non-Pharmacological Cognitive Enhancement." *Neuropharmacology* 64: 529–543.

Dunstan, D.W., B. Howard, G.N. Healy, and N. Owen. 2012. "Too Much Sitting—A Health Hazard." *Diabetes Research and Clinical Practice.*

Francois, M.E., J.C. Baldi, P.J. Manning, S.J.E. Lucas, J.A. Hawley, M.J.A. Williams, and J.D. Cotter. 2014. "'Exercise Snacks' before Meals: A Novel Strategy to Improve Glycaemic Control in Individuals with Insulin Resistance." *Diabetologia.* In press.

Freburger, J.K., G.M. Holmes, R.P. Agans, A.M. Jackman, J.D. Darter, A.S. Wallace, L.D. Castel, W.D. Kalsbeek, and T.S. Carey. 2009. "The Rising Prevalence of Chronic Low Back Pain." *Archives of Internal Medicine* 169 (3): 251–258.

Gebel, K., A.E. Bauman, B. Reger-Nash, and K.M. Leyden. 2011. "Does the Environment Moderate the Impact of a Mass Media Campaign to Promote Walking?" *American Journal of Health Promotion* 26 (1): 45–48

Gibala, M.J., and S.L. McGee. 2008. "Metabolic Adaptations to Short-Term High-Intensity Interval Training: A Little Pain for a Lot of Gain?" *Exercise and Sport Sciences Reviews* 36 (2): 58–63.

Goetzel, R.Z., S.R. Long, R.J. Ozminkowski, K. Hawkins, S. Wang, and W. Lynch. 2004. "Health, Absence, Disability, and Presenteeism Cost Estimates of Certain Physical and Mental Health Conditions Affecting U.S. Employers." *Journal of Occupational and Environmental Medicine* 46 (4): 398-412.

Haskell, W.L., I.-M Lee, R.R. Pate, K.E. Powell, S.N. Blair, B.A. Franklin, C.A. Macera, G.W. Heath, P.D. Thompson, and A. Bauman. 2007. "Physical Activity and Public Health: Updated Recommendation for Adults From the American College of Sports Medicine and the American Heart Association." *Circulation* 116 (9): 1081–1093.

Healthy People 2020. 2010. Department of Health and Human Services (U.S.), Office of Disease Prevention and Health Promotion, ODPHP publication no. B0132. www.healthypeople.gov/2020/TopicsObjectives2020/pdfs/HP2020_brochure_with_LHI_508.pdf

Healy, G.N., Dunstan, D.W., Salmon, J., Cerin, Shaw, J.E., Zimmet, P.Z., and Owen, N. 2007 "Objectively Measured Light-Intensity Physical Activity Is Independently Associated With 2-h Plasma Glucose." *Diabetes Care* 30 (6): 1384–1389.

Healy, G.N., K. Wijndaele, D.W. Dunstan, J.E. Shaw, J. Salmon, P.Z. Zimmet, and N. Owen 2008. "Objectively Measured Sedentary Time, Physical Activity, and Metabolic Risk: The Australian Diabetes, Obesity and Lifestyle Study (AusDiab)." *Diabetes Care* 31 (2): 369–371.

Herbert, R.D., and M. de Noronha. 2008. Stretching to Prevent or Reduce Muscle Soreness After Exercise (Review). *The Cochrane Collaboration* 4: 1–32.

Houmard, J.A., C.J. Tanner, C.A. Slentz, B.D. Duscha, J.S. McCartney, and W.E. Kraus. 2004. "Effect of the Volume and Intensity of Exercise Training on Insulin Sensitivity." *Journal of Applied Physiology* 96 (1): 101–106.

How Much Physical Activity Do Adults Need? 2014. U.S. Centers for Disease Control and Prevention. www.cdc.gov/physicalactivity/everyone/guidelines/adults.html

Hu, G., N.C. Barengo, J. Tuomilehto, T.A. Lakka, A. Nissinen, and P. Jousilahti. 2004. "Relationship of Physical Activity and Body Mass Index to the Risk of Hypertension: A Prospective Study in Finland." *Hypertension* 43 (1): 25–30.

Hughes-Dawson, B. 2010. "Bad for Bones." *Nutrition Action Healthletter* 10: 1–7.

Jago, R., K. MacDonald-Wallis, J.L. Thompson, A.S. Page, R. Brockman, and K.R. Fox. 2011. "Better With a Buddy: Influence of Best friends on Children's Physical Activity." *Medicine and Science in Sports and Exercise* 43 (2): 259–265.

Johannsen, D.L., N.D. Knuth, R. Huizenga, J.C. Rood, E. Ravussin, and K.D. Hall. 2012. "Metabolic Slowing With Massive Weight Loss Despite Preservation of Fat-Free Mass." *Journal of Clinical Endocrinology and Metabolism* 97 (7): 2489–2496.

Kabat-Zinn, Jon. 2013. *Full Catastrophe Living*. New York: Dell Bantam.

Kelley, G.A., K.S. Kelley, and W.M. Kohrt. 2012. "Effects of Ground and Joint Reaction Force Exercise on Lumbar Spine and Femoral Neck Bone Mineral Density in Postmenopausal Women: A Meta-Analysis of Randomized Controlled Trials." *BMC Musculoskeletal Disorders* 13.

Kim, Y.S., Y.S. Park, J.P. Allegrante, R. Marks, H. Ok, K. Ok Cho, and C. E. Garber. 2012. "Relationship between Physical Activity and General Mental Health." *Preventive Medicine* 55 (5): 458-463

Law, R.Y.W., and R.D. Herbert. 2007. "Warm-Up Reduces Delayed-Onset Muscle Soreness but Cool-Down Does Not: A Randomised Controlled Trial." *Australian Journal of Physiotherapy* 53 (2): 91–95.

Levine, J.A., and J.M. Miller. 2007. "The Energy Expenditure of Using a 'Walk-and-Work' Desk for Office Workers With Obesity." *British Journal of Sports Medicine* 41 (9): 558–561.

Levinger, I., C. Goodman, D.L. Hare, G. Jerums, T. Morris, and S. Selig. 2009. "Psychological Responses to Acute Resistance Exercise in Men and Women Who Are Obese." *Journal of Strength and Conditioning Research* 23 (5): 1548–1552.

Loprinzi, P. D. and B. J. Cardinal. 2013. "Association between Biologic Outcomes and Objectively Measured Physical Activity Accumulated in ≥10-Minute Bouts and <10-Minute Bouts." *American Journal of Health Promotion* 27 (3): 143-151.

Mammen, G. and G. Faulkner. 2013. "Physical Activity and the Prevention of Depression: A Systematic Review of Prospective Studies." *American Journal of Preventive Medicine* 45 (5): 649-657.

McArdle, W.D., F.I. Katch, V.L. Katch. 2009. *Exercise Physiology* (7th ed.). Baltimore: Williams & Wilkins.

Murphy, M.H., A.M. Nevill, E.M. Murtagh, and R.L. Holder. 2007. "The Effect of Walking on Fitness, Fatness and Resting Blood Pressure: A Meta-Analysis of Randomised, Controlled Trials." *Preventive Medicine* 44 (5): 377–38.

Nielson Company. 2012. "State of the Media: Trends in TV Viewing—2011 TV Up Front." http://blog.nielsen.com/nielsenwire/

Pate, R.R., M. Pratt, S.N. Blair, W.L. Haskell, C.A. Macera, C. Bouchard, D. Buchner, et al. 1995. "Physical Activity and Public Health: A Recommendation From the Centers for Disease Control and Prevention and the American College of Sports Medicine." *Journal of the American Medical Association* 273 (5): 402–407.

Paul, G. 2007. "An Integrated Approach to Training Core Stability." *Strength and Conditioning Journal* 29: 58–68.

Peters, L.W.H., G. Kok, G.T.M. Ten Dam, G.J. Buijs, and T.G.W.M. Paulussen. 2009. "Effective Elements of School Health Promotion Across Behavioral Domains: A Systematic Review of Reviews." *BMC Public Health* 9.

Peterson, M.D., A. Sen, and P.M. Gordon. 2011. "Influence of Resistance Exercise on Lean Body Mass in Aging Adults: A Meta-Analysis." *Medicine and Science in Sports and Exercise* 43 (2): 249–258.

Phillips, E.M. (Ed). 2011. *Core Exercises*. Boston: Harvard Health Publications.

Physical Activity Guidelines for Americans. 2008. U.S. Department of Health and Human Services.

Physical Activity and Health: A Report of the Surgeon General. 1996. U.S. Department of Health and Human Services.

Reger, W., T.G. Allison, and R. Kurucz. 1984. "Exercise, Post-Exercise Metabolic Rate, and Appetite." *Proceedings of the 1984 Olympics*. Champaign, IL: Human Kinetics.

Ryan, R.M., Frederick, C.M., Lepes, D., Rubio, N., and Sheldon, K.M. 2008. "Intrinsic Motivation and Exercise Adherence." *International Journal of Sport Psychology* 28: 335–54.

Sherwood, N.E., and R.W. Jeffery. 2000. "The Behavioural Determinants of Exercise: Implications for Physical Activity Interventions." *Annual Review of Nutrition* 20: 21–44.

Siahkouhian, M., D. Khodadadi, and K. Shahmoradi. 2013. "Effects of High-Intensity Interval Training on Aerobic and Anaerobic Indices: Comparison of Physically Active and Inactive Men." *Science and Sports* 28 (5): e119–e125.

Stessman, J., R. Hammerman-Rozenberg, A. Cohen, E. Ein-Mor, and J.M. Jacobs. 2009. "Physical Activity, Function and Longevity Among the Very Old." *Archives of Internal Medicine* 169 (16): 1476–1483.

Tappe, K., E. Tarves, J. Oltarzewski, and D. Frum. 2013. "Habit Formation among Regular Exercisers at Fitness Centers: An Exploratory Study." *Journal of Physical Activity and Health* 10 (4): 607-613.

Van Dyck, D., J. Veitch, I. De Bourdeaudhuij, L. Thornton, and K. Ball. 2013. "Environmental Perceptions as Mediators of the Relationship Between the Objective Built Environment and Walking Among Socio-Economically Disadvantaged Women." *International Journal of Behavioral Nutrition and Physical Activity* 10.

Veerman, J.L., G.N. Healy, L.J. Cobiac, T. Vos, E.A.H. Winkler, N. Owen, and D.W. Dunstan. 2012. "Television Viewing Time and Reduced Life Expectancy: A Life Table Analysis." *British Journal of Sports Medicine* 46 (13): 927–930.

"Vital Signs: Walking Among Adults—United States, 2005 and 2012." 2012. *Morbidity and Mortality Weekly Report* 61 (31): 595–601.

Wilmot, E.G., C.L. Edwardson, F.A. Achana, M.J. Davies, T. Gorely, L.J. Gray, K. Khunti, T. Yates, and S.J.H. Biddle. 2012. "Sedentary Time in Adults and the Association With Diabetes, Cardiovascular Disease and Death: Systematic Review and Meta-Analysis." *Diabetologia*: 1–11.

Chapter 7

"Arsenic in Your Food: Our Findings Show a Real Need for Federal Standards for This Toxin." 2012. *Consumer Reports* 77 (11): 22–27.

"Arsenic in Your Juice: How Much Is Too Much? Federal Limits Don't Exist." 2012. *Consumer Reports* 77 (1): 22–27.

Albers, S. 2011. "Using Mindful Eating to Treat Food Restriction: A Case Study." *Eating Disorders* 19 (1): 97–107.

Benetou, V., P. Orfanos, D. Zylis, S. Sieri, P. Contiero, R. Tumino, M.C. Giurdanella, et al. 2011. "Diet and Hip Fractures Among Elderly Europeans in the EPIC Cohort." *European Journal of Clinical Nutrition* 65 (1): 132–139.

Bhutani, S., and K.A. Varady. 2009. "Nibbling Versus Feasting: Which Meal Pattern Is Better for Heart Disease Prevention?" *Nutrition Reviews* 67 (10): 591–598.

Bolton, R.P., K.W. Heaton, and L.F. Burroughs. 1981. "The Role of Dietary Fiber in Satiety, Glucose, and Insulin: Studies With Fruit and Fruit Juice." *American Journal of Clinical Nutrition* 34 (2): 211–217.

Brandeis University. 2007. "New Fat, Same Old Problem With An Added Twist? Replacement For Trans Fat Raises Blood Sugar In Humans." ScienceDaily. www.sciencedaily.com/releases/2007/01/070116131545.htm

Bybee, J., E. Zigler, D. Berliner, and R. Merisca. 1996. "Guilt, Guilt-Revoking Events, Depression and Eating Disorders." *Current Psychology* 15 (2): 113–127.

Campbell, W.W., C.A. Johnson, G.P. McCabe, and N.S. Carnell. 2008. Dietary Protein Requirements of Younger and Older Adults. *American Journal of Clinical Nutrition* 88 (5): 1322–1329.

CDC Guide to Strategies for Reducing the Consumption of Sugar-Sweetened Beverages. 2014. Centers for Disease Control and Prevention. www.cdph.ca.gov/SiteCollectionDocuments/StratstoReduce_Sugar_Sweetened_Bevs.pdf

Choi, H.K., W. Willett, and G. Curhan. 2010. "Fructose-Rich Beverages and Risk of Gout in Women." *Journal of the American Medical Association* 304 (20): 2270–8.

Cotton, P.A., A.F. Subar, J.E. Friday, and A. Cook. 2004. "Dietary Sources of Nutrients Among U.S. Adults, 1994 to 1996." *Journal of the American Dietetic Association* 104 (6): 921–930.

Coxson, P.G., N.R. Cook, M. Joffres, Y. Hong, D. Orenstein, S.M. Schmidt, and K. Bibbins-Domingo. 2013. "Mortality Benefits From US Population-Wide Reduction in Sodium Consumption: Projections From Three Modeling Approaches." *Hypertension*.

de Koning, L., V.S. Malik, and M.D. Kellogg, et al. 2012. "Sweetened Beverage Consumption, Incident Coronary Heart Disease, and Biomarkers of Risk in Men." *Circulation* 125 (14): 1735–41.

Dellavalle, D.M., L.S. Roe, and B.J. Rolls. 2005. "Does the Consumption of Caloric and Non-Caloric Beverages With a Meal Affect Energy Intake?" *Appetite* 44 (2): 187–193.

de Oliveira, M.C., A. Alonso, D.H. Lee, G.L. Delclos, A.G. Bertoni, R. Jiang, et al. 2012. "Dietary Intakes of Zinc and Heme Iron From Red Meat." *Journal of Nutrition* 142 (3): 526–33.

Deshmukh-Taskar, P., T.A. Nicklas, J.D. Radcliffe, C.E. O'Neil, and Y. Liu. 2013. "The Relationship of Breakfast Skipping and Type of Breakfast Consumed With Overweight/Obesity, Abdominal Obesity, Other Cardiometabolic Risk Factors and the Metabolic Syndrome in Young Adults. The National Health and Nutrition Examination Survey (NHANES): 1999–2006." *Public Health Nutrition* 16 (11): 2073–2082.

Dietary Guidelines for Americans, 2010. 2011. United States Department of Agriculture. www.cnpp.usda.gov/Publications/DietaryGuidelines/2010/DGAC/Report/B-2-TotalDiet.pdf

Dietary Reference Intakes for Water, Potassium, Sodium, Chloride, and Sulfate. 2005. Institute of Medicine. Washington, DC: National Academies Press.

Djoussé, L., and J.M. Gaziano. 2007. "Breakfast Cereals and Risk of Heart Failure in the Physicians' Health Study I." *Archives of Internal Medicine* 167 (19): 2080–2085.

Djoussé, L., A.O. Akinkuolie, J.H.Y. Wu, E.L. Ding, and J.M. Gaziano. 2012. "Fish Consumption, Omega-3 Fatty Acids and Risk of Heart Failure: A Meta-Analysis." *Clinical Nutrition* 31 (6): 846–53.

Eriksson, M., L. Holmgren, U. Janlert, J.-H Jansson, D. Lundblad, B. Stegmayr, S. Söderberg, and M. Eliasson. 2011. "Large Improvements in Major Cardiovascular Risk Factors in the Population of Northern Sweden: The MONICA Study 1986-2009." *Journal of Internal Medicine* 269 (2): 219-231.

Farshchi, H. R., M. A. Taylor, and I. A. Macdonald. 2005. "Deleterious Effects of Omitting Breakfast on Insulin Sensitivity and Fasting Lipid Profiles in Healthy Lean Women." *American Journal of Clinical Nutrition* 81 (2): 388-396.

Flegal, K.M., D. Carroll, B.K. Kit, and C.L. Ogden. 2012. "Prevalence of Obesity and Trends in the Distribution of Body Mass Index Among U.S. Adults, 1999–2010." *Journal of the American Medical Association* 307 (5): 491–497.

Flock, M. R. and P. M. Kris-Etherton. 2011. "Dietary Guidelines for Americans 2010: Implications for Cardiovascular Disease." *Current Atherosclerosis Reports* 13 (6): 499-507.

Forman, E.M., M.L. Butryn, K.L. Hoffman, and J.D. Herbert. 2009. "An Open Trial of an Acceptance-Based Behavioral Intervention for Weight Loss." *Cognitive and Behavioral Practice* 16 (2): 223–235.

Fung, T.T., F.B. Hu, M.A. Pereira, S. Liu, M.J. Stampfer, G.A. Colditz, and W.C. Willett. 2002. "Whole-Grain Intake and the Risk of Type 2 Diabetes: A Prospective Study in Men." *American Journal of Clinical Nutrition* 76 (3): 535–540.

Fung, T.T., M. Schulze, J.E. Manson, W.C. Willett, and F.B. Hu. 2004. "Dietary Patterns, Meat Intake, and the Risk of Type 2 Diabetes in Women." *Archives of Internal Medicine* 164 (20): 2235–2240.

Gaziano, J., H.D. Sesso, W.G. Christen, et al. 2012. "Multivitamins in the Prevention of Cancer in Men: The Physicians' Health Study II Randomized Controlled Trial." *Journal of the American Medical Association* 1–10. doi:10.1001/jama.2012.14641.

Gearhardt, A.N., C.M. Grilo, R.J. DiLeone, K.D. Brownell, and M.N. Potenza. 2011. "Can Food Be Addictive? Public Health and Policy Implications." *Addiction* 106 (7): 1208–1212.

Gillen, M.M., and E.S. Lefkowitz. 2011. "The 'Freshman 15': Trends and Predictors in a Sample of Multiethnic Men and Women." *Eating Behaviors* 12 (4): 261–266.

Halton, T.L., and F.B. Hu. 2004. "The Effects of High Protein Diets on Thermogenesis, Satiety and Weight Loss: A Critical Review." *Journal of the American College of Nutrition* 23 (5): 373–385.

Halweil, B. 2002. *Home Grown: The Case for Local Food in a Global Market*. Worldwatch Paper no. 163.

Hanh, T.N., and L. Cheung. 2010. *Savor: Mindful Eating, Mindful Life*. New York, Harper Collins.

He, K., Y. Song, M.L. Daviglus, K. Liu, L. Van Horn, A.R. Dyer, and P. Greenland. 2004. "Accumulated Evidence on Fish Consumption and Coronary Heart Disease Mortality: A Meta-Analysis of Cohort Studies." *Circulation* 109 (22): 2705–2711.

Healthy People 2020. 2010. www.healthypeople.gov/2020/default.aspx

Henney, J.E. C.L. Taylor, and C.S. Boon (Eds). 2010. Strategies to Reduce Sodium Intake in the United States, Food and Nutrition Board, Institute of Medicine. Retrieved July 14, 2014, from www.nap.edu/catalog.php?record_id=12818

Hu, F.B. 2005. "Protein, Body Weight and Cardiovascular Health." *American Journal of Clinical Nutrition* 82 (1 Suppl): 242S–247S.

Johnson, R.K., L.J. Appel, M. Brands, B.V. Howard, M. Lefevre, R.H. Lustig, F. Sacks, L.M. Steffen, and J. Wylie-Rosett. 2009. "Dietary Sugars Intake and Cardiovascular Health: A Scientific Statement From the American Heart Association." *Circulation* 120: 1011–1020.

Kelley, A.E., V.P. Bakshi, S.N. Haber, T.L. Steininger, M.J. Will, M. Zhang. 2002. "Opioid Modulation of Taste Hedonics Within the Ventral Striatum." *Physiology and Behavior* 76: 365–377.

King, D.E., A.G. Mainous, and C.A. Lambourne. 2012. "Trends in Dietary Fiber Intake in the United States, 1999–2008." *Journal of the Academy of Nutrition and Dietetics* 112 (5): 642–648.

Kris-Etherton, P. M., W. S. Harris, and L. J. Appel. 2002. "Fish Consumption, Fish Oil, Omega-3 Fatty Acids, and Cardiovascular Disease." *Circulation* 106 (21): 2747-2757.

Kushner, R.F., and D. Ognar. 2006. "How to Counsel Patients About Diet: Sorting Fact From Fiction, Part 1." *Consultant* 46 (2): 171–176.

Lee, R.E., K.M. Heinrich, A.V Medina, G.R. Regan, J.V. Reese-Smith, Y. Jokura, and J.E. Maddock. 2010. "A Picture of the Healthful Food Environment in Two Diverse Urban Cities." *Journal of Environmental Health Insights* 4: 49–60.

Levine, J., J.D. Gussow, D. Hastings, and A. Eccher. 2003. "Authors' Financial Relationships With the Food and Beverage Industry and Their Published Positions on the Fat Substitute Olestra." *American Journal of Public Health* 93 (4): 664–669.

Liebman, B. 2006. "Whole Grains: The Inside Story." *Nutrition Action Healthletter* May: 1–7. www.cspinet.org/nah/05_06/grains.pdf

Liebman, B. 2008. "Fiber Free-for-All: Not All Fibers Are Equal." *Nutrition Action Healthletter* July/August: 1–7.

Liebman, B., and J. Hurley. 2007. "Healthy Foods: Your Guide to the Best Basic Foods." *Nutrition Action Healthletter.*

Lloyd-Jones, D.M., Y. Hong, D. Labarthe, D. Mozaffarian, L.J. Appel, L. Van Horn, K. Greenlund, et al. 2010. "Defining and Setting National Goals for Cardiovascular Health Promotion and Disease Reduction: The American Heart Association's Strategic Impact Goal Through 2020 and Beyond." *Circulation* 121 (4): 586–613.

Malik, V.S., B.M. Popkin, G.A. Bray, J.P. Després, W.C. Willett, and F.B. Hu. 2010. "Sugar-Sweetened Beverages and Risk of Metabolic Syndrome and Type 2 Diabetes: A Meta-Analysis." *Diabetes Care* 33 (11): 2477–2483.

Maroon, J.C., and J.W. Bost. 2006. "Omega-3 Fatty Acids (Fish Oil) as an Anti-Inflammatory: An Alternative to Nonsteroidal Anti-Inflammatory Drugs for Discogenic Pain." *Surgical Neurology* 65 (4): 326–331.

Marriott, B. P., L. Olsho, L. Hadden, and P. Connor. 2010. "Intake of Added Sugars and Selected Nutrients in the United States, National Health and Nutrition Examination Survey (NHANES) 2003-2006." *Critical Reviews in Food Science and Nutrition* 50 (3): 228-258.

Mattes, R.D., and D. Donnelly. 1991. "Relative Contributions of Dietary Sodium Sources." *Journal of the American College of Nutrition* 10: 383–393.

McDougall, John, and Mary McDougall. 2012. *The Starch Solution.* Emmaus, PA: Rodale Press.

McIntosh, G.H., M. Noakes, P.J. Royle, and P.R. Foster. 2003. "Whole-Grain Rye and Wheat Foods and Markers of Bowel Health in Overweight Middle-Aged Men." *American Journal of Clinical Nutrition* 77 (4): 967–974.

Meyer, K.A., L.H. Kushi, D.R. Jacobs Jr., J. Slavin, T.A. Sellers, and A.R. Folsom. 2000. "Carbohydrates, Dietary Fiber and Incident Type 2 Diabetes in Older Women." *American Journal of Clinical Nutrition* 71 (4): 921–930.

Morris, M.C., D.A. Evans, C.C. Tangney, J.L. Bienias, and R.S. Wilson. 2005. "Fish Consumption and Cognitive Decline With Age in a Large Community Study." *Archives of Neurology* 62 (12): 1849–1853.

Moss, Michael. 2013. *Salt Sugar Fat: How the Food Giants Hooked Us.* New York: Random House.

Mourao, D.M., J. Bressan, W.W. Campbell, and R.D. Mattes. 2007. "Effects of Food Form on Appetite and Energy Intake in Lean and Obese Young Adults." *International Journal of Obesity* 31 (11): 1688–1695.

Mursu, J., K. Robien, L.J. Harnack, K. Park, and D.R. Jacobs Jr. 2011. "Dietary Supplements and Mortality Rate in Older Women: The Iowa Women's Health Study." *Archives of Internal Medicine* 171 (18): 1625–1633.

National Nutrient Database for Standard Reference Release 26. 2010. U.S. Department of Agriculture. http://ndb.nal.usda.gov/ndb/search/list

Nedeltcheva, A.V., J.M. Kilkus, J. Imperial, K. Kasza, D.A. Schoeller, and P.D. Penev. 2009. "Sleep Curtailment Is Accompanied by Increased Intake of Calories From Snacks." *American Journal of Clinical Nutrition* 89 (1): 126–133.

Neuhouser, M.L., S. Wassertheil-Smoller, C. Thomson, A. Aragaki, G.L. Anderson, J.E. Manson, R.E. Patterson, et al. 2009. "Multivitamin Use and Risk of Cancer and Cardiovascular Disease in the Women's Health Initiative Cohorts." *Archives of Internal Medicine* 169 (3): 294–304.

Niemeier, H.M., T. Leahey, K. Palm Reed, R.A. Brown, and R.R. Wing. 2012. "An Acceptance-Based Behavioral Intervention for Weight Loss: A Pilot Study." *Behavior Therapy* 43 (2): 427–435.

Norat, T., S. Bingham, P. Ferrari, N. Slimani, M. Jenab, M. Mazuir, K. Overvad, et al. 2005. "Meat, Fish and Colorectal Cancer Risk: The European Prospective Investigation Into Cancer and Nutrition." *Journal of the National Cancer Institute* 97 (12): 906–916.

Nutrition Facts Label Programs & Materials. nd. U.S. Food and Drug Administration. www.fda.gov/Food/ IngredientsPackagingLabeling/LabelingNutrition/ucm20026097.htm

Ohr, L.M. 2012. "Little Packages, Big Nutrition." *Food Technology* 66 (2): 61–64.

Ornish, Dean. 1990. *Dr. Dean Ornish's Program for Reversing Heart Disease.* New York: Random House.

Puhl, R.M., and C.A. Heuer. 2009. "The Stigma of Obesity: A Review and Update." *Obesity* 18 (5): 941–964.

Remig, V., B. Franklin, S. Margolis, G. Kostas, T. Nece, and J.C. Street. 2010. "Trans-Fats in America: A Review of Their Use, Consumption, Health Implications and Regulation." *Journal of the American Dietetic Association* 110 (4): 585–592.

Rolls, B.J. 2007. *The Volumetrics Eating Plan.* New York: Harper Paperbacks.

Sacks, F.M., L.P. Svetkey, W.M. Vollmer, L.J. Appel, G.A. Bray, D. Harsha, E. Obarzanek, et al. 2001. "Effects on Blood Pressure of Reduced Dietary Sodium and the Dietary Approaches to Stop Hypertension (Dash) Diet." *New England Journal of Medicine* 344 (1): 3–10.

Sallis, J.F., N. Owen, and E.B. Fisher. 2008. "Ecological Models of Health Behavior" in K. Glanz, B.K. Rimer, and K. Viswanath (Eds.), *Health Behavior and Health Education: Theory, Research, and Practice*, 4th ed., 465–485. San Francisco, CA: Jossey-Bass.

San Giovanni, J.P., E.Y. Chew, T.E. Clemons, M.D. Davis, F.L. Ferris III, G.R. Gensler, N. Kurinij, et al. 2007. "The Relationship of Dietary Lipid Intake and Age-Related Macular Degeneration in a Case-Control Study: AREDS Report No. 20." *Archives of Ophthalmology* 125 (5): 671–679.

Schulze, M.B., J.E Manson, D.S. Ludwig, et al. 2004. "Sugar-Sweetened Beverages, Weight Gain, and Incidence of Type-2 Diabetes in Young and Middle-Aged Women." *Journal of the American Medical Association* 292: 927–934.

Shields, D.S. 2010. "Prospecting for Oil." *Gastronomica: The Journal of Food and Culture* 10 (4): 25–34.

Subar, A.F., S.M. Krebs-Smith, A. Cook, and L.L. Kahle. 1998. "Dietary Sources of Nutrients Among U.S. 1989 to 1991." *Journal of the American Dietetic Association* 98 (5): 537–547.

Subway US Product Ingredient. 2014. www.subway.com/Nutrition/Files/usProdIngredients.pdf

Tang, B.M., G.D. Eslick, C. Nowson, C. Smith, and A. Bensoussan. 2007. "Use of Calcium or Calcium in Combination With Vitamin D Supplementation to Prevent Fractures and Bone Loss in People Aged 50 Years and Older: A Meta-Analysis." *Lancet* 370 (9588): 657–666.

Tate, D.F., G. Turner-McGrievy, E. Lyons, J. Stevens, K. Erickson, K. Polzien, M. Diamond, X. Wang, and B. Popkin. 2012. "Replacing Caloric Beverages With Water or Diet Beverages for Weight Loss in Adults: Main Results of the Choose Healthy Options Consciously Everyday (CHOICE) Randomized Clinical Trial." *American Journal of Clinical Nutrition* 95 (3): 555–563.

Theuwissen, E., and R.P. Mensink. 2008. "Water-Soluble Dietary Fibers and Cardiovascular Disease." *Physiology and Behavior* 94 (2): 285–292.

Thomson, A.B.R., R.H. Hunt, and N.L. Zorich. 1998. "Review Article: Olestra and Its Gastrointestinal Safety." *Alimentary Pharmacology and Therapeutics* 12 (12): 1185–1200.

Wansink, B., K. Van Ittersum, and C.R. Payne. 2014. "Larger Bowl Size Increases the Amount of Cereal Children Request, Consume, and Waste." *Journal of Pediatrics* 164 (2): 323–326.

White, B.A., C.C. Horwath, and T.S. Conner. 2013. "Many Apples a Day Keep the Blues Away Daily Experiences of Negative and Positive Affect and Food Consumption in Young Adults." *British Journal of Health Psychology.* doi: 10.1111/bjhp.12021.

Willett, W.C. *Eat, Drink, and Be Healthy: The Harvard Medical School Guide to Healthy Eating* Boston: Simon and Shuster, 2005.

Wing, R. R. and S. Phelan. 2005. "Long-Term Weight Loss Maintenance." *The American Journal of Clinical Nutrition* 82 (1 Suppl): 222S-225S.

Ye, E.Q., S.A. Chacko, E.L. Chou, M. Kugizaki, and S. Liu. 2012. "Greater Whole-Grain Intake Is Associated With Lower Risk of Type 2 Diabetes, Cardiovascular Disease and Weight Gain." *Journal of Nutrition* 142 (7): 1304–1313.

Yuan, Y., G. Marshall, C. Ferreccio, C. Steinmaus, S. Selvin, J. Liaw, M.N. Bates, and A.H. Smith. 2007. "Acute Myocardial Infarction Mortality in Comparison With Lung and Bladder Cancer Mortality in Arsenic-Exposed Region II of Chile From 1950 to 2000." *American Journal of Epidemiology* 166 (12): 1381–1391.

Chapter 8

2010 Traffic Safety Culture Index Survey. American Automobile Association Foundation. www.aaafoundation.org/pdf/2010TSCIndexFinalReport.pdf

Abramson, J. 2004. *Overdosed America: The Broken Promise of American Medicine.* New York: Harper Collins.

Adult Sleep Habits. 2002. National Sleep Foundation. www.sleepfoundation.org/article/sleep-america-polls/2002-adult-sleep-habits

Alcohol-Impaired Drivers Involved in Fatal Crashes, by Gender and State, 2007–2008. 2009. U.S. Department of Transportation, National Highway Traffic Safety Administration. www.nhtsa.gov/DOT/NHTSA/reports/811095.pdf

Andersen, S.R., H. Würtzen, M. Steding-Jessen, J. Christensen, K.K. Andersen, H. Flyger, C. Mitchelmore, C. Johansen, and S.O. Dalton. 2013. "Effect of Mindfulness-Based Stress Reduction on Sleep Quality: Results of a Randomized Trial Among Danish Breast Cancer Patients." *Acta Oncologica* 52 (2): 336–344.

Asaoka, S., T. Abe, Y. Komada, and Y. Inoue. 2012. "The Factors Associated With Preferences for Napping and Drinking Coffee as Countermeasures for Sleepiness at the Wheel Among Japanese Drivers." *Sleep Medicine* 13 (4): 354–361.

Belleville, G. 2010. "Mortality Hazard Associated With Anxiolytic and Hypnotic Drug Use in the National Population Health Survey." *Canadian Journal of Psychiatry* 55 (9): 558–567.

Bonnet, M.H., and D.L. Arand. 1997. "Hyperarousal and Insomnia." *Sleep Medicine Reviews* 1 (2): 97–108.

Bonnet, M.H., and D.L. Arand. 2000. "Activity, Arousal, and the MSLT in Patients With Insomnia." *Sleep* 23 (2): 205–212.

Bootzin, R.R., and S J. Stevens. 2005. "Adolescents, Substance Abuse and the Treatment of Insomnia and Daytime Sleepiness." *Clinical Psychology Review* 25 (5): 629–644.

Brand, S., Gerber, M., Beck, J., Hatzinger, M., Pühse, U., Holsboer-Trachsler, E. 2010. "High Exercise Levels Are Related to Favorable Sleep Patterns and Psychological Functioning in Adolescents: A Comparison of Athletes and Controls." *Journal of Adolescent Health* 46: 133–141.

Brown, K.W., and R.M. Ryan. 2003. "The Benefits of Being Present: Mindfulness and Its Role in Psychological Well-Being." *Journal of Personality and Social Psychology* 84 (4): 822–848.

Brown, W.D. 2009. "Insomnia: Prevalence and Daytime Consequences." In T.L. Lee-Chiong, *Sleep Medicine Essentials* (pp. 23–30). Hoboken, NJ: Wiley.

Brunborg, G.S., R.A. Mentzoni, H. Molde, H. Myrseth, K.J.M. Skouverøe, B. Bjorvatn, and S. Pallesen. 2011. "The Relationship Between Media Use in the Bedroom, Sleep Habits and Symptoms of Insomnia." *Journal of Sleep Research* 20 (4): 569–575.

Caffeine and Sleep. n.d. National Sleep Foundation. www.sleepfoundation.org/article/sleep-topics/caffeine-and-sleep

Campbell, S.S., and P.J. Murphy. 2007. "The Nature of Spontaneous Sleep Across Adulthood." *Journal of Sleep Research* 16 (1): 24–32.

Campbell, S.S., P.J. Murphy, and T.N. Stauble. 2005. "Effects of a Nap on Nighttime Sleep and Waking Function in Older Subjects." *Journal of the American Geriatrics Society* 53 (1): 48–53.

Carlson, L.E., M. Speca, K.D. Patel, and E. Goodey. 2004. "Mindfulness-Based Stress Reduction in Relation to Quality of Life, Mood, Symptoms of Stress and Levels of Cortisol, Dehydroepiandrosterone Sulfate (DHEAS) and Melatonin in Breast and Prostate Cancer Outpatients." *Psychoneuroendocrinology* 29 (4): 448–474.

Curcio, G., M. Ferrara, and L. De Gennaro. 2006. "Sleep Loss, Learning Capacity and Academic Performance." *Sleep Medicine Reviews* 10: 323–337.

Dinges, D.F., F. Pack, K. Williams, K.A. Gillen, J.W. Powell, G.E. Ott, C. Aptowicz, and A.I. Pack. 1997. "Cumulative Sleepiness, Mood Disturbance, and Psychomotor Vigilance Performance Decrements during a Week of Sleep Restricted to 4–5 Hours Per Night." *Sleep* 20 (4): 267–277.

Drowsy Driving. n.d. National Sleep Foundation. www.sleepfoundation.org/article/sleep-topics/drowsy-driving

Fulda, S., and H. Schulz. 2001. "Cognitive Dysfunction in Sleep Disorders." *Sleep Medicine Reviews* 5: 423–445.

Garcia-Rill, E., T. Wallace-Huitt, M. Mennemeier, A. Charlsworth, D.E. Heister, M. Ye, and C. Yates. 2009. "Neuropharmacology of Sleep and Wakefulness." In T.L. Lee-Chiong, *Sleep Medicine Essentials* (pp. 23–30). Hoboken, NJ: Wiley.

Gradisar, M., A.R. Wolfson, A.G. Harvey, L. Hale, R. Rosenberg, and C.A. Czeisler. 2013. "The Sleep and Technology Use of Americans: Findings From the National Sleep Foundation's 2011 Sleep in America Poll." *Journal of Clinical Sleep Medicine* 9 (12): 1291–1299.

Greene, J.A., and E.S. Watkins. 2012. "The Prescription in Perspective." In *Prescribed: Writing, Filling, Using, and Abusing the Prescription Modern America*, Greene and Watkins (eds.), 1–22. Baltimore: Johns Hopkins University Press.

Gross, C.R., M.J. Kreitzer, M. Reilly-Spong, M. Wall, N.Y. Winbush, R. Patterson, M. Mahowald, and M. Cramer-Bornemann. 2011. "Mindfulness-Based Stress Reduction Versus Pharmacotherapy for Chronic Primary Insomnia: A Randomized Controlled Clinical Trial." *Explore: The Journal of Science and Healing* 7 (2): 76–87.

Healthy Sleep Tips. 2011. National Sleep Foundation. www.sleepfoundation.org/article/sleep-topics/healthy-sleep-tips

Heath, A. C., K. S. Kendler, L. J. Eaves, and N. G. Martin. 1990. "Evidence for Genetic Influences on Sleep Disturbance and Sleep Pattern in Twins." *Sleep* 13 (4): 318-335.

Howell, A.J., N.L. Digdon, and K. Buro. 2010. "Mindfulness Predicts Sleep-Related Self-Regulation and Well-Being." *Personality and Individual Differences* 48 (4): 419–424.

How Much Sleep Do Adults Need? 2014. National Sleep Foundation. www.sleepfoundation.org/article/white-papers-how-much-sleep-do-adults-need

How Much Sleep Do We Really Need? 2014. National Sleep Foundation. www.sleepfoundation.org/article/how-sleep-works/how-much-sleep-do-we-really-need

Kabat-Zinn, Jon. 2013. *Full Catastrophe Living.* New York: Dell Bantam.

Knutson, K.L., and F.W. Turek. 2006. "The U-Shaped Association Between Sleep and Health: The 2 Peaks Do Not Mean the Same Thing." *Sleep* 29 (7): 878–9.

Kripke, D.F., R.D. Langer, and L.E. Kline. 2012. "Hypnotics' Association With Mortality or Cancer: A Matched Cohort Study." *BMJ Open* 2 (1).

Kripke, D.F., R.N. Simons, L. Garfinkel, and E.C. Hammond. 1979. "Short and Long Sleep and Sleeping Pills: Is Increased Mortality Associated?" *Archives of General Psychiatry* 36 (1): 103–116.

Lowden, A., A. Anund, G. Kecklund, B. Peters, and T. Åkerstedt. 2009. "Wakefulness in Young and Elderly Subjects Driving at Night in a Car Simulator." *Accident Analysis and Prevention* 41: 1001–1007.

McKnight-Eily, L.R., Y. Liu, A.G. Wheaton, J.B. Croft, G.S. Perry, C.A. Okoro, and T. Strine. 2011. "Unhealthy Sleep-Related Behaviors—12 States, 2009." *Morbidity and Mortality Weekly Report* 60 (8): 233–238.

Mets, M.A.J., D. Baas, I. Van Boven, B. Olivier, and J.C. Verster. 2012. "Effects of Coffee on Driving Performance During Prolonged Simulated Highway Driving." *Psychopharmacology* 222 (2): 337–342.

Moore-Ede, M. 1994. *Twenty-Four Hour Society: Understanding Human Limits in a World That Never Stops.* New York: Addison-Wesley.

Monk, T.H. 2005. "Aging Human Circadian Rhythms: Conventional Wisdom May Not Always Be Right." *Journal of Biological Rhythms* 20 (4): 366–374.

Muzet, A. 2007. "Environmental Noise, Sleep, and Health." *Sleep Medicine Reviews* 11: 135–142.

Napping. 2014. National Sleep Foundation. www.sleepfoundation.org/article/sleep-topics/napping

National Center on Sleep Disorder Research. n.d. *Test Your Sleep IQ.* National Heart Blood Lung Institute. www.nhlbi.nih.gov/about/ncsdr/patpub/patpub-a.htm

Nedergaard, M. 2013. "Garbage Truck of the Brain." *Science* 340 (6140): 1529–1530.

Ohayon, M.M., and T. Roth. 2003. "Place of Chronic Insomnia in the Course of Depressive and Anxiety Disorders." *Journal of Psychiatric Research* 37: 9–15.

Ong, J.C., C.S. Ulmer, and R. Manber. 2012. "Improving Sleep With Mindfulness and Acceptance: A Metacognitive Model of Insomnia." *Behaviour Research and Therapy* 50 (11): 651–660.

Ong, J.C., S.L. Shapiro, and R. Manber. 2008. "Combining Mindfulness Meditation With Cognitive-Behavior Therapy for Insomnia: A Treatment-Development Study." *Behavior Therapy* 39 (2): 171–182.

Pan, L., Z. Lian, and L. Lan. 2012. "Investigation of Sleep Quality Under Different Temperatures Based on Subjective and Physiological Measurements." *HVAC and R Research* 18 (5): 1030–1043.

Passos, G.S., D. Poyares, M.G. Santana, S.A. Garbuio, S. Tufik, and M.T. Mello. 2010. "Effect of Acute Physical Exercise on Patients With Chronic Primary Insomnia." *Journal of Clinical Sleep Medicine* 6 (3): 270–275.

Passos, G.S., D.L.R. Poyares, M.G. Santana, S. Tufik, and M.T. de Mello. 2012. "Is Exercise an Alternative Treatment for Chronic Insomnia?" *Clinics* 67 (6): 653–659.

Petersen, A. 2011. "Dawn of a new sleep drug?" *Wall Street Journal*, D1e4.

Poudel, G.R., C.R.H. Innes, P.J. Bones, R. Watts, and R.D. Jones. 2014. "Losing the Struggle to Stay Awake: Divergent Thalamic and Cortical Activity During Microsleeps." *Human Brain Mapping* 35 (1): 257–269.

Schwarz, J.F.A., M. Ingre, C. Fors, A. Anund, G. Kecklund, J. Taillard, P. Philip, and T. Åkerstedt. 2012. "In-Car Countermeasures Open Window and Music Revisited on the Real Road: Popular but Hardly Effective Against Driver Sleepiness." *Journal of Sleep Research* 21 (5): 595–599.

Sleep in America Poll: Planes, Trains, Automobiles and Sleep. 2012. National Sleep Foundation. Washington: National Sleep Foundation. www.sleepfoundation.org/2012poll

Sleep in the Bedroom Poll. 2013. American Sleep Foundation. www.sleepfoundation.org/article/2013internationalbedroompoll

Spiegel, K., J.F. Sheridan, and E. Van Cauter. 2002. "Effect of Sleep Deprivation on Response to Immunization." *Journal of the American Medical Association* 288: 1471–72.

Tang, Y., Y. Ma, J. Wang, Y. Fan, S. Feng, Q. Lu, Q. Yu, D. Sui, M.K. Rothbart, M. Fan, and M.I. Posner. 2007. "Short-Term Meditation Training Improves Attention and Self-Regulation." *Proceedings of the National Academy of Sciences* 104 (4): 17152–17156.

Taylor, D.J, and A.D. Bramoweth. 2010. "Patterns and Consequences of Inadequate Sleep in College Students: Substance Use and Motor Vehicle Accidents." *Journal of Adolescent Health* 46: 610–612.

Tefft, B.C. 2010. "AAA Foundation for Traffic Safety. Sleep at The Wheel: The Prevalence and Impact of Drowsy Driving." Washington, DC: AAA Foundation for Traffic Safety. www.aaafoundation.org/pdf/2010/drowsydrivingreport.pdf

Tefft, B.C. 2012. "Prevalence of Motor Vehicle Crashes Involving Drowsy Drivers, United States, 1999–2008." *Accident Analysis and Prevention* 45: 180–186.

Tremaine, R., J. Dorrian, L. Lack, N. Lovato, S. Ferguson, X. Zhou, and G. Roach. 2010. "The Relationship Between Subjective and Objective Sleepiness and Performance During a Simulated Night-Shift With a Nap Countermeasure." *Applied Ergonomics* 42 (1): 52–61.

Vinson, D.C., B.K. Manning, J.M. Galliher, L. Miriam Dickinson, W.D. Pace, and B.J. Turner. 2010. "Alcohol and Sleep Problems in Primary Care Patients: A Report From the AAFP National Research Network." *Annals of Family Medicine* 8 (6): 484–492.

Vitiello, M.V. 2012. "Sleep in Normal Aging." *Sleep Medicine Clinics* 1 (2): 539–544.

Vuori, I., H. Urponen, J. Hasan, and M. Partinen. 1988. "Epidemiology of Exercise Effects on Sleep." *Acta Physiologica Scandinavica* 134 (Suppl. 574): 3–7.

Watson, N. 2014. "Sleep Duration and Depressive Symptoms: A Gene-Environmental Interaction." *Sleep* 37 (2): 351–358.

Watson, N.F., K.P. Harden, D. Buchwald, M.V. Vitiello, A.I. Pack, D.S. Weigle, and J. Goldberg. 2012. "Sleep Duration and Body Mass Index in Twins: A Gene-Environment Interaction." *Sleep* 35 (5): 597–603.

Winbush, N.Y., C.R. Gross, and M.J. Kreitzer. 2007. "The Effects of Mindfulness-Based Stress Reduction on Sleep Disturbance: A Systematic Review." *Explore* 3: 585–591.

Youngstedt, S.D., and C.E. Kline. 2006. "Epidemiology of Exercise and Sleep." *Sleep and Biological Rhythms* 4 (3): 215–221.

Zaharna, M., and C. Guilleminault. 2010. "Sleep, Noise and Health: Review." *Noise & Health* 12 (47): 64–69.

Chapter 9

Advisory Committee for Immunization Practices (ACIP). 2010. *General Recommendations on Immunizations*. 2010. Centers for Disease Control and Prevention. www.cdc.gov/vaccines/pubs/ACIP-list.htm

American Academy of Family Physicians (AAFP). n.d. www.aafp.org/online/en/home.html

American Academy of Pediatrics (AAP). n.d. www.aap.org/

American Congress of Obstetricians and Gynecologists (ACOG). n.d. www.acog.org/

Bagdasarov, Z., S. Banerjee, K. Greene, and S. Campo. 2008. "Indoor Tanning and Problem Behavior." *Journal of American College Health* 56 (5): 555–561.

Berlin, E., and W. Fowkes. 1983. "A Teaching Framework for Cross-Cultural Health Care: Application in Family Practice." *Western Journal of Medicine*. 139: 934–938.

Boulos, R., E.K. Vikre, S. Oppenheimer, H. Chang, and R.B. Kanarek. 2012. "ObesiTV: How Television Is Influencing the Obesity Epidemic." *Physiology and Behavior* 107 (1): 146–153.

Breast Cancer Risk in Women. n.d. National Cancer Institute. www.cancer.gov/cancertopics/factsheet/detection/probability-breast-cancer

Campbell T, L Labelle, S Bacon, P Faris, and L Carlson. 2012 Impact of Mindfulness-Based Stress Reduction (MBSR) on attention, rumination, and resting blood pressure in women with cancer: a waitlist controlled study. Journal of Behavioral Medicine Vol 35(3): 262-271.

Cates, J.R., N.L. Herndon, S.L. Schulz, and J.E. Darroch. 2004. *Our Voices, Our Lives, Our Futures: Youth and Sexually Transmitted Diseases*. Chapel Hill: University of North Carolina at Chapel Hill School of Journalism and Mass Communication.

CMS (Center for Medicare and Medicaid Services). Table 1. www.cms.gov/Research-Statistics-Data-and-Systems/Statistics-Trends-and-Reports/NationalHealthExpendData/Downloads/Proj2011PDF.pdf

Donaldson, Stewart, Mihaly Csikszentmihalyi, and Jeanne Nakamura. 2011. *Applied Positive Psychology: Improving Everyday Life, Health, Schools, Work, and Society* (Applied Psychology Series). New York: Routledge.

Eisenberg, D., R. Kessler, C. Foster et al. 1993. "Unconventional Medicine in the U.S.: Prevalence, Costs and Patterns of Use." *New England Journal of Medicine* 328 (4): 246–252.

Elster, A.B., and N. Kuznets. 1994. *Guidelines for Adolescent Preventive Services (GAPS): Recommendations and Rationale*. Chicago: American Medical Association.

English, A. 2010. *The Patient Protection and Affordable Care Act of 2010: How Does It Help Adolescents and Young Adults?* Chapel Hill, NC: Center for Adolescent Health and the Law; San Francisco: National Adolescent Health Information and Innovation Center. http://nahic.ucsf.edu/wp-content/uploads/2011/02/HCR_Issue_Brief_Aug2010_Final_Aug31.pdf

Ewing, J.A. 1984. "Detecting Alcoholism: The CAGE Questionnaire." *Journal of the American Medical Association* 252: 1905–1907.

Ford, E.S., W.H. Giles, and W.H. Dietz. 2002. "Prevalence of Metabolic Syndrome Among US Adults: Findings From the Third National Health and Nutrition Examination Survey." *Journal of the American Medical Association* 287 (3): 356–359.

Fortuna, R.J., B.W. Robbins, and J.S. Halterman. 2009. "Ambulatory Care Among Young Adults in the United States." *Annals of Internal Medicine* 151 (6): 379–385.

Genital HPV Infection—Fact Sheet. n.d. Centers for Disease Control and Prevention. www.cdc.gov/cancer/cervical/index.htm

Gilman, S.E., E.J. Bromet, K.L. Cox, L.J. Colpe, C.S. Fullerton, M.J. Gruber, S.G. Heeringa, et al. 2014. "Sociodemographic and Career History Predictors of Suicide Mortality in the United States Army 2004–2009." *Psychological Medicine*. Published online.

Hagan, J.F., J. Shaw, and P. Duncan. 2008. *Bright Futures: Guidelines for Health Supervision of Infants, Children, and Adolescents*. http://brightfutures.aap.org/pdfs/Guidelines_PDF/18-Adolescence.pdf

Hillhouse, J., R. Turrisi, and A.L. Shields. 2007. "Patterns of Indoor Tanning Use: Implications for Clinical Interventions." *Archives of Dermatology* 143 (12): 1530–1535.

Holland, S., S.D. Silberstein, F. Freitag, D.W. Dodick, C. Argoff, and E. Ashman. 2012. "Evidence-Based Guideline Update: NSAIDs and Other Complementary Treatments for Episodic Migraine Prevention in Adults Report of the Quality Standards Subcommittee of the American Academy of Neurology and the American Headache Society." *Neurology* 78 (17): 1346–1353.

Horricks, S., E. Anderson, and C. Salisbury. 2002. "Systematic Review of Whether Nurse Practitioners Working in Primary Care Can Provide Equivalent Care to Doctors." *British Medical Journal* 324: 819–23.

Huffman, J.C., C.M. DuBois, B.C. Healy, J.K. Boehm, T.B. Kashdan, C.M. Celano, J.W. Denninger, and S. Lyubomirsky. 2014. "Feasibility and Utility of Positive Psychology Exercises for Suicidal Inpatients." *General Hospital Psychiatry* 36 (1): 88–94.

Karliner, L., E. Jacobs, A. Chen, and S. Mutha S. 2007. "Do Professional Interpreters Improve Clinical Care for Patients With Limited English Proficiency? A Systematic Review of the Literature." *Health Services Research* 42 (2): 727–54.

Klein, E.A., I.M. Thompson; C. Tangen; J.J. Crowley, M.S. Lucia, et al. 2011. "Vitamin E and the Risk of Prostate Cancer—The Selenium and Vitamin E Cancer Prevention Trial (SELECT)." *Journal of the American Medical Association* 306 (14):1549–1556.

Klein, N.P., J. Bartlett., A. Rowhani-Rahbar., B. Fireman., and R. Baxter. 2012. "Waning Protection After Fifth Dose of Acellular Pertussis Vaccine in Children." *New England Journal of Medicine* 367: 1012–1019.

Kountz, D. 2009. "Strategies for Improving Low Health Literacy." *Postgraduate Medicine* 121 (5): 171–7.

Kroenke, K., R.L. Spitzer, and J.B. Williams. 2001. "The PHQ-9: Validity of a Brief Depression Severity Measure." *Journal of General Internal Medicine* 16 (9): 606–613.

Le, T.N., and J.M. Gobert. 2013. "Translating and Implementing a Mindfulness-Based Youth Suicide Prevention Intervention in a Native American Community." *Journal of Child and Family Studies*: 1–12.

Liddon NC, JS Leichliter, and LE Markowitz 2012 "Human papillomavirus vaccine and sexual behavior among young and adolescent women" American Journal of Preventative Medicine 42(1): 44-52.

McGinnis JM, P Williams-Russo, JR Knickman March 2002 " The case for more active policy attention to health promotion" Health Affairs Vol 21(2): 78-93.

McKay, B. 2011. "Lesbian, Gay, Bisexual, and Transgender Health Issues, Disparities, and Information Resources." *Medical Reference Services Quarterly* 30 (4): 393–401.

Morone, N.E., and D.K. Weiner. 2013. "Pain as the Fifth Vital Sign: Exposing the Vital Need for Pain Education." *Clinical Therapeutics* 35 (11): 1728–1732.

Myers, D., T. Wolff, K. Gregory, et al. 2008. "USPSTF Recommendations for STI Screening." *American Family Physician* 77 (6): 819–24.

National Standards for Culturally and Linguistically Appropriate Services in Health Care (CLAS). 2001. U.S. Office of Minority Health, U.S. Department of Health and Human Services. http://minorityhealth.hhs.gov/assets/pdf/checked/finalreport.pdf

Ozer, E.M., J.T. Urquhart, C.D. Brindis, et al. 2012. "Young Adult Preventive Health Care Guidelines: There but Can't Be Found." Archives of Pediatrics and Adolescent Medicine 166 (3): 240–247.

Physical Activity Guidelines for Americans. 2008. U.S. Department of Health and Human Services.

Preston, S.H., and A. Stokes. 2011. "Contribution of Obesity to International Differences in Life Expectancy." *American Journal of Public Health*. doi/10.2105/AJPH.2011.300219.

Prochaska, J.O., and C.C. DiClemente. 1983. "Stages and Processes of Self-Change of Smoking: Toward an Integrative Model of Change." *Journal of Consulting and Clinical Psychology* 51: 390–395.

Ricketts, T.C. 2005. "Work Force Issues in Rural Areas: A Focus on Policy Equity." *American Journal of Public Health* 95 (1): 42–8.

Rolls, B.J. 2007. *The Volumetrics Eating Plan*. New York: Harper Paperbacks.

Sachs, B.D., J.R. Ni, and M.G. Caron. 2014. "Sex Differences in Response to Chronic Mild Stress and Congenital Serotonin Deficiency." *Psychoneuroendocrinology* 40 (1): 123–129.

Schroeder, S.A. 2005. "What to Do With a Patient Who Smokes?" *Journal of the American Medical Association* 294 (4): 482–7.

Serdar, K.L., S.E. Mazzeo, K.S. Mitchell, S.H. Aggen, K.S. Kendler, and C.M. Bulik. 2011. "Correlates of Weight Instability Across the Lifespan in a Population-Based Sample." *International Journal of Eating Disorders* 44 (6): 506–514.

Skin Cancer Information. n.d. www.skincancer.org/skin-cancer-information

Strasburger, C., R.T. Brown, and P.K. Braverman. 2006. *Adolescent Medicine: A Handbook for Primary Care*. Philadelphia: Lippincott Williams & Wilkins.

"Suicide Trends Among Youth and Young Adults." 2007. *Morbidity and Mortality Weekly Report* 56 (35): 905–908.

Testicular Cancer Society. n.d. www.testicularcancersociety.org/tc_101.html

Unequal Treatment: Confronting Racial/Ethnic Disparities in Health Care. 2002. Institute of Medicine. Washington, DC: National Academies Press.

U.S. Preventive Services Task Force (USPSTF). 2010. *USPSTF A and B Recommendations*. www.uspreventiveservicestaskforce.org

Williams, K., J. Petronis, D. Smith, D. Goodrich, J. Wu, N. Ravi, E. Doyle, G. Juckett, M. Kolar, R. Gross, and L. Steinberg. 2005. "Effects of Iyengar Yoga Therapy for Chronic Low Back Pain." *Pain* 115: 107–117.

Chapter 10

AA Fact File. 2012. Prepared by the General Services Office of Alcoholics Anonymous. New York. www.aa.org/pdf/products/m-24_aafactfile.pdf

Abramson, J. 2004. *Overdosed America: The Broken Promise of American Medicine*. New York: Harper Collins.

Adams, C.E., M.T. Tull, and K.L. Gratz. 2012. "The Role of Emotional Nonacceptance in the Relation Between Depression and Recent Cigarette Smoking." *American Journal on Addictions* 21 (4): 293–301.

Alcoholics Anonymous (4th ed.). 2001. New York: Alcoholics Anonymous World Service. 2001.

Alcoholics Anonymous World Services, Inc. 2012. *The Twelve Steps of Alcoholics Anonymous*. www.aa.org/en_pdfs/smf-121_en.pdf

Anderson, M.L., M.S. Nokia, K.P. Govindaraju, and T.J. Shors. 2012. "Moderate Drinking? Alcohol Consumption Significantly Decreases Neurogenesis in the Adult Hippocampus." *Neuroscience* 224: 202–209.

Bill, B. 1981. *Compulsive Overeater: The Basic Text for Compulsive Overeaters*. Minneapolis, MN: CompuCare.

Biondo, G., and H.D. Chilcoat. 2014. "Discrepancies in Prevalence Estimates in Two National Surveys for Nonmedical Use of a Specific Opioid Product Versus Any Prescription Pain Reliever." *Drug and Alcohol Dependence* 134 (1): 396–400.

Boulos, R., E.K. Vikre, S. Oppenheimer, H. Chang, and R.B. Kanarek. 2012. "ObesiTV: How Television Is Influencing the Obesity Epidemic." *Physiology and Behavior* 107 (1): 146–153.

Cami, J., and M. Farre. 2003. "Drug Addiction." *New England Journal of Medicine* 349 (10): 975–986.

Carnes, P. 1983. *Out of the Shadows: Understanding Sexual Addiction*. Minneapolis, MN: CompCare.

Centers for Disease Control and Prevention. 2010. *Alcohol-Related Disease Impact (ARDI)*. Atlanta, GA www.cdc.gov/alcohol/ardi.htm

Centers for Disease Control and Prevention. 2014a. *Alcohol and Public Health*. www.cdc.gov/alcohol/faqs.htm#drinkingProblem

Centers for Disease Control and Prevention. 2014b. *Binge Drinking*. www.cdc.gov/alcohol/fact-sheets/binge-drinking.htm

Centers for Disease Control and Prevention. 2014c. *Smoking and Tobacco Use*. http://www.cdc.gov/tobacco/

Childress, A.R., R.N. Ehrman, Z. Wang, Y. Li, N. Sciortino, J. Hakun, W. Jens, et al. 2008. "Prelude to Passion: Limbic Activation by 'Unseen' Drug and Sexual Cues." *PLoS ONE* 3 (1).

Commonweal Cancer Help Program. 2014. www.commonweal.org/program/commonweal-cancer-help-program/

Connolly, G.N., and H.R. Alpert. 2008. "Trends in the Use of Cigarettes and Other Tobacco Products, 2000–2007." *Journal of the American Medical Association* 299 (22): 2629–2630.

Corsica, J.A., and M.L. Pelchat. 2010. "Food Addiction: True or False?" *Current Opinion in Gastroenterology* 26 (2): 165–169.

Corwin, R.L., N.M. Avena, and M.M. Boggiano. 2011. "Feeding and Reward: Perspectives From Three Rat Models of Binge Eating." *Physiology and Behavior* 104 (1): 87–97.

Diagnostic and Statistical Manual of Mental Disorders (5th edition) (DSM-5). 2013. American Psychiatric Association.

Dietary Guidelines for Americans 2010. 2011. U.S. Department of Agriculture and U.S. Department of Health and Human Services. Washington, DC: U.S. Government Printing Office.

Freud, Sigmund. 1900. *The Interpretation of Dreams*. Translator A.A. Brill. New York: MacMillan.

Garland, E. L., A. Roberts-Lewis, K. Kelley, C. Tronnier, and A. Hanley. 2014. "Cognitive and Affective Mechanisms Linking Trait Mindfulness to Craving among Individuals in Addiction Recovery." *Substance use and Misuse* 49 (5): 525-535.

Geiger, B.M., M. Haburcak, N.M. Avena, M.C. Moyer, B.G. Hoebel, and Pothos. 2009. "Deficits of Mesolimbic Dopamine Neurotransmission in Rat Dietary Obesity." *Neuroscience* 159 (4): 1193–9.

Gearhardt, A.N., W.R. Corbin, and K.D. Brownell. 2009. "Preliminary Validation of the Yale Food Addiction Scale." *Appetite* 52 (2): 430–436.

Goldstein, R.Z., A.D.(Bud). Craig, A. Bechara, H. Garavan, A.R. Childress, M.P. Paulus, and N.D. Volkow. 2009. "The Neurocircuitry of Impaired Insight in Drug Addiction." *Trends in Cognitive Sciences* 13 (9): 372–380.

Griffiths, M. 2005. "A 'Components' Model of Addiction Within a Biopsychosocial Framework." *Journal of Substance Use* 10 (4): 191–197.

Health Statistics. 2014. www.nlm.nih.gov/medlineplus/health-statistics.html

Healthy People 2020. 2010a. "Substance Abuse." U.S. Department of Health and Human Services. http://healthypeople.gov/2020/topicsobjectives2020/overview.aspx?topicid=40

Heatherton, T.F., and D.D. Wagner. 2011. "Cognitive Neuroscience of Self-Regulation Failure." *Trends in Cognitive Sciences* 15 (3): 132–139.

Huang, P. -H, C. X. Kim, A. Lerman, C. P. Cannon, D. Dai, W. Laskey, W. F. Peacock, et al. 2012. "Trends in Smoking Cessation Counseling: Experience from American Heart Association-Get with the Guidelines." *Clinical Cardiology* 35 (7): 396-403.

Johnston, L.D., P.M. O'Malley, J.G. Bachman, and J.E. Schulenberg. 2009. "Monitoring the Future: National Survey Results on Drug Use 1975–2008." Volume I, *Secondary School Students*. Bethesda, MD: National Institute on Drug Abuse. www.monitoringthefuture.org/pubs.html

Kabat-Zinn, Jon. 2013. *Full Catastrophe Living*. New York: Dell Bantam.

Liebman, B. 2012. "Food and Addiction." *Nutrition Action Healthletter* May: 1–7.

McIlwraith, R., R.S. Jacobvitz, R. Kubey, R., and A. Alexander. 1991. "Television Addiction: Theories and Data Behind the Ubiquitous Metaphor." *American Behavioral Scientist* 35: 104–121.

Merikangas, K.R., and V.L. McClair. 2012. "Epidemiology of Substance Use Disorders." *Human Genetics* 131 (6): 779–789.

Methven, L., E. Langreney, and J. Prescott. 2012. "Changes in Liking for a No Added Salt Soup as a Function of Exposure." *Food Quality and Preference* 26 (2): 135–140.

Meule, A., and A. Kübler. 2012. "Food Cravings in Food Addiction: The Distinct Role of Positive Reinforcement." *Eating Behaviors* 13 (3): 252–255.

Mokdad, A.H., J.S. Marks, D.F. Stroup, and J.L. Gerberding. 2004. "Actual Causes of Death in the United States, 2000." *Journal of the American Medical Association* 291 (10): 1238–1245.

Nakken, C. 1990. "An Addictive Personality." In J.A. Christen and A.G. Christen, *Defining and Addressing Addictions: A Psychological and Sociocultural Perspective*, pp. 13–18. Indianapolis: Indiana University School of Dentistry.

National Institute on Drug Abuse. 2010. "Are There Effective Treatments for Tobacco Addiction?" www.nida.nih.gov/researchreports/nicotine/treatment.html

Nestler, E.J. 2005. "Is There a Common Molecular Pathway for Addiction?" *Nature Neuroscience* 8 (11): 1445–1449.

O'Flaherty, M., I. Buchan, and S. Capewell. 2013. "Contributions of Treatment and Lifestyle to Declining CVD Mortality: Why Have CVD Mortality Rates Declined So Much Since the 1960s?" *Heart* 99 (3): 159–162.

Olshansky, S.J., D.J. Passaro, R.C. Hershow, J. Layden, B.A. Carnes, J. Brody, L. Hayflick, R.N. Butler, D.B. Allison, and D.S. Ludwig. 2005. "A Potential Decline in Life Expectancy in the United States in the 21st Century." *New England Journal of Medicine* 352 (11): 1138–1145.

Ornish, Dean. 1990. *Dr. Dean Ornish's Program for Reversing Heart Disease.* New York: Random House.

Peele, S., and A. Brodsky. 1975. *Love and Addiction.* New York: Taplinger.

Prescription Drug Abuse. 2014. www.nlm.nih.ov/medlineplus/prescriptiondurgabuse.html

Preventing Tobacco Use Among Youth and Young Adults. 2014. U.S. Department of Health and Human Services. www.surgeon-general.gov/library/reports/preventing-youth-tobacco-use/factsheet.html

Prochaska, J.O., J.C. Norcross, and C.C. DiClemente. 1994. *Changing for Good.* New York: Morrow.

Results From the 2011 National Survey on Drug Use and Health: Summary of National Findings. 2012. NSDUH Series H-44, HHS Publication No. (SMA) 12-4713, pp. 20, 31. Substance Abuse and Mental Health Services Administration. Rockville, MD: Substance Abuse and Mental Health Services Administration.

Terry, A., A. Szabo, and M. Griffiths. 2004. "The Exercise Addiction Inventory: A New Brief Screening Tool." *Addiction Research and Theory* 12: 489–499.

The Health Consequences of Smoking—50 Years of Progress, Surgeon General's Report on Tobacco and Health. 2014. U.S. Department of Health and Human Services. www.surgeongeneral.gov/library/reports/50-years-of-progress/exec-summary.pdf

Twelve Steps and Twelve Traditions. 1981. New York: Alcoholics Anonymous World Services.

Vaillant, G.E. 2013. Psychiatry, Religion, Positive Emotions and Spirituality. *Asian Journal of Psychiatry* 6 (6):590–594.

Vaillant, George E. 1995. *The Natural History of Alcoholism Revisited.* Cambridge, MA: Harvard University Press.

Viguier, F., B. Michot, V. Kayser, J.-F. Bernard, J.-M. Vela, M. Hamon, and S. Bourgoin. 2012. "GABA, but Not Opioids, Mediates the Anti-Hyperalgesic Effects of 5-HT 7 Receptor Activation in Rats Suffering From Neuropathic Pain." *Neuropharmacology* 63 (6): 1093–1106.

Volkow, N.D., G.-J Wang, J.S. Fowler, and D. Tomasi. 2012. "Addiction Circuitry in the Human Brain." *Annual Review of Pharmacology and Toxicology* 52: 321–336.

Waller, M.W., B.J. Iritani, S.L. Christ, C. Tucker Halpern, K.E. Moracco, and R.L. Flewelling. 2013. "Perpetration of Intimate Partner Violence by Young Adult Males: The Association With Alcohol Outlet Density and Drinking Behavior." *Health and Place* 21: 10-19.

Chapter 11

Agostinho, F., and L. Pereira. 2013. "Support Area as an Indicator of Environmental Load: Comparison Between Embodied Energy, Ecological Footprint, and Energy Accounting Methods." *Ecological Indicators* 24: 494–503.

Aldo Leopold Foundation. www.aldoleopold.org/AldoLeopold/leopold_bio.shtml

"Arsenic in Your Food: Our Findings Show a Real Need for Federal Standards for This Toxin." 2012. *Consumer Reports* 77 (11): 22–27.

Blaine, J.G., B.W. Sweeney, and D.B. Arscott. 2006. "Enhanced Source-Water Monitoring for New York City: Historical Framework, Political Context, and Project Design." *Journal of the North American Benthological Society* 25 (4): 851–866.

Carson, Rachel. 1962. *Silent Spring.* New York: Houghton Mifflin.

Chang, N. B, C. Qi, and Y.J. Yang. 2012. "Optimal Expansion of a Drinking Water Infrastructure System With Respect to Carbon Footprint, Cost-Effectiveness and Water Demand." *Journal of Environmental Management* 110: 194–206.

Clark, M.S., A. Greenberg, E. Hill, E.P. Lemay, E. Clark-Polner, and D. Roosth. 2011. "Heightened Interpersonal Security Diminishes the Monetary Value of Possessions." *Journal of Experimental Social Psychology* 47 (2): 359–364.

Clegg, N. 2012. "Rio's Reprise Must Set Hard Deadlines for Development." *Guardian.* June 19. www.guardian.co.uk/comment-isfree/2012/jun/19/rio-earth-summit-development-deadlines

Clemmens, A.J. 2008. "Accuracy of Project-Wide Water Uses From a Water Balance: A Case Study From Southern California." *Irrigation and Drainage Systems* 22 (3–4): 287–309.

Daily, G.C., and Ehrlich, P.R. 1992. "Population, Sustainability and Earth's Carry Capacity." *BioScience* 42: 761-771.

Dennehy, K.F. 2000. *High Plains Regional Ground-Water Study: U.S. Geological Survey Fact Sheet FS-091-00.* USGS. http://co.water.usgs.gov/nawqa/hpgw/factsheets/DENNEHYFS1.html

Diamond, Jarrod. 1997. *Guns, Germs, and Steel.* New York: Norton.

Diaz, J.H. 2011. "The Legacy of the Gulf Oil Spill: Analyzing Acute Public Health Effects and Predicting Chronic Ones in Louisiana." *American Journal of Disaster Medicine* 6 (1): 5–22.

"Ecosystems and Human Well-Being." 2005. *Millennium Ecosystem Assessment.* Washington, DC: Island Press.

EnvironmentalChemistry.com 2004. www.EnvironmentalChemistry.com

Feinberg, M., and R. Willer. 2013. "The Moral Roots of Environmental Attitudes." *Psychological Science* 24: 56–62.

Fereres, E., and M.A. Soriano. 2007. "Deficit Irrigation for Reducing Agricultural Water Use." *Journal of Experimental Botany* 58 (2): 147–159.

Foley, C.M.R. 2013. "Management Implications of Fishing Up, Down, or Through the Marine Food Web." *Marine Policy* 37 (1): 176–182.

Fuller, R.J., and U.M. de Jong. 2011. "The Cost of Housing: More Than Just Dollars." *Open House International* 36 (3): 38–48.

Geiger, F., J. Bengtsson, F. Berendse, W.W. Weisser, M. Emmerson, M.B. Morales, P. Ceryngier, et al. 2010. "Persistent Negative Effects of Pesticides on Biodiversity and Biological Control Potential on European Farmland." *Basic and Applied Ecology* 11 (2): 97–105.

General Services Administration. 2009. *The New Sustainable Frontier.* Washington, DC: General Services Administration. www.gsa.gov/graphics/ogp/2009_New_Sustainable_Frontier_Complete_Guide.pdf

Gilbert, Geoffrey, ed. 1999. *Thomas R. Malthus, an Essay on the Principle of Population.* Oxford World's Classics, p. 61.Oxford: Oxford University Press.

Global Footprint Network. 2014. *Ecological Sustainability.* www.footprintnetwork.org

Goleman, Daniel. 2009. *Ecological Intelligence*. New York: Broadway Books.

Greenhouse Gas Overview. 2010. Environmental Protection Agency. http://epa.gov/climatechange/ghgemissions/gases. html

Hall, C.A.S., and J.W. Day. 2009. "Revisiting the Limits to Growth After Peak Oil." *American Scientist* 97: 230–237.

Halweil, B. 2002. "Home Grown: The Case for Local Food in a Global Market." *Worldwatch Paper* (163): 5–79.

Hansen, E., B. Gilmer, A. Varrato, and A. Rosser. 2014. *Potential Significant Contaminant Sources Above West Virginia American Water's Charleston Intake: A Preliminary Assessment*. Down-Stream Strategies Report. Morgantown, WV.

Hönisch, B., A. Ridgwell, D.N. Schmidt, E. Thomas, S.J. Gibbs, A. Sluijs, R. Zeebe, et al. 2012. "The Geological Record of Ocean Acidification." *Science* 335 (6072): 1058–1063.

Hopton, M.E., and D. White. 2012. "A Simplified Ecological Footprint at a Regional Scale." *Journal of Environmental Management* 111: 279–286.

Hoyt, Erich. 1996. *The Earth Dwellers*. New York: Simon and Schuster.

Hunt, R.G., and W.E. Franklin. 1996. "LCA—How It Came About—Personal Reflections on the Origin and the Development of LCA in the USA." *International Journal of Life Cycle Assessment* 1 (1): 4–7.

Indoor Air: Report on the Environment. 2013. Environmental Protection Agency. http://cfpub.epa.gov/eroe/index. cfm?fuseaction=list.listBySubTopic&ch=46&s=343

Intergovernmental Panel on Climate Change. 2007. *Climate Change Fourth Assessment Report of the Intergovernmental Panel on Climate Change*. Cambridge, UK: Cambridge University Press.

Intergovernmental Panel on Climate Change, Fifth Assessment Report, United Nations. 2014. *Climate Change 2014: Impacts, Adaptation and Vulnerability*. http://www.ipcc.ch/report/ar5/wg2/

Jay-Russell, M.T. 2013. "What Is the Risk From Wild Animals in Food-Borne Pathogen Contamination of Plants?" *CAB Reviews: Perspectives in Agriculture, Veterinary Science, Nutrition and Natural Resources* 8.

Keitsch, M.M. 2010. *Sustainability and science – challenges for theory and practice*. Sustainable Development, 18 (5): 241-317.

Kenworthy, T., J.D. Weiss, L. Kaufman, and C.C. DiPasquale. 2011. *Drilling Down on Natural Gas Fracking Concerns*. http://climateprogress.org/2011/03/21/drilling-down-on-natural-gas-fracking-concerns/

King, K.W., N.R. Fausey, R. Dunn, P.C. Smiley Jr., and B.L. Sohngen. 2012. "Response of Reservoir Atrazine Concentrations Following Regulatory and Management Changes." *Journal of Soil and Water Conservation* 67 (5): 416–424.

Koellner, T., and R.W. Scholz. 2007. "Assessment of Land Use Impacts on the Natural Environment: Part 1: An Analytical Framework for Pure Land Occupation and Land Use Change." *International Journal of Life Cycle Assessment* 12 (1): 16–23.

Law, K.L., and Thompson, R.C., "Microplastics in the Seas." Science 345 (6193), 144-145.

Leitch, K.R., C. Koop, M. Messer, and A. Payne. 2013. "Green Construction in Civil Engineering Instruction." *Proceedings—Frontiers in Education Conference*, pp. 24–28.

Leverkus, A.B., C. Puerta-Piñero, J.R. Guzmán-Álvarez, J. Navarro, and J. Castro. 2012. "Post-Fire Salvage Logging Increases Restoration Costs in a Mediterranean Mountain Ecosystem." *New Forests* 43 (5–6): 601–613.

Lucas, Robert E. 2002. *Lectures on Economic Growth*, pp. 109–110. Cambridge: Harvard University Press.

Maslow, Abraham. 1954. *Motivation and Personality* (3rd ed.) New York: Harper and Row.

McDonnough, William, and Michael Braungart. 2002. *Cradle to Cradle*. New York: North Point Press.

McEntire, J. 2013. "Foodborne Disease. The Global Movement of Food and People." *Infectious Disease Clinics of North America* 27 (3): 687–693.

McKenzie, J.F., R.R. Pinger, and J.E. Kotecki. 2012. *An Introduction to Community Health* (7th ed.) Sudbury, MA: Jones & Bartlett Learning.

Meadows, Donella H., Dennis L. Meadows, Jorgen Randers, and William W. Behrens. 1972. *Limits to Growth*. New York: Universe Books.

Meadows, Donella, Jorgen Randers, and Dennis Meadows. 2004. *Limits to Growth: The 30-Year Update*. White River Junction, VT: Chelsea Green.

Moore, R., and C.M. Burns. 2011. "The Effect of Oil Spills on Workers Involved in Containment and Abatement: The Role of the Occupational Health Nurse." *AAOHN Journal* 59 (11): 477–482.

Nicholls, R.J., and A. Cazenave. 2010. "Sea-Level Rise and Its Impact on Coastal Zones." *Science* 328 (5985): 1517–1520.

Pollan, Michael. 2006. *The Omnivore's Dilemma: A Natural History of Four Meals*. New York: Penguin Press.

Product Policy Institute. 2014. www.productpolicy.org/content/history-waste

Rosen, G. 1975. *Preventive Medicine in the United States, 1900–1975*. New York: Science History

Rudiak-Gould, P. 2011. "Climate Change and Anthropology: The Importance of Reception Studies." *Anthropology Today* 27 (2): 9–12.

Ryff, C.D., and B.H. Singe. 2008. "Know Thyself and Become What You Are: A Eudaimonic Approach to Psychological Well-Being." *Journal of Happiness Studies* 9:13–39.

Stratospheric Ozone and Surface Ultraviolet Radiation. 2010. United Nations Environment Programme, Ozone Secretariat. http://ozone.unep.org/Assessment_Panels/SAP/Scientific_Assessment_2010/04-Chapter_2.pdf

SustainAbility.com. 2014. *Non-Profit Consulting*. www.sustainability.com

The Endocrine Disruptor Exchange. 2014. www.EndrocrineDisruption.org

Tompkins, C.F. and K. Levin, 2014. "Four Takeaways from IPCC Report Reveal Worsening Impacts of Climate Change." World Resources Institute Report. www.wri.org/blog/2014/03/4-takeaways-ipcc-report-reveal-worsening-impacts-climate-change.

Travel Trends: Train Travel in the USA. 2010. Gadling. www.gadling.com/2010/05/27/train-travel-in-the-usa/

United States Green Building Council. 2012. http://new.usgbc.org

Wilson, A., and J. Boehland. 2005. "Small Is Beautiful: U.S. House Size, Resource Use, and the Environment." *Journal of Industrial Ecology* 9 (1–2): 277–287.

World Bank Institute. 2013. *World Bank Data: Motor Vehicles (Per 1,000 People)*. http://data.worldbank.org/indicator/IS.VEH.NVEH.P3

World Commission on Environment and Development. 1987. *Our Common Future*. Oxford: Oxford University Press.

Wright, L., S. Kemp, I. Williams. 2011. "Carbon Footprinting: Towards a Universally Accepted Definition." *Carbon Management* 2 (1): 61–72.

Yan, Y. 2012. "Food Safety and Social Risk in Contemporary China." *Journal of Asian Studies* 71 (3): 705–729.

Chapter 12

Abeysekara, A. 2010. "The Im-Possibility of Secular Critique: The Future of Religion's Memory." *Culture and Religion* 11 (3): 213–246.

A Course in Miracles (3rd ed.). 2007. Mill Valley, CA: Foundation for Inner Peace.

Anastasi, B.S., and A.B. Newberg. 2008. "A Preliminary Study of the Acute Effects of Religious Ritual on Anxiety." *Journal of Alternative and Complementary Medicine* 14 (2): 163–165.

Antonovsky, A. 1987. *Unraveling the Mystery of Health—How People Manage Stress and Stay Well*. San Francisco: Jossey-Bass.

Antonovsky, A. 1993. "The Structure and Properties of the Sense of Coherence Scale." *Social Science and Medicine* 36: (6) 725–33.

Brazier, C. 2013. "Roots of Mindfulness." *European Journal of Psychotherapy and Counselling* 15 (2): 127–138.

Bridges, K.R., R.J. Harnish, and D. Sillman 2012. "Teaching Undergraduate Positive Psychology: An Active Learning Approach Using Student Blogs." *Psychology Learning & Teaching* 11 (2): 228–237.

Cavanagh, K., C. Strauss, L. Forder, and F. Jones. 2014. "Can Mindfulness and Acceptance be Learnt by Self-Help?: A Systematic Review and Meta-Analysis of Mindfulness and Acceptance-Based Self-Help Interventions." *Clinical Psychology Review* 34 (2): 118–129.

Chodron, P. 2012. *Living Beautifully With Uncertainty and Change*. Ed. J.D. Oliver. Boston: Shambala.

Christopher, A. N. and B. R. Schlenker. 2004. "Materialism and Affect: The Role of Self-Presentational Concerns." *Journal of Social and Clinical Psychology* 23 (2): 260-272.

Covey, Steven R. 1989. *The 7 Habits of Highly Effective People: Restoring the Character Ethic*. New York: Simon & Schuster.

Covey, Steven R. 1997. *The 7 Habits of Highly Effective Families*. New York: Golden Books.

Csikszentmihalyi, M. 1990. *Flow: The Psychology of Optimal Experience*. New York: Harper Perennial.

De Chardin, T. 1955. *The Phenomenon of Man*. Translated by Bernard Wall. New York: Harper Perennial Modern Thought.

Doswell, W.M., M. Kouyate, and J. Taylor. 2003. "The Role of Spirituality in Preventing Early Sexual Behavior." *American Journal of Health Studies* 18 (4): 195–199.

Feher, S., and R.C. Maly, 1999. "Coping With Breast Cancer in Later Life: The Role of Religious Faith." *Psychooncology* 8: 408–416.

Feldman, R. 2007. "Parent-Infant Synchrony: Biological Foundations and Developmental Outcomes." *Current Directions in Psychological Science* 16 (6): 340-345.

Frankl, V.E. 1959. *Man's Search for Meaning*. Boston: Beacon Press.

Freud, S. 1922. *Group Psychology and the Analysis of the Ego*. Chapter IX, "The Herd Instinct." Translated by James Strachey. New York: Boni and Liveright.

Grossman, P., L. Niemann, S. Schmidt, and H. Walach. 2004. "Mindfulness-Based Stress Reduction and Health Benefits: A Meta-Analysis." *Journal of Psychosomatic Research* 57 (1): 35–43.

Guilherme, A. 2012. "God as Thou and Prayer as Dialogue: Martin Buber's Tools for Reconciliation." *Sophia* 51 (3): 365–378.

Hays, J.C., K.G. Meador, P.S. Branch, and L.K. George. 2001. "The Spiritual History Scale in Four Dimensions (SHS-4): Validity and Reliability." *Gerontologist* 41 (2): 239–249.

Hodge, D.R. 2007. "A Systematic Review of the Empirical Literature on Intercessory Prayer." *Research on Social Work Practice* 17 (2): 174–187.

Hood, R.W., P.C. Hill, and B. Spilka. 2009. *The Psychology of Religion*. New York: Guilford Press.

Hugo, Victor. 1862. *Les Miserables*. New York: Ballantine Books.

Hummer, R. A., R. G. Rogers, C. B. Nam, and C. G. Ellison. 1999. "Religious Involvement and U.S. Adult Mortality." *Demography* 36 (2): 273-285.

Jager, R. 1997. "Afrocultural Integrity and the Social Development of African American Children: Some Conceptual, Empirical, and Practical Considerations." *Journal of Prevention and Intervention in the Community* 16: 7–31.

Jones, D.L. 2012. *Joy Awaits*. Bloomington: Balboa Press.

Kabat-Zinn, J. 2013. *Full Catastrophe Living: Using the Wisdom of Your Body and Mind to Face Stress, Pain and Illness*. New York: Dell Bantam.

Keown, David. 2013. *Buddhism: A Very Short Introduction*. Oxford: Oxford University Press.

Kohlberg, L. 1973. "Stages and Aging in Moral Development: Some Speculations." *Gerontologist* 13 (4): 497–502.

Koomey, J.G. 2001. *Turning Numbers Into Knowledge: Mastering the Art of Problem Solving*. Oakland, CA: Analytics Press.

Kornfield, J. 2011. *A Lamp in the Darkness*. Boulder: Sounds True.

Krakauer, Jon. 2004. *Under the Banner of Heaven*. New York: Anchor Books.

Krause, N. 2008. "The Social Foundation of Religious Meaning in Life." *Research on Aging* 30 (4): 395-427.

Larson, D. B. and H. G. Koenig. 2000. "Is God Good for Your Health? the Role of Spirituality in Medical Care." *Cleveland Clinic Journal of Medicine* 67 (2): 80, 83-84.

Lindholm, J. 2013. A. "Students at Catholic Universities: Their Spiritual Development," In J.R. Wilcox (Ed.). *Revisioning Mission: The Future of Catholic Higher Education*, pp 117-143. North Charleston, SC: CreateSpace Independent Publishing Platform.

Maslow, A. 1961. "Past Experiences as Acute Identity Experiences." *American Journal of Psychoanalysis* 21: 254–260.

Menninger, K.A. 1963. *The Vital Balance: The Life Process in Mental Health and Illness*. New York: Viking Penguin.

Murphy, S.A., L.C. Johnson, and J. Lohan. 2003. "Finding Meaning in a Child's Violent Death: A Five-Year Prospective Analysis of Parents' Personal Narratives and Empirical Data." *Death Studies* 27: 381–404.

Nakamura, J., and M. Csikszentmihalyi. 2001. "Flow Theory and Research." In *Handbook of Positive Psychology*, eds. Snyder, Wright, and Lopez, pp. 195–206. New York: Oxford University Press.

Oman, D. 2011. "Spiritual Practice, Health Promotion, and the Elusive Soul: Perspectives From Public Health." *Pastoral Psychology* 60 (6): 897–906.

Oman, D. and C. E. Thoresen. 2002. "'does Religion Cause Health?': Differing Interpretations and Diverse Meanings." *Journal of Health Psychology* 7 (4): 365-380.

Pargament, K.I. 2008. "The Sacred Character of Community Life." *American Journal of Community Psychology* 41 (1–2): 22–34.

Piaget, J. 1974. "The Future of Developmental Child Psychology." *Journal of Youth and Adolescence* 3 (2): 87–93.

Pransky, J. 2003. *Prevention From the Inside-Out*. First Book Library.

Savundranayagam, M.Y. 2014. "Receiving While Giving: The Differential Roles of Receiving Help and Satisfaction With Help on Caregiver Rewards Among Spouses and Adult-Children." *International Journal of Geriatric Psychiatry* 29 (1): 41–48.

Schultz, J.M., E. Altmaier, S. Ali, and B. Tallman. 2014. "A Study of Posttraumatic Spiritual Transformation and Forgiveness Among Victims of Significant Interpersonal Offences." *Mental Health, Religion and Culture* 17 (2): 122–135.

Seligman, Martin. 2002. *Authentic Happiness: Using the New Positive Psychology to Realize Your Potential for Lasting Fulfillment*. New York: Free Press.

Seligman, Martin. 2006. *Learned Optimism: How to Change Your Mind and Your Life*. New York: Vantage Books.

Seligman, Martin. 2011. *Flourish: A Visionary New Understanding of Happiness and Well-Being*. New York: Free Press.

Sirgy, M. J., E. Gurel-Atay, D. Webb, M. Cicic, M. Husic, A. Ekici, A. Herrmann, I. Hegazy, D. -J Lee, and J. S. Johar. 2012. "Linking Advertising, Materialism, and Life Satisfaction." *Social Indicators Research* 107 (1): 79-101.

Sobel, D., and R. Ornstein. 1989. *Healthy Pleasures*. Woburn, MA: Addison-Wesley.

Spilka, B., R.W. Hood, B. Hunsberger, and R. Gorsuch. 2003. *The Psychology of Religion: An Empirical Approach* (3rd ed.). New York: Guilford Press.

State of the World's Indigenous Populations. 2009. New York: United Nations. ISBN 92-1-13028307.

Szekeres, R.A., and E.H. Wertheim. 2014. "Evaluation of Vipassana Meditation Course Effects on Subjective Stress, Well-Being, Self-Kindness and Mindfulness in a Community Sample: Post-Course and 6-Month Outcomes." *Stress and Health*.

Thérèse of Lisieux. 1957. *Autobiography of Saint Thérèse of Lisieux: The Story of a Soul*. Translated by J. Beevers. New York: Doubleday.

Thomas, B. 1952. *Abraham Lincoln, A Biography*. New York: Knopf.

Tolle, E. 2005. *A New Earth: Awakening to Your Life's Purpose*. New York: Plume.

Travis, J.W., and R.S. Ryan. 2004. *The Wellness Workbook: How to Achieve Enduring Health and Vitality* (3rd ed.). New York: Ten Speed Press.

Turner-Musa, J., and L. Lipscomb. 2007. "Spirituality and Social Support on Health Behaviors of African American Undergraduates." *American Journal of Health Behavior* 31 (5): 495–501.

Vail III, K. E., J. Arndt, and A. Abdollahi. 2012. "Exploring the Existential Function of Religion and Supernatural Agent Beliefs among Christians, Muslims, Atheists, and Agnostics." *Personality and Social Psychology Bulletin* 38 (10): 1288-1300.

Vaillant, G. 2008. "Positive Emotions, Spirituality and the Practice of Psychiatry." Mens Sana Monographs 6 (1): 48-62.

Vaillant, G.E. 2013. "Psychiatry, Religion, Positive Emotions and Spirituality." *Asian Journal of Psychiatry* 6 (6): 590–594.

Ventres, W., and S. Dharamsi. 2013. "Beyond Religion and Spirituality: Faith in the Study and Practice of Medicine." *Perspectives in Biology and Medicine* 56 (3): 352–361.

Wapnick, K. 1989. *Love Does Not Condemn*. Roscoe, NY: Foundation for a Course in Miracles.

Wapnick, K. 2011. *Healing the Unhealed Mind*. Temecula, CA: Foundation for a Course in Miracles.

Welwood, J. 1991. *Journey of the Heart: Intimate Relationship and the Path to Love*. Chapter: "Relationship as a Spiritual Path." Perennial Publishers.

Yangarber-Hicks, N. 2004. "Religious Coping Styles and Recovery From Serious Mental Illnesses." *Journal of Psychology and Theology* 32: 305–317.

Young, J.S., C.S. Cashwell, and J. Sheherbakova. 2000. "The Moderating Relationship of Spirituality on Negative Life Events and Psychological Adjustment." *Counseling and Values* 45: 49–57.

INDEX

Note: Page numbers followed by italicized *f* and *t* indicate information contained in figures and tables, respectively.

ABOUT THE AUTHORS

Bill Reger-Nash, EdD, is emeritus professor in the School of Public Health at West Virginia University. He has been a wellness professional for more than 30 years and has served as research coordinator for the Cardiac and Wellness Center of Wheeling Hospital; director of the Bayer Wellness Program in Wellsburg, West Virginia; director of wellness for the Ohio Valley Medical Center; and founding director of wellness for West Virginia University.

Reger-Nash has more than 10 first-author peer-reviewed publications and has presented his work in health promotion throughout the world. He has received numerous awards and distinctions, including being named among the 100 best minds by *US News & World Report* in 2004, the 2006 Ethel and Gerry Heebink Award for Distinguished State Service, and the 1996 Health Advocate of the Year Award presented by the State Health Education Council of West Virginia.

Gregory Juckett, MD, MPH, is a professor of family medicine at West Virginia University, Morgantown, where he provides clinical services for the WVU Health Service and also directs the University's International Travel Clinic. He received his medical degree from Pennsylvania State University College of Medicine at Hershey and a master's degree in public health from West Virginia University. He completed his family medicine residency at the Medical University of South Carolina, Charleston. Dr. Juckett's interests include tropical and travel medicine, dermatology, and cross-cultural health care. In addition, Dr. Juckett has extensive international experience in Africa, Asia, Latin America, and the Pacific.

Meredith Smith, MS, MA, has master's degrees in sport and exercise psychology and community counseling from West Virginia University. She has worked as a family and marriage therapist as well as a drug and alcohol counselor. She works for the State of New Mexico as a health educator to decrease the burden of chronic disease in the state. She and her husband, Sean, also own and operate a small farm that emphasizes sustainable and organic practices. In addition, Meredith is a certified yoga teacher. She strives to live both her professional and personal life in accordance to wholistic wellness and enjoys helping others do the same.